CERTIFIED PROFESSIONAL SECRETARY®
CERTIFIED ADMINISTRATIVE PROFESSIONAL®
EXAMINATION REVIEW SERIES

OFFICE ADMINISTRATION

FIFTH EDITION

Betty L. Schroeder, Ph.D.
Northern Illinois University

Diane Routhier Graf CPS, Ed.D.
Northern Illinois University

Carol Mull
Series Editor

A joint publication of
International Association of Administrative Professionals®

International Association of
Administrative Professionals®

and

PEARSON
Prentice
Hall

Upper Saddle River, New Jersey 07458

Library of Congress Cataloging-in-Publication Data

Schroeder, Betty L.

   CPS exam review office administration / Betty L. Schroeder, Diane Routhier Graf.—5th ed.

       p. cm. — (Certified professional secretary examination review series)

   Rev. ed. of: Office systems & administration. c2001.

   Includes index.

   ISBN 0-13-114551-7

   1. Office practice—Automation. 2. Office management. I. Routhier Graf, Diane, 1943-

II. Schroeder, Betty L. Office systems & administration. III. Title. IV. Series.

HF5547.5S364 2005

651.3'076—dc22

                                                 2004003525

Executive Editor: Elizabeth Sugg
Director of Production and Manufacturing: Bruce Johnson
Editorial Assistant: Cyrenne Bolt de Freitas
Marketing Manager: Leigh Ann Sims
Development Editor: Deborah Hoffman
Managing Editor—Production: Mary Carnis
Manufacturing Buyer: Ilene Sanford
Production Liaison: Denise Brown
Production Editor: Lori Dalberg, Carlisle Publishers Services
Composition: Carlisle Communications, Ltd.
Design Director: Cheryl Asherman
Senior Design Coordinator/Cover Design: Christopher Weigand
Cover Printer: Phoenix Color
Printer/Binder: Banta/Harrisonburg

Pearson Prentice Hall™ is a trademark of Pearson Education, Inc.
Pearson® is a registered trademark of Pearson plc
Prentice Hall® is a registered trademark of Pearson Education, Inc.

Pearson Education Ltd.
Pearson Education Singapore, Pte. Ltd.
Pearson Education Canada, Ltd.
Pearson Education—Japan
Pearson Education Australia PTY, Limited
Pearson Education North Asia Ltd.
Pearson Educacíon de Mexico, S.A. de C.V.
Pearson Education Malaysia, Pte. Ltd.

10 9 8 7 6 5 4 3 2 1
ISBN 0-13-114551-7

Contents

Preface

The Certified Professional Secretary (CPS) and Certified Administrative Professional (CAP) Examination Review Series, a four-volume set of review manuals that consists of one review manual for the first three parts of the CPS and CAP Examinations and one for Part 4 the CAP Examination, is a joint publication of Prentice Hall and the International Association of Administrative Professionals (IAAP). The content of each review manual is based on the current Certification Review Guide published by the IAAP.

CPS and CAP Examinations

The rewards for achieving the Certified Professional Secretary (CPS) and Certified Administrative Professional (CAP) certifications are numerous, as attested to by the more than 65,000 CPS and CAP holders. These rewards include pride in accomplishment, increased self-esteem, greater respect from employers and peers, and confidence to assume greater responsibilities as well as possible college credit toward a degree, pay increases, bonuses, and opportunities for advancement. In today's workplace, having the CPS or CAP credentials can enhance assurance of employability and career advancement.

The CPS Examination is a one-day, three-part examination which includes

Part 1: Office Systems and Technology
Part 2: Office Administration
Part 3: Management

The CAP Examination is a 1½ day, four-part examination which includes

Parts 1, 2, and 3 above
Part 4: Advanced Organizational Management

To apply for the CPS or CAP Examination, the candidate must meet certain educational and professional experience requirements. Visit the IAAP Web site at _www.iaap-hq.org/_ to obtain detailed information concerning testing centers, testing dates, application packets, and other information relative to applying for certification candidacy.

CPS and CAP Examination Review Series

The CPS and CAP Examination Review Series provides valuable assistance to the administrative professional preparing for the CPS and CAP Examinations, whether this series is used for group review sessions or self-study. The series provides an excellent learning tool that is focused on key topics necessary for passing the examinations.

The format used in Parts 1, 2, and 3 (Office Systems and Technology, 5E; Office Administration, 5E; and Management, 5E) of the CPS and CAP Examination Review Series is an outline format with multiple-choice review questions. The format used in Part 4, Advanced Organizational Management for the CAP Examination Review, is slightly different based on the scenario-oriented nature of Part 4 of the CAP Examination. The CPS and CAP Examination Review Series provides relevant information to help the candidate prepare for both the CPS and CAP Examinations. However, this does not imply that all information presented in this series will be included on the examinations. Further review is encouraged for the candidate by studying selected titles from the bibliography supplied by IAAP.

Each review manual in the CPS and CAP Examination Review Series includes:

- An overview introducing the reader to the chapter contents.
- Key terms that reinforce essential vocabulary.
- Text in outline form, with examples highlighted in italics, to enhance the explanation given in the text.
- Key examples emphasized.
- Difficult concepts illustrated.
- Check Point sections within each chapter that offer reviews of key concepts.
- For Your Review section at the end of each chapter with practice questions similar to those found on the CPS and CAP Examinations.
- A glossary at the end of each book that provides accessible reference.
- A comprehensive practice exam that simulates the testing environment and provides even more practice.
- Solutions to all check points and review questions, including references to the chapter outline where the answers are explained.

  For example:

  Answer   Reference

  1. *(B)*   *[A-2]* (Section of Chapter)
- An index with page references provided in the Office Systems and Technology, 5E, and the Office Administration, 5E, review manuals.

NEW Online eLearning Format for CPS and CAP Examination Review

The NEW online eLearning format includes all material found in Parts 1–3 of the CPS and CAP Examination Review Series plus assessment feedback. You can purchase each title separately or receive a quantity discount when all three titles are purchased.

- Office Systems and Technology, 5E, eLearning version
- Office Administration, 5E, eLearning version
- Management, 5E, eLearning version
- CPS Examination Review Series, eLearning version (includes all three titles)

CPS and CAP Examination Review Guide

The Certification Review Guide should be used to direct any course of study. This guide includes the examination outline, sample questions, bibliography of recommended study materials, and suggestions for exam review. The Certification Review Guide is available free of charge on the IAAP Web site: http://www.iaap-hq.org, then Professional Certification, Forms.

Acknowledgments

The fifth edition of the *Certified Professional Secretary*® *and Certified Administrative Professional*® *Examination Review for Office Administration* complements the current revised study outline developed for the Certified Professional Secretary® and Certified Administrative Professional® Examinations. Like the other reviews available in the series, *Office Administration* will be a successful review tool because of the contributions, critiques, and dedicated efforts of a number of individuals who are interested and involved in the certification of secretaries and administrative professionals.

The International Association of Administrative Professionals (IAAP), through the Institute for Certification, has not only provided the incentive for the development of the fifth edition of this review but also valuable input during the review process. We are sincerely grateful for the continued support and endorsement of IAAP and the Institute in the development and revision of the series.

Specifically, we acknowledge the contributions of Dr. Dolores Kelly, Neumann College; Evelyn Mattison, Ergon Corporation; Carol Mull, Greenville Technical College; and Pam Silvers, Asheville-Buncombe Technical Community College, for their helpful reviews and critiques of the manuscript. In addition, the continued support of Kathy L. Schoneboom CPS/CAP, Certification Manager, IAAP, is much appreciated.

The Illinois Division of IAAP and, in particular, those members of the Kishwaukee Chapter, DeKalb, Illinois, who are pursuing or have received their professional certification deserve a special acknowledgment. These groups continue to be extremely supportive and positive about the need for secretaries and administrative professionals to become certified and to participate in professional organizations. Their friendship and encouragement is very much appreciated.

Lastly, we appreciate the leadership demonstrated by Elizabeth Sugg, Prentice Hall, and the many contributions of Deborah Hoffman, Project Manager, and Carol Mull, the Series Editor, in coordinating the reviews and critiques of the manuscript. With their help, we were able to identify and interpret the kinds of information needed by secretaries and administrative professionals to appropriately prepare for the CPS and CAP Examinations.

We hope that all the input provided by professionals and incorporated in the manuscript content for this review will help candidates everywhere in their preparation for the CPS and CAP Examinations.

Betty L. Schroeder, Ph.D.

Diane Routhier Graf CPS, Ed.D.

SECTION ONE
Records Management

Chapter 1
Filing Systems

OVERVIEW

The management of information, an extremely important office support function, enables paper, image, and digital information to continue to serve their purposes effectively within an organization. Records are the products of office work, and they serve as the "memory" of the organization. The average cost of each misfiled record or filing error is more than $100.

Filing systems are an integral part of records management. The basic premise for establishing filing systems within an organization is the ability to retrieve records. Appropriate storage of records is the key to records retrieval; a means to an end, with the end being retrieval. If a record cannot be located when needed, the filing system is at fault.

KEY TERMS

Active records, 2
Constant information, 8
Cuts, 28
Data integrity, 11
Fiche, 13
Guides, 28
Important records, 2
Inactive records, 2
Index record, 11
Individual folder, 26

Intelligent retrieval, 20
Microform, 12
Miscellaneous folder, 27
Nonessential records, 3
Nonrecords, 2
Optical character recognition (OCR), 21
Out folder, 27
Periodic transfer, 6
Perpetual transfer, 6

Posted record, 11
Primary value, 5
Purging, 6
Records, 2
Relative index, 11
Secondary value, 5
Tab, 28
Useful records, 3
Variable information, 8
Vital records, 2

1

A. Analyzing Records and Records Systems

In any business organization, information in the form of documents can be categorized as **records** or **nonrecords.** The term *records* refers to official documents of the company or organization valuable enough to be retained and stored in a format for future use and distribution. Documents prepared for the organization's convenience or temporary use but normally not saved and disposed of after use are called *nonrecords*. Records need to be analyzed to determine what the nature of the present records system is in the organization. Records analysis consists of examining the types of records and the records cycle in use.

1. *Classifying Records:* Individual records are classified according to either the record activity (use) or the importance of particular records used within the business, or both.

   a. *Record activity or use:* Records are either active records or inactive records. The length of time active and inactive records will be retained is determined when the record is created or as the record is used.

      (1) *Active records:* Those records that are accessed and utilized in the current administration of business functions are known as **active records.** They are often used to generate more business, to follow-up on current transactions of the organization, and to develop more information on the organization and its activities.

      (2) *Inactive records:* Those records no longer referred to on a regular basis but still of limited importance are called **inactive records.** They do not relate to current business activities of the organization and are usually transferred to inactive status in a central records storage facility. Such a facility could have computer storage as well as physical storage space for files, boxes, and other media.

   b. *Importance of records:* Typically, records are classified as vital, important, useful, or nonessential records.

      (1) *Vital records:* Records classified as **vital records** are essential for the effective, continuous operation of the firm. Vital records are irreplaceable records.

      EXAMPLES:

      Accounts payable

      Accounts receivable

      Copyrights

      Insurance policies

      Leases

      Legal documents

      Patents

      Property deeds

      Trademarks

      (2) *Important records:* Records classified as **important records** contribute to the continued smooth operation of an organization and can be replaced or duplicated if lost or destroyed in a disaster but with a considerable expenditure of time and money. Copies of important records are usually available, but extra time may be involved in requesting and locating them, causing delays in use. Many of these records are available on microforms, magnetic tapes, compact discs, or computer disks.

EXAMPLES:

> *Case files*
> *Customer orders*
> *Financial records*
> *Tax records for previous years*

(3) *Useful records:* Records used in the operation of the organization that can be easily replaced are called **useful records.** In case of a disaster, the loss of useful records would not prevent routine operation of the business, only temporary delay or inconvenience in trying to locate pertinent documents and information.

EXAMPLES:

> *Business reports*
> *Complaint letters received from customers*
> *Customer requests for product information*

(4) *Nonessential records:* Records that are not necessary for the restoration of the business and have no predictable value are known as **nonessential records.** These records probably should be destroyed once their usefulness is over.

EXAMPLES:

> *Subscriptions for external publications*
> *Survey results received from suppliers*
> *Telephone messages*

2. ***The Records Cycle:*** A record's life cycle extends from the moment the record is created until its final disposition. An initial decision is made when a record is created as to its life; that is, how long the record must be retained either in active or inactive storage. Decisions are made at various times during the records cycle as to the continued use of the record, the procedure to be used in filing the record, and its retention or disposal. Figure 1–1 highlights the key steps in the records cycle: creation of the record, utilization of the record, retention of the record, transfer of the record, and disposal of the record. Manual filing and electronic filing form the basis for a total records cycle since both manual and electronic procedures must be applied to the information and documents involved.

   a. *Creation of records:* Only people with the authority to create records within an organization should be permitted to do so. Central control of records stems from careful monitoring of all records as they are created. Basic considerations in the creation of new records should include the following:

   (1) Format of the new record

   (2) Procedures established for creating the record

   (3) Justification (rationale) for the new record

   (4) Purpose of the new record

   (5) Cost of producing the record

   (6) Increased office productivity likely to result

   (7) Estimated life of the record

FIGURE 1–1   The Records Cycle

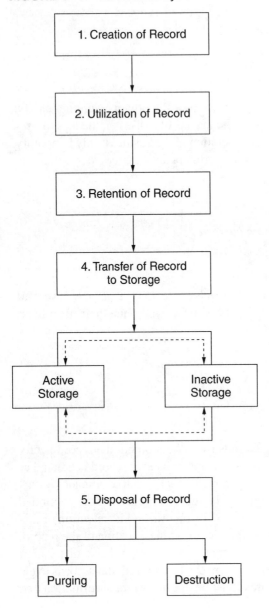

b. *Utilization of records:* Efficient procedures must be developed so that the record that has been created may be used, stored, and retrieved for the purpose(s) intended. A records inventory will help determine the actual use to which the record will be put as well as the cost of using and retaining the record.

c. *Retention of records:* The life of a particular record is based on the record's value. In this phase of the records cycle, retention schedules are developed and the value of specific records determined.

(1) *Development of retention schedules:* A records retention schedule is an agreement among the department creating the record, the user, and the records manager that identifies the records of the organization being kept in active, semiactive, and inactive storage. Such a schedule estimates the period of time each type of record is to be held in active storage for day-to-day reference, in inactive storage for occasional reference, and if and when records may be purged

or destroyed. A retention schedule approved for use within the organization helps to ensure that federal, state, and local regulations are considered in deciding how important specific records are and how long to keep records on file.

(2) *Appraisal of records:* In the process of establishing retention schedules, records are evaluated in terms of their primary and secondary value. Value assigned to records depends on the utilization of those records in ongoing operations. Once their value has been determined, a set number of years for retaining those records can be established.

    (a) *Primary value:* Records that are active in nature and needed for current operations are said to have **primary value.** Records may have administrative, legal, fiscal, or research value.

- *Administrative value:* Records that have administrative value are needed for a business to conduct current business operations.
  EXAMPLES: *Policies and procedures, executive directives, purchase requisitions, inventory records, personnel records*

- *Legal value:* Those documents that have legal value contain provisions or agreements that relate to the legal rights and obligations of the business.
  EXAMPLES: *Contracts, agreements to purchase new property or equipment, leases for business property*

- *Fiscal value:* Records of fiscal value usually refer to those documents that relate to the financial transactions of the organization.
  EXAMPLES: *Budgets, vouchers, tax returns, sales reports*

- *Research value:* Records consisting of technical information that results from primary or secondary research will have research value to the organization.
  EXAMPLES: *Records of procedures used in conducting a research project, records of step-by-step procedures in analyzing the historical development in information equipment over the past ten years*

    (b) *Secondary value:* Records that are held in semiactive or inactive storage are said to have **secondary value** and may have historical or archival importance.

- *Information value:* Over a period of years, any organization will accumulate records that contain information relating to people, places, events, and other phenomena.
  EXAMPLES: *Copyrights, patents, blueprints, photographs, maps*

- *Evidence value:* Records that trace the development of an organization from its beginning to the present may have evidentiary value in providing proof of policies, procedures, and practices during the organization's lifetime.
  EXAMPLES: *Organizational charts, policies and procedures manuals, articles of incorporation, minutes books*

d. *Transfer of records:* During its life, a record may be transferred from active to inactive storage or from inactive to active storage, depending on the record activity. A record may be physically removed from the premises and transferred to remote storage in a centralized records center, an off-site records facility, or within a computer system. Two methods of records transfer are the **perpetual transfer** and **periodic transfer** methods.

(1) *Perpetual transfer method:* Using the perpetual method, records can be transferred at any time that the event has been completed or the case closed, and future referral to the records will be infrequent and limited.

EXAMPLE: *A perpetual method of records transfer is used in the Lawrence & Brown law firm. Once a court case has been closed, the file is moved immediately to inactive storage. With this method, a case sometimes remains open for two or more years before it can be closed and becomes inactive.*

(2) *Periodic transfer method:* Records are transferred as of a specific date each year. All files for a specific period of time are transferred at that time.

EXAMPLE: *The Powell Seed Company uses a periodic transfer method because this particular type of business lends itself to a periodic rather than a perpetual method. On July 1 and December 31 of each year, the files are transferred from active to inactive storage. Of course, on those particular dates, all records are perused to see whether they are needed for future reference or can be destroyed.*

e. *Disposal of records:* When a record is no longer needed, it may be purged or destroyed. Before this is done, however, the department that created and/or used the record is contacted to determine whether the record indeed can be deleted or destroyed. The records retention schedule specifies the period of time a given record should be retained before disposal.

(1) *Purging of records:* The process of automatically deleting the contents of an electronically stored record is known as **purging.** As purging takes place, each record is examined to determine whether it still has value or can be eliminated. Deleting an electronic copy of a document, however, does not mean that the information has been destroyed. The information is removed from, or deleted at, the stored location but may still remain somewhere within the system.

EXAMPLE: *Each week Grayson creates a disk copy of all correspondence prepared. After a one-week period, she reviews the contents of each disk to see whether any of the records can be purged (deleted) from the disk. She labels each disk carefully and keeps all correspondence relating to a particular project or task on the same disk.*

(2) *Destruction of paper records:* The method of destruction is very important since many records, even though ready to be destroyed, contain confidential information. Common ways of destroying paper records include shredding, pulverizing, and incinerating.

(3) *Destruction of microform and magnetic records:* Common ways of destroying microform or magnetic records include shredding, pulverizing, and incinerating. Because these types of records may also contain confidential information, destruction is essential to eliminate the chance that the information might become public.

Most business organizations are now participating in recycling programs for paper, cardboard, and shredded or pulverized materials.

Check Point—Section A

Directions: For each question, circle the correct answer.

A–1. Individual business records are classified according to the

   A) steps in the record cycle
   B) form of the record
   C) method used for creating the record
   D) use of the record

A–2. Which one of the following types of records would be classified as a vital record?

   A) A report stored on a computer disk
   B) Copyright for a software program

   C) Tax records for the previous year
   D) Customer request for product information

A–3. The series of steps from the time the record is created until final disposition is called the

   A) document preparation
   B) utilization of records in business activities
   C) records cycle
   D) records transfer from active to inactive storage

B. Records Creation, Design, and Control

Business records must be controlled throughout the records cycle to ensure efficient handling and security of the records. The design of the record enhances the ability of the records manager to control the use of that record within the organization. Once the record has been designed for either manual or electronic use, appropriate steps must be taken to ensure that the record will be used as intended. Any record created for organizational use should be planned carefully before actual creation. Control in the creation and design phase results in increased quality, improved productivity, reduced costs, and more effective storage and retrieval. Records are created in both conventional and unconventional formats.

1. *Conventional Formats:* Correspondence, business forms, and business reports typically appear in conventional formats that result in hard copies (paper copies) or soft copies (electronic copies). Appropriate formatting of these types of records makes control of the information contained in these records an easier task.

   a. *Correspondence:* Written messages in the form of business letters (external communication) and electronic mail and memorandums (internal communication) are referred to as *correspondence.*

      (1) *Letter design:* Many companies use logos, standardized letter formats, and letter styles to create a positive image as well as to reduce letter-writing costs. Letters merged with variable information from databases reduce the average cost of correspondence while still permitting personalization of letters with individual addresses, salutations, and inserted information.

         EXAMPLE: *Since 1930, when the cost of a business letter was estimated at 30 cents, the Dartnell Corporation's Institute of Business Research has conducted research into the cost of producing a business letter. By 1960, this cost had increased to $1.83; and the 1983 figure increased to well over $7 per letter. This computation included all labor costs (executive and secretary), overhead costs, and indirect costs.*

Dartnell's 1991 estimate was a range from $12 to $18 depending on the use of dictation equipment, personal computers, or typewriters to produce the letter. The cost of producing a one-page, 185-word letter that was machine dictated and transcribed on a personal computer was $11.77. The same letter transcribed on an electric typewriter was $17.71.

A 1994 study indicated that the cost ranged from $12.64 to $19.13, depending on the technology used to produce the letter. Dartnell's research suggested that transcribing from dictation on a personal computer is the fastest, most cost-effective way to produce a business letter. No further research study on business letter costs has been published by Dartnell since 1994.

(2) *Memorandum design:* Standardized formats that speed up production and reduce costs are also used for memorandums. Decisions are made within departments on whether memorandums, the telephone, or electronic mail will be used for internal communication. Electronic mail has become a very popular means of transmitting information internally throughout the organization and externally to other organizations. With e-mail, a record of e-memos sent, received, and deleted as trash is kept by the system, making the task of knowing what e-mails are in the system relatively easy. The sender knows whether the message was received and viewed. The receiver can respond to the e-memo if a response is required.

(3) *Maintaining document flow:* Control of the movement of written messages through the organization is very important. In large firms, a central distribution area or mail center controls all incoming and outgoing written correspondence. In smaller firms, an individual is typically assigned the task of distributing incoming correspondence and processing outgoing correspondence.

(4) *Development of correspondence manuals:* With so much more information being communicated through various means, many firms have developed recommended procedures for the preparation and handling of written and electronic correspondence. This enables a more concerted effort to standardize procedures throughout the organization.

b. *Business forms:* Forms used in business procedures need to be analyzed on a regular basis to determine whether they are still in use, need to be revised, or can be eliminated. A *business form* is a record that contains **constant information** (printed or electronically imaged) and space for **variable information** to be filled in and inserted.

EXAMPLE: *Electronic copies of forms (templates) are often provided on the firm's intranet to be opened and filled in with variable information. Completed forms can then be printed and saved under appropriate file names.*

Before a form is redesigned, any problems resulting from either its design or its use should be analyzed.

(1) *Classifications of forms:* Business forms may be classified in two ways: according to specific business functions (external or internal) for which they are intended, and the physical way in which they are constructed (single copy, multiple copy, or view copy).

EXAMPLE: *Business forms designed for specific business functions include human resource forms (application for employment, interview evaluation form), accounting forms (purchase requisition, purchase order, invoice, check), and sales or customer service forms (customer order form, repair requisition).*

The physical design of a business form depends on its physical size, paper stock used, type styles used for constant information, and space required to insert variable information.

(2) *Types of business forms:* Forms may be referred to by the type of form, either a flat form (a single sheet of paper that may be interleaved with other sheets to produce multiple copies), a specialty form (one that requires special equipment to produce or use), or an electronic form (one that requires a computer to fill in the required information).

(3) *Forms design:* The process of designing a business form depends on what information needs to appear on the form and the sequence of that information. Sound forms design should be based on the actual use of the form and the standardization of the form in relation to others used in the business. Forms may be designed for completion through manual and electronic means.

EXAMPLES OF MANUAL FORMS:

Snap-out or unit-set forms: *A multiple-copy form is used when more than one copy of the same form is needed; carbon paper is interleaved between the copies or the paper is specially treated to produce carbonless copies.*

Spot-carbon forms: *Certain areas on each copy of the form are carbonized so that only the information to be transferred to other copies will be copied.*

Carbonless (NCR) forms: *Specially treated (coated) paper permits the pressure of a pen or pencil on the original copy to create the same images on the other copies.*

EXAMPLES OF AUTOMATED FORMS:

Continuous forms: *Forms are used with printers to produce multiple numbers of forms that will have to be separated on the perforations between forms after printing.*

Unit-record forms: *Forms, either in continuous form or in tab-card sets, are used as input and output records in electronic systems.*

Magnetic-ink character recognition (MICR) form: *Coded information on the form, such as MICR numbers on checks, can be read by automated equipment and transmitted to a computer for processing.*

Optical-character recognition (OCR) forms: *Data typed, written, or mark sensed on the form can be interpreted by OCR readers and scanners for computer processing.*

Templates or view forms: *Templates, created with word processing, spreadsheet, or graphics software, that have been stored (hard disk, diskette, compact disc) can be retrieved as needed for fill-in and processing.*

Electronic forms: *Access to the firm's intranet enables system users to download forms needed, fill in the information required, and forward copies of the completed forms to other departments within the firm for processing.*

   c. *Business reports:* A business report is the final outcome of a specific information-gathering activity within the organization that summarizes the problem or topic, background of the research, procedures, and results of a business project or research. A business report conveys information to top-level management for decision-making purposes or to external sources who need the information to further their own work. The report tends to be the most expensive type of record created within most organizations because of its originality, time involved, and other research and writing costs.

     (1) *Content of reports:* Reports may be either formal or informal. A formal report may be informational or analytical and usually follows a standard format or structure for the specific content. The style of writing is more formal in nature. Such a report is typically more than five pages in length and may be prepared in letter format if directed to a specific company or organization or in manuscript format.

         An informational report would most likely include the following sections:

- Introduction and background of the topic
- Facts and findings
- Summary and conclusions

         An analytical report would most likely include the following sections:

- Introduction to the problem
- Facts and findings
- Discussion and analysis
- Conclusions and recommendations

         An informal report is used primarily for internal communication and is prepared for a single purpose within the organization—to provide additional information on a specific topic. The informal report is rather short, perhaps less than five pages, and may be prepared in a memorandum format if distributed only within the organization.

     (2) *Reports design:* As with correspondence, standardized formats are very important in the preparation of business reports. Most reports will be generated through the use of software (word processing, spreadsheet, and graphics) using a computer system. Particularly in these cases, the more standardized the format, the easier it is to control the actual preparation of the report. Only information absolutely needed should be included in the report.

         EXAMPLE: *Format features affect the way the final document will look. Some format decisions can be made before the text is keyed in, such as margins (top, bottom, left, right), vertical spacing (single or double spacing), inclusion of headings within the text, and left justification of the text. Other format decisions are best made immediately prior to printing the document. These decisions include the placement of headers, footers, and page numbers.*

     (3) *Preparation costs:* Costs incurred as a result of preparing a business report include the research involved in gathering the information and data for the report, the writer's salary, the time involved in researching and writing the report, the length and involvement of the report, fixed costs, and office support and word/information processing costs.

d. *Card systems:* In records management, cards (3 by 5 inches, 4 by 6 inches, 5 by 8 inches) are used as a means of filing information or referencing information filed elsewhere. Card systems are used for two primary purposes: to create index records and to create posted records.

(1) *Index records:* Cards may be used as a **relative index** for files using a numeric or alphanumeric classification system. As an **index record,** the card contains only *reference* information. An individual would examine the index record to find out where the original file or document is located.

EXAMPLES OF INDEX RECORDS:

> *Names and addresses of clients or customers*
> *Employee lists*
> *Price lists*
> *Membership lists*
> *Stockroom item locations*
> *Telephone numbers frequently used*
> *Subscription lists*

EXAMPLE: *Burton & Smith, a local law firm, uses a numeric system for filing. Each client or case is assigned a separate file number. A relative index is kept on cards in a special card drawer in alphabetical order. If a file needs to be located, the first step is to look in the index under the client's name or the case name to see what number has been assigned to the file. Once the number of the file is located, the file can be located easily in the file.*

Such a system may also be computerized by creating a database to organize or manage files electronically. A database may be accessed by keying in the name of the file desired or conducting a search for the individual name or file number. Electronic lists have the advantage of storing all data in one location, making data available to more than one user, and improving **data integrity** when properly maintained. [Data integrity refers to the maintenance of accurate data within the system.]

(2) *Posted records:* Card records may be used to record (post) information (update, change, delete, add to) to bring the record up to date. New information posted on the card form may be entered manually or by computer. Since a source document, the original record, is used to obtain the information to be posted, the **posted record** is sometimes called a *secondary record.*

EXAMPLES OF POSTED RECORDS:

> *Stock control cards*
> *Payroll cards*
> *Repair and maintenance cards for office equipment*
> *Automobile service records*
> *Hospital and medical records*
> *Dental records*

EXAMPLE: *All records at Prairie View Animal Hospital were kept on individual owner cards before the system was computerized. Whenever a pet received some type of treatment, medication, or examination, an entry was posted on the card form, indicating the date, the diagnosis, the prescribed treatment or medication, the charge, and any other relevant information. In this way, a perpetual record was kept with the medical history of the pet.*

Recently, the records were converted to a computer system. Now, when a pet owner enters the office, the name is keyed into the system to obtain a file number; the appropriate file folder can then be pulled from an open-shelving unit for reference during the examination. The complete medical history of the pet is helpful in making appropriate diagnoses and prescribing medication or treatment. The billing is immediate, too, with the pet owner presented with a statement for payment before leaving the office.

(3) *Design of card forms:* Many card forms are preprinted with descriptors (key words), horizontal and vertical rulings, and directions for completion. Preprinted card forms are designed so that the user will be able to locate information easily. The descriptors, key words, or phrases preprinted on the form are called *constant information* since those words appear the same on all copies of a particular form. *Variable information* consists of the words or text inserted on the card form that will change for each user or situation. Card forms must be created on card stock that will be durable, compact, and easy to handle.

e. *Other conventional records:* In addition to correspondence, business forms, reports, and cards, other types of conventional records include engineering documents, maps, charts, drawings, technical catalogs, and manuals (policies, procedures, and operations). The design and use of any of these types of records need to be controlled as well.

2. **Nonconventional Formats:** Increased use of automation in offices has resulted in a greater variety of unconventional formats. Microforms, audiovisual media, videotapes, compact discs, digital videodiscs, and information and image processing media are becoming more versatile in substituting for paper documents.

Note: The word *disks,* with a *k,* typically refers to magnetic disks, whereas the word *discs,* with a *c,* typically refers to compact discs, optical discs, and videodiscs.

a. *Microforms:* Any record that contains reduced images on film is known as a **microform.** Perhaps the greatest advantage of using microform records is saving storage space. Microforms also appear to be advantageous in preserving records over time. The most commonly used microforms are microfilm and fiche; microforms may be inserted into aperture cards or packaged in cartridges, cassettes, or jackets.

(1) *Microfilm:* The oldest type of microform is *microfilm*, which stores images of document pages side by side on 16-, 35-, 70-, or 105-millimeter film. Each reel of film has a standard size of 100 feet and can hold up to 2,500 letter-size images or up to 30,000 smaller-size images. When a document that is stored on microfilm needs to be read, the film images are enlarged and projected on a visual display screen.

(a) *Computer output microfilm (COM):* In the past several years, computer output microfilm (COM) has become an efficient method of working with data stored on electronic storage media. Ordinarily, data are electronically stored in a computer and printed out on continuous-form paper. With COM, only the data needed are obtained in printout form rather than all of the data in a particular file. The greatest advantage of using COM is the saving of space that occurs since only those images needed are printed out. Other advantages include the following:

- More standardized formats for large volumes of information
- Time saved in printing out paper copies
- Economics of producing large office manuals that need to be updated frequently
- Use of an indexing system to locate images

(b) *Computer input microfilm (CIM):* A relatively recent development, computer input microfilm (CIM), is considered a low-cost method for automatically reading files of information contained on microfilm into the computer for storage. With CIM, the information contained in the document does not need to be converted into any other form before processing takes place. A general procedure is illustrated in Figure 1–2.

(2) *Fiche:* A **fiche** is a sheet of film containing miniature images arranged in rows and columns on a card. The number of images that can be arranged on one fiche depends on the reduction ratio being used. The standard size of a fiche is 6 by 4 inches, with the fiche coded for retrieval purposes.

(a) *Microfiche:* A standard 6- by 4-inch fiche can hold up to 98 images in 7 rows, with 14 images in each row, when the standard 24X reduction ratio is applied. Each sheet of *microfiche* is coded to identify its contents.

(b) *Ultrafiche:* An *ultrafiche* is like a microfiche except that the page images are reduced more than 90 times. On a standard 6- by 4-inch fiche, hundreds of images can be stored in a similar pattern to that used on a microfiche, from left to right in rows, and from top to bottom of the sheet. Ultrafiche stores the largest number of images of any microform.

FIGURE 1–2 Conversion Procedure for Microfilming Documents

Large Quantity of Paper Documents

↓

Paper Documents are Microfilmed (with Certificate of Authenticity)

↓

Microfilmed Documents Pass Through Optical Sensing (Recognition)

↓

Data Contained on Microfilmed Documents are Stored in Computer

(3) *Aperture cards:* An *aperture card* is a punched card that contains a slot into which at least one microform can be inserted. Usually, text is punched into the card and/or interpreted on the face of the card. A set of aperture cards can be easily duplicated. The explanation on the card with the microforms is an added advantage.

(4) *Microform packaging:* Microforms are packaged in cartridges, cassettes, and jackets.

  (a) *Cartridge:* A roll of microfilm may be housed inside a cartridge. Cartridges are convenient to handle, and the microfilm is protected from fingerprints and possible damage. A cartridge must be rewound before it can be removed from a microfilm reader.

  (b) *Cassette:* A cassette contains two reels: a feed reel and a take-up reel. The microfilm is protected from possible damage by being encased in the cassette. A cassette does not have to be rewound before it can be removed from a microfilm reader.

  (c) *Jacket:* A *jacket* is a plastic unitized record the same size as a microform. Strips of film can be inserted in single or multiple channels on the jackets. As many as 60 images (5 strips with 12 images each) can be inserted into a 6- by 4-inch jacket. Its primary advantage is the ease with which microfilm can be updated. A strip of film can be removed and quickly replaced with a new one. Each jacket is coded for storage and retrieval purposes.

b. *Audiovisual media:* Another category of nonconventional records is audiovisual media. Photographs, 33-millimeter slides, electronic slides, compact discs, cassette tape recordings, videodiscs, videotapes, and transparencies are included in this group. Special attention must be given in the indexing, coding, and storing of these types of records since many times special filing cabinets are required for adequate protection. Special equipment is also needed to view or listen to the information contained in these kinds of records.

EXAMPLES:

> *Compact discs, a compact disc player (for listening to recorded text or music) or a compact disc drive on the computer (for accessing recorded text or music stored on compact discs)*
>
> *Electronic slides: a computer, a screen, or a projection system*
>
> *Videotapes: a videocassette recorder-player (VCR) with a television screen*
>
> *Transparencies: an overhead projector*
>
> *Videodiscs: a videodisc player with a television screen*

c. *Electronic media:* Information processing media are receiving more attention from records managers. Information recorded on magnetic disks and tapes or compact discs (soft copies) is extremely sensitive. Therefore, the electronic media must be handled carefully to protect the stored information from possible damage. The authenticity of the information contained on the media must be able to be certified as accurate and the integrity of the information maintained.

Backup copies are routinely prepared for important documents or for the most recent business transactions (for a specified period of time, e.g., a day or a week) in case the original records are lost, damaged, or destroyed. Electronic media are especially helpful in planning and creating databases of information for application throughout the organization. A *database* is an electronic method of organizing facts and data in one or more computer data files.

(1) *Preliminary planning:* The following types of questions will be helpful in deciding what types of information will be essential or useful as the creation of a database is being planned:

- What types of information will be included in the database?
- Who will be the database users?
- How often will specific types of data and information be accessed?
- Will the information be used to process transactions such as sales?
- Will the information be used as part of a decision support system?

(2) *Database creation:* The creation of an electronic database expedites the efficient use of information and data. Typically, a database consists of two or more related computer data files. To design an electronic database, a database management system (DBMS) is required. Typical microcomputer database systems are Microsoft Access® and dBase®.

The use of database files should be related to the overall efficiency of systems used within the entire organization. People throughout the organization should be aware of the availability of information through the use of computer databases.

Check Point—Section B

Directions: For each question, circle the correct answer.

B–1. Which one of the following records is typically designed in a conventional format?

A) An invoice
B) One sheet of microfiche
C) An electronic slide
D) A computer disk

B–2. Reduced images captured on film are stored on a/an

A) magnetic disk
B) videotape

C) OCR process
D) microform

B–3. Which one of the following records is designed in a nonconventional format?

A) A business letter
B) A 3- by 5-inch card for equipment repair
C) A set of electronic slides
D) A three-page business report

C. Records Management Equipment Systems

In addition to procedures for filing records for future use, records storage equipment and supplies must be used to guarantee safety of records during their useful life. The costs of maintaining adequate floor space for paper records is encouraging businesses to investigate other methods of records storage such as micrographics and computer storage. The actual cost of records storage equipment and supplies is approximately 20 percent of the overall cost of maintaining a records storage and retrieval system.

1. ***Filing Equipment for Paper Storage:*** Conventional storage systems are used in many offices where paper is the primary medium for storage. File cabinets, usually three- or four-drawer models, are generally the most common filing equipment used.

    a. *Vertical file cabinet:* Paper documents are stored on end in a vertical fashion in vertical files. These file cabinets may hold letter-size or legal-size documents. Each filing unit may contain anywhere from two to six drawers, and each drawer may be 24, 26, or 28 inches in length. A standard 26-inch drawer can hold up to 5,000 sheets of paper plus guides and folders. Generally, file cabinets such as these are easy to set up and use.

    b. *Lateral file cabinet:* Lateral files are available from two-drawer (usually placed by the side of a desk) to five-drawer capacity. Folders can be stored in two ways: facing the front of the file or facing the side of the cabinet. Each drawer may be pulled out to a maximum of 16 inches. Less aisle space is needed to accommodate the lateral file. The unit may be placed flush with the wall, and most materials can be filed sideways rather than frontwise, as is true of vertical files.

    c. *Stationary shelving unit:* Stationary open-shelf units are a form of lateral file characterized by the "open" view of all the files in the system. The equipment may be completely open shelf, without door enclosures, or doors may be pulled down over each shelf and locked for overnight security. Some units have closed backs to keep files or books from slipping behind the shelving units. Open shelves allow "through" shelving for the storage of larger materials. Up to 50 percent savings of floor space usage results from using this system. Typically, labor costs are reduced because of the increased efficiency of the records personnel in working with this type of storage unit. Numeric filing with color coding is the most common classification system used with open-shelf files.

       EXAMPLE: *Prairie View Animal Hospital has a large open-shelving unit that contains color-coded files for each client (pet owner). Each time a client brings in a pet the veterinarian is given the appropriate folder so that the pet's medical history is immediately available. These file folders are coordinated with records that are stored on the computer. With approximately 5,000 clients, a four-digit color code, representing the client number, is assigned to each file folder to help in refiling the folder. The office staff is currently revising all records on the computer system so that initial access by client name at the terminal will give the code number of the file folder.*

    d. *High-density mobile storage:* Mobile storage systems include sets of storage units on wheeled carriages that slide on tracks embedded in or attached to the floor. Mobile systems commonly in use in business today include programmable, powered, mechanically assisted, or manual systems. The shelving units can be moved together when not in use or can be moved apart to create aisle space when a person needs to locate a file. Safety systems typically activate automatically when records personnel are working with the files. Mobile systems are available in custom designs to match office décor.

       (1) *Programmable systems:* The aisles of storage in a programmable system can be opened at the touch of a button. LCD displays on each shelving unit indicate the status of the system (e.g., whether portions of the system are in use

and certain sections of the mobile storage cannot be moved). Programmable features of the system allow accessibility to stored files and records by moving sections of the mobile system and opening aisle space where desired. Aisle widths can be programmed to accommodate personnel in wheelchairs.

(2) *Powered systems:* Aisles in a powered system can be opened with levers located on the sides of the individual shelving units. Similar safety features as those on programmable systems are used in powered systems. The power allows the storage units to move more easily along the floor tracks. Aisles may be entered as soon as the mobile units are moved to save time in storing and retrieving files.

(3) *Mechanically assisted or manual shelving systems:* Individual storage units, resembling book shelves, are used to store documents and other materials. With mechanically assisted or manual shelving systems, a pull handle is used to open aisles between the units. Regardless of the weight of the contents, the units are easy to move along the floor tracks. A variety of safety features protect the user and the documents stored in the system.

EXAMPLE: *Spacesaver Corporation has a QuickSpace™ storage system that consists of pull-out shelving units. This type of system is especially suited for creating storage space in narrow areas between walls or in alcoves.*

(4) *Lateral mobile storage:* When floor space for storage is limited, a lateral mobile storage system provides side-to-side storage. One storage unit is mounted to the wall with one or two rows of movable shelving mounted to the floor directly in front. The sliding shelving units move laterally to allow access to the fixed shelving in the back.

EXAMPLE: *Lateral Bi-file® or Tri-file® systems are designed for narrow storage areas, with two or three storage units, respectively. These systems are especially useful in narrow storage areas.*

(5) *Open-faced shelving:* The open design of this type of shelving enables office personnel to access records easily and quickly. When comparing cost per filing inch, open-faced shelving is considered the most cost-effective type of storage equipment.

e. *Rotary (carousel) file:* The greatest advantage of the rotary file is that the operator can bring a file or document to the point of use by turning or rotating the file. *Rotary files* are available for either vertical or horizontal operation. The entire file rotates like a Lazy-Susan around a central hub. Large rotary files may be powered, permitting the operator to control the movement of the file with a push button.

EXAMPLE: *Rotary storage from Spacesaver Corporation may be used to store computer discs, microforms, compact discs, video- and audiocassettes, and other standard filing applications. The storage units range from low-height units used in private offices to larger units for teams or for the entire organization (central storage).*

f. *Automated filing system:* With an automated system, the operator must enter an electronic or computer command (code) to let the system know which file is desired. The conveyor revolves around its track, like a Ferris wheel, and automatically stops at the desired location. This type of system uses vertical space for maximum storage in a minimum amount of floor space.

EXAMPLE: *A system such as a Lektriever system uses movable carriers to actually bring the file folders to the point of use.*

The time involved is relatively short (within a minute or two) if only one file must be located. If numerous files need to be located at one time, time can be saved by locating files with similar codes at the same time.

g. *Card file equipment:* When information is stored on cards, the size of the cards used for storage will help determine the type of filing equipment that can be used. The most common types of equipment are vertical, visible, wheel, and rotary card file equipment.

   (1) *Vertical card files:* Like vertical correspondence files, vertical card files allow the cards to stand upright and to be compressed tightly within the file drawer. These files may be individual card file drawers or special card file drawers that are part of a vertical correspondence file. The size of the drawer will determine the size of the cards to be used with that drawer.

   EXAMPLE: *The most common sizes for cards are 3 by 5 inches, 4 by 6 inches, and 5 by 8 inches. File drawers meant for cards of these sizes should be used.*

   (2) *Visible card files:* With visible files, cards are positioned so that one line of information appears in the *visible margin* that overlaps at the front edge of the file. Visible files are stored in flat drawers and trays or suspended on panels so that the operator has ready access to the card records at any time. Color coding may be used so that the cards may represent different groups of records. The biggest advantage is that the visible card files may be updated at any time simply by removing the "old" card or adding "new" cards.

   (3) *Wheel card files:* Information that needs to be accessible for quick reference may be kept on cards inserted into a wheel card file. This type of file looks like a miniature Ferris wheel with the cards inserted in a particular alphabetic or numeric order. Usually, these files use cards up to 5 by 8 inches and take up very little space on a work surface.

   (4) *Rotary card files:* Rotary files move horizontally around a central hub and may be used for correspondence, cards, or both, depending on specific office needs.

h. *Filing equipment for noncorrespondence storage:* In addition to paper documents and electronic media, numerous other types of noncorrespondence items need to be stored properly. Each item needs to be examined to see what kind of storage system would provide the protection and durability needed. Typical noncorrespondence items might include plans, drawings, blueprints, maps, photographs, audiotapes, videotapes, compact discs, slides, and computer printouts. Here are some types of storage equipment that might be used for some of these applications:

   (1) *File storage with horizontal drawers:* Flat storage provides the best storage for maps, blueprints, and photographs.

   (2) *Suspension open-shelf files:* Computer printouts require a suspension (or "hanging") type of storage area because of the bulkiness of the printouts and the necessity to keep these files close at hand for each reference.

   (3) *Rolled files:* Maps, plats, blueprints, or posters may be encased in cardboard rolls for safe storage.

2. ***Equipment for Microforms Preparation and Storage:*** Special equipment is needed
   to prepare microforms for a micrographics system and to view these microforms once
   they have been developed.

   a. *Microform cameras:* A microform camera records a miniaturized image of each full
      page of a document onto film. The most commonly used microform cameras are
      the rotary microfilm camera, the planetary camera, and the step-and-repeat camera.

      (1) *Rotary microfilm camera:* This camera films documents as they pass through
          an open area within the camera. This is the least expensive method of filming
          records.

      (2) *Planetary camera:* The *planetary camera* is an overhead flatbed camera used
          to photograph flat stationary objects. Filming is more expensive with a plan-
          etary camera than with a rotary camera, but a better-quality image results.

      (3) *Step-and-repeat camera:* The purpose of the *step-and-repeat camera* is to
          film microfiche. This camera films images onto a 4-inch-wide film that can
          be cut in the standard-size master microfiche of 6 by 4 inches.

   b. *Processor:* The film used to record images for microforms must be developed in
      a darkroom on a processor.

   c. *Microfilm reader:* A microfilm reader displays the image of a microform on a
      viewing screen (much the same as a visual display screen on a computer termi-
      nal). Readers are either front projection or rear projection, which refers to the lo-
      cation of the viewing screen.

   d. *Fiche reader:* Because a fiche has multiple images, the reader is designed to help
      the operator locate particular images needed through the use of reader pads and
      pointers. A "zoom" lens also assists the operator in enlarging or reducing the size
      of the image reproduced on the screen.

   e. *Microform reader-printer:* Many times not only is it important to be able to view
      the image on the viewing screen but also to obtain a printed copy of that image.
      With a reader-printer, the operator may obtain a hard copy whenever needed
      merely by locating the image, displaying the image on the screen, and pushing a
      control button that activates the printing mechanism.

   f. *Microform storage equipment:* Microforms are stored in special containers
      (boxes, cases, binders, and cabinets). Equipment should be selected primarily be-
      cause it enables the user to retrieve stored microforms more easily.

   g. *Automated microform retrieval equipment:* Two types of automated retrieval
      equipment are used to store and retrieve microforms: self-contained equipment
      and remote-controlled equipment.

      (1) *Self-contained equipment:* Documents stored as microforms can be housed
          within self-contained equipment that will allow electronic scanning when at-
          tempting to retrieve a needed record. Retrieval begins when an operator keys
          in a request on the keyboard of the retrieval equipment. The computer pro-
          gram directs the system to scan the stored microforms, responding with the
          image of the document showing on the visual display screen or a request for
          additional information.

      (2) *Remote-controlled equipment:* Another type of automated microform retrieval
          equipment searches for microforms that are stored external to the retrieval

equipment. The request for a needed microform is keyed into a terminal equipped with a visual display screen and then transmitted to a microform file located in the central storage for the organization. When the record is found in the central file, the image is displayed on the visual display screen. If a hard copy of the image is needed, the central storage system can provide this service as well.

Equipment is also available for updating stored images in case an image contained on a microfilm reel or a fiche becomes obsolete or is inaccurate. One of the techniques used is similar to the splicing process used with other types of film.

3. ***Equipment for Optical Disc Preparation and Storage:*** Special equipment is needed to transfer images and computer-generated information to optical disc storage.

   a. *Optical character recognition (OCR) scanners:* Documents that are not in digital form (computer generated) can be scanned with OCR scanners and converted to digital images.

   b. *Discs:* Two types of optical discs are glass and polymer, with the glass disc weighing more. Glass discs cost more and do not spin as fast as polymer, reducing data access speed. Polymer discs have the same life span as glass discs.

   c. *Storage equipment:* Most optical discs are stored in devices called "jukeboxes," which can hold 5 to 200 discs.

   d. *Computer:* Information stored on optical disc is accessed through special software housed on a microcomputer or within a network. In such a document management system, documents can be full-text indexed. Content words (descriptors) are used to build the index so that more efficient searching is possible. This process is also called **intelligent retrieval.**

4. ***Equipment for Digital Storage:*** The major types of equipment used in storing information in digital form are the computer, office systems software, optical character recognition (OCR) equipment, and optical disc technology.

   a. *Computers:* Most automated data management systems need computer assistance in order to be effective storage systems. The administrative professional's microcomputer of the present and into the future is a desktop PC or laptop to access any stored data or document available through databases developed for the organization. The vital link between users and the information contained in files and records is the computer.

      EXAMPLE: *Infolinx*™ *is an example of a custom software package designed specifically for records and document management. Spacesaver Systems, Inc., has designed this program to track and retrieve any document stored in a database. The program can be adapted to specific client requirements and provide access to organizational records and documents.*

   b. *Office systems software:* Records prepared with office systems software are stored on electronic storage media, primarily magnetic disk storage (hard disk, diskette, compact disc, Zip or Jaz cartridge), compact disc (CD or DVD), or computer network storage. File management is a crucial issue in word/information processing because of the need to retain needed documents and to purge the electronic storage of any unneeded documents.

c. *Optical character recognition (OCR):* With **optical character recognition (OCR)**, a document is scanned, and the data are converted to digital form for processing by the computer. The transmission rate is very fast, approximately 300 to 400 characters per second. The OCR system can read typewritten, printed, or handwritten information that is prepared in acceptable formats.

d. *Optical disc technology:* A recent technology to come under records management scrutiny is the optical disc or optical disc memory, a very popular image-based form of storage. Optical disc development is a major step in digital storage technology. The compact disc read-only memory (CD-ROM) is the least expensive type of optical disc. Today's microcomputer typically has a CD-ROM drive as well as a disk drive for 3 1/2-inch magnetic disks. The optical disc has the advantage of having high-density storage and rapid random access. Another positive aspect of the technology is the capability of providing graphics, color video, and stereo sound. In the development process, pictures and sound tracks are recorded in digital form on the optical disc with a laser beam.

Optical discs may be utilized to store the following kinds of documents: source documents with original information for business transactions or ventures, bulky computer printout pages, and handwritten documents, photographs, and other graphics.

These are only a few of the ways in which computers with office systems software influence the way in which documents recorded on electronic storage are managed and stored.

5. ***Non-computer-assisted Storage/Retrieval Systems:*** Not all automated systems require the use of the computer. Non-computer-assisted storage and retrieval systems refer to those equipment systems that are used to store and retrieve paper documents or data stored on microforms without the need for computerized retrieval.

a. *Paper storage/retrieval systems:* Systems consisting of banks of metal file containers for holding paper documents of any acceptable size (usually in file folders) are used to automate the storage of paper documents. The system is a *closed system*; this means that the system is controlled from a keyboard either at an operator workstation or near the files. Records in paper form are advantageous to many business operations. Here are a few selected advantages of this type of system:

(1) *File security:* The security and file integrity make these retrieval systems very popular. The files should contain the documents requested if the files have been maintained properly.

(2) *Space-saving system:* These types of systems tend to take up less floor space because they fit either into wall storage areas or within cabinets that permit access from both sides. The files will move toward the operator workstation or rotate within the walls or cabinets until the file requested can be removed from the storage area for a particular bank of files.

(3) *Automatic charge-out features:* Some systems have automatic charge-out features so that an accurate record is kept of the authorized person removing the record or file and the date it is due back. If the file is requested by another person before it is returned, the system will indicate that the file is not available. This eliminates much unnecessary time searching for missing files.

(4) *Standardized filing procedures:* A specific set of filing procedures must be established, with each person within the organization responsible for following

these procedures. Color-coded labels based on an alphabetic or numeric system enhance the possibility of keeping the files in order.

b. *Microform storage/retrieval units:* Any record that contains reduced images on film is known as a microform. Microforms include microfilm, fiche, and aperture cards. The equipment needed for microform storage includes the following:

- A reader-printer for scanning, reading, and producing hard copies of microform images
- A microfilm camera for filming documents and creating the microform images
- An indexing system for microforms that will allow for quick retrieval of information contained on microforms

6. ***Computer-assisted Storage/Retrieval Systems:*** The computer is especially useful in applying effective file management systems to accommodate the vast amount of information to be stored and to assist in accessing, updating, or retrieving data or documents. Here are some descriptions of computer-assisted storage and retrieval procedures that are now being used:

a. *Automated indexing:* Whenever an office information system is used to create a file, an indexing system is required to name, code, number, or classify the file so that it will be retrievable through electronic means.

(1) *File inventory:* The index for a computer-assisted system identifies every file and record in the system. The complete inventory of all files and records should include the following:

- The retention period designated for each file or record
- The date by which the file or record must be examined for retention
- Code numbers for retrieval
- Key words (descriptors and identifiers) for the file or record that describe the stored document and assist in the retrieval of the file or record

(2) *Records usage:* With the help of a computer, a complete record can be available specifying the exact use of records:

- The number of times files or records have been retrieved and/or viewed
- By whom records have been retrieved and/or viewed
- The number of times files or records have been revised and/or updated
- By whom files or records have been revised and/or updated

(3) *File management:* A set of file management techniques are needed for computer-assisted storage and retrieval systems so that the files can be maintained for efficient and effective use. User needs must also be kept in mind when developing a file management system.

(a) *Record indexes:* All stored records must be included in electronic indexes that are updated by the file management software as new files or records are added or existing files or records are purged.

(b) *Document access:* Individuals should be able to access records in many different ways: by name of correspondent, by type of record, by date, by topic or subject, or by descriptors or identifiers.

(4) *Bar code indexes:* Bar codes can be used on file folders as file identification measures. These codes label the files much as other types of bar codes are used on products in a supermarket. This file identification information can be read by a computer or by optical character recognition (OCR) equipment, creating a tracking and managing procedure that will be helpful.

b. *Electronic filing:* Documents may be stored, using digital electronic document storage, without any rekeying of the original information. Electronic filing systems may require combinations of word processing, information processing, and micrographics technologies.

(1) *Storage of incoming documents:* Documents that have been received in paper form are scanned by OCR devices in order to store the contents electronically on computer storage media. In other words, all incoming records are converted to digital form, without any intermediate rekeying of the information, and stored in the computer.

(2) *Storage of in-house documents:* Documents prepared within the office may be stored electronically as they are being created. Terminals used for keying in original information become part of the electronic network in the office, and electronic storage takes place directly on the computer's external storage devices such as hard drives, magnetic disks, optical discs, USB flash drives, or network secondary storage.

(3) *Document imaging:* Signatures, photographs, and other types of images can also be stored with electronic filing systems. Security of electronically stored information is enhanced through precautionary measures like these.

(4) *Database management:* The existence of a database management system facilitates the creation of electronically filed records as well as verification, retrieval, updating, and printing of those records. Records must be retrievable, whether they are paper documents converted to microform or electronically produced. In the retrieval process, specific records stored in a database often need to be selected and sorted into particular sequences. The database management system serves as a directory, telling the user the location of the document that is stored within the computer memory. The user, however, still has to be able to retrieve the stored document, with appropriate security clearance, to access the needed information.

c. *Electronic mail:* Any messages that are transmitted by electronic mail to other locations are electronically stored in the receiver's and sender's mailboxes. These electronic documents need to be managed by purging (deleting) from the In and Sent files when no longer needed or moved to electronic file folders for long-term storage. The Trash/Recycle Bin (discarded) file folder must periodically be emptied by the user to maintain efficient use of the electronic storage space.

Input to a computer-assisted storage and retrieval system consists of both internal and external messages. Internal messages are created electronically, with users keying information into the records system. External messages need to be converted into digital form for storage within available electronic storage. Two storage areas are needed in the system: active storage (to house those electronic files and records that would be accessed often) and remote storage (to house those electronic files that would be accessed occasionally). The user accesses files or records only through active storage; this would mean that if a record stored in remote storage is needed, the user might have

FIGURE 1–3   A Computer-assisted Storage and Retrieval System

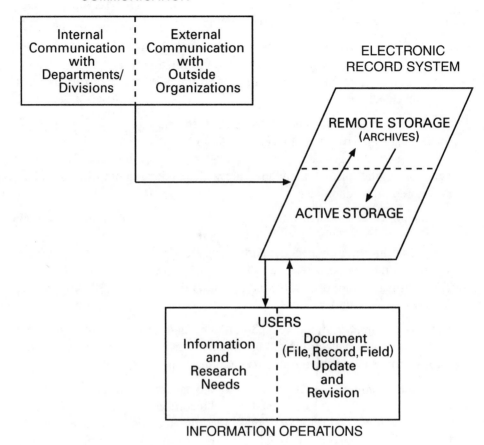

to wait until that record had been transferred into active storage. With appropriate security clearances, the user would have direct access to electronic information for research purposes or be able to update and revise the stored information when necessary.

EXAMPLE: *Figure 1–3 shows an example of a computer-assisted storage and retrieval system.*

Electronically stored information may be transmitted in a number of different ways: telecommunications, microwave or satellite transmission, cable networks, data communication network, fax, or electronic message centers.

Check Point—Section C

Directions: For each question, circle the correct answer.

C–1. Mathers is conducting an analysis of the floor space required for the conventional files presently being used in her office. The greatest savings in floor space would result from using which one of the following types of files?

A) Open-shelf units
B) Lateral file cabinets

C) Vertical file cabinets

D) Powered shelving system

C–2. Microform technology enables retrieved documents to be viewed

A) without any special micrographics equipment

B) if a reader-printer is available

C) if the microform is housed in self-contained equipment

D) if the microform is stored in an internal system

C–3. A document in paper form

A) can be converted to digital storage through an optical scanning procedure

B) will remain in paper form until that information is no longer needed

C) can be converted to digital storage only by keying in the information on a terminal

D) will become part of the organizational database

D. Utilizing Filing Classification Systems

Classification systems are established so that records will be filed or stored according to a documented set of rules. Records need to be retrievable when needed. Determining the type of filing arrangement appropriate for an organization depends on how records will be utilized.

1. *Needs Analysis for Filing Systems:* A knowledge of records practices currently being used will help in determining an appropriate classification system. The following types of information need to be analyzed:

   a. *Identification of records problems:* In the existing records system, a number of problems may be identified, such as overcrowded files, misfiles, or the lack of a tracking system for records removed from the files.

   b. *Identification of records and their use:* Recognizing the kinds of records that are being created will help to trace their use throughout the organization. The specific uses of these records will help to identify their usefulness in daily operations.

   c. *Retrieval of records:* Knowing how records will be retrieved (accessed) will help in determining the best filing arrangement. Records access might be by name or by number.

   d. *The number of records maintained:* If the volume of records is relatively small, access with an alphabetic filing arrangement may be adequate. However, if a larger volume of records exists, a numeric or alphanumeric filing system may provide a better filing arrangement.

   e. *The size of the organization:* The larger the organization the more people who will need to have access to the records. In addition, more records personnel may be needed to maintain the records.

   f. *Users of the records:* The classification system selected must be appropriate for people who will be accessing and using the records.

   g. *The possibility of expansion:* A futuristic look is necessary to determine the ways in which the filing system can be expanded.

2. ***Types of Filing Arrangements:*** The selection of a filing arrangement depends on the records management needs of the organization. Here are the most common filing systems in use:

   a. *Alphabetic systems:* Records are filed by name of correspondent or document alphabetically. Typically, this is a direct access system; a person can locate a specific record by going directly to the files and looking under the name of the record.

   b. *Numeric systems:* Numbers in various combinations are used as codes and assigned to records and files. Numbers representing dates are used in chronological filing systems. This type of filing arrangement is an indirect access system. An index would be necessary to determine the code or number assigned to a record.

   c. *Alphanumeric systems:* In an alphanumeric system, records will be coded with a combination of letters and numbers that indicate the placement of the records within the files. This type of system would also be indirect access; an index would need to be accessed to find out the code or number under which the record is filed.

   d. *Subject systems:* Sometimes records are filed by the topic rather than a name. Records are filed alphabetically by subject, but an index of the subjects used in the files would be accessed first when looking for a particular record.

   e. *Geographic systems:* In some organizations, a geographic filing system is used because of the nature of the business. Perhaps there are branch offices in different parts of the country or the world, and documents are filed according to these regions. Such a system is generally an alphabetic system. An index of the geographic subdivisions within the files is needed.

3. ***Standardization of Classification Systems:*** Consistency in utilizing a classification system in setting up files and records is the key to an effective records management program.

   a. *Standardization of filing terms:* The terms used within the firm's classification plan need to be constant throughout the organization. All personnel need to identify and describe records in exactly the same words and terms.

   b. *Documentation of filing procedures:* All records personnel need to follow the same rules and procedures in working with the records and files of the organization. Documented procedures or a records manual will provide assistance to all personnel within the firm who come in contact with records.

4. ***Identification Aids and Supplies:*** Proper techniques must be used to index, code, and store documents so that they can be retrieved easily. Otherwise, the storage system, whether manual or electronic, will be ineffective. Correspondence filed in conventional formats requires an identification system consisting of guides and folders prearranged in a sequential manner, depending on the classification system used. Guides tell where the folders are located. Here is a quick review of some of the identification aids that are needed for records storage systems:

   a. *File folders:* Individual folders are used to store the documents pertaining to one correspondent, case, or account.

      (1) *Individual folders:* Located behind a primary guide, an **individual folder** includes all correspondence for one correspondent, subject, or account. In some systems, a minimum number of documents is needed to open an individual folder.

FIGURE 1–4 The Arrangement of Guides and Folders in a Correspondence System

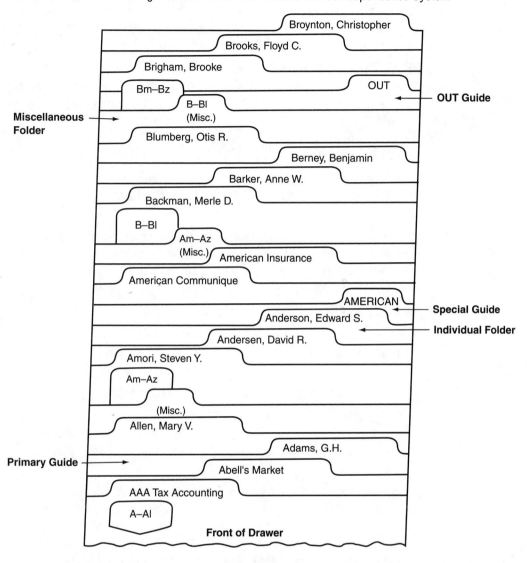

EXAMPLE: *In Figure 1–4, individual file folders are included for each correspondent (i.e., AAA Tax Accounting, Abell's Market). Each file is established when a minimum number of documents are accumulated, typically three to five.*

(2) *Miscellaneous folders:* Located at the end of each file group, a **miscellaneous folder** houses the group of records that have not yet been assigned individual file folders. These records may be filed alphabetically or numerically, depending on the system used.

EXAMPLE: *The alphabetical file shown in Figure 1–4 illustrates the use of a miscellaneous folder at the end of each alphabetic section within the file (i.e., at the end of the A-Al section, the Am-Az section, the B-Bl section, and the Bm-Bz section).*

(3) *Out folder:* An **out folder** is inserted into the file when someone charges out an entire file folder.

b. *Folder tabs:* Each file folder or guide has a projection or **tab** for placement of a *label* with a typed *caption*. Common **cuts** of folders are single-cut (only one tab extending across the folder), third-cut (positioning of three tabs in a set of folders), or fifth-cut (positioning of five tabs in a set of folders).

EXAMPLE: *The folders shown in Figure 1–4 are third-cut so that three folders would fit across the file drawer and all three can be seen easily. The folder for* AAA Tax Accounting *appears in the first position, since it is the first file in the drawer;* Abell's Market *is in the second position, since it is the second file; and* Adams, G.H. *is in third position as the third file. The folder for* Allen, Mary V. *is first position. Additional folders may be added in order from that point on.*

c. *Guides:* File **guides** form an outline of the classification system used, indicate the sections of the file, and serve as dividers for groups of records. Guides are either primary guides or secondary guides.

    (1) *Primary guides:* These guides highlight the major divisions and subdivisions of records stored in a file drawer or on a shelf and should appear in first position—to the left.

        EXAMPLE: *The primary guide for the A section in the file appears before the file folders in the section in first position.*

    (2) *Secondary guides:* These guides represent subdivisions within major divisions of the file and are typically placed in first or second position.

        EXAMPLE: *In Figure 1–4, the A section of the file is subdivided into A-Al and Am-Az. A secondary guide is included for A-Al and another one for Am-Az to show this subdivision of the file.*

    (3) *Out guides:* This special guide substitutes for a folder or a record that has been temporarily removed from the file. The tab on this guide is typically in fifth position.

    (4) *Special guides:* These guides are placed in front of a section of file folders and are used to highlight frequently referenced sections of records, such as *Applications for Employment* or if a number of files begin with the same word, such as *American.* These guides are typically placed in fifth position so that they are relatively easy to locate behind the alphabetic files in that section.

d. *Color coding:* Colored tabs are placed on the sides of file folders to represent numeric or alphanumeric codes. This identification system is of particular value in an open-shelf filing system.

Check Point—Section D

Directions: For each question, circle the correct answer.

D–1. Which one of the following classification systems assumes that direct-access procedures will be used to retrieve records?

    A) An alphabetic system
    B) A numeric system
    C) A color-coded system
    D) A subject system

D–2. In establishing a classification system for files and records, each user within the organization needs to

    A) develop his or her own procedures for working with the files and records

B) keep a written record of any inconsistent use of the files and records

C) follow the standard filing rules for the organization but note any inconsistencies that may occur

D) use an indirect-access system to locate specific files and records

D–3. When a minimum number of documents has accumulated for a specific person or organization, these documents will be filed in a/an

A) primary guide
B) out folder
C) miscellaneous folder
D) individual folder

E. Electronic Records Systems

Computer-based records management systems consist of data files and records tracking systems. *Data files* are collections of specific records needed for business functions. A data management system utilizes the computer to store records and files throughout the life cycle of the records. Computer-based records management systems are an important component of information processing systems.

1. *Collection of Data Files:* A database is a collection of data files containing all records and data fields available. In a computer database, data stored in separate files can be integrated and managed. The number of data files from which information can be drawn varies. Unique field names are needed for information integration and retrieval. Gathering all organization data into one database may not be possible. Basic considerations in developing a computer database consisting of a number of data files include the following items:

   a. *Data entry:* Once a data item is entered correctly, it will not have to be entered again to be ready for user access.

   b. *Volume of information:* The storage capacity within each database is a primary consideration. The storage media used will have to be able to handle the volume of information stored. A database management system is the software that governs files, records, and data/field storage and retrieval and the way users will be permitted to work with the information.

2. *Databases for a Variety of Topics:* A database holds information in the form of data files on different topics. The advantage of having a database system is that it reduces the duplication of data fields that would exist from one set of files to another.

3. *Quick Access to Data:* Data can be accessed quickly by users (subscribers) as they need the information to supplement their own knowledge. For public databases, people or organizations pay an annual subscription fee for access to the information on a regular basis. One important feature of a database management system is that information from multiple databases can be merged with information from our sources.

4. *Records Tracking Systems:* These systems track records automatically by tracking in-and-out filing activity. By using bar codes and automated equipment, an organization can keep accurate records of the location of all files. As a result, activity reports for better cost efficiency can be prepared; and inactive records, retention periods, and disposal of records can be managed more effectively.

a. *Types of systems:* Three types of computer-based records management (CBRM) systems are available: database management software, commercial CBRM systems, and in-house developed software.

(1) Database management software can be adapted to specific company needs.

EXAMPLES: *Microsoft Access®, dBASE V®, and Paradox®*

(2) Commercial CBRM systems that handle one or more aspects of records management are available. Active records management may be the only function needed, or integrated systems that handle several functions are also available.

EXAMPLES: *Inform Software® and Frolic®*

(3) In-house developed software is highly specialized and written to suit a company's specific needs. This alternative is more time-consuming and expensive.

b. *Considerations in CBRM system selection:* A thorough needs assessment must be done to determine the volume of active and inactive records and the specific electronic procedures being considered. Basic considerations in system selection include the following:

- Ease of learning
- Vendor reputation
- Other installations in the area
- Simple, easy-to-understand instructional and operational manuals
- Training needed and availability of training
- Free or inexpensive assistance with problem solutions
- Data security
- Cost and/or add-on cost
- Maintenance of the system

5. **Integration with Other Systems:** Records management and computer technology team up in several different types of computer-assisted storage and retrieval systems. Optical disc technology and micrographics technology, in particular, provide an excellent opportunity for the integration of business information systems. In computer-assisted retrieval systems (CARS), documents are stored on microforms and are accessible through the computer system. Four primary types of CARS are currently in operation:

a. *CAR system with off-line indexes and off-line reader:* An off-line index is one that is maintained by a computer but printed out on paper or COM-generated fiche for use by the operator of a stand-alone reader-printer. [COM is an acronym for computer output microform.]

b. *CAR system with online index and off-line reader:* The index is maintained online by the computer system, but the microform retrieval device is a stand-alone reader-printer.

c. *CAR system with online index and online reader:* An online index is maintained on the computer system, and the microform reader is electronically attached to the computer terminal. Information is usually document based and retrieved primarily for reference purposes. The reader will be directed by the computer to find the correct microform image and display it on the visual display screen.

d. *CAR system with online reader and minicomputer:* This method utilizes a minicomputer rather than a mainframe computer. The minicomputer may be dedicated to index retrieval for a microfilming operation. The integration of records management technology with office systems and computer technologies is occurring as a result of the procedures used in creating and filing documents electronically, developing information banks for access by researchers, and the need for people to be given access to such stored information.

Records management technology is an integral part of management information systems (MIS) and office information systems (OIS). The ways in which documents are created, stored, retrieved, and purged are vital aspects of information systems that have been developed. As new technologies are developed, the systems used for document and records management will be refined as well.

Check Point—Section E

Directions: For each question, circle the correct answer.

E–1. A database is a

   A) single field of information on a specific topic
   B) directory of document files stored electronically in the system
   C) collection of data files, all relating to the same type of information available
   D) cross-reference for items included in a set of data files

E–2. Determining the volume of active and inactive records being processed through a system is a component of

   A) a thorough needs assessment
   B) a database management system
   C) in-house software development
   D) a records tracking system

E–3. Micrographics technology and computer technology link together in a/an

   A) optical disc system
   B) optical character recognition system
   C) electronic mail system
   D) computer-assisted retrieval system

For Your Review

Directions: For each question, circle the correct answer.

1. Primarily, filing systems are established within an organization so that records will be
   A) accessible
   B) stored
   C) analyzed
   D) retrievable

2. Documents that are used temporarily and then disposed of are called
   A) nonrecords
   B) inactive records
   C) important records
   D) records

3. The loss of which one of the following documents would cause only a temporary delay or inconvenience in maintaining routine business operations?
   A) A patent obtained for the design of a chair-lift device
   B) The deed for the North Avenue property where the new chair-lift plant is being built
   C) A client's request for information about the new chair-lift device
   D) A customer order for the first 500 chair-lift devices

4. A database of current employees that includes personal information such as name, address, home telephone number, and Social Security number would have
   A) legal value
   B) administrative value
   C) research value
   D) fiscal value

5. Semiactive or inactive records that provide proof of the policies and procedures in effect throughout an organization's lifetime are known to have
   A) legal value
   B) primary value
   C) fiscal value
   D) secondary value

6. If a perpetual method of records transfer is in use, the records for a specific project could be transferred
   A) at the end of each fiscal year
   B) whenever the project has been completed
   C) as each phase of the project is completed
   D) when the records are no longer needed

7. A records retention schedule specifies the
   A) process to be used in deleting the contents of an electronically stored document
   B) method to be used in destroying a specific group of records
   C) period of time a record should be stored
   D) physical movement of a record from active to inactive storage

8. Control of records during the creation and design phase results in
   A) less effective records storage
   B) increased costs of records storage
   C) improved productivity in using records
   D) the need for more conventional formats

9. When producing a one-page, average-length business letter with electronic technology, the letter is estimated to cost
   A) less than the cost of having the letter prepared on an electric typewriter
   B) about the same as the cost of having the letter prepared on an electric typewriter
   C) higher than the same letter produced on an electric typewriter
   D) an undetermined amount because no cost comparisons are available

10. Electronic copies of business forms provided on an organization's intranet may be
    A) opened and completed with constant information provided by the user
    B) printed and variable information filled in later
    C) opened and saved under appropriate file names
    D) opened and completed with variable information provided by the user

11. The effective design of a business form depends most on the
    A) special equipment needed to complete the form
    B) sequence of the information that needs to appear on the form
    C) external use of the form
    D) electronic storage of the form

12. Information conveyed to top-level management who need to make informed business decisions results in the development of
    A) a business form with variable information included
    B) a memorandum conveying basic information about the research topic
    C) a business report presenting a literature review and a summary of the research conducted
    D) data analysis highlighting primary data collected

13. An index record is used to
    A) record information to update or revise the record
    B) make information contained in the record available to a limited number of users
    C) store all information pertaining to a given subject in one location
    D) indicate the location of the original file or document

14. The authenticity of information recorded on magnetic disks, magnetic tapes, or compact discs must be able to be certified to
    A) prepare backup copies of the information
    B) maintain the integrity of the information
    C) create a stored copy of the information
    D) create a database with specific types of information

15. Organizing related facts and data in one or more computer files can be achieved by creating a
    A) posted record
    B) compact disc
    C) database
    D) microform

16. When floor space available for storage units is limited, side-to-side storage is provided with
    A) a rotary file
    B) a powered high-density storage system
    C) lateral mobile storage units
    D) lateral file cabinets

17. Which one of the following equipment systems is considered a conventional filing system?
    A) Rotary file
    B) Desktop PC or laptop computer
    C) Optical disc technology
    D) Microform storage system

18. Information stored on optical discs can be full-text indexed, which means that
    A) an abstract of the document is available and indexed by key content words
    B) the entire text of the document is available and indexed by key content words
    C) key content words are used to access a summary of the document
    D) searching the text of the document can be done line by line

19. Records available in paper form are advantageous to business operations because of the
    A) minimal need for records control
    B) open access to the files by any user
    C) need for file indexing
    D) file integrity

20. A computer-assisted storage and retrieval system requires precautionary measures such as
    A) an electronic index that is updated as new records are added
    B) imaging of signatures and photographs included with a stored document
    C) a bar code index used in a tracking procedure
    D) accessing files directly by name of correspondent or name of document

21. A filing classification system is established to
    A) identify the types of problems that occur with the present system
    B) document a set of rules for storing records and files
    C) recognize the types of records that are being created in the organization
    D) determine the volume of records to maintain within the system

22. An indirect-access system requires that
    A) a specific record can be located by going to the files and looking under the name of the record
    B) records are filed by topic rather than the name of the correspondent
    C) a numeric code be assigned to records and files
    D) records are filed by the name of the correspondent

23. A group of records that have not yet been assigned individual file folders will be filed
    A) in an individual folder placed within an alphabetical section of the file
    B) after a special guide placed in front of the folder
    C) after an out guide placed within an alphabetical section of the file
    D) in a miscellaneous folder placed at the end of an alphabetical section of the file

24. Selection of a computer-based records management system depends on the outcome of a needs assessment to determine the
    A) volume of active and inactive records
    B) availability of highly specialized in-house developed software
    C) retention schedule for records and files in the system
    D) manual procedures that will be eliminated with the new system

25. Records management technology is an integral part of computer-assisted retrieval systems in which documents are
    A) stored as paper documents and later scanned into the computer-assisted retrieval system
    B) stored as data files in a computer database management system
    C) stored on microforms and accessible through the computer system
    D) indexed and stored electronically for user access

Solutions

Solutions to Check Point—Section A

Answer	Refer to:
A–1. (D)	[A-1]
A–2. (B)	[A-1-b (1)]
A–3. (C)	[A-2]

Solutions to Check Point—Section B

Answer	Refer to:
B–1. (A)	[B-1-b]
B–2. (D)	[B-2-a]
B–3. (C)	[B-2-b]

Solutions to Check Point—Section C

Answer	Refer to:
C–1. (D)	[C-1-d (2)]
C–2. (B)	[C-2-e, and C-5-b]
C–3. (A)	[C-3-a]

Solutions to Check Point—Section D

Answer	Refer to:
D–1. (A)	[D-2–a]
D–2. (B)	[D-3]
D–3. (D)	[D-4–a(1)]

Solutions to Check Point—Section E

Answer	Refer to:
E–1. (C)	[E-1]
E–2. (A)	[E-4-b]
E–3. (D)	[E-5]

Solutions to For Your Review

Answer	Refer to:
1. (D)	[A-Overview]
2. (A)	[A]
3. (C)	[A-1–b (3)]
4. (B)	[A-2–c (2) (a)]
5. (D)	[A-2–c (2) (b)]
6. (B)	[A-2–d (1)]
7. (C)	[A-2–e]
8. (C)	[B]
9. (A)	[B-1–a (1)]
10. (D)	[B-1–b]
11. (B)	[B-1–b (3)]
12. (C)	[B-1–c]
13. (D)	[B-1–d (1)]

14. (B)   [B-2-c]
15. (C)   [B-2-c]
16. (C)   [C-1-d (4)]
17. (A)   [C-1-e]
18. (B)   [C-3-d]
19. (D)   [C-5-a (1)]
20. (B)   [C-6-b (3)]
21. (B)   [D]
22. (C)   [D-2-b]
23. (D)   [D-4-a (2)]
24. (A)   [E-4-b]
25. (C)   [E-5]

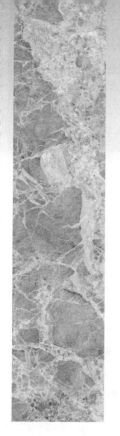

Chapter 2

File Management

OVERVIEW

If records that have been stored in the records system cannot be found, then the records system in use, whether it is a manual or an electronic system, is probably inadequate to handle the organization's records. Records must be stored so that they can be located easily and quickly as needed. Records that have been stored according to a basic set of procedures and a classification system must be retrievable at any time. The information contained in the organization's records must be secure so that the integrity of the records will not be compromised.

KEY TERMS

Accession register, 45
Authenticity, 43
Biometric identification
    system, 46
Business archive, 45
Charge-out (tracking)
    system, 42
Coding, 41
Color coding, 41
Confidentiality, 44

Constant information, 48
Cross-reference, 41
Decryption, 46
Digital signature, 46
Direct access, 40
Encryption, 46
Files integrity, 43
Indexing, 41
Indirect access, 40
Inspecting, 41

Logical security, 45
Microprinting, 47
Passwords, 46
Physical security, 45
Private key, 46
Public key, 46
Records center, 44
Relative index, 40
Variable information, 48

A. Procedures for Records Storage

Before records can be retrieved, they must be stored (filed) according to a prescribed set of procedures and rules. An organization will adopt a set of rules and procedures to be used in storing manual as well as electronic records. Each person coming in direct contact with records is expected to use the filing rules and procedures established for the organization.

EXAMPLE: *A set of filing rules necessary for proper records management procedures to be used is similar in nature to a set of golfing rules prescribed for playing a good game of golf. If you know how to index and code a name alphabetically, you can proceed from one name to another. In golf, you move from hole to hole in a systematic manner as you follow the rules of the game.*

1. *Accessing Files:* Records may be accessed through either direct- or indirect-access procedures.

   a. *Direct-access procedures:* A **direct-access** file permits a person to go directly to the storage system (file cabinet or computer storage) and locate the file.

      EXAMPLE: *An alphabetic filing system is a direct-access system. Without referring to any other information, you can go directly to the storage unit and locate the file. If a file folder is labeled* Smith, John, *all you need to do is look under "S" in order to find the file, which is filed alphabetically first according to the last name,* Smith.

   b. *Indirect-access procedures:* An **indirect-access** filing system requires a person to consult a *relative index* to locate the name, subject, or number under which the file is stored.

      (1) *Manual procedures:* A **relative index** serves as a backup for numeric and alphanumeric systems. The index consists of cards filed alphabetically, providing a complete list of names or subjects already included in the filing system.

      EXAMPLE: *In a numeric filing system, you would consult the relative index first to see what number has been assigned to the file you need. If you are looking for a file under* Smith, John, *you would look in the relative index under "S" to locate the card for* Smith, John *(filed alphabetically). This card will indicate something like this:*

Smith, John	1028

      The number assigned to the file for John Smith is File No. 1028. You can proceed to the storage unit containing that file, and the file should be there in numeric order unless someone else has charged out the file.

      (2) *Electronic procedures:* Electronic systems permit quick storage of records as well as retrieval. As a record is being created or saved in the system, the operator is prompted to provide a file name for the document. Later access to the document requires the operator to view an index or a directory listing first to select the correct record or, if the file name is known, that name can be keyed into the computer and the document should appear on the screen in a matter of seconds. Random access allows direct access to the document without having to view all other documents stored on that disk or tape.

2. *Inspecting, Indexing, and Coding Records:* Before a record can be filed, it must be *inspected* to ensure that it has been released for filing by an appropriate authority

within the firm. Usually, an inspection mark or initials are written on the document to indicate that **inspecting** has taken place. **Indexing** is the term used to indicate the decision making that is necessary in deciding what names, numbers, or character strings to use in filing. **Coding** refers to making notations on the record itself as to exactly how the record will be stored (under what names, numbers, or character strings).

EXAMPLE: *Summerfield has the responsibility of examining each record to be sure that it has been released for filing and is ready to be indexed and coded. Once he has decided the name under which the record will be filed, he codes the name as it appears on the document in this way:*

2	3	1	4
James	*G.*	*Blair*	*Jr.*

The first filing unit should be underlined and the number 1 written above it. Then the numbers 2, 3, and 4 (in this case) can be written above the subsequent filing units.

3. *Color Coding:* Many organizations find that **color coding** the files improves office efficiency and effectiveness in locating and refiling records. A color-coded system requires identifying the topic areas within the organization and/or division. All folders pertaining to one particular topic are of the same color. Pendaflex is a common color-coded filing system used by many organizations.

EXAMPLE: *At Waubonsee College, the Business Division color coded the major academic programs like this:*

Accounting—green

Management (Human Resources)—purple

Management Information Systems—yellow

Marketing—red

Operations and Logistics—orange

General—gray

4. *Cross-referencing Records:* Whenever a record could be filed in more than one place in the files, a cross-reference is needed. The **cross-reference** indicates where the original document or complete file can be located. In a card file, the cross-reference is another card coded as a cross-reference card. The cross-reference in a document file is indicated on a cross-reference sheet or folder.

EXAMPLE: *Sarah Lou Masterson is married to John L. Masterson. In an alphabetic file, the caption for her file would read*

MASTERSON, SARAH LOU (Mrs.)

A cross-reference will appear under

MASTERSON, JOHN L. (Mrs.)

See MASTERSON, SARAH LOU (Mrs.)

to let file users know where the original file can be found. If Sarah prefers to keep her maiden name as part of her married name, she may want her name to appear as

HUGHES-MASTERSON, SARAH LOU (Mrs.)

In this case, two cross-references may be needed: one under Masterson, Sarah Lou (Mrs.) and another under Masterson, John L. (Mrs.). The cross-reference under her husband's name would appear as

> MASTERSON, JOHN L. (Mrs.)
>
> See HUGHES-MASTERSON, SARAH LOU (Mrs.)

In this way, if someone knew only her husband's name, her file could still be located.

5. **Charging Out Records:** A **charge-out (tracking) system** must be in place for any records that have been borrowed from hard-copy files. While these records are temporarily removed from the files, a record must be kept identifying the following types of information:

   - The name of the person or department borrowing the record or file
   - The date the record or file was borrowed
   - The probable return date of the record or file

   A set of charge-out forms should be maintained for use with the files. Whenever someone needs to charge out a particular record, a charge-out request form should be completed and presented to the records clerk in charge. Whenever an individual record is removed from a file, an *out guide* should take its place in the file. If an entire file folder is borrowed, an *out folder* should be substituted in the file for that particular folder.

   Files that are filed electronically can be accessed only by those who have authorization to do so. The database management system (DBMS) establishes the creation, use, and maintenance of all information in the database. Security procedures that are established include the use of log-in names and passwords to gain access to specific files.

Check Point—Section A

Directions: For each question, circle the correct answer.

A–1. An indirect-access filing system requires the use of a relative index to locate the

   A) order in which the files are stored
   B) directory showing where a file is stored
   C) color coding used for the files
   D) subject under which a file is stored

A–2. Making notations on the record itself indicating exactly how the record will be stored is referred to as

   A) inspecting
   B) indexing
   C) coding
   D) classifying

A–3. Whenever a record can be filed in more than one place in the files,

   A) a duplicate copy of the record should be filed in each place
   B) a cross-reference to the original record should be prepared
   C) a cross-reference should be noted on the original record
   D) the record should be filed in a special location within the file

B. Files Integrity and Confidentiality

Records management is concerned primarily with the protection of information contained in the files and records of the organization. The integrity of the files and records and the confidentiality with which they are handled are at stake. Appropriate organizational and governmental controls must be in place so that the truthfulness and accuracy of the records will be maintained.

1. **Files Integrity:** Organizational records must be maintained in such a way that they remain factual, accurate, and truthful, as reflected in the term **files integrity.** Information in the files can only be accessed and/or modified by those who are authorized to do so. Specific types of files and records, whether they be hard or soft copies, need to be certified as to their authenticity.

    a. *Verifying record authenticity:* The document must be the work of the stated author or source. The name(s) of the author(s) (individuals or organizations) must be a part of the document or attached to the document to assure the **authenticity** of the document.

    - No alteration of the contents of the document should have occurred without permission of the author and/or copyright holder.
    - The document was issued or released by an authorized individual or organization.
    - A certificate of authenticity might accompany the document, with the signature of an authorized official attached. [This is particularly true of microforms that have been released for storage.]

    b. *Use of online processes:* Organizations must ensure that online business processes do not compromise the integrity and appropriate use of documents that contain sensitive information.

    EXAMPLE: *A time stamp embedded in an electronic document provides an auditable time record so that a person authorized to view the document will know exactly when the document was created and stored. This is a feature that is currently available in word processing software programs.*

    c. *Controlled access to records:* Access to and use of records must be controlled by authorized and trained personnel and continuously monitored in order to maintain authenticity of the records. Records should only be seen by the intended audience and used for specific purposes.

    EXAMPLES:

    > *Medical records in a hospital*
    > *Financial records in a public accounting firm*
    > *Educational records in the records and registration division of a university*

    Within an organization, electronically stored documents must be protected so that they can be safely shared internally and externally as needed.

2. **Confidentiality of Records:** The information contained in business records needs to be used only for intended purposes. Documents may contain extremely sensitive information that deserves to be kept private. Other documents pertain to research and development activities that lead to patents and copyrights. Giving away "trade secrets" such as ingredients or recipes may compromise further development of new products or services.

EXAMPLES:

A patient's medical records

Last year's income tax returns for a client

Preliminary information about a new software product being developed

a. *Need for controlled access:* Strict controls are needed to limit access only to authorized individuals who have permission to do the following:

- View the contents of documents.
- Modify the content of the documents as needed.
- Store the documents according to a prescribed set of standards.

b. *Maintaining confidentiality:* Administrative professionals whose responsibility it is to maintain information **confidentiality** must adhere to a very high standard. Part of an orientation program for new employees should be an explanation of the confidential nature of the business and the need for everyone in the organization to treat information contained in documents in a discreet manner. Drastic measures are often taken when these ideals are compromised.

Check Point—Section B

Directions: For each question, circle the correct answer.

B–1. An organization's records that are factual, accurate, and truthful are said to have

    A) information confidentiality
    B) files integrity
    C) document authenticity
    D) cross-references

B–2. A certificate of authenticity might accompany a document to

    A) indicate that the document has been inspected for storage

    B) specify the document return date and time
    C) verify the contents of the document along with the author's signature
    D) verify the date and time the document was created

B–3. The confidentiality of information is the responsibility of

    A) the information administrator
    B) the author of the document
    C) everyone in the organization
    D) the records manager

C. Maintaining Records Centers and Archives

Records centers and archives are specific types of depositories for records deemed to be important to retain for given periods of time.

1. *Maintaining Records Centers:* The **records center** is the depository for the organization's vital, inactive, and/or active records. Vital records may be classified as active or inactive, depending on the current use. Many times, sets of duplicate records exist in the form of electronic disks and tapes (soft copy), paper copies (hard copy), or microforms. *Dispersal* is the term used to indicate the duplication of hard copies and their storage in other locations.

a. *On-site storage:* In-house records centers, file rooms, or vaults provide records storage on the company's premises. Vital records are sometimes stored in highly protected vaults or in underground storage at different locations for even greater security.

b. *Off-site storage:* Records storage in off-premises locations may be in space owned by the organization or rented from other commercial firms. Usually, off-site storage is in a lower-rent area and, therefore, will result in a lower records storage cost. A higher degree of security exists in off-site facilities, primarily because these locations are not publicized by the organization.

2. *Maintaining Archives:* A **business archive** is a facility that houses records being retained for research or historical value. Archives may be *public* (may be accessed by the general public) or *private* (may be used only by members of the organization). An **accession register** identifies the records in the archive and controls access to documents and retrieval of documents from the archive. Here are some of the basic reasons for the maintenance of archives by organizations:

a. The organization's history can be preserved for posterity.

b. The public image of an organization may be enhanced by permitting the public to use its archives.

c. Relevant administrative, fiscal, or legal information may be maintained for later research and reference.

Documents maintained in an archive are preserved in special storage containers to deter further deterioration. Access to an archive is limited to those individuals whose reasons for using the archive are approved by appropriate officials of the organization.

Check Point—Section C

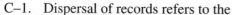

Directions: For each question, circle the correct answer.

C–1. Dispersal of records refers to the

A) duplication and storage of hard copies in various locations
B) destruction of active and inactive records
C) storage of active and inactive records in a central location
D) depository for an organization's vital records

C–2. A higher degree of record storage security exists when using

A) electronic disks and tapes
B) microforms
C) off-site storage
D) vaults

C–3. Matthews needs to find an historical document to use in obtaining information for his speech. Matthews would be able to find out where the document is archived by checking the

A) accession register
B) business archive
C) records procedures manual
D) records center

D. Security of Records

Records management issues arise from concerns for **physical security,** which restricts access through the use of hardware, facilities, or electronic storage, and **logical security,** which relates to procedures embedded in software programs to restrict individual access to records.

Some of the security measures organizations are using include establishing user identification systems, assigning security codes, and documenting user procedures to keep company records secure.

1. ***User Identification Systems:*** For records to remain secure, users need to be accurately identified through specific procedures before they can be granted access to information. Identification systems that have been successful include the following:

    a. *User identification and passwords:* A relatively traditional method of gaining access to records is with the assignment of user IDs (string of characters) and **passwords.** The user ID tends to remain the same, but the passwords may change. These procedures provide a few simple rules to follow in regard to passwords:

       - Never tell anyone else your password.
       - Never write down your password so that another person can use it.
       - Change your password often using a combination of mnemonics and numbers so the password is easily remembered.

    b. *Digital signatures and seals:* A **digital signature** proves that the document has never been altered since it was signed. Identity information, document fingerprints, and date/time information are used as verification.

    c. *Encryption and decryption of messages:* Perhaps the most effective way of achieving data security is through encryption and decryption.

       (1) *Encryption of messages:* **Encryption** is the translation of the data into a secret code that is unintelligible without a deciphering device. This technique is used to ensure that data stored in a computer will not be read or compromised by people who should not have access to the information. When a sender encodes (encrypts) a message, a **public key** that is available to everyone is used as the basis for encrypting the message. A **private key,** known only to the recipient of the message, is used to decode (decrypt) the message.

       (2) *Decryption of message:* **Decryption** is the process of decoding data that has been encrypted into a secret format. Decryption requires the use of a private (secret) key or password.

       Unencrypted data are called *plain text,* and encrypted data are called *cipher text.* A safe storage system is needed for storage of public and private keys.

       EXAMPLE: *Encryption of file formats prevents a hacker from casual hacking (using a computer to view files and information on another computer) or a malicious hacker (a cracker) from sabotaging or changing information contained in important records.*

    d. *Biometric identification system:* When a **biometric identification system** is in effect, certain unique physical characteristics of a person are matched against a database as an authentication technique to permit access to files and records.

       EXAMPLES: *Fingerprints, palm prints, iris scans, speech patterns, and faceprints; the most secure biometric system is the iris of one's eye.*

    e. *Magnetic-card based systems:* An electronic system that is used to provide access to a secured area by swiping the magnetic strip on a readable card is known as a *magnetic-card* based system.

2. ***Need for Trusted Custodian:*** A trusted custodian is needed to maintain a secure, well-managed records management system. This individual, often called the records manager, needs to be able to perform the following responsibilities, along with other records personnel, to maintain and retain records appropriately.

   a. *Physical records security:* The custodian must ensure the physical security of the active and inactive records of the organization.

   b. *Preservation of organizational memory:* Another duty of the custodian is to preserve the "memory" of the organization. This "memory" constitutes the history and development of the organization to the present time.

   c. *Protection of documents:* A variety of threats affect the protection of the valuable records of the organization. Such threats include fire, flood, theft, damage due to environmental problems, and terrorism.

   d. *Protection of storage media:* Since a variety of media are used for information storage, the custodian must be able to provide protection for the different types of media used. This protection includes damage due to the environment (heat, light, dust, pollutants, moisture) as well as from disasters such as flood, fire, or storms.

3. ***User Procedures to Secure Records:*** Users may be issued security clearances or use special security codes that will allow them access to certain records within the organization. Written procedures need to be established and approved so that all users are aware of the procedures to use. All office professionals have the responsibility to safeguard these procedures in handling information internally within the organization and externally to other organizations.

4. ***Document Security Features:*** A record or document can be designed to include specific security features that will deter anyone from wanting to alter or forge a document. The application of these types of features will add to the authenticity of the document.

   a. *Security papers:* Papers used in creating original documents can be chemically reactive to bleach and solvent alterations, contain fluorescent fibers, or have artificial watermarks. These features offer security against duplication and scanning of the document. Unique watermarks, in addition to the watermark usually imprinted by the paper manufacturer, can be a company logo or other special identifier.

   b. *Security pantograph:* A *pantograph* is an instrument used for copying, enlarging, or reducing line drawings that are used as a security device on a printed record or form. On the original document, a security word, such as VOID, is blocked and cannot be readily seen. When a user attempts to duplicate that document (record or form) on a copier, the result is a copy that is distorted from the original. Hidden words like VOID in the original document will appear on the copy, making it unusable.

      EXAMPLE: *Checks are printed on security or safety paper. If a payee tries to "raise" the amount of the check by erasing or using some other type of correction device, the hidden word VOID will appear on the original document where the alteration was attempted.*

   c. *Microprinting:* An area on the document can be imprinted with microscopic words that appear to the casual reader as a solid line. On the originals, the words can be read under magnification. On copies, the **microprinting** is unreadable.

d. *Use of thermochromic ink:* Use of heat-sensitive ink, *thermochromic ink*, will cause a change in color of text or will cause text to disappear when heat is applied to the ink.

e. *Bleed-through numbering:* When a specially inked ribbon comes into contact with paper, the numbers appearing on the right side of the document, such as on a check, bleed through and appear red on the reverse side. An example is a check protector, an instrument that is often used to stamp the amount of a check into the paper. The *bleed-through numbering* makes it impossible to "raise" the amount of the check.

The factual and accurate information contained on records must be maintained in such a way that the file integrity is not compromised. The maintenance of accurate, truthful information is the basis for any successful records management program.

Check Point—Section D

Directions: For each question, circle the correct answer.

D–1. Procedures embedded in software programs that restrict access to records is referred to as the
- A) certificate of authenticity
- B) logical security
- C) physical security
- D) relative index

D–2. Messages can be encrypted to ensure that only the receiver can read the message. The receiver is able to decrypt the message by using a
- A) magnetic card
- B) password
- C) private key
- D) public key

D–3. A chemical reaction that occurs when a specially inked ribbon comes into contact with paper, making the numbers appear red on the reverse side, is a document security feature known as
- A) bleed-through numbering
- B) pantograph
- C) security paper
- D) thermochromic ink

E. Forms Management

Because gathering and processing information is critical in every organization, a forms management program yields important benefits. When procedures are established for ordering, designing, procuring, storing, distributing, reviewing, and disposing of each type of form used within the organization, costs for administrative processing can be controlled. An office form consists of a format with **constant information** (information that remains the same on each document) and **variable information** (information that is inserted on the document and changes each time the form is filled in). Forms may be paper copies (typewritten or printed copies) or displayed on a computer screen in the form of a template (electronic copy) stored on disk or the system.

1. *Key Factors in Forms Management:* In some organizations, forms management is controlled through one person, the records manager or information administrator, or one specific work unit. These units control the organization's forms analysis, design, production, and use. Some organizations contract with firms offering commercial

services in forms management. Other companies, however, have not viewed forms as a vital element in the records management process and have not initiated any kind of forms management program. As an organization grows, forms management becomes more important. Some key factors in developing a forms management program include the following:

a. *Top-management support:* Any forms management program must have the support of top management in actively promoting the program. Top management can provide appropriate directives to employees at all levels so that everyone in the organization plays an important part in forms management.

b. *Forms control:* To be effective, forms control must go into effect as soon as possible. Time must be devoted to the proper administration and design of forms used within the organization.

c. *Training for employees:* Administrative professionals must be trained so they can assist with updating procedures for the organization's forms management program. A training plan must be developed and implemented as part of the program.

2. ***Organizing a Forms Management System:*** Forms management is one of the most important elements of a total records management program. Here are some of the primary components of a successful program:

a. *Establishing forms management policy:* Policies for managing forms must be developed and supported by top management. Procedures for creating, reviewing, and producing forms must be identified as well as personnel who will be responsible for forms management.

b. *Forms analysis:* Forms designed for use within the company need to be analyzed to determine their importance. Those forms that receive high usage need to be analyzed first, hopefully resulting in improvements that lead to cost-effective use of the form. Legal compliance is another purpose for forms analysis.

c. *Forms specifications:* Decisions must be made about how the forms are to be produced: the size of the form, the type of paper stock and ink to use, the number of plies (copies), directions for producing the form, the method used to produce copies or templates of the form for individual use, and the packaging of the printed forms.

d. *Forms design:* The layout of the form is another very important forms management function. Forms may be designed by professional forms designers or by people within the organization who have expertise with the specific form being designed. The use of forms design software enables the creation of forms on a computer system. A variety of type styles and design features are easily incorporated into the printing process.

3. ***Controlling a Forms Management System:*** Forms control procedures ensure that the objectives of the forms management program are being achieved. No system is effective without controls for production, recording, filing, storage, and distribution being in effect.

a. *Forms production:* Forms may be produced and printed in an in-house reproduction center or by an outside commercial printer. The decision can also be made about using forms that are stored on disk or on a network and accessed for fill-in and completion. Forms are considered a part of the office supplies inventory, with some forms classified as *stock forms* and others as *nonstock forms.*

(1) *Stock forms:* Usually, stock forms are those that are used by more than one department. More than 1,000 copies of a stock form are needed per year. A quantity of stock forms is always kept available in a warehouse area.

(2) *Nonstock forms:* Typically, nonstock forms are used by only one individual or one department within an organization. Small quantities of less than 1,000 are needed per year. Therefore, nonstock forms are produced as needed.

b. *Forms recording and filing:* As forms are created for use within the organization, master sets of these forms should be maintained, recorded, and filed by the forms manager. For each form, printing specifications, information as to its use within the firm, and the department or individual for whom it is produced are part of the form's record. When the form is created, a decision also needs to be made relative to its retention; that is, how long this particular record will be kept on file. In addition, the form needs to be reviewed periodically for possible revision. These reviews are often conducted by records committees within the organization.

c. *Forms storage and distribution:* Storage and distribution of forms are also very important. Because of high storage costs, estimating the quantities of forms to have on hand is vital. Users must be provided with forms as needed, where needed, and in sufficient quantity. Storage may be as stock forms (hard copies, paper) or soft copy (disk or network).

d. *Forms control:* A forms control program is designed to involve representatives from all the departments or divisions of the organization in the process of creating, updating, and revising forms. Policies and procedures need to be established that benefit the entire organization.

(1) *Primary purposes:* A forms control program typically includes the following primary purposes.

(a) Maximize forms control throughout the entire organization.

(b) Reduce the cost of forms production and usage throughout the firm.

(c) Reduce forms duplication in various departments or divisions of an organization.

(d) Implement technology to hopefully increase operational efficiency.

(2) *Procedures and policies for forms control:* One important procedure that is needed is periodic review of forms for update and revision. In many organizations specific records committees perform this type of review process.

(a) *Approval of forms changes:* The design and use of new forms usually involves approval by the organizational forms committee as well as the manager of the department or division requesting the form. When a form that is already being used is reordered, the department that originated the form is asked for any revisions that might be needed.

(b) *Reproducing copyrighted forms:* The reproduction of copyrighted forms must be approved by the copyright holder. Often these forms would have to be ordered from or through the copyright holder.

(c) *Justification for forms design:* The cost of new or revised forms designs must be justified by the department responsible for the forms. Sometimes consultants are available to help with the forms design. The annual forms usage must be estimated, and appropriate approvals must be obtained from appropriate administrators.

The forms control system also involves the requisition procedures that will be followed by the various departments of the organization in obtaining stock and non-stock forms needed for day-to-day operations.

4. ***Integration with Other Systems:*** Forms control systems interface with a number of other systems, such as inventory control, warehousing, procurement, reproduction services, and various departmental office systems.

   a. *Inventory control:* Forms inventories are typically managed by materials management personnel within the organization. Inventories of stock and nonstock forms will need to be anticipated so that adequate supplies of forms will be available as needed.

   b. *Warehousing:* Forms that are kept in stock are those forms that are used in large quantities each year. Therefore, they must be stored or warehoused either in central storage within the organization or at the production location by the supplier until needed.

   c. *Purchasing:* Some forms may need to be produced by commercial printing services or through a publisher or vendor that holds the copyright for specific forms. Purchase requisitions must be initiated any time that the organization needs to procure a new supply of forms or to outsource for printing services. Once the purchase requisition has been approved, a purchase order is forwarded to the supplier. In some organizations, the purchase order is sent directly to a central supplier where orders are processed. A reorder point for forms needs to be predetermined so that a supply of forms is available as needed. Purchasing a large quantity of forms at one time will reduce the per-unit cost.

   d. *Reproduction services:* The printing of an organization's stock forms is typically handled through centralized printing services. A predetermined reorder point for forms should ensure that an adequate supply of forms is always available. Reproducing a large quantity of forms at one time will reduce the per-unit production costs. Specialists in central printing can also be very helpful in terms of layout and design of business forms.

   e. *Office systems:* Most of the forms design can be done in-house with word processing and desktop publishing software programs. In addition to brochures, product pamphlets, and announcements, forms that will be available in print or electronic format can be designed with these types of software programs. The latest electronic development is the availability of electronic forms on the intranet for fill-in, completion, and transmitting to appropriate administrators for approval.

Forms management within an organization involves controlling information contained on forms as well as access to forms. Only those individuals who need to have access to specific forms will be permitted to do so. Electronic access to forms is one way of providing more efficient forms control.

Check Point—Section E

Directions: For each question, circle the correct answer.

E–1. The Able Corp., a mid-sized organization, had approximately 150 forms for processing its traditional as well as Web transactions. One of the plant employees recommended that a system of forms management be established. If a forms management program is to be successful, it must have the support of

A) all plant employees
B) the records manager
C) the plant manager
D) top management

E–2. When establishing a forms management program, a primary component is to ensure legal compliance, which would be addressed when

A) conducting forms analyses
B) determining forms specifications
C) determining forms design
D) using forms design software

E–3. The Human Resource Division wants to reduce the cost of storage for the expense form that all managers use weekly to process reimbursements. The best recommendation would be to

A) place the expense form on a forms display rack to be picked up and used when needed, with extra copies stored in the human resources filing cabinet
B) provide all managers with 52 copies of the expense form every January
C) store the document on the organization's network for access and completion when needed
D) store large quantities of the expense form in Central Printing Services and a smaller quantity in the Human Resource Division

For Your Review

Directions: For each question, circle the correct answer.

1. Before a business record can be retrieved from active files, the record must be filed according to
   A) direct-access procedures
   B) the integrity of the record
   C) a prescribed set of rules and procedures for the organization
   D) the individual requirements of people who have access to the record

2. A person can go directly to the records storage system and locate the file or record if records may be accessed through
   A) a relative index
   B) indirect-access procedures
   C) records indexing
   D) direct-access procedures

3. An indirect-access filing procedure requires a user to consult a relative index to locate
   A) the number that has been assigned to the record or file
   B) the filing classification system under which the record is filed
   C) the original document (record)
   D) the manual procedures for accessing the record

4. In a direct-access filing system, what would be the *first* filing unit for the name Juan Carlos Rodriguez, Jr.?
   A) Juan
   B) Jr.
   C) Rodriguez
   D) Carlos

5. Inspecting a record means that the record has been
   A) reviewed to determine the indexing that will be used
   B) coded for filing
   C) assigned a file number
   D) released for filing by an authorized person

6. One advantage of color coding files is that
   A) a charge-out system is not necessary
   B) greater efficiency in locating and refiling records occurs
   C) one particular topic or subject can have two different color codes
   D) a cross-reference indicates where the original record is filed

7. When a record could be filed in more than one file location,
   A) color coding the original document will be necessary
   B) a tracking system is used to locate the original document
   C) copies of the document need to be placed at each file location
   D) a cross-reference is needed to indicate where the original document is filed

8. Documents in the organization's files can only be modified by a/an
   A) user within the organization
   B) authorized person
   C) records administrator
   D) administrative professional

9. An authentic document is one that is the work of the

A) copyright holder
B) users of the document
C) publisher of the document
D) author or source

10. A document's contents should not be altered without the express permission of the

A) major source of the information
B) copyright holder
C) records manager
D) president of the organization

11. Microforms that have been approved for filing must include a

A) verification of document content
B) certificate of authenticity
C) time stamp
D) copyright

12. Which one of the following types of records requires controlled access?

A) A university's student records
B) Inquiry letters from consumers about a new product
C) Published articles about an organization's program for employee career development
D) An organization's financial report to the stockholders

13. Confidentiality of information contained in records and documents must be observed in which one of the following situations?

A) Reading the announcement of Microsoft's new software program just on the market
B) Reviewing the newly published book, *Living History*, by Hillary Rodham Clinton
C) Obtaining the recipes for Emeril Lagasse's new salad dressings
D) Viewing a performance of the play, *The Lion King*

14. Which one of the following classifications of records would likely be stored in underground storage at a different location than the organization's headquarters?

A) Important records
B) Nonessential records
C) Vital records
D) Useful records

15. Storing records in an off-site facility usually results in

A) lower cost for storage of semiactive and inactive records
B) lower degree of records security
C) higher rent for the off-site facility
D) quick access to semiactive and inactive files stored off site

16. The records being held in an archive are identified or listed in a/an

A) direct-access system
B) cross-reference
C) relative index
D) accession register

17. Procedures embedded in software programs that restrict individual access to records are known as

A) passwords
B) logical security measures
C) user identification systems
D) physical security measures

18. The process of translating data into a secret code that can only be decoded by the recipient of the message is called

A) decryption of the message
B) indirect-access procedures
C) physical security for the message
D) encryption of the message

19. When a sender encrypts a message,

A) casual hacking is easily accomplished
B) a public key is available only to the recipient to decode the message
C) a private key is used by the recipient to decode the message
D) a message in plain text is the result

20. Use of an iris scan or a speech pattern to permit records access to an authorized user is part of a
   A) biometric identification system
   B) magnetic-card based system
   C) password identification system
   D) decryption system

21. The custodian of an organization's records has the responsibility to maintain and retain records in such a way to
   A) encrypt business information to be sent to selected recipients
   B) decode information received by the organization
   C) use security codes only to allow access to certain records
   D) ensure the physical security of active and inactive records of the organization

22. Information that remains the same on a set of business forms is referred to as
   A) plain text
   B) constant information
   C) microprinting
   D) variable information

23. To ensure that employees at all levels in the organization actively support the program, an effective forms management program requires
   A) no specific employee training
   B) the organization to remain relatively small
   C) support of top management
   D) assistance from an external forms management consultant

24. The development of forms specifications for a new business form involves decisions about the
   A) design and layout of the form
   B) general forms management policy of the organization
   C) use of forms design software
   D) way the form is produced

25. Which one of the following is a purpose of forms control?
   A) Reduce the number of forms that are duplicated in different departments of an organization
   B) Increase the use of forms throughout the organization
   C) Maintain the present cost level for production of forms
   D) Implement manual procedures to increase business efficiency

Solutions

Solutions to Check Point—Section A

Answer	Refer to:
A–1. (D)	[A-1-b]
A–2. (C)	[A-2]
A–3. (B)	[A-4]

Solutions to Check Point—Section B

Answer	Refer to:
B–1. (B)	[B-1]
B–2. (C)	[B-1-a]
B–3. (C)	[B-2-b]

Solutions to Check Point—Section C

Answer	Refer to:
C–1. (A)	[C-1]
C–2. (C)	[C-1-b]
C–3. (A)	[C-2]

Solutions to Check Point—Section D

Answer	Refer to:
D–1. (B)	[D]
D–2. (C)	[D-1-c (1)]
D–3. (A)	[D-4-e]

Solutions to Check Point—Section E

Answer	Refer to:
E–1. (D)	[E-1-a]
E–2. (A)	[E-2-b]
E–3. (C)	[E-3-a]

Solutions to For Your Review

Answer	Refer to:
1. (C)	[A]
2. (D)	[A-1-a]
3. (A)	[A-1-b]
4. (C)	[A-2]
5. (D)	[A-2]
6. (B)	[A-3]
7. (D)	[A-4]
8. (B)	[B-1]
9. (D)	[B-1-a]
10. (B)	[B-1-a]
11. (B)	[B-1-a]
12. (A)	[B-1-c]

13. (C)   [B-2]

14. (C)   [C-1-a]

15. (A)   [C-1-b]

16. (D)   [C-2]

17. (B)   [D]

18. (D)   [D-1-c (1)]

19. (C)   [D-1-c (1)]

20. (A)   [D-1-d]

21. (D)   [D-2-a]

22. (B)   [E]

23. (C)   [E-1-a]

24. (D)   [E-2-c]

25. (A)   [E-3-d (1) (c)]

Chapter 3

Filing Rules and Standards

OVERVIEW

Records are filed for easy retrieval. Filing rules applied within an organization need to be standardized so that all personnel who have the responsibility for filing and retrieving documents will follow the same procedures. Consistency in filing records occurs when the rules to be followed are documented (written) in the form of standardized procedures for everyone to know and follow.

The primary classification systems for filing are based on alphabetic, numeric, and alphanumeric procedures. Sets of filing rules are typically contained in all standard office procedures and records management references. The leading authority for establishing alphabetic filing rules is the Association of Records Managers and Administrators, Inc. (ARMA), which has published filing standard rules that may be adopted when filing personal, business, governmental, or political names.

KEY TERMS

A. Alphabetic Filing Systems

The **alphabetic filing system** is the oldest form of classification system and serves as the basis for all other types of classification systems. Even a numeric system must have a relative index that is in alphabetical order or can be accessed alphabetically. The 26 letters of the alphabet are the primary divisions within an alphabetic system.

1. *Alphabetic Filing Rules:* The Association of Records Managers and Administrators, Inc. (ARMA), a major professional organization for records management professionals, recommends the following Simplified Filing Standard Rules as an initial step to creating appropriate filing and retrieval procedures.

    a. *Arrangement of alphabetic files:* Files need to be arranged alphabetically in unit-by-unit order and letter by letter within each unit.

        • A **filing unit,** as defined by ARMA, may be a number, a letter, a word, or any combination of those.

        • A **filing segment** consists of one or more filing units (the total name, a number, or a subject) used for filing purposes.

    b. *Filing units and segments:* Each filing unit in a filing segment is to be considered, except for *a, an, the, any prepositions,* the *ampersand (&),* and *any conjunctions.* These words are placed in parentheses to indicate that they need not be used in filing if they are understood. When the word *the* is the first word in a business or organization name, *the* is placed in parentheses at the end of the name and is not considered a filing unit. Symbols like *$* and *#* are spelled out and filed alphabetically.

    EXAMPLES:

    Filing segment: Bonnie Louise Nichols

    > *Unit 1: Bonnie*

    > *Unit 2: Louise*

    > *Unit 3: Nichols*

    Filing segment: The Country Inn

    > *Unit 1: Country*

    > *Unit 2: Inn*

    The word The *is placed in parentheses at the end of the filing units: Country Inn (The)*

    c. *Filing nothing before something:* When filing documents, "nothing comes before something." Single-unit filing segments are filed before multiple-unit filing segments.

    EXAMPLES:

    > *White*

    > *White House*

    > *White, James Russell*

    d. *Ignoring punctuation in filing:* All marks of punctuation are ignored when alphabetizing filing segments. This includes periods, commas, dashes, hyphens, apostrophes, and any other punctuation mark that is included in a filing segment. Hyphenated words are considered one filing unit.

EXAMPLES:

Filing segment: Charlie's Home Improvements, Inc.

>   *Unit 1: Charlies*
>   *Unit 2: Home*
>   *Unit 3: Improvements*
>   *Unit 4: Inc*

Filing segment: Qwik-Copy Services

>   *Unit 1: QwikCopy*
>   *Unit 2: Services*

e. *Arabic numbers and Roman numerals:* Filing segments that begin with Arabic numbers and Roman numerals are filed sequentially in numeric order (not spelled out) before names with alphabetic characters. All names beginning with Arabic numbers precede names beginning with Roman numerals.

EXAMPLES:

>   *12 Building Rentals*
>   *1450 LaSalle Center*
>   *V Paramount Films, Inc.*
>   *LV Antique Books*
>   *ABC Corporation*
>   *Brooks Academic Services*

f. *Acronyms, abbreviations, and station names:* Acronyms, abbreviations, and radio and television station call letters are filed as one unit.

EXAMPLES:

Filing segment: ABC, Inc.

>   *Unit 1: ABC*
>   *Unit 2: Inc*

Filing segment: Mr. Crumb's Cookies

>   *Unit 1: Mr*
>   *Unit 2: Crumbs*
>   *Unit 3: Cookies*

Note: *Ignore punctuation marks when determining the filing units for a filing segment.*

g. *Names and titles:* The most commonly used name or title is the one that should be used when filing. Cross-reference filing segments under other names or titles that might be used when searching for documents or information.

EXAMPLE:

>   *Filing segment:*   *Jayne Mayfield-Bristol*
>   *Cross-reference:*   *Mayfield, Jayne*
>   *Bristol, Roger (Mrs.)*
>   *(See Bristol, Jayne Mayfield [Mrs.])*

2. ***Filing Personal Names:*** Personal names are filed with the surname considered as the first filing unit, followed by first name or initial and middle name or initial.

EXAMPLES:

Name	Unit 1	Unit 2	Unit 3
JoAnn Smith Robinson	Robinson	JoAnn	Smith
Carter L. MacGregor	MacGregor	Carter	L

If a married woman chooses to keep her maiden name, a cross-reference to her spouse's name may be necessary.

EXAMPLES:

Roseanne Marie Johnson
 (See Peterson, James L. [Mrs.])

Roseanne Johnson-Peterson
 (See Peterson, James L. [Mrs.])

a. *Surnames with prefixes:* A surname with a prefix (Da, De, Fitz, L', Mac, Mc, St.) is filed as one filing unit. If the prefix is followed by a space or punctuation, the space or punctuation is ignored in indexing (St. James = StJames).

EXAMPLES:

Name	Unit 1	Unit 2	Unit 3
Manuel De La Torre	DeLaTorre	Manuel	
Denise Jo FitzPatrick	FitzPatrick	Denise	Jo
Bradley R. MacDonald	MacDonald	Bradley	R
James Patrick O'Leary	OLeary	James	Patrick
Beth Rose St. James	StJames	Beth	Rose
Thomas John Van der Heide	VanderHeide	Thomas	John

When a number of names start with the same prefix, such as Mac or St., the prefixes are filed as a separate letter group preceding the other name.

EXAMPLES:

Name	Unit 1	Unit 2	Unit 3	Unit 4
James de La Rosa	de	La	Rosa	James
Manuel De La Torre	De	La	Torre	Manuel
Bradley R. Macdonald	Mac	donald	Bradley	R
Rosemary J. MacDonald	Mac	Donald	Rosemary	J

Another variation concerns prefixes that are pronounced the same but spelled differently, such as M', Mac, and Mc (pronounced "mac"). These names are filed as if they were all spelled "Mac."

EXAMPLES:

M'Cardow, Joan C.

McGovern, G. Alan

MacNamara, Roy Louis

Any decision to handle names in this way needs to be documented.

b. *Personal names with professional titles and suffixes:* Titles and suffixes are not considered filing units unless two or more individuals have the same surname.

EXAMPLES:

Name	Unit 1	Unit 2	Unit 3	Unit 4
Phyllis Jane Mueller, CPS	*Mueller*	*Phyllis*	*Jane*	*CPS*
Mrs. Phyllis Jane Mueller	*Mueller*	*Phyllis*	*Jane*	*Mrs*
Phyllis Jane Mueller, Ph.D.	*Mueller*	*Phyllis*	*Jane*	*PhD*
Paul J. Mueller, CPA	*Mueller*	*Paul*	*J*	*CPA*
Paul J. Mueller, Jr.	*Mueller*	*Paul*	*J*	*Jr*
Paul J. Mueller, M.D.	*Mueller*	*Paul*	*J*	*MD*
Mr. Paul J. Mueller	*Mueller*	*Paul*	*J*	*Mr*

c. *Hyphenated personal names:* When a personal name is hyphenated, the hyphen should be ignored and the two words considered one filing unit. Place the hyphen in parentheses so that the name is written correctly, however.

EXAMPLES:

Name	Unit 1	Unit 2	Unit 3
Mary-Jane Hadley	*Hadley*	*Mary(-)Jane*	
Ida Mae Ritz-Maurice	*Ritz(-)Maurice*	*Ida*	*Mae*
Jon-Lyn C. Carter	*Carter*	*Jon(-)Lyn*	*C*
Carter M. Hixon-Gates	*Hixon(-)Gates*	*Carter*	*M*

d. *Names that are pseudonyms:* A fictitious name or a pen name, known as a pseudonym, is indexed in the order written, with each word treated as a separate filing unit.

EXAMPLES:

Name	Unit 1	Unit 2
Father Time	*Father*	*Time*
Uncle Sam	*Uncle*	*Sam*
Mother Goose	*Mother*	*Goose*

e. *Names with royal and religious titles:* Personal names that begin with a royal or religious title and follow with only a given name are filed as written.

EXAMPLES:

Name	Unit 1	Unit 2	Unit 3
King Arthur	*King*	*Arthur*	
Prince William	*Prince*	*William*	
Queen Elizabeth II	*Queen*	*Elizabeth*	*II*
Father Flanagan	*Father*	*Flanagan*	
Mother Teresa	*Mother*	*Teresa*	

However, when numerous files use religious titles, the title may become the last filing unit.

EXAMPLES:

Name	Unit 1	Unit 2	Unit 3	Unit 4
Sister Katherine Mary	Katherine	Mary	Sister	
Sister Mary Margaret	Mary	Margaret	Sister	
Sister Mary Teresa	Mary	Teresa	Sister	
Father William Murphy	Murphy	William	Father	
Father Thomas O'Donnell	ODonnell	Thomas	Father	
Father Joseph J. Scaparelli	Scaparelli	Joseph	J	Father

f. *Foreign personal names:* File the name with the surname first, as in any other name, if you can identify the word that is the surname. If you question which part of the name is the surname, use the last word in the name as the first filing unit; but cross-reference under the first word in the name. In Asian countries as well as other parts of the world, the surname may be placed as the first unit. In the name *Tao Sung, Tao* is the surname rather than *Sung.*

EXAMPLES:

Name	Unit 1	Unit 2	Unit 3
Kim Son Yung	Kim	Son	Yung
		(See Yung, Kim Son)	

Name	Unit 1	Unit 2	Unit 3
Sri Pak Onro	Sri	Pak	Onro
		(See Onro, Sri Pak)	

g. *Nicknames:* A nickname that is commonly used by the person (and recognized by other people) as a first name should be used as a filing unit.

EXAMPLES:

Name	Unit 1	Unit 2
Fuzzy Zoeller	Zoeller	Fuzzy
	(See Zoeller, Frank Urban, Jr.)	

Name	Unit 1	Unit 2
Jimmy Carter	Carter	Jimmy
	(See Carter, James Earl, Jr.)	

3. **Filing Business and Organization Names:** Company names are filed using each word in the name as an indexing unit but not the words *a, an, &, and, the,* prepositions, and conjunctions. If the word *The* appears as the first word, it is transposed and placed in parentheses to indicate that the word need not be used as an indexing unit. Spell out abbreviations like *Inc., Co.,* and *Ltd.*

EXAMPLES:

Name	Unit 1	Unit 2	Unit 3
The Royale Corp.	Royale	Corporation (The)	
Center of the World Restaurant	Center (of the)	World	Restaurant
Blake & Sons, Inc.	Blake (&)	Sons	Incorporated
BP Oil, Inc.	BP	Oil	Incorporated

Note: The, of the, *and & are not used as filing units, but these words need to be inserted within the name in the correct place within parentheses.*

a. *Cross-references:* When necessary, cross-reference business acronyms with the complete business name.

EXAMPLE:

> *IBM*
> *(See International Business Machines Corporation)*

Subsidiaries of businesses will be filed under their own names with a cross-reference to the parent company.

EXAMPLE:

> *Taco Bell*
> *(See Yum!Brands, Inc.)*
> *Pizza Hut*
> *(See Yum!Brands, Inc.)*

b. *Geographic names:* Each filing unit in a geographic place name will be treated as a separate unit; similar rules are followed as with personal names.

EXAMPLES:

Name	Unit 1	Unit 2	Unit 3	Unit 4
St. Paul Museum of Industry	StPaul	Museum (of)	Industry	
New York Metro System	New	York	Metro	System
Wisconsin Power & Light Co.	Wisconsin	Power (&)	Light	Company
The Empire District Electric Co.	Empire	District	Electric	Company (The)

c. *Names with compass terms:* Each word or filing unit containing compass terms is considered a separate filing unit.

EXAMPLES:

Name	Unit 1	Unit 2	Unit 3	Unit 4
South Eastern Products, Inc.	South	Eastern	Products	Incorporated
South Florida Com-Networks	South	Florida	Com(-)Networks	
Southeast Innovative Media	Southeast	Innovative	Media	
Southern Bell Communications	Southern	Bell	Communications	
Southwestern Publishers, Ltd.	Southwestern	Publishers	Limited	

4. **Filing Names by Addresses:** When the same business or organization name may apply to more than one location, filing order will be determined by the location (the address). When using an address, these filing units are considered in this order:

- City
- State or province
- Street name
  - Numbered streets appear in numeric order before streets with alphabetical names
  - Streets with compass directions are alphabetized as written
- House or building number

EXAMPLES:

Name	Unit 1	Unit 2	Unit 3	Unit 4
Chamber of Commerce, Peoria, Illinois	Chamber (of)	Commerce	Peoria	Illinois
Chamber of Commerce, Sycamore, Illinois	Chamber (of)	Commerce	Sycamore	Illinois
St. Anthony's Hospital, Madison, Wisconsin	StAnthonys	Hospital	Madison	Wisconsin
St. Anthony's Hospital, Rockford, Illinois	StAnthonys	Hospital	Rockford	Illinois

Name	Unit 1	Unit 2	Unit 3	Unit 4	Unit 5	Unit 6	Unit 7	Unit 8	Unit 9
Mary L. Anderson, 123 23rd Avenue, LaCrosse, Wisconsin	Anderson	Mary	L	LaCrosse	Wisconsin	23rd	Avenue	123	
Mary L. Anderson, 4280 Concord Drive, La Crosse, Wisconsin	Anderson	Mary	L	LaCrosse	Wisconsin	Concord	Drive	4280	
Mary L. Anderson, 892 Warwick Avenue, Manchester, New Hampshire	Anderson	Mary	L	Manchester	New	Hampshire	Warwick	Avenue	892

5. **Individual Names in Company Names:** A company name that begins with the full name of an individual should be included with surname first, followed by first name and the rest of the company name.

EXAMPLES:

Name	Unit 1	Unit 2	Unit 3	Unit 4
R.L. Lawrence Transfer	Lawrence	R	L	Transfer
Susan Klein Flowers	Klein	Susan	Flowers	

When a company named for an individual becomes well known, the words in the name can be considered as written. Otherwise, using the surname first may be too confusing. Cross-reference names only if necessary. Disregard punctuation marks.

EXAMPLES:

Name	Unit 1	Unit 2	Unit 3	Unit 4
J.C. Penney Company	J	C	Penney	Company
Marshall Field's	Marshall	Fields		

6. **Hyphenated Business Names:** When two or more words, initials, or names in a business name are joined by a hyphen, the hyphen should be disregarded so that each part of the name is treated as a separate unit. Cross-reference names only if necessary. Although the hyphens are disregarded in filing, they need to be inserted in parentheses and kept with the name.

EXAMPLES:

Name	Unit 1	Unit 2	Unit 3
A-Z QwikCopy	A(-)	Z	QwikCopy
B-J Decorators	B(-)	J	Decorators
Bern-Well Distributors	Bern(-)	Well	Distributors

Each article, preposition, or conjunction that is joined to another word by a hyphen is treated as a separate unit.

EXAMPLES:

Name	Unit 1	Unit 2	Unit 3	Unit 4	Unit 5
X-and-Y Transport, Inc.	X(-)	and(-)	Y	Transport	Incorporated
Dari-Ripple Drive-In	Dari(-)	Ripple	Drive(-)	In	

When a hyphen joins two parts of a single word, both parts are considered together as one unit.

EXAMPLES:

Name	Unit 1	Unit 2	Unit 3
Inter-Continental Automotive Associates	Inter(-)Continental	Automotive	Associates
Trans-Atlantic Systems, Ltd.	Trans(-)Atlantic	Systems	Limited
Quad-City Recycling, Inc.	Quad(-)City	Recycling	Incorporated

7. **Filing Names of Governmental and Political Organizations:** Governmental organizations are filed first under the name of the government, then the name of the department

or agency, in sequential order of authority. Words such as *and*, *the*, and *of* are placed in parentheses and are not regarded as indexing units.

    a. *Federal government names:* The name of the government comes first:

EXAMPLE:

Name	Unit 1	Unit 2	Unit 3
United States Government	United	States	Government

followed by department (if known):

EXAMPLE:

Name	Unit 4	Unit 5
Department of the Treasury	Treasury	Department (of the)

followed by the service bureau within the department:

EXAMPLE:

Name	Unit 6	Unit 7	Unit 8
Internal Revenue Service	Internal	Revenue	Service

The above example has eight filing units in the entire name of the service/bureau. The following example has six filing units in the name of the agency.

EXAMPLES:

Unit 1	Unit 2	Unit 3	Unit 4	Unit 5	Unit 6
United	States	Government	Environmental	Protection	Agency

    b. *Military names:* File the names of camps, forts, bases, and other military names after the prefix, "United States Government."

EXAMPLES:

Unit 1	Unit 2	Unit 3	Unit 4	Unit 5
United	States	Government	Camp	Lejeune
United	States	Government	Fort	Jackson
United	States	Government	Fort	McCoy

8. **State and Local Government Names:** State, county, municipal, and township governments and other political divisions are filed by their distinctive names. The words *county*, *city*, and *department* may be used for clarity as separate filing units.

EXAMPLES:

Name	Unit 1	Unit 2	Unit 3	Unit 4
DeKalb County Highway Department	DeKalb	County	Highway	Department
State of Michigan Department of Health	Michigan	State (of)	Health	Department (of)
City of Reedsburg Zoning Commission	Reedsburg	City (of)	Zoning	Commission
Village of Rock Springs Treasurer	Rock	Springs	Village (of)	Treasurer

9. **Foreign Governments:** The first filing unit is the distinctive English name of the country. Continue with the rest of the official name. Divisions or departments within the government follow in sequential order.

EXAMPLES:

Unit 1	Unit 2	Unit 3	Unit 4	Unit 5	Unit 6	Unit 7	Unit 8
Great	Britain	Commonwealth (of)	Defense	Department	Royal	Air	Force
China	Republic (of)	Commerce (and)	Trade	Division	Exports (and)	Imports	
Canada	Government (of)	Alberta		Province (of)	Edmonton	City (of)	Public	Safety

Check Point—Section A

Directions: For each question, circle the correct answer.

A–1. Hoffman uses an alphabetic classification system based on the ARMA rules in which correspondence is filed alphabetically by name of client. Which one of the following names would be filed *first*?

A) Roberta L. Bernard
B) Bernarde Robot Company
C) Robert Louis Bernard
D) The Bernard Recreation Association

A–2. When an alphabetic classification system is used, which one of the following names would be filed *last*?

A) U.S. Department of Labor
B) United Airlines

C) U.S. Department of Education
D) United States of America

A–3. Bromley files correspondence alphabetically, with all correspondence for a particular client filed chronologically, with the most recent date first. Which one of the following pieces of correspondence will be filed *first* (on top) in the file?

A) A letter from George R. Johnson dated February 4, 2004
B) A letter from G. R. Johnson dated January 3, 2004
C) A letter to George R. Johnson dated March 14, 2004
D) A letter to G. R. Johnson dated December 28, 2003

B. Numeric Filing Systems

A **numeric filing system** is an indirect-access system that consists of various combinations of numeric codes assigned to names of individuals, organizations, or subjects. An **accession record** (an official log listing the names to which numbers have already been assigned) and a **relative index** (individual cards or computer listing of all names to which numbers have been assigned in alphabetic order) are necessary elements of the numeric system. Typically, a key field in computerized systems tends to be numeric (e.g., employee number, part number, product code) because that field must contain unique information pertinent only to the individual or item.

When numeric files are used within a business, correspondents are usually encouraged to put the numeric code (file number, account number) on each piece of correspondence relating to a business transaction. There are many different types of numeric systems. Those presented here are examples of some of the more commonly used numeric systems.

1. **Straight Numeric:** Files are arranged in consecutive order, from the lowest number to the highest number. **Sequential** or **serial files** are other terms used for a straight-numeric system. Color coding can be used to tab folders in a straight-numeric system for quick access when folders are stored in open shelving. The following colors are used in one color-coding system:

0 = red	5 = blue
1 = pink	6 = lavender
2 = yellow	7 = brown
3 = orange	8 = silver
4 = green	9 = gold

EXAMPLE: *An administrative assistant who codes the four-digit customer number, 1249, on a file folder would place the following color tabs vertically on the folder tab:*

1 = pink
2 = yellow
4 = green
9 = gold

A folder for customer number 1250 would have the following color tabs:

1 = pink
2 = yellow
5 = blue
0 = red

One of the primary advantages of color coding files is that misfiled folders can be spotted easily because of the arrangement of the color tabs. A color-coded system for paper files can be coordinated with customer databases stored on the computer.

2. **Duplex Numeric:** File numbers may have two or more sets of code numbers separated by a dash, comma, period, or space when a **duplex numeric system** is used. A relative index is needed so that a complete list of the primary numbers assigned to the major categories within the system can be maintained.

EXAMPLE: *The file set up for Administration is assigned the number 20. Subsections within that file for budgets, business travel, costs, personnel, and research include a second set of numbers. If any of those subsections is divided, a third set of numbers is applied. The folders within the file are arranged alphabetically by subject.*

Administration	*20*
Budgets	*20–10*
Business Travel	*20–11*

Costs	20–12
Administrative	20–12–01
Operating	20–12–02
Personnel	20–13
Research	20–14

3. **Block Codes:** Blocks of numbers called **block codes** may be reserved for records that have a common feature or characteristic.

EXAMPLE:

Administration	201–299
Production	301–399
Sales and Marketing	401–499

4. **Middle Digit:** Records are filed numerically by the middle digits, not necessarily according to the number as it appears on the record. The file numbers in the accession record are still listed in straight-numeric sequence.

EXAMPLE:

File No. 482311

Indexing Units:

48	23	11
Secondary	Primary	Tertiary
(2)	(1)	(3)

The record will be filed under 23 first, then 48 within the 23 section, and finally in folder 11.

Drawer:	23
Guide:	48
Folder:	11

The **middle-digit system** is very effective if file numbers have six or fewer digits. When file numbers are more than six digits, other numeric systems would probably be more effective.

5. **Terminal Digit:** Records are filed by the *last digits* (the terminal digits) in the **terminal-digit system,** which tends to be a more efficient system than middle-digit. The code number is divided into sets of two or three digits as a general rule. File numbers are listed consecutively in the accession record so that a record of the file numbers already assigned in the system is kept. A primary advantage of the terminal-digit system is security in the handling of confidential files or information.

EXAMPLE:

File No. 482311628

Indexing Units:

482	311	628
Tertiary	Secondary	Primary
(3)	(2)	(1)

The record will be filed under 628 first, then 311 within the 628 section, and finally in folder 482.

Drawer:	*628*
Guide:	*311*
Folder	*482*

If the number 482311 is grouped in sets of three digits, the coding would be like this:

482	*311*
Secondary	*Primary*
(2)	*(1)*

EXAMPLE: *The catalog stores for a prominent retailer use a very simple terminal-digit system to file the orders waiting for customer pickup. When a customer orders catalog merchandise, the customer's telephone number is entered on the order form along with other information such as name, address, account number, items ordered, and unit prices. When the customer picks up the merchandise, the clerk asks for the customer's telephone number. The last two digits (the terminal digits) are used to locate the order in the storage area.*

6. *Decimal Numeric:* A **decimal-numeric system** permits a subject (topic) to be subdivided, thus expanding a simple numeric arrangement for the file.

   a. *Subdividing subjects:* Major divisions of a subject (topic) are assigned a number. A decimal point followed by one digit is placed after the number of the first subdivision, a second digit after the second subdivision, and so on.

   EXAMPLE: *The major division, Motor Vehicles, is assigned the number 350. Within that division, specific types of motor vehicles can be assigned decimal numbers.*

Motor Vehicles	*350*
Sedan	*350.1*
Coupe	*350.11*
Sport Coupe	*350.12*
Van	*350.2*
Conversion	*350.21*
Minivan	*350.22*

   b. *The Dewey Decimal System:* The **Dewey Decimal System** is perhaps the most widely known decimal-numeric filing system. Developed in 1873 primarily for cataloging library books, the system includes ten general categories:

000	General Works
100	Philosophy
200	Religion
300	Social Science
400	Philology
500	Pure Science
600	Applied Science or Useful Arts
700	Arts and Recreation

800   Literature

900   History

Each of these ten categories is then divided into ten parts, with a further subdivision into ten more subdivisions. A typical decimal used in cataloging a book and placed on a tab on the book would look like this:

650.231 (a book within the Applied Science or Useful Arts category)

7. ***Coded Numeric:*** Sometimes records are given numeric codes where the codes are really numbers telling something about the person or item. When the codes used take on additional meaning about the item, we say that a **mnemonic code** is being used.

   a. *ZIP Codes:* Used by the U.S. Postal Service for mail delivery, the Zone Improvement Program (ZIP) Codes are an example of a coded numeric system. The **ZIP + 4 Codes** (9-digit numbers), the expanded code established in 1981, are an extension of the original system.

   EXAMPLE:

   ZIP Code = 60115–2623

   > *6 = area within United States*
   >
   > *01 = sectional center*
   >
   > *15 = local delivery area*
   >
   > *26 = geographic portion of a zone or a portion of a rural route, part of a box section, or official designation*
   >
   > *23 = a specific block face, apartment house, bank of boxes, firm, building, or other specific delivery locations*

   b. *Area codes:* Telephone networks across the United States are divided into geographic zones called **area codes.** The area code serves as a prefix so that a telephone number can be dialed directly (without intervention by an operator) anywhere in the United States.

   EXAMPLE:

   > *(312) 445–2189*
   >
   > *312 = an area code within the city of Chicago, Illinois*
   >
   > *445–2189 = individual or business telephone number within that area code*

   International codes are also in use for calling individual telephone numbers in foreign countries.

   c. *Catalog numbers and product codes:* Product numbers included in catalogs and on bar codes for merchandise represent information about the items.

   EXAMPLES:

   The catalog number for a specific item may represent the following types of information about the item:

   > *110 22 1260–8 = 110 item category*
   >
   > *22 catalog number*
   >
   > *1260 item style*
   >
   > *8 color*

In grocery stores, produce is individually tagged with a numeric code (e.g., 4409 for Bartlett pears, 4016 for red delicious apples). This makes the job of the cashier easier for all he or she has to do is enter the code number for the product, weigh the item, and view the price that appears on the computer screen.

8. **Chronological System:** Often, records need to be filed according to *date*. A filing system that utilizes calendar dates as the significant divisions of the system is known as a **chronological system.**

EXAMPLES:

A tickler file is arranged according to dates, with the most recent date first. Reminder notes are recorded/entered on cards or files for particular dates.

A business calendar is arranged by chronological dates (and times). If appointments are entered onto a small handheld computerized calendar system called a personal digital assistant (PDA), *the calendar can be accessed by entering an appropriate code. The appointments will appear on a small screen in chronological order according to times.*

Check Point—Section B

Directions: For each question, circle the correct answer.

B–1. The primary purpose for using a relative index with a numeric classification system is so that
   A) cross-references can be located easily
   B) the record can be retrieved using a direct-access procedure
   C) a particular record or file can be located quickly
   D) blocks of numbers can be reserved for certain record categories

B–2. If you were filing the following numbered records using a middle-digit filing system that divides the numbers into two-digit groups, which one of the following numbers would be filed *first*?
   A) 204573
   B) 134591
   C) 105424
   D) 115429

B–3. The following numbered records are filed using a terminal-digit system, containing two-digit groupings of numbers. Which record would be filed *second*?
   A) 115119
   B) 154517
   C) 225891
   D) 334717

C. Alphanumeric Filing Systems

Alphanumeric filing systems combine the elements contained in alphabetic and numeric systems. Whenever a combination of alphabetic characters and numbers is used in a filing code, the code is referred to as **alphanumeric code.** In a system like this, it is possible to have the alphanumeric designations on primary guides as well as individual folders. A relative index lists the codes assigned to each letter of the alphabet and any subdivisions.

1. **Soundex Codes:** A **Soundex code** is an alphanumeric code that includes an alphabetic letter (the first letter of the name being coded) and three numbers representing the con-

sonant sounds in the name. Vowel sounds and silent letters are omitted. Additional information numerically coded follows these first four code digits. This code is commonly used for such numbers as driver's license numbers.

EXAMPLE:

S636 = S – r – d – r Schrader

The letters c-h-a-e are omitted in the rules for the Soundex code.

2. ***The Library of Congress System:*** One of the systems for cataloging library books, the **Library of Congress system,** uses an alphanumeric code that includes one or two alphabetic letters and series of numbers that designate subdivisions within categories.

EXAMPLE:

FK889.3 F = History K = Law 889.3 = indicates specific code for book

Check Point—Section C

Directions: For each question, circle the correct answer.

C–1. A relative index for an alphanumeric filing system lists the codes assigned to
  A) each alphabetic letter and any subdivisions
  B) subjects or topics in the file
  C) names of correspondents
  D) geographic regions for an organization

C–2. An alphanumeric code that includes an alphabetic letter (the first letter of the name being coded) and numbers representing the consonant sounds in the name is called

  A) terminal-digit system
  B) Soundex code
  C) block code
  D) straight numeric system

C–3. The classification system used for cataloging library books that uses an alphanumeric code is the
  A) Dewey Decimal System
  B) Soundex code
  C) Library of Congress classification system
  D) middle-digit system

D. Subject and Geographic Filing Systems

Two other classification systems that use alphabetic filing systems to store documents are subject filing and geographic filing. In subject filing, each document is analyzed first to see what subject it should be filed under. In geographic filing, each document is analyzed to determine the location of the transaction or the task performance.

1. ***Subject Filing:*** Another classification system that uses the alphabetic system as a base is a **subject filing system.** Instead of arranging records by names of individuals or business names, records are arranged in alphabetical order according to topics or categories.

EXAMPLE:

Administration
    Budgets
    Business travel
    Costs—administrative
    Costs—operating
    Human resources
    Research

a. *Advantages of subject filing:* Subject filing is used primarily when it is advantageous to file documents by topic rather than by names of individuals or companies. An index of all the topics (subjects) used in the system must be kept either manually or electronically. When a user needs to find information on a specific subject, this type of filing system is particularly helpful.

b. *Disadvantages of subject filing:* Subject filing can be rather cumbersome because a user needs to be able to access the index first and see if a subject file has already been established. Another disadvantage might be that the file for a particular subject may become too large and need to be subdivided into smaller files.

2. ***Geographic Filing:*** In a **geographic filing system,** records are arranged alphabetically according to geographic locations. Filing by geographic locations may be particularly useful in a company or organization with branch offices or divisions in different parts of the country.

EXAMPLES:

Canada
    Atlantic Provinces
        New Brunswick
        Newfoundland
        Nova Scotia
        Prince Edward Island
    Quebec
    Ontario
    Prairie Provinces
        Alberta
        Saskatchewan
        Manitoba
    British Columbia
    Territories
        Yukon Territory
        Northwest Territories
United States
    Central region

North-Central region

Northeastern region

Northwestern region

Southeastern region

Southwestern region

Western region

Great Britain, Commonwealth (of)

England

Northern Ireland

Scotland

Wales

a. *Advantages of geographic systems:* One of the greatest advantages for using a geographic system is in the marketing and selling of products or providing services, which usually take on a regional or international flavor. This type of system provides the opportunity to set up financial, advertising, and public relations information on a regional basis so that management can easily determine how various areas of the country are being served.

b. *Disadvantages of geographic systems:* Again, a geographic system may become too cumbersome if all correspondence and reports for a given region are included in one section of the files. Files for clients with whom an organization does business will no doubt still have to be set up.

Check Point—Section D

Directions: For each question, circle the correct answer.

D–1. When records are filed according to specific topics, what type of classification system is being used?

A) alphabetic filing system
B) geographic filing system
C) numeric filing system
D) subject filing system

D–2. Which one of the following is an advantage of a subject filing system?

A) records are retrievable from files based on names of correspondents and clients
B) records can be filed according to geographic regions of the country
C) records can be accessible for different products a company is marketing or selling

D) a subject file will be limited as to the quantity of the contents within that file

D–3. A geographic filing system is based upon

A) the products or services offered by an organization
B) business transactions taking place in different regions of the country or world
C) direct access to records pertaining to the business transactions of the organization
D) an alphabetic list of clients for the business.

E. Filing Standards

A **filing standard** is a procedure to follow in establishing consistent filing rules. Such standards provide the documentation needed to support the rules applied within a given organization. Here are some standards that organizations are currently following in ensuring consistency in handling files and records.

1. ***Documentation of Use of Rules:*** A written set of filing rules to be applied within the organization is essential in establishing consistency in how office professionals throughout the firm will practice records management techniques. If these rules are placed in a filing or records manual for all to see, they will be much easier to question as well as follow. Exceptions that vary from the filing rules will need to be documented as well.

   EXAMPLE: *Inconsistencies can sometimes be resolved at the time data are entered into a database. When the information is being input directly from file folders, data entry personnel can be directed to input the data the way it is to be written. "St." should be keyed in as "Saint."*

2. ***Training of Records Personnel:*** Individuals who are assigned the responsibility of working with files and records need to be trained. Only those who are trained should be allowed access to the records (the "memory") of the organization.

3. ***Use of Cross-References:*** The records management program needs to emphasize the use of cross-references whenever a record or document could possibly be filed under more than one name or subject. The cross-reference must lead the user to the record in a minimum amount of time.

4. ***Manual and Electronic Procedures:*** An organization needs to design both manual and electronic procedures and include these procedures in appropriate operations manuals. The practices of the current manual filing system will help to serve as a basis for the electronic filing system to be developed.

   Even though some filing systems still require manual procedures, as time goes on, these systems will continue to become more automated and computer-assisted. Therefore, records management personnel within the organization need to be cognizant of the ways in which the records systems can be upgraded toward more electronic applications.

   EXAMPLE: *In alphabetic filing, names that begin with Arabic numerals come before names that begin with alphabetic letters. If these names are converted to an electronic system, left-margin zeroes may need to be added to the numbers so that the same number of digits will be used. "2nd Avenue Market" may have to be entered as "0002 Avenue Market" to correspond with 0015 Street Deli ("15th Street Deli").*

   When automating a records system, it is important to know the sorting capabilities of the particular software and hardware being used. Most computers can more easily apply simplified rather than complex indexing rules. Therefore, rules such as those proposed by ARMA are versatile enough to form the basis for a set of filing standards and rules that an entire organization can well benefit from putting into place.

Check Point—Section E

Directions: For each question, circle the correct answer.

E–1. Documentation of filing rules to be implemented within an organization will be beneficial in providing

    A) reasons for filing names a particular way

    B) consistency in the way office professionals make decisions about files and records

    C) a method for inputting names of correspondents and clients

    D) a basis for converting to an electronic system

E–2. Administrative professionals who are assigned responsibility for managing the records of the organization need to be

    A) trained to make appropriate filing and retrieval decisions

    B) versatile in the use of electronic filing systems

    C) experienced in working with both manual and electronic records systems

    D) use cross-references when there is one best way to file a specific record

E–3. A records manual for the organization will provide

    A) training needed to become a records professional

    B) guidelines for consistent application of filing rules and standards throughout the organization

    C) absolute answers to questions that may arise about the filing system

    D) the opportunity for the organization to develop a unique set of filing rules and standards

For Your Review

Directions: For each question, circle the correct answer.

1. In an alphabetic filing system, files need to be arranged in
   A) a relative index
   B) filing segments
   C) filing-unit order
   D) cross-referencing

2. A filing unit in an alphabetic system is defined as
   A) a person's full name
   B) a string of characters or a word
   C) the official name of an organization
   D) another name under which the record could be filed

3. When determining the filing units in the name *The Clothes Horse, Inc.*, the word
   A) *The* is not considered a filing unit and is placed in parentheses
   B) *Clothes* is considered a filing segment
   C) *Inc.* is placed in parentheses and is not considered a filing unit
   D) *Horse* is the first filing unit in the name

4. Which one of the following demonstrates the "nothing comes before something" rule?
   A) John Bensen comes after Jonathan Benson
   B) Shirley MacMurray comes before Shirley MacLaine
   C) LaSalle comes before LaSalle Builders
   D) Xavier Thompson comes before Xavier Thomas

5. In an alphabetical file, the filing segment *728 Park Center* should be filed
   A) after a name beginning with a Roman numeral
   B) under the number (seven hundred twenty-eight) spelled out
   C) with five filing units
   D) before a name beginning with a Roman numeral

6. Kristin Alyce Timlon is also known by her married name, Mrs. Jacob L. Stein. The cross-reference should be filed under
   A) Jacob L. Stein (Mrs.)
   B) Timlon, Kristin Alyce
   C) Stein, Jacob L. (Mrs.)
   D) Timlon-Stein, Kristin Alyce

7. The prefix O', as in the surname O'Brien, is
   A) filed as one filing unit with the rest of the surname (O'Brien)
   B) filed as a separate filing unit (O')
   C) placed in parentheses and not included as a filing unit
   D) disregarded in indexing the filing units in the name

8. Which one of the following personal names would be filed *second* in an alphabetic file?
   A) Roy Louis MacNamara, Sr.
   B) Mrs. Roberta L. Macdonald
   C) Dr. Robert MacDonald
   D) Charles Lawrence MacNamee, Jr.

9. The pseudonym *Dr. Seuss* would be indexed
   A) last name first (i.e., *Seuss*, *Dr.*)
   B) under only the last name *Seuss*
   C) in two filing units in the order written
   D) Dr. would be placed in parentheses

10. Index the names shown below. Which one of the names would be filed *third*?
    A) King George VI
    B) Pope John Paul
    C) Sister Mary Teresa
    D) Father Flanagan

11. Which one of the following names requires a cross-reference?
    A) Museum of Natural History, Chicago, Illinois
    B) Western Bell Communications Network
    C) Maureen M. O'Connelly
    D) KFC, a subsidiary of Yum!Brands, Inc.

12. When two or more names are identical, the next filing unit is the name of the
    A) street
    B) state or province
    C) city
    D) house number

13. Index each of the names shown below. Which one of the following names would be filed *last*?
    A) James Collier's Construction Co.
    B) Collier Construction, Ltd.
    C) J-C Construction Company
    D) James-Collier Construction, Inc.

14. Index the following names into filing units. Which one will be filed *third*?
    A) U.S. Department of the Treasury
    B) U.S. Air Express, Inc.
    C) United Parcel Service
    D) *USA Today*

15. In a numeric filing system, a relative index is used to
    A) file documents in numeric order
    B) locate the number assigned to a specific name or case

C) purge the system of unneeded files
D) assign a number to the file of a specific correspondent

16. When a numeric system is used, color coding can be applied to each folder so that
    A) the folders can be seen easily when stored on open shelves
    B) the computer system can locate individual folders more easily
    C) misfiled folders can be more easily spotted on the open shelves
    D) the files can be arranged in different filing sequences

17. A duplex numeric system requires the maintenance of a list of numbers assigned to the major categories within the system in a/an
    A) relative index
    B) sequential filing system
    C) accession record
    D) filing segment

18. A numeric system in which each file number is six digits (e.g., 692103) and initial filing is under the 21 is called a
    A) terminal-digit system
    B) system of block codes
    C) middle-digit system
    D) straight numeric system

19. The ZIP + 4 Codes used by the U.S. Postal Service for mail delivery (e.g., 90547–2623) are an example of a/an
    A) area code
    B) block code
    C) decimal numeric code
    D) mnemonic code

20. Appointments entered on a business calendar using a personal digital assistant (PDA) appear on a small screen in
    A) numeric order
    B) chronological order
    C) terminal-digit order
    D) sequential order

21. A system for creating driver's license numbers that applies an alphabetic-numeric sequence for the person's last

name plus additional numbers representing personal data uses a

A) block code
B) decimal-numeric code
C) Soundex code
D) straight numeric code

22. In a subject filing system, records are arranged in alphabetical order

A) according to names of individual correspondents
B) by mnemonic code
C) by topics or categories
D) according to business or organization names

23. The opportunity to establish regional advertising and public relations information in marketing a product or service is one advantage of a/an

A) subject filing system
B) alphanumeric filing system

C) coded numeric filing system
D) geographic filing system

24. An established procedure to follow resulting in filing rules that will be applied consistently throughout an organization is referred to as

A) a filing standard
B) documentation of the filing rules
C) a filing or records manual
D) electronic filing procedures

25. When a records system is being automated,

A) few cross-references will be needed
B) the manual records system will no longer be needed
C) the sorting capabilities of the software and hardware need to be determined
D) the ARMA filing rules and standards need to be adopted as quickly as possible

Solutions

Solutions to Check Point—Section A

Answer	*Refer to:*
A–1. (D)	[A-2 and A-3]
A–2. (A)	[A-3 and A-7]
A–3. (B)	[A-2 and B-8]

Solutions to Check Point—Section B

Answer	*Refer to:*
B–1. (C)	[B]
B–2. (B)	[B-4]
B–3. (D)	[B-5]

Solutions to Check Point—Section C

Answer	*Refer to:*
C–1. (A)	[C]
C–2. (B)	[C-1]
C–3. (C)	[C-2]

Solutions to Check Point—Section D

Answer	Refer to:
D–1. (D)	[D-1]
D–2. (C)	[D-1-a]
D–3. (B)	[D-2]

Solutions to Check Point—Section E

Answer	Refer to:
E–1. (B)	[E-1]
E–2. (A)	[E-2]
E–3. (B)	[E-4]

Solutions to For Your Review

Answer	Refer to:
1. (C)	[A-1-a]
2. (B)	[A-1-a]
3. (A)	[A-1-b]
4. (C)	[A-1-c]
5. (D)	[A-1-e]
6. (C)	[A-1-g and A-2]
7. (A)	[A-2-a]
8. (B)	[A-2-a]
9. (C)	[A-2-d]
10. (B)	[A-2-e]
11. (D)	[A-3-a]
12. (C)	[A-4]

13. (D)   [A-5 and A-6]

14. (A)   [A-3 and A-7-a]

15. (B)   [B]

16. (C)   [B-1]

17. (A)   [B-2]

18. (C)   [B-4]

19. (D)   [B-7 and B-7-a]

20. (B)   [B-8]

21. (C)   [C-1]

22. (C)   [D-1]

23. (D)   [D-2-a]

24. (A)   [E]

25. (C)   [E-4]

Chapter 4

Verbal Communication: Fundamentals

OVERVIEW

As the lifeblood of any organization, communication represents the uniting force that directs many activities and efforts toward reaching both organizational and personal goals. The importance of effective oral (verbal) communication cannot be overstated. The key to effective communication is understanding the message being conveyed and its intended meaning. However, so many factors and elements are associated with the communication process that one can easily appreciate how and why misunderstandings arise.

The telephone requires that administrative professionals use appropriate techniques for receiving calls, placing calls, and using appropriate reference materials. Taking and delivering complete messages takes little time but is extremely important to the smooth operation of an office. Domestic and international telephone calls are a daily occurrence, as are specialized calls like conference calls.

Nonverbal communication must not be neglected. The workplace will continue to take on both a cross-cultural flavor with the diverse domestic population and an international emphasis with global trade. Therefore, learning the effective use of nonverbal communication with an awareness of diversity is very important. Those in business need to realize that their messages are being received and responded to by people from different backgrounds.

KEY TERMS

Body language, 112
Calling card call, 99
Channel, 93
Collect call, 99
Conference call, 103
Content listening, 108

Credit card call, 99
Critical listening, 108
Criticism, 105
Decoding, 94
Direct-distance dialing, 99
Direct personal channels, 93
Empathic listening, 108

Encoding, 90
Environment, 95
Feedback, 90
Impersonal channels, 93
Intended meaning, 89
Interactive channels, 93

A. Oral Communication as a Process

Oral communication is a process of sharing information and intended meaning, both knowingly and unknowingly, that requires the verbal response of a receiver. As an ongoing process, **oral communication** involves an exchange of information between speakers (senders) and listeners (receivers) in which those roles are shared. Thus, speakers and listeners simultaneously send and receive messages. When you are not conversing with someone else, you are communicating internally, even talking to yourself. Sometimes you "speak" to yourself while you are listening to and even talking with another person.

EXAMPLE: *Hernandez is busy organizing the work on her desk when Struthers stops by to ask how her granddaughter is feeling. While Hernandez gives Struthers a report on her granddaughter's condition, she is thinking to herself that she needs to mail a birthday card to her aunt. During the conversation, Hernandez is attentive to Struthers and responds to her questions. When Struthers leaves, Hernandez immediately writes herself a note and puts it with her daily calendar so she does not forget to mail the card.*

1. ***The Importance of Verbal Communication:*** Communication is vital to any organization's successful existence. When communication within an organization becomes ineffective, the organization will encounter problems and will probably experience a decline in effectiveness. Communication is very important in all interpersonal relationships. The following highlights are important communication outcomes for the workplace:

    a. *Influencing task performance:* Leaders and managers use verbal communication to attempt to influence others to perform tasks required for achieving organizational goals.

    b. *Linking plans and actions:* Communication activates an organization by serving as a linking pin between plans and actions. Developing the plan is often called the "talking" step while performing the desired action is called the "doing" step. Some people in the organization are excellent at planning a task whereas others prove to be "doers"—people who actually carry out the task. An organization can have a clear and understandable mission, general objectives for implementation, and specific work plans explaining the role of each person in goal achievement. However, if the mission and plans are not shared and understood in basically the same way, chaos and inaction result. Managers cannot act effectively if they do not know what to do and what performance standards are expected.

    c. *Making effective decisions:* Communication ensures that relevant information necessary for effective decision making is shared. The decisions are then passed along verbally to the appropriate office professionals.

    d. *Enhancing effective working relationships:* Most jobs require work with others, often in a team environment. Without effective oral communication skills, a person cannot relate appropriately with other people. Effective communication enables people to resolve office conflicts in a more productive way. Positive communication skills can make the office a less stressful and more enjoyable place to work.

e. *Sharing emotions:* Through verbal communication, workers can share their feelings of excitement and frustration with their peers and with management.

f. *Fulfilling social need for belonging:* Communication permits people to share mutual experiences, preferences, likes and dislikes, and to become part of informal groups, thus satisfying the basic need for belonging.

g. *Providing training aids:* Teaching new office professionals or temporary office workers what they must do in their positions requires clear and complete communication.

h. *Assisting in problem solving:* Work groups are becoming more prevalent, especially in business today. Managers and subordinates are expected to engage in give-and-take discussion sessions to help solve problems. This task can be accomplished more efficiently through effective group communications.

2. ***Sharing and Transmitting Information:*** Communication requires you as the sender to share a message with a receiver. You purposely select words and symbols that you think have a shared meaning with the person with whom you are communicating. You would not choose to speak or write in a language unfamiliar to the receiver of the message; otherwise, you would be wasting your time and energy as well as that of the receiver. In addition, if an understanding is not reached, complete communication does not really occur. Transmission without reciprocal understanding is not communication.

a. *Intended meaning of message:* Communication requires some meaning to be attached to the message that has been sent or received. One of the biggest problems associated with verbal communication is that the sender's **intended meaning** may not be the receiver's **perceived meaning**. Cultural backgrounds and previous experiences help to shape the meaning people attach to words. In the communication process, a preconceived notion of what a person is going to say often exists. When this happens, you tend not to hear the words that are actually spoken. Instead, you fulfill your own expectations of the conversation. Participants in a conversation must always attempt to understand what others are saying and hearing. This active participation in verbal communication will improve the full understanding of the message.

b. *Transmission of information:* When you communicate, you transmit information both knowingly and unknowingly. Although the right words are usually carefully selected when speaking, people seldom think about the *way* they are speaking. People often fail to realize that *how* something is said is often more important than *what* is actually said. Therefore, not only should you concentrate on the words (the verbal aspect of communication), but you must also think about that part of the communication consisting of nonverbal cues or actions that is beyond words (e.g., tone of voice, posture, and facial expressions). Because intentional as well as unintentional messages may be sent, the receiver can easily get confused as to the "real" meaning that is being conveyed. When this happens, the listener often makes assumptions or jumps to conclusions that might be far from the truth.

EXAMPLE: *Running a little late for work this morning, Wilson was not as careful in selecting her attire. In her rush, she selects a suit that is less flattering than others in her wardrobe. Consequently, she felt rather self-conscious the entire morning. After lunch, another administrative professional in the office asked Wilson whether she has lost some weight. Sure that Cooper is indicating that the suit makes Wilson look heavier, she gave him a nasty glance, commented that he looked like he was the one who has gained weight, and then turned back to her work. Cooper returned to his desk wondering why Wilson did not like the report submitted that morning. Pulling on his belt, he began to make plans to start a new diet and exercise program as soon as possible.*

    c. *Response of the receiver:* For effective communication to take place, the receiver needs to respond to the message that is sent. This response, referred to as **feedback**, helps the sender determine whether the message sent was truly received and understood. The listener's response can take any form, including words, action, thinking to oneself, and even silence. If you have ever contacted someone for information, you know the frustration of not receiving a response to your comments and questions. When communicating face to face, you can often tell whether someone is confused about what is being said. Sometimes, however, the receivers of messages pretend to understand, walk away, and then become confused. Although many reasons might exist for this, some people are too self-conscious to ask questions or make comments that would clarify a misunderstanding. Depending on cultural background, others believe that asking questions of a superior is a sign of disrespect or incompetence.

3. *The Communication Process:* Verbal communication is conducted through a complex process. This transactional process consists of distinct factors interacting together, often simultaneously. Problems can occur as a result of breakdowns during the interactions between any of the elements, although many communication misunderstandings are the result of failures occurring within the process at the same time. The worst assumption anyone can make about a message just sent or received is that the message was conveyed as intended. Since so many things can go wrong, you should always assume that something will! Recognizing the presence of communication obstacles is by far the biggest battle in achieving understanding. For you to be a successful speaker and listener, you must first recognize the barriers that create misunderstandings and that must be overcome within each element of the communication process. The major components of the communication process shown in Figure 4–1 are the speaker, the message, the channel, the listener(s), feedback, distractions, and the communication environment.

    a. *The speaker:* Oral communication begins with a **speaker** who is the source of a message. The speaker can be anyone. Administrative professionals may communicate with top-level managers, maintenance personnel, administrative assistants, clients, suppliers, public officials, and lay citizens. The speaker has an idea or information that needs to be shared with others.

        (1) *Encoding the message:* Before any communication occurs, the idea, feeling, information, or action the speaker is purposely trying to transmit needs to be formed into symbols that the other person understands. The process of assigning and organizing symbols (e.g., words or gestures) to formulate the message you want to send is called **encoding**.

        (2) *Encountering communication problems:* Numerous communication problems may be associated with the speaker. Here are some typical problems that speakers encounter and some recommended solutions.

           (a) *Planning the message:* The speaker needs to plan what message to convey. Without planning, messages can be vague and/or inconsistent, thus

FIGURE 4–1   The Communication Process

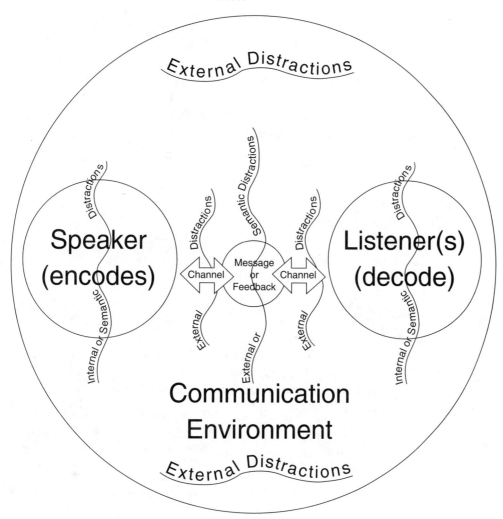

confusing the listener(s). Here are some helpful pointers to remember as you plan your message:

- Think about the intent of the message before speaking.
- Consider your audience (the listeners) and their point of view.
- Consider your own point of view as the presenter.
- Select words that are as specific and descriptive as possible.
- Ask the listeners to paraphrase what they heard or understood.
- Have the listeners repeat your directions.

In turn, when the speaker becomes the listener, verification of understanding is very important.

(b) *Speaking distinctly:* Speaking too quickly or too softly or not enunciating clearly affects the listener's ability to understand the message. Obviously, the key is to speak distinctly. Again, verify how well your listeners understood the message. Often, facial expressions and posture of the listener can help determine whether the message has been understood. The listener's understanding of the message does not mean that the listener is in agreement with the information presented.

(c) *Paying attention to nonverbal messages:* Concentrate on the nonverbal messages being sent. If speakers do not pay attention to nonverbal messages that they are sending when they speak, interference and conflict with verbal messages may occur that will confuse the listener. Nonverbal messages sent by the listener may indicate how attentive or interested the listener is. Nonverbal cues, an important part of all communication encounters, should enhance the communication process. Paying attention to all aspects of the message is vital for communication to take place.

b. *The message:* The result of the encoding process is the development of the message to be sent.

(1) *Selection of symbols:* The symbols you select to convey the message can be verbal (spoken or written words), nonverbal (facial expressions, gestures, and physical movements), or a verbal-nonverbal combination.

(2) *Source of misinterpretation:* The message can become the cause for the listener's misinterpretation of the intended meaning.

(a) *Multiple word meanings:* Many people believe words have an innate meaning that is understood and agreed upon by all who use them. Words may have different meanings for each person. This dilemma is especially true for people from diverse backgrounds. Can you think of a word that has different meanings depending on what region of the United States you grew up in or what country you are from?

EXAMPLES: *Harrington, a Minnesotan, is visiting friends in California. While shopping in a mall, he suddenly gets thirsty. Harrington asks a clerk where the nearest "bubbler" is. Where Harrington lives, a water fountain is a "bubbler."*

Soft drinks may be referred to as "soda" or "pop" in some parts of the country.

(b) *Semantics:* Sometimes the problem may simply be semantics. The word **semantics** refers to the meanings assigned to the words that we use when we communicate with others. When words are not chosen carefully or the listener does not have the vocabulary to understand them, a problem of semantics is encountered. The words you select may also be technical terms. People outside the discipline may not understand these words. Remember, the goal is communication; simple words that enhance understanding affect the listener more than a string of words that illustrate an extensive vocabulary in a certain profession.

(c) *Vague terms or phrases:* Difficulty in interpreting a message may stem from the use of vague terms or nonspecific phrases.

EXAMPLE: *Castle sends her administrative assistant to the office supply store to buy a large envelope to mail a report to a client. Assuming that Steinway will remember the report she showed him two days ago, Castle does not bother to give specific measurements. When Steinway returns, Castle is irritated because he bought an envelope that is too small. By not being more specific in describing the size of the material to be mailed, an extra trip to the supply store was necessary. These types of extra activities cost more time and money.*

c. *The channel:* The connecting device between the speaker and the listener(s) is the **channel** through which the message is sent.

   (1) *Types of communication channels:* Many different types of communication channels are available to the speaker (e.g., telephone, memorandum, bulletin board, face-to-face conversation, electronic mail, and fax messages). One of the major considerations during the communication process is to ensure that the proper channel has been selected.

   (a) *Impersonal channels:* Written memoranda, notices on bulletin boards, and electronic mail messages are best for clear, simple, and routine messages. These **impersonal channels** are considered to be useful when a small amount of information about a single topic needs to be communicated in a simple, straightforward manner. In these situations, personal contact is not deemed necessary.

   (b) *Direct personal channels:* Face-to-face conversations, telephone calls, meetings, and conferences are **direct personal channels**. Such channels are best used when personal contact is necessary for sharing lengthy, complex, ambiguous, and nonroutine messages.

   (2) *Number of channels used:* Another consideration is the number of channels a message may have to go through to reach all the people involved. The amount of time allocated to get the information out is also important.

   (a) *Retention of intended meaning:* You cannot expect to communicate information, especially through a multiplicity of channels or to a large number of people, and still retain the extended meaning. Every time you pass a message on to others, the message is filtered through the receivers' own perceptions; some pieces are added while others are left out. Eventually, the message can get so changed that the sender may not even recognize it. A message that must go through a number of people is best put in writing, video- or audiotaped, or electronic alternatives.

   (b) *Interactive channels:* The shorter the time allowed for communicating, the more important face-to-face conversations, telephone calls, and meetings become. These **interactive channels** allow for questions and concerns to be immediately addressed.

d. *The listener:* The person to whom the message is directed is the listener. The speaker must take the listener into account when encoding the message and selecting the channel for transmission.

   (1) *Receiving the message:* Often, the listener may not receive the message, persons other than the intended receiver may receive it, or the receiver and unintended people accept the message simultaneously. The speaker must be cautious to ensure that proprietary (confidential) messages designed for and addressed to specific people are received only by the intended parties. The medium and symbols used can play important roles in this respect.

   EXAMPLES:

   During the recent war in Iraq, the coalition troops led by American military forces used sophisticated systems for sending messages so that the Iraqis would not be able to determine what invasions were being planned. At the same time, the communication systems of the Iraqis were destroyed so that their efforts would be hindered.

Recent events in the United States concerning insider trading focused especially on oral communication between stockbrokers and clients prior to stock trading.

(2) *Decoding the message:* The process by which the listener interprets the meaning(s) of the message is known as **decoding**. If the speaker (or source) has used symbols, words, or gestures unfamiliar to the receiver, errors in interpretation can easily occur.

Effective listening is a skill that can be practiced and enhanced. As people learn how to increase their listening effectiveness, the interactive communication process improves.

e. *Feedback:* The listener's response to the message is valuable in letting the speaker know how the message was interpreted. This response is known as feedback.

(1) *Indication of feedback:* Feedback may be as simple as a nod, a return call, or an e-mail message or memorandum sent in response.

(2) *Sources of misunderstanding:* Since feedback is in essence a message, too, the same sources of misunderstanding previously attributed to messages apply equally when giving and receiving feedback. Feedback is greatly affected in these two ways:

(a) *Feedback delays:* Usually feedback does not follow the original message quickly enough. Thus, the feedback is not received in a timely or sufficient manner to aid the speaker. The speaker needs to ask the listener to respond promptly. The listener should make every effort to respond as soon as possible after the message is received. To reinforce understanding, asking questions or having the speaker repeat ideas and information will help to clarify the meaning of the message.

(b) *Need for specific feedback:* The feedback needs to be specific enough to help the speaker know how to adapt the message to increase understanding and its total impact. When providing feedback, respond in detail and give specific examples. The speaker should ask for precise comments.

EXAMPLE: *Fakoury has to give an important presentation to a prospective client. He asked the office staff to listen and critique his sales "pitch." After Fakoury finished, everyone complimented him on his presentation. Only after watching a videotape did he realize the little distractions he could have corrected if he had only been aware of them. When he asked staff members whether they had noticed any of these problem areas, they reluctantly said "yes." They explained their concern about affecting his enthusiasm if they pointed out these distractions that he should correct.*

f. *Distractions in communication:* Barriers, blocks, problems, and interferences are some of the names attributed to distractions that interfere with effective communication and affect understanding. Distractions, often referred to as **noise**, can occur at virtually any time or point in the communication process. These distractions may be categorized as external, internal, or semantic distractions.

(1) *Time as a distraction:* Time is a common problem, especially when the time allotted to decode a message might not be comparable to the proper amount of time required. Also, the time of day or the timeliness of the transactions might interfere with understanding.

(2) *External distractions:* Within the communication channel or environment, external distractions can occur while communication is taking place.

EXAMPLES:

Radio static, television "ghosts," and blurred fax messages are common examples of channel noise.

Some people are better able to concentrate in the morning, whereas others don't even begin to function effectively until the afternoon.

After a disaster, listeners who have been directly affected are not able to focus their attention on other matters.

Disturbances (people moving around, background noise, extraneous sounds, bright lights or colors, obnoxious smells) can impair the speaker's and the listener's abilities to concentrate on the communication exchange that is taking place.

(3) *Internal distractions:* Internal distractions are often difficult to identify because they take place within the minds of the speaker and/or the listener. Even when you have a close relationship with the person, you cannot always tell whether he or she may be suffering from depression or low self-esteem. In addition, people do not always tell others when they are experiencing physical discomfort or illness. Prejudices, biases, and preoccupation with other issues are often hidden. Occasionally, a person's attitude reflects the true inner feelings of the communicator. It is important to work at understanding and addressing internal distractions that may adversely affect verbal communication.

(4) *Semantic distractions:* Words and gestures have different meanings around the world as well as within subcultures of a society. Many books have been written to help travelers learn the perspectives of the languages of other cultures. A person only needs to travel across the United States to see that people in different geographic regions within the same country may interpret the same words in different ways. Also, words can have unique meanings depending on the professional environment in which they are used. Since meanings differ among individuals, the words used can create misunderstandings.

EXAMPLES:

At some transportation companies, semi-tractor trailer trucks are called "feeders." Yet, in a manufacturing environment, a "feeder" could be a belt that feeds materials into a particular piece of machinery.

A study of a major dictionary showed that an average of 28 separate meanings were listed for each of the 500 most widely used words in the English language.

g. *The communication environment:* The **environment** is the context in which communication encounters take place. The place may be relaxing, as in an office with low background music, or the place may be stressful, as in a high-powered meeting.

(1) *Context of the situation:* Context refers to the rationale for the communication encounter in the first place. A friendly chat during a break occurs within a different communication climate than a disagreement between a manager and a subordinate in the manager's office.

(2) *Personal moods:* The environment encompasses the moods of the people involved in the conversation. Messages may be interpreted differently, depending on where and when the communication event is taking place and to whom and how a message is being communicated.

Check Point—Section A

Directions: For each question, circle the correct answer.

A–1. The key to effective communication is

    A) understanding a shared meaning

    B) creating a relaxed atmosphere

    C) solving conflicts

    D) watching for nonverbal cues

A–2. The human resources manager pauses during an office meeting because she notices several quizzical expressions on the faces of the staff. She is illustrating that communication

    A) is irreversible

    B) is a process

    C) is not always verbal

    D) requires the attention of the listeners

A–3. Feedback occurs when

    A) an outside noise interferes with communication

    B) the channel chosen is appropriate for the message

    C) the speaker selects the appropriate words to communicate a message

    D) the listener responds to the message sent

B. Telephone Communication Techniques

You become the voice of the organization when you use the telephone to communicate with others. Every time you speak over the telephone, you create an impression of the organization in the minds of the people with whom you are communicating. By applying some very specific techniques as you use the phone, you will be able to influence the impressions you and your organization make to others.

1. *Applying Effective Speaking Skills:* The caller begins to form an opinion about you and your organization the moment you begin speaking on the telephone. Your voice projects your attitude, which is hopefully pleasant, courteous, and businesslike. The tone of your voice and the words you use must be clear for you to be an effective communicator.

    a. *Projecting voice quality:* A number of factors, including speed, volume, and enunciation, affect the way you will be perceived as you speak. These techniques will help you keep your voice as conversational as possible.

        • Visualize the other person as you speak, and speak as though you were talking in person.

        • Speak at a rate that is moderate—not too fast nor too slow. If you speak too fast, the caller will not be able to keep up with you and will probably ask you to repeat information. If you speak too slowly, you may give the impression of being uncertain or hesitant.

        • Use the caller's name as you speak to personalize your response and get the caller involved in the conversation, thus leaving a positive impression.

- Vary the tone of your voice to emphasize the meaning you are trying to convey.
- Speak clearly and distinctly, enunciating words and pronouncing names correctly, so that your message will be more easily understood.

By paying attention to the way you speak and the quality of your voice, you will project your own confidence in handling a business matter or your enthusiasm for being helpful to the person with whom you are talking.

b. *Answering incoming calls:* When you answer an incoming telephone call, you represent your organization by the way in which you handle the call. Following basic techniques like these will help you respond in a businesslike and professional manner.

   (1) *Responding quickly:* When you receive a telephone call, respond by the second or third ring. Most voice-mail messaging takes over on the third or fourth ring.

   (2) *Attending to the caller:* The caller deserves your full, courteous attention. If you are speaking with someone in your office when the phone rings, say, "Excuse me, please" to the person and pick up the phone. When your phone call is over, you may then continue your conversation with the person in your office. If the call is confidential, politely ask the person who is in your office to return in a few minutes. If that is not possible, ask the caller if you can return the call in a short time.

   (3) *Identifying yourself on the phone:* When you receive a call, identify your department by saying, "Management Department, Shirley Atkins speaking," or identify yourself by saying, "Good morning, Shirley Atkins speaking." When answering someone else's telephone, say "Mrs. Keenan's office, Shirley Atkins speaking," so that the caller knows immediately what office or department has been reached. Include your name so that the caller knows who is answering the phone. You save an enormous amount of time by answering in this way. Never answer with only "Hello" or "Accounting Department."

c. *Taking telephone messages:* When you answer the telephone, you need to be ready to take a message in case the call is for someone else in your office. Your options include keeping a message pad or notebook handy for writing down messages, using your computer to key in the information directly onto an e-mail message form, or forwarding the call to the intended receiver's voice-mail box. Taking a message seems like a simple task; however, the biggest challenge is to write down accurate and complete information about the call.

   (1) *Message information:* The following list includes the types of key information that need to be included in a message:

   - Date and time of the call
   - Complete name of the caller, with title and business identified
   - Telephone number with area code
   - The message—generally, what the call is about—and any files or documents needed for reference
   - The best time to return the call
   - Your initials or signature if you are one of several people who take messages in the office

FIGURE 4–2 Examples of Telephone Messages

```
Message

Date        3-14-0x

Time        3:20 p.m.

To          Roberta Lindsey

M           Max Lindbergh

Of          Office Renovation Inc.

Phone       (414) 555-2010

☐ Telephoned          ☐ Please call
☐ Called to see you   ☒ Returned your call
☐ Will call again

Message     Mr. Lindbergh has info you requested on
modular desk units -- also has a computer desk for
you to look at. He will be in his office all day today.


Message Taker   B. Lawrence
```

```
        Appointment │ Task │ Note │ Phone │
To:
Roberta Lindsey                                         Send
CC:                              BC:                     Send Options
                                                         Address Book
Subject:                                                 Spell Check
PHONE MESSAGE —Max Lindbergh                            Attach
                                                         Cancel
Message:
Dear Roberta:

Max Lindbergh of Office Renovation, Inc., returned your call at 3:20 p.m. today. He has
information you requested on modular desk units - - also has a computer desk for you to look
at. He will be in his office all day today.

Beth Lawrence
```

(2) *Techniques for recording the message:* After the caller gives you the message, restate it so that the caller knows how you have received and recorded it. In addition, make sure that the name of the caller is spelled accurately and the area code is included with the callback number. Find out from the caller what time is best for the return call. Write the message clearly as you are talking to the caller. You do not want to have to rewrite it.

Figure 4–2 shows examples of a properly written telephone message and an e-mail message based on the same information.

d. *Delivering messages:* When you are taking another person's calls and recording messages, be sure to deliver them to that person promptly. If you write the messages on message forms, place them in a designated mailbox or location so that the person can access them easily. Telephone messages in the form of e-mail messages should be sent to the individual immediately so that they will be available the next time that person opens his or her e-mail.

e. *Placing telephone calls:* When you are placing domestic or international telephone calls, prepare yourself before you make the call. A little research ahead of time will help to optimize the time you spend on the telephone.

(1) *Techniques for placing calls:* Here are a few techniques that will help you organize your thoughts and materials before you call:

- Place your own telephone calls. Having someone else place them for you is too time-consuming.

- Look up telephone numbers in directories or in address files.

- Assemble and organize any files or documents that you will need to refer to as you speak.

- Write down any specific questions you want to be sure to ask during your conversation.

- When the call is answered, identify yourself immediately to the person who answers: "Good afternoon, this is Betty Reynolds at Apex Accounting Services."
- Then, ask for the person to whom you wish to speak: "May I please speak to Joseph Della Rosa?"
- Be prepared to leave a message if the called person is not in. This is especially important if the voice-mail system "kicks in" to receive the message.
- When you are not sure to whom you need to speak, give the reason for your call so that the call can be transferred more easily and quickly to the appropriate person.

(2) *Leaving voice-mail messages:* You may be able to leave a voice-mail message if the person you are calling is not in. A **voice-mail system** stores messages digitally. Using suitable etiquette is very important when leaving voice-mail messages. Instead of someone answering the telephone in person, you hear a recording with directions for leaving a message; or the recording puts you through several steps (using a touch-tone phone) until finally you are connected with an office, a person, or a voice-mail system.

(3) *Placing long-distance calls:* Long-distance telephone service assists many office professionals in handling business matters from the office.

   (a) *Direct-distance dialing (DDD):* **Direct-distance dialing** is used to place a long-distance call to another telephone number without the intervention of an operator. A long-distance access (1), plus an area code, plus the number of the party with whom you wish to speak needs to be dialed. (The United States and Canada are divided into approximately 275 calling areas, each one represented by a three-digit *area code*.) DDD results in a **station-to-station call**, which is one telephone number to another telephone number.

   EXAMPLE: *Dial 1 + area code + phone number to place a station-to-station call (a "number-to-number" call). You will speak to anyone who answers the phone. If the call is in the same area code from which the call is being placed, but is a long-distance call, the area code needs to be dialed.*

   (b) *Person-to-person call:* An operator-assisted call charged to the caller is a **person-to-person call**. The charge is made only if the person being called is able to come to the phone.

   (c) *Collect call:* An operator-assisted call that will be paid by the person or company receiving the call is known as a **collect call**.

   (d) *Card call:* A long-distance call that allows the caller to charge the service to a specific account number is called a **credit card call** or a **calling card call**. The card company assigns personal identification numbers (PINs) so the account number can be verified before the card call is completed and the account charged. Card calls from rotary-dialed phones require operator assistance and a service charge. Service charges are also accrued when using pay-telephones. Touch-tone systems are programmed to accept the card number to which the call should be charged, the PIN, and the number being called.

   EXAMPLE: *Dial 0 + area code + telephone number if the call is operator assisted (e.g., person-to-person or collect calls).*

For card calls from a touch-tone telephone, the card calling number (a toll-free telephone number) plus the PIN must be entered; follow the prompts before entering the telephone number being called.

(4) *Placing international calls:* International direct-distance dialing (IDDD) is available from North America to a number of foreign countries. When you are placing a call to an organization outside North America, dial 011 (the international access code), the code for the country you are calling, the city or area code, and the local telephone number. After dialing, you might have to wait 40 to 50 seconds for the call to be completed. If IDDD is not available to your organization, you may place a call through your international long-distance carrier.

   (a) *Assisted calls:* An international call with assistance would be placed in a similar fashion. The caller uses the international access number for the country where the call is placed followed by the code number for the country called (i.e., United States), the city or area code, and the local telephone number. Most local telephone directories have listings of country codes.

   (b) *Overseas calling cards:* Many individuals take advantage of overseas calling cards. Using an overseas calling card is the same as using a long-distance calling card.

   (c) *Computer calls:* Using the computer for calling requires specialized hardware and software; the Internet has made this service attractive to many individuals.

(5) *Telephoning to other time zones:* Placing long-distance telephone calls requires you to have basic information about time zones in different parts of the country and the world. Timing of calls is very important in attempting to reach business associates during working hours. Here is some basic information about time zones that may be helpful.

   (a) *Standard and local time:* The time at any particular place in the world is called *local time.* To avoid confusion in establishing local time, *standard time zones* were established so that there would be a difference of one hour between a place on the eastern edge of a time zone and a place on the western edge of the neighboring time zone. The local time at the meridian of longitude that runs through the center of the zone is used for all places within the time zone. Therefore, time throughout the time zone is the same.

   EXAMPLE: *A telephone call placed by Doyle at Hankscraft Co. in Reedsburg, Wisconsin, on Monday at 10:07 A.M. within the Central Time Zone would be received within a few minutes by Spiers at the Kelly-Springfield Company in Freeport, Illinois. Both cities are in the Central Time Zone.*

   (b) *Standard time zones:* The United States and Canada have six standard time zones. The time in each time zone is one hour different from the neighboring zone. The time is earlier to the west of each zone and later to the east. In the United States and Canada, the standard time zones are Eastern, Central, Mountain, and Pacific Time Zones. In addition, the Hawaii-Aleutian Time Zone includes Hawaii and the western Aleutian Islands, which are part of Alaska. The rest of Alaska is in the Alaska Time Zone. The Atlantic and Newfoundland Time Zones affect the easternmost Canadian provinces.

EXAMPLE: *Doyle places another call at 2 P.M. CST to McDonald in San Diego, California, which is in the Pacific Time Zone, hoping to catch McDonald before lunch. The time in San Diego is 12 noon, a difference of two hours. McDonald had already left for lunch and will not be able to return the call until after 1 P.M. PST, which would be 3 P.M. CST.*

(c) *World time zones:* When the world time zones were established in 1884, the meridian of longitude passing through the Greenwich Observatory in England was chosen as the starting point. The Greenwich meridian is also called the *prime meridian.* An international conference set up 12 time zones west of Greenwich and 12 to the east, which divided the world into 23 full zones and two half-zones. The two half-zones are on either side of the International Date Line, which is halfway around the world from Greenwich. A traveler crossing the International Date Line while headed west loses a day. A traveler who crosses the International Date Line traveling eastward gains a day.

EXAMPLE: *After talking with McDonald, Doyle needs to place a call to Schmidt, a distributor in Sydney, Australia. The time now is Monday at 3:30 P.M. CST in Reedsburg, Wisconsin. The time in Sydney is Tuesday at 7:30 A.M. If Schmidt does not report for work until 8 A.M., Doyle will have to wait a half hour before placing the call.*

Attention to time zones is very important for the administrative professional who needs to communicate with business associates in other states or countries. Using electronic mail and telephoning procedures effectively in making business contacts will help business ventures succeed across time zones.

f. *Listening to voice-mail messages:* To hear your message, dial your voice-mail number from any touch-tone phone anywhere. Prompt the system with your pass code, and then listen to each recorded message.

(1) *Advantages of voice-mail systems:* Voice mail makes it possible to send and receive messages, thus eliminating the telephone tag that many of us have experienced. **Telephone tag** occurs when two people keep trying to reach each other by telephone without success. Often, you can take care of a business matter if the message you receive is complete enough, without the need for actually speaking with the other person. Messages may be sent and received 24/7 anywhere in the world.

EXAMPLE: *Stevens, the human resources manager, can send a message to the entire staff (a predefined "group") at once regardless of the day or time.*

(2) *Disadvantages of voice-mail systems:* Users who do not access their voice mailboxes on a regular basis may miss receiving important information or announcements. Unless the telephone has a signaling device, as many telephones today have, the user may be unaware that a message is waiting. With most phone systems, you are told how many messages are waiting when you access your voice mailbox.

g. *Techniques for using voice mail:* Here are some techniques that will be useful to you in using your voice-mail system more effectively:

- Personalize your voice-mail message by updating your recorded message.

EXAMPLE: *Thank you for calling. I am out in the field today meeting with a client. Your call is very important. Please leave your name, telephone number, and a brief message so I can return your call as soon as possible. If you need to speak to someone immediately, please dial 0 and one of our office professionals will help you.*

- Check your voice mail regularly. Some people check their voice mail two or three times a day. Decide what will work for you, but be sure you can handle the calls on a per-day basis.

- Leave brief but detailed voice-mail messages. Indicate the phone number with area code and perhaps the time of day when you definitely will be in your office to respond. When giving the phone number, make sure to speak slowly and clearly.

  EXAMPLE: *This is Carmen Suarez from the A & M Company. I need to speak with you about one of the terms of our new contract with your company. My telephone number is 312–555–2010. The best time to return my call is between 2 and 4 P.M. this afternoon. I hope to hear from you then.*

- Record your telephone number clearly. Some people speed up when giving the number, making it difficult to understand the numbers. Repeating the telephone number a second time in the message is usually a good idea.

Good organizational skills will help you complete your outgoing calls and leave messages with a minimum of time and effort.

h. *Techniques for using Internet phones:* Internet phones are also used for placing long-distance calls. Computer equipment needed includes a microcomputer with microphone, speakers, and software for audio conversations over the Internet. This system can be used for audio conferences as well as long-distance domestic and international telephoning. The same techniques would be used for placing calls, receiving calls, and leaving messages as noted earlier in this chapter for telephone usage. Message service is also available with an Internet phone system. One specific caution when calling worldwide is to be aware that certain countries may restrict, regulate, block, or prohibit telephone calls that originate from a computer.

2. *Using Telephone Directories and the Internet:* Administrative professionals find various telephone directories and the Internet helpful in locating such information as telephone numbers, ZIP Codes, and area codes. Web sites on the Internet can be helpful, too, when information pertaining to a particular organization is needed.

   a. *White and Yellow Pages:* Alphabetic (White Pages) and classified (Yellow Pages) sections of public telephone directories provide information about listed telephone numbers.

      (1) *White Pages:* The alphabetic listing of all telephone numbers assigned within a given city or area is included in the **White Pages**. These numbers are only those that are available as listed numbers of businesses, individuals, and governmental agencies. Unlisted telephone numbers are private numbers not available to the general public in a telephone directory. Directories for a number of larger cities divide the White Pages into sections for business, government, and individual names.

      (2) *Yellow Pages:* The classified section of the telephone directory, better known as the **Yellow Pages**, uses a subject index of products and services as the ba-

sis for presenting information about provider organizations. Listed companies can furnish toll-free numbers for clients or customers to call. Toll-free calls to 800, 888, 877, 866, and 855 numbers are paid for by the company that is issued the number.

b. *Telephoning procedures:* The telephone company includes basic telephoning procedures in the front pages of the directory along with emergency numbers, community information, and other telephone services available.

c. *Government listings:* Telephone numbers for government offices are available under the label given to that level of government.

   (1) *Federal listings:* Federal offices are listed under the words *United States Government* first.

   (2) *State listings:* State government offices are listed under the name of the state first.

   (3) *County and local listings:* Other government offices are listed under the name of the county or municipality first.

   Sometimes government listings are in a special section of the directory highlighted in another color, such as blue.

d. *Locating information on the Internet:* The Internet provides access to a wealth of information about an organization, including telephone numbers and other contact data. Accessing organization Web sites and online directories for Yellow Pages or searching the Web by using key words will assist in finding calling information. The Web addresses *www.planetpages.com* and *www.yellowbook.com* lead to specific listings for individual and business telephone numbers.

3. ***Other Telephoning Techniques:*** Telephone communications technologies permit users to track telephone usage and arrange special kinds of telephone calls.

a. *Computer long-distance log:* Specialized computer software analyzes computer reports for long-distance telephone calls for accuracy to be sure that all costs are accountable to a specific department or division.

b. *Conference calls:* When three or more people in different locations need to discuss a business transaction or project, they can arrange for a **conference call** through a firm providing conference call services. The operator then places the call to the appropriate telephone numbers at the appointed time, or each participant is asked to call a specific telephone number at the appointed time to connect with the conference call. A conference call is sometimes called an audio conference.

c. *Transferred calls:* The office professional must learn the procedures for transferring calls to other people within the organization. Too often a call is not transferred because the person answering the call does not know the procedure. Before a call is transferred, give the caller the name of the person to whom you are transferring the call and the extension. This ensures that if the call is prematurely terminated for any reason, the caller can call back the person he or she intended to call.

d. *Use of cellular phones:* Perhaps the greatest change in recent years is the use of cellular phones to conduct day-to-day business. The cell phone that the busy executive carries is a helpful communication tool in keeping communication lines open—with the office, with clients or customers, or even with family members. Many of the same techniques highlighted in the previous sections apply to the use of cell phones as well. However, privacy issues may arise if the cell phone communication is overheard by a secondary audience or is interrupted by noise in the channel. With increased cell phone use, cellular telephone etiquette, such as the following simple guidelines, has become extremely important:

- Switch off the cell phone when attending public events or use the silent mode to be notified of calls. The cell phone displays a light or produces a sensation; some cell phones are capable of displaying a short message (SMS service).

- Activate the silent mode or switch off the cell phone when its use can cause an annoyance in public places.

- When in an enclosed space, such as buses or elevators, be discreet with your conversation and speak in low tones.

- When the cell phone ring is active, set the ring on a low setting and answer promptly to avoid disturbing others.

- For safety protection when driving, use a hands-free telephone kit in your vehicle.

- When necessary, forward calls to office mail so the call can be handled in the privacy of your office.

Telephone communication is more important today than ever before. New technologies are enabling business professionals to conduct business anywhere at any time. The human element—the voice—is the real key to effective telephone communication. Techniques for personalized communication still need to be applied effectively.

Check Point—Section B

Directions: For each question, circle the correct answer.

B–1. When you answer a telephone call, the caller

A) forms an impression about you and your organization

B) knows instantly that you are ready and willing to be of assistance

C) senses from the speed of your voice that you are knowledgeable about the message topic

D) understands the intended meaning of the information you are conveying

B–2. Which one of the following is the *best* way to answer an incoming telephone call?

A) "Good morning . . . Peterson Systems. May I help you?"

B) "Good morning . . . Peterson Systems . . . Joanne Whitely speaking."

C) "Hello . . . Joanne speaking."

D) "Peterson Systems . . . good afternoon."

B–3. The classified section of a public telephone directory, which includes a subject index of products and services available in the area, is called the

A) White Pages

B) Internet section

C) community information

D) Yellow Pages

C. Giving and Receiving Praise or Criticism

Two diametrical opposites in interpersonal communication are praise and criticism. Studies have found that both areas have potential as positive motivators.

1. *Communicating Praise:* Acknowledging the effective work of others is **praise**. Most people like to work in an environment where their hard work is complimented. Studies on motivation have found that numerous people place more value on recognition than money. Yet for many people, the only thing that seems to be harder than giving praise is graciously accepting it.

   a. *Giving praise:* Although criticism should be a private matter, praise should be a public event. Many organizations have incorporated recognition as a reward for excellence. When you give compliments, be specific. Tell the person what she or he did to deserve your commendations. Also, you must be sincere. People quickly learn that praise is basically worthless if compliments are given to everyone for just about anything.

   b. *Receiving praise:* When someone gives you a compliment for a job well done or an extraordinary effort, say "thank you." People who are being complimented should not be embarrassed or make demeaning remarks about themselves or their efforts, such as "That was nothing" or "I was just lucky, I guess." The most gracious response is a simple appreciation for the recognition.

2. *Communicating Criticism:* Unfortunately, criticism conjures up a negative image in most people's minds. Yet, when done correctly, **criticism** helps to enhance a person's knowledge and skills. Constructive criticism is what we want to achieve. As people strive for excellence, they need to know what areas of their performance require improvement.

   a. *Giving constructive criticism:* Constructive criticism starts with respect. First, we need to recognize the positive contributions the person makes to the organization. Using the "sandwich" theory, constructive criticism is balanced between positive remarks about the person's overall efforts. The goal is to "sincerely" assist the office professional to improve in certain aspects of job performance. Maintaining self-esteem and motivation is important. Giving criticism should be a "learning" event allowing everyone to speak and listen. If the participants attempt to understand an agreed-upon outcome and discuss the circumstances with respect and sincerity, criticism can be a positive influence.

   b. *Receiving criticism:* For many people, the natural tendency when criticized is to become defensive. Their reaction is self-defense; people want to protect their self-esteem. To truly learn from a critique, the following guidelines need to be applied. By adhering to these suggestions, people will seek open and honest input from others.

      (1) *Responding to criticism:* Whenever someone criticizes you, first attempt to understand that person's perspective. If you have ever critiqued someone else's performance, you know how important it is to put the criticism into context. Let the person know that you appreciate his or her taking the time and caring enough to approach you with the issue. You need to appreciate honesty. Let your superior know how much you want to know where your problem areas are so that you can improve. Being open to accepting criticism and putting it into a positive context will help you become a better contributor to the organization.

(2) *Seeking other opinions:* Just because someone has given you advice, however, does not mean that he or she is correct. After thanking the person for the advice, you may want to go to other people whose confidence you trust and ask for their opinions on the matter. Remember, others like you will think like you and agree with you. Now is the time to obtain diverse opinions and to weigh and balance the input you receive. Through the process of verification by others, you can decide what is right for you.

(3) *Modifying personal behavior:* As you evaluate opinions and contributions from others, the changes you may or may not make are personal and collective. If you realize that you have been criticized fairly, you will decide what needs to be changed. Let the person who brought the criticism to your attention, as well as others who provided input, know how you addressed the issue. Make sure to offer thanks for their concerns.

Check Point—Section C

Directions: For each question, circle the correct answer.

C–1. Studies show that praise and criticism can be

A) a source of misunderstandings
B) easy-to-use techniques for encouraging work teams
C) effective when used often and equally with all employees
D) positive motivators in the workplace

C–2. Constructive criticism starts with

A) discussing the issues with colleagues who are most like you
B) realizing that the advice (critique) cannot be modified
C) respect between the parties involved
D) self-confidence in realizing you do not need to change

C–3. You prepared last week's sales report and distributed it Tuesday morning to all the sales representatives. Brown, the sales manager, criticized you for not having the report ready Monday morning as usual and indicated that next week you need to be on time. Which one of the following is your *best* response?

A) Become defensive and blame Cooper, another administrative professional, for not collecting the data on time
B) Indicate to Brown that you understand how important the report is, especially in Brown's work with the sales representatives
C) Listen to Brown's words, nod, and return to your work area
D) Tell Cooper, who collects the sales data, to get the data to you by Thursday of this week without fail

D. The Effective Listener

Research indicates that most office professionals spend approximately 40 percent of their workday listening. Yet, very few people have studied the listening process. Although many people judge themselves to be good listeners, studies have found that, without formal training in listening, the average person listens at a 25 percent efficiency level. Operating a business requires more than a 25 percent effort from employees.

1. ***The Listening Process:*** In addition to hearing what someone has said, **listening** is a mental process that involves sensing, seeing, and interpreting what is being communicated. The **listening process** involves a set of related physical and mental activities usually considered in sequence and involves different types of listening. Effective listening is an active, energetic process, not a passive one. To really listen requires concentration and hard work. This process demands that a high degree of energy be expended to maintain an appropriate attention level.

   a. *The listening sequence:* As in any other process, listening consists of phases that advance the listener from a mere awareness of the message (information presented) to a more complete understanding of the content and the presenter's point of view. As the listener becomes more involved in the process, she or he will be capable of determining the importance of the content to a particular task or job.

      (1) *Receiving the message:* The presentation has been prepared by the speaker, and the listener is seated in the audience and gets ready to listen and possibly take notes.

      (2) *Perceiving the message:* The listener gains an initial perception of the message or senses what the message is about. Sometimes a written program or handout material is distributed to members of the audience. Conference proceedings include a summary or copy of each presentation. Looking over these materials results in an initial reaction to the message.

      (3) *Interpreting the message:* The listener determines what the speaker means by assigning meaning to verbal and nonverbal symbols received. In other words, the listener begins to attach meaning to the speaker's words and behaviors.

      (4) *Remembering the message:* Retention of the content of the message enables the listener to recall and apply some or all of the information included in the message. The typical question is just how much of the message a listener will retain and be able to use. Most people retain only 50 percent of what was learned the day before. And two days after a presentation, most people remember only about 20 percent of the information presented.

      (5) *Evaluating the message:* In this stage of the process, the listener weighs the facts, opinions, and recommendations and attempts to formulate conclusions about the message. The application of critical thinking skills will enable the listener to evaluate the quality of the information presented.

      (6) *Reacting to the message:* Feedback is one way in which a listener responds to the message. As an active listener, you might ask questions of the speaker to see how best to apply what you have heard. Applause, a standing ovation, or silence might be other reactions to the message.

      Figure 4–3 illustrates these steps in the listening process, along with possible barriers that arise within this process.

   b. *Types of listening:* Applying the physical, mental, and emotional elements inherent in listening permits the listener to become totally involved in the process. Sometimes the listener will be more focused on the content; at other times, the speaker's emotional appeal may be in the forefront. Another reason we listen is to evaluate how this information will help in our work lives. The ultimate goal of effective listening is to apply all three types of listening when we are audience participants.

FIGURE 4–3   The Listening Process and Barriers

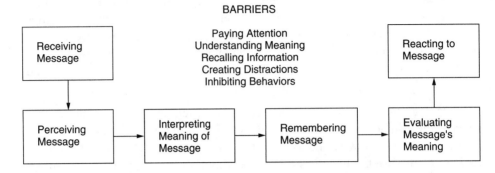

BARRIERS

Paying Attention
Understanding Meaning
Recalling Information
Creating Distractions
Inhibiting Behaviors

Receiving Message → Perceiving Message → Interpreting Meaning of Message → Remembering Message → Evaluating Message's Meaning → Reacting to Message

(1) *Content listening:* The listener is interested in the content of the presentation. The main purpose is to gain an understanding of the information, **content listening**, not to evaluate it or to agree with it.

(2) *Critical listening:* As you listen critically to a message, your task changes from gaining information to evaluating that information in terms of logic, validity, and implications for your own performance. **Critical listening** affects your ability to improve the way you communicate and perform particular duties.

(3) *Empathic listening:* With **empathic listening**, your primary task is to understand the speaker's emotions and feelings about the topic of the presentation. You do not have to share the speaker's point of view, but you are trying to "put yourself in that person's shoes" and understand his or her point of view without the need for giving advice or evaluating right and wrong.

2. ***Problems Inherent in the Listening Process:*** Poor listening habits result in communication problems that can be costly to the organization; missed meetings, errors in shipments, or inaccurate correspondence can occur as a result of poor listening. A good listener recognizes these problems and works at developing techniques to help improve personal listening effectiveness.

The first step in correcting any communication problem is to recognize the issues involved. In listening, the way that people's minds function creates a dilemma in and of itself. Three problems are inherent in the listening process: paying attention, understanding the meaning, and remembering information. The word *inherent* means that these obstacles are established as a part of the auditory system, "built in," so to speak.

a. *Paying attention:* The first problem inherent in the listening process involves paying attention. No matter how excited you are about the subject, by nature paying attention for an extended period of time is difficult.

(1) *Attention span:* Studies have determined the attention span for adults to be approximately 20 minutes. With the development of modern technology to test brain functions, scientists have found that the brain takes a "break" from whatever it is the person is concentrating on every two to three *seconds*!

(2) *Attention wandering:* When the brain is taking a respite from the duties at hand, attention automatically wanders to other tasks you need to complete that day, such as an upcoming meeting or a parent who is hospitalized.

(3) *Concentrating on the speaker's message:* Sometimes you become more interested in the "side trips" your mind is taking than concentrating on what the

speaker has to say, especially if the presenter has not taken the audience into consideration. At that point the internal message you are listening to becomes more appealing, which makes refocusing on the message being received much more difficult.

b.   *Understanding the meaning:* Understanding is the key to effective communication. Without understanding, effective communication cannot really take place.

   (1)   *Comprehending the message:* Obviously, if the participant's mind is not focused on what is being said, problems will arise in comprehending the entire message. The real dilemma comes when directions from a superior are misunderstood.

   EXAMPLE: *A divergent train of thought distracted Edwards when her manager said, "Do not order the extra part." Edwards heard only ". . . order the extra part." This lack of comprehension can become a costly and time-consuming problem.*

   (2)   *Speaking and listening:* Another issue related to both attention and understanding has to do with the rate of speech compared with the rate of listening. The average person speaks at a rate of 125 words per minute. Yet the average listener can follow and understand information up to a rate of 350 words per minute! The gap time between these two speeds is usually filled with "daydreaming" of some sort. Often, the listener's attention is not completely on what is being said. Part of the message is missed, thus affecting complete understanding.

c.   *Remembering information:* At the end of most conversations, only a portion of what was said is remembered. Even as participants leave staff meetings, they forget what was talked about the moment they walk out the door. This situation, as frustrating as it is, is not uncommon. As previously discussed, research shows that the average person remembers only 50 percent of what he or she heard in the listening process.

   (1)   *Attention:* Part of the difficulty is related to attention and understanding.

   (2)   *Short-term memory:* Another factor concerns the way short-term memory functions.

   •   When you hear information and then decode the meaning, you place the idea into your short-term memory. Short-term memory is limited in its storage capacity.

   •   If the listener or the speaker relates new information to knowledge previously acquired or uses some other memory aid, the information is transferred to long-term memory, where later recall is greater.

   (3)   *Information recall:* Visual aids that accompany presentations (electronic slides and handouts) or written reports (graphs and charts) can be extremely helpful in recalling specific information. Often a visual aid enables a person to remember and associate with a specific fact or bit of information.

3.   ***Behaviors That Inhibit Listening:*** In addition to the problems inherent in the listening process, people engage in poor listening behaviors that compound listening ineffectiveness. Because most people have not been trained to be better listeners, they are not even aware that their actions detract from the communication process.

Studies have concluded that the average person has several listening habits that may need to be changed.

a. *Calling the subject uninteresting:* When topics are not interesting to the listener, paying close attention is nearly impossible. Concentrating on a message is hard enough; therefore, when something is not interesting, the listener needs to make an extra effort to listen to the entire presentation. During time gaps, ask yourself questions such as "What is this person saying that I can use?" Identify information you already know that relates to what the speaker is presenting. This can make the topic more interesting. In this way, every listening encounter becomes a learning experience.

b. *Judging delivery instead of content:* Many people excuse themselves from listening to what is being said because of the way the presenter looks, sounds, or moves. The good listener looks beyond the "cover" and seeks to "read" the message.

c. *Jumping to conclusions:* Learn to withhold judgment until you hear the entire message. At times this suggestion may seem extremely difficult to follow. The natural tendency for most people is to start planning a rebuttal or response as soon as a speaker gives an opposing viewpoint. Key points can be missed when someone concentrates on the response instead of listening first to the opposing view. If you believe the presenter is mistaken, the best approach is to respond to the opponent's reasoning. If you are not listening, you will not know what points were brought up and discussed. Keep an open mind during the presentation. When appropriate, ask questions in an attempt to clarify the issue or better understand the points made during the presentation. Issues need to be discussed openly and with respect for diverse perspectives.

d. *Listening for details instead of the "big" picture:* Poor listeners try to commit too many facts to memory too rapidly. A good listener, however, works at understanding the central ideas. Once those principles are recognized, it is easier to remember the details that support them.

e. *Taking excessive notes:* Although you can listen at a much faster rate than anyone can talk, you cannot take notes at a quick enough pace to keep up with even a relatively slow speaker unless you have excellent note-taking skills. Jotting down the key points, interesting phrases, and memorable quotes helps you keep a focus on the presentation. In the process, you improve your opportunity to learn and to remember important points from the presentation.

f. *Attentive listening:* Listening needs to be active. In the work setting, we typically listen to gain information that will be useful in specific tasks. When we concentrate on the information being presented, we show speakers that we respect them, value their opinions, and really care about them.

    (1) *Physiological changes while listening:* When you are actively listening, your body goes through the same physiological changes as when you are engaged in physical activity. Your heart rate increases, your blood circulates faster, and your body temperature rises slightly.

    (2) *Listening and concentrating:* Various studies support the fact that when you *look* like you are listening, people believe you are paying attention. Demon-

strating your concentration helps to keep you focused, and this behavior is courteous and encouraging to the speaker. Here are some ways you can show that you are listening:

- Establish and maintain eye contact with the person who is speaking.
- Jot down a few notes during the presentation.
- Face the speaker, and lean forward slightly.
- Nod occasionally to demonstrate your understanding of the message.
- With your facial expressions, show your interest in gaining as much as you can from the presentation.
- When appropriate, ask relevant questions.
- Where appropriate, switch roles. While you speak, others should actively listen to you.

g. *Creating or tolerating distractions:* Not only are poor listeners easily distracted, but many times they are the cause of distractions. A good listener works at overcoming interference by closing a door; shutting off television, radio, or other equipment; and, if necessary, moving closer to the person who is talking or asking the speaker to talk louder. Sometimes, however, the disruption cannot be eliminated. In that case, concentration is the key.

h. *Failing to listen to difficult material:* A good listener gains invaluable experience by taking the time to listen to a variety of material no matter how difficult or unfamiliar. New material challenges mental capacities, thus strengthening the mind for other difficult listening endeavors.

4. ***Techniques for Improving Listening:*** Effective listening is a skill that, through practice, can be improved. Listening effectively can be increased by following these recommendations:

a. *Deciding to listen:* Before meeting with the person with whom you will be communicating, set listening as your goal. Decide ahead of time to focus your attention on the message. As best you can, clear your mind of extraneous thoughts (things to do, people to see, places to visit).

b. *Getting rest and food:* Concentrating is easier when you are well rested. Also, eating properly contributes to a healthy life both mentally and physically. Too much to eat can make you sleepy; however, not eating can affect you physically, and hunger pangs can become distracting.

c. *Finding comfortable seating close to the speaker:* When seated in the back of the room, the tendency is for the mind to wander. When you sit closer to the speaker, you will be able to focus more attention on the presentation. In addition, other people in the audience are less likely to disturb your concentration when you are seated closer to the front. A firm but comfortable chair allows you to sit for a longer period of time before becoming fatigued.

Look at every communication encounter as a learning experience. If you are having trouble concentrating, try and analyze why this is happening. Change anything you can that will help increase your attention. Look for the precious gems of knowledge hidden under all the rough spots. With learning, every listening activity will be a positive experience.

Check Point—Section D

Directions: For each question, circle the correct answer.

D–1. The listener's initial perception of the information presented is affected *most* by

A) meaning assigned to the verbal and nonverbal cues by the listener

B) the facts and opinions presented by the speaker

C) the listener's readiness to participate in the session

D) reviewing the summary of the session in the conference proceedings prior to the speaker's presentation

D–2. Evaluating information gained from listening to a presentation to improve performance on the job is termed

A) empathic listening

B) critical listening

C) content listening

D) interpretive listening

D–3. Which one of the following behaviors inhibits the capacity of the listener to pay attention?

A) Concentrating on a topic the listener is interested in

B) Memorizing details, facts, and data presented

C) Withholding judgment until the entire message has been heard

D) Jotting down the main points of the presentation

E. Nonverbal Communication—Listening Between the Words

Effective communication skills are important for success in business. One area that is often overlooked is the important role the various elements of nonverbal communication play in this success.

Many communicators believe that if they carefully choose the right *words*, their messages will be understood. Receivers often believe that if they carefully listen to the spoken words or read a document thoroughly, they do all that is necessary to effectively communicate with others. Nonverbal factors *do* affect the message and its reception.

1. ***Nonverbal Cues in Communication:*** According to research in nonverbal communication, as much as 90 percent of the impact of messages is based on nonverbal aspects. Thus, those who want success in business and in their personal lives should improve their awareness of nonverbal cues.

   That part of communication that is beyond words is referred to as **nonverbal communication**. The old axiom—*It's not what you say, but how you say it and what you are doing when you say it!*—is true. Although many different nonverbal cues are present in any encounter, you especially need to be aware of the major ones to increase your communication effectiveness and clarity of messages.

   a. *Body language:* The most prominent element in nonverbal communication, **body language**, refers to posture, facial expressions, eye contact, gestures, and physical movements. By watching another person, you can determine a great deal about his or her attitude toward you and the situation. The study of nonverbal body motions and communication is known as *kinesics*.

EXAMPLE: *Before movies had sound, body language was how actors and actresses "talked."*

b. *Paralanguage:* Vocal attributes add a new dimension to words. The sound of a speaker's voice adds variety and excitement. **Paralanguage** is the communication effect of speed, intensity, volume, accent, and even silence on spoken words in the message. Even the nonverbal utterances like "oh," "ah," and "um" send a message.

c. *Space and distance:* The distance you stand away from someone communicates your degree of comfort. Even the way you arrange your work space and living space demonstrates certain personality attributes. **Proxemics** is the term that indicates the way people structure their space or territory.

   (1) *Close proximity:* Usually, only those considered to be close friends are comfortable within the range of *intimate space* (physical contact to 18 inches) or *personal space* (18 inches to 4 feet). Sometimes circumstances require us to intrude or to enter others' personal space. In a small area with strangers, most people stiffen, stand up straight, and stare ahead or at the floor. Americans are especially uncomfortable standing close together but are tolerant of the situation for short periods of time. Many people feel much more comfortable with *social space* (from 4 to 12 feet) and *public space* (from 12 feet to hearing and seeing range).

   EXAMPLES: *An elevator, a crowded bus, a group of people waiting to enter an auditorium or theater*

   (2) *Effect of culture:* In some cultures, people expect to stand close to those with whom they are talking. Being unaware of such a background, you may think that someone standing so close is trying to be intimidating or too friendly. Being sensitive to the space of others is an important part of communicating effectively with people of other cultures.

   EXAMPLE: *Maxim was involved with a conversation with Azdiz who always stood very close to her. When Maxim stepped back to give herself some room to breathe, Azdiz took the movement as rudeness and became insulted.*

d. *Touch:* With the increased concern over sexual harassment in the workplace, touch has become taboo in most offices. Still, communication can occur through a pat on the back or a "high five." The most common form of touch in the business environment is the handshake. If you want to give a favorable impression, a firm but brief handshake is best regardless of whether the other person is a man or a woman.

e. *Clothing and accessories:* In today's business world, the emphasis is on "dressing for success." Appropriate business attire is affected by changes in styles, but conservative classic styles have remained constant over the years. The "latest rage," when extreme, should be reserved for personal life outside the office. Accessories also communicate certain messages.

   (1) *Making character judgments:* Studies show that many people make character judgments of others based on their clothes, shoes, or jewelry. The influence clothing and accessories have on others as they make these judgments is something over which you have control. Being aware of the impact that clothing and accessories make is important. In today's diverse environment, firms expect employees to work together collaboratively—with respect and overcoming

stereotyping. However, first impressions do have an impact on communication. Therefore, by being aware of the tendency for people to judge you based on appearance, assess your current style, and adapt it to communicate the message you want to send.

(2) *Social status:* In some cultures, clothing and accessories help to identify the social status of the wearer. Bright colors, expensive fabric, and an abundance of jewelry may look gaudy to some. Yet others might judge that these items represent a creative, happy nature. Traditional business attire may be seen as "stuffy" by some, and some viewers might even consider the person wearing an outfit like this as uncreative or boring.

Dressing for success in the global marketplace requires administrative professionals to be aware of acceptable business attire when dealing with business people from other countries and cultures. "Casual Friday" is an event many organizations have initiated so that business professionals can relax the strict dress standards for at least one day. However, caution should be exercised in selecting appropriate casual clothes to wear to the office.

EXAMPLES:

Sweatshirts and jeans are not considered "casual business" attire.

Some businesses that initiated "Casual Friday" reverted to traditional business attire for every day after employees began to dress too casually every day of the week.

f.   *Time:* The way you spend time and how you treat time communicates a message about responsibility.

(1) *Paying attention to time:* Time management is important to an efficient office operation. Having the office open during office hours tells co-workers and clients that you assume the responsibility of accessibility. Completing projects on time demonstrates your ability to assume responsibility, prioritize tasks, and meet deadlines.

EXAMPLE: *Are you always on time for an appointment? Do you maintain a strict time schedule during the day?*

(2) *Relating to time in other geographic regions:* Some countries have a more relaxed view of time and time limits than others. These cultural differences need to be respected, particularly if international communication commences with businesses in these countries. Some regions of the United States also have a more relaxed attitude about time. An agreed-upon working style is important when doing business with companies in diverse areas. For effective working relationships to develop, open and respectful communication must occur.

EXAMPLE: *People who get transferred from a slow-paced community may complain if their relocation work ethic is different. Similarly, those who have spent most of their lives in a fast-paced environment may become frustrated when they are transferred to a region where life is slower and they have to wait for their slower-moving co-workers. These new opportunities require people to be open, flexible, and adaptable for their own satisfaction as well as that of their co-workers.*

2. **Interpreting Nonverbal Cues:** Looking at one or two nonverbal cues does not necessarily give an accurate picture of what is happening. Imagine someone standing in the

corner of the office away from everyone else with arms crossed and head lowered. Is the person angry . . . or sad? Before interpreting what we see (the nonverbal cues), remember that a complete picture is necessary. To more accurately interpret nonverbal cues exhibited by others, both consciously and unconsciously, you need to consider the four Cs of nonverbal behavior (clusters, consistency, culture, and communication). Also, remember that nonverbal cues are clues, not facts.

a. *Clusters:* Nonverbal signs do not happen in isolation. You need to look at and receive as many cues as possible. When examined together as one big picture, the nonverbal message can be read more accurately.

b. *Consistency:* Another area of nonverbal behavior is consistency which assesses how consistent nonverbal signals are with other cues and how consistent these signals are with the person's personality.

(1) *Consistency of signals with other cues:* The first area has to do with how consistent the nonverbal cues are with other signals. To obtain a more accurate picture, determine whether the signals point to the same conclusion.

EXAMPLE: *If you see a person with arms crossed and an intense facial expression, you might infer that the person is angry. When you talk with the person, you discover a pleasant tone of voice. The two signals are not consistent. Understanding what the nonverbal message means will require more information about the person, situation, and setting.*

(2) *Consistency of signals with personality:* The second area has to do with how consistent the nonverbal cues are with the personality of the person. If you already know the person, you should have an idea as to what constitutes that person's normal behavior.

EXAMPLE: *When Jensen-Koch walks into a room and she is sad-faced, you might get concerned since she is normally smiling and happy. However, when Bertrand walks in with a sad face, you know Bertrand's facial expression looks sad, but she really is a pleasant, positive person.*

c. *Culture:* A person's cultural upbringing influences the way she or he communicates. Today's global workplace is diverse. Even people who are born in the same country can assign different meanings to nonverbal cues. Many books address various methods of communicating nonverbally with a diverse workforce.

EXAMPLE: *Kragan enjoys working with Ching-she; however, she notes that Ching-she never looks at her when they talk. Kragan has always believed that failure to establish eye contact means you are lying or trying to hide something. She cannot figure out what Ching-she could be hiding. One day Kragan asked Ching-she why she never looks at her when they talk. Ching-she said that in her culture the act of staring at someone or looking them directly in the eyes is a sign of disrespect. Now that Kragan understands Ching-she's motives, she is no longer uncomfortable carrying on a conversation with Ching-she. Kragan attempts to modify her eye contact while Ching-she knows she can look at Kragan when they are talking and Kragan will not be insulted. Both women learned something new through their friendship by being respectful and open with one another.*

d. *Communication:* The only way to find out what message someone is intending to send with nonverbal cues is to ask. Often, questioning is not necessary. Before judging someone's incomplete message or when conflicting messages are detected between and among nonverbal and verbal elements, you should obtain more information from the sender. When in doubt, the best thing to do is to be respectful and seek additional information.

Check Point—Section E

Directions: For each question, circle the correct answer.

E–1. Physical movements, gestures, and posture are called
   A) body language
   B) communication distractors
   C) the language of space and distance
   D) vocal enhancements

E–2. When you are in a face-to-face conversation, the distance you stand from someone communicates your
   A) ability to handle diverse groups
   B) body language
   C) degree of comfort with that person
   D) interest in the topic

E–3. The reason you should consider nonverbal messages as clues rather than facts is
   A) nonverbal clues are similar from one culture to another
   B) nonverbal signs do not happen in isolation
   C) the context of the communication encounter does not always have to be considered
   D) communication is a process

For Your Review

Directions: For each question, circle the correct answer.

1. The exchange of information between speakers and listeners requires that
   A) only the intended meaning is conveyed
   B) such communication is external in nature
   C) the roles of speakers and listeners are shared
   D) nonverbal communication becomes less important

2. Which one of the following is an important communication outcome for the workplace?
   A) Developing a plan for completing a particular task or project
   B) Influencing others to work toward achieving organizational goals
   C) Performing a given task or project
   D) Deciding on the performance standards once the task or project has been completed

3. Effective use of positive communication skills will most likely result in
   A) the productive resolution of office conflicts
   B) a more productive work environment but also a more stressful one
   C) less training needed for administrative professionals
   D) more individual problem solving expected of administrative professionals

4. As the sender of a message, you have control over
   A) the language of the receiver of the message
   B) selection of words that the person you are contacting will understand
   C) the receiver's perceived meaning
   D) the receiver's preconceived notion of what the message is about

5. The responsibility of the participants in a conversation, both speaker and listener, is to
   A) convey information that will clarify a point
   B) concentrate on the words being spoken at the time
   C) focus on the nonverbal cues or actions of the participants
   D) attempt to understand what others are saying and hearing

6. Feedback assists the sender in finding out if
   A) the intended meaning of the message that was sent was understood
   B) the message was encoded appropriately
   C) the receiver sends a response to someone else
   D) the receiver asks someone else to respond to the message

7. For communication to take place, an idea has to be formulated into a message during the part of the communication process called
   A) transmitting the message
   B) encoding
   C) interpreting
   D) decoding

8. The listener's ability to understand the message is affected most by
   A) the development of the message to be sent
   B) the attention being paid to the speaker
   C) the speaker's ability to enunciate words clearly
   D) nonverbal messages sent by the listener to the speaker

9. The words or symbols selected to convey the message can be
   A) spoken (verbal)
   B) gestures or facial expressions (nonverbal)
   C) a combination of verbal and nonverbal communication
   D) encoded in more than one way

10. The meanings assigned to the words we use when communicating with others are referred to as
    A) nonverbal cues
    B) semantics
    C) decoding
    D) communication channels

11. Which one of the following is an example of an impersonal communication channel?
    A) A telephone call
    B) A face-to-face conversation
    C) An e-mail message
    D) An office meeting

12. As you answer the telephone, your voice projects
    A) an image of the organization as well as your attitude toward the caller
    B) your skill in being able to handle telephone communication effectively
    C) the topic of the conversation
    D) the technique you apply to telephone communication

13. When you receive a telephone call, respond by
    A) returning the call after you listen to the voice-mail message
    B) the time that voice mail takes over

C) the second ring if possible
D) the fourth ring

14. You receive a confidential telephone call while you are talking to a co-worker in your office. Which one of the following is the most appropriate response to your co-worker?
    A) "Excuse me, Clarice, while I take care of this call."
    B) "Clarice, would you be kind enough to return in a few minutes so we can continue our conversation?"
    C) "Clarice, please get us some coffee while I finish this call."
    D) "Excuse me for a moment. I'll be back with you as soon as I can."

15. When you place a call and you are not sure to whom you need to speak,
    A) ask whoever answers to take a message
    B) ask to leave a voice-mail message
    C) ask that the call be transferred
    D) give the reason for your call

16. If the person you are calling is not in, you may be able to leave a message by
    A) giving your name and telephone number
    B) the voice-mail system
    C) calling back later with more information
    D) placing a station-to-station call

17. When you are placing a call to an organization outside North America, the first number dialed is the
    A) local telephone number you are calling
    B) city or area code
    C) international access code
    D) code of the country being called

18. The time in one of the standard time zones around the world is
    A) the same time as the time zone to the east
    B) one hour later to the west of that time zone

C) one hour earlier to the east of that time zone

D) one hour earlier to the west of that time zone

19. Studies on motivation have found that people often place more value on receiving

A) public recognition than monetary rewards

B) criticism than praise

C) monetary rewards than praise

D) monetary rewards than public recognition

20. After reviewing the report you finished yesterday, Evans compliments you on the quality of your writing. Which one of the following is your best response?

A) "That was nothing. Let me know if you have any questions."

B) "Thank you, Evans. I really enjoyed doing the research."

C) "Now I'm ready to start on the Jones file."

D) "I did just what you told me to do."

21. The listening process advances the listener from awareness of the information presented to the highest level in the process, which is

A) responding to the information presented

B) recalling some or all of the information in the message

C) perceiving what the message or information is about

D) determining the speaker's intended meaning

22. "Putting yourself in another person's shoes" allows you the opportunity to

A) improve your ability to perform a given task

B) gain an understanding of a basic area of knowledge

C) understand another person's point of view

D) evaluate the accuracy of the information presented

23. Which one of the following behaviors tends to compound listening ineffectiveness?

A) Understanding the central ideas first, then concentrating on details

B) Asking questions to clarify or better understand a specific issue

C) Identifying information already known that relates to the content of the speaker's presentation

D) Planning a rebuttal when the speaker presents an opposing view

24. The communication effect of vocal attributes such as volume, silence, or speed is known as

A) kinesics

B) proxemics

C) paralanguage

D) body language

25. To interpret nonverbal cues of others more accurately, you need to consider

A) making a final decision on the information you have

B) how inconsistent the nonverbal cues are with other signals

C) isolated nonverbal signs as primary indicators

D) obtaining more information from the sender

Solutions

Solutions to Check Point—Section A

Answer	Refer to:
A–1. (A)	[A and A-2]
A–2. (C)	[A-3-a (2) (c)]
A–3. (D)	[A-2-c and A-3-e]

Solutions to Check Point—Section B

Answer	Refer to:
B–1. (A)	[B and B-1]
B–2. (B)	[B-1-b (3)]
B–3. (D)	[B-2-a (2)]

Solutions to Check Point—Section C

Answer	Refer to:
C–1. (D)	[C]
C–2. (C)	[C-2-a]
C–3. (B)	[C-2-b (1)]

Solutions to Check Point—Section D

Answer	Refer to:
D–1. (D)	[D-1-a (2)]
D–2. (B)	[D-1-b (2)]
D–3. (B)	[D-3-d]

Solutions to Check Point—Section E

Answer	Refer to:
E–1. (A)	[E-1-a]
E–2. (C)	[E-1-c]
E–3. (B)	[E-2-a]

Solutions to For Your Review

Answer	Refer to:
1. (C)	[A]
2. (B)	[A-1-a]
3. (A)	[A-1-d]
4. (B)	[A-2]
5. (D)	[A-2-a]
6. (A)	[A-2-c]
7. (B)	[A-3-a (1)]
8. (C)	[A-3-a (2) (b)]
9. (C)	[A-3-b (1)]
10. (B)	[A-3-b (2) (b)]
11. (C)	[A-3-c (1) (a)]

12.	(A)	[B-1]
13.	(C)	[B-1-b (1)]
14.	(B)	[B-1-b (2)]
15.	(D)	[B-1-e (1)]
16.	(B)	[B-1-e (2)]
17.	(C)	[B-1-e (4)]
18.	(D)	[B-1-e (5) (b)]
19.	(A)	[C-1]
20.	(B)	[C-1-b]
21.	(A)	[D-1-a (6)]
22.	(C)	[D-1-b (3)]
23.	(D)	[D-3-c]
24.	(C)	[E-1-b]
25.	(D)	[E-2-d]

Chapter 5

Verbal Communication: Professional Communication Applications

OVERVIEW

Many executives are involved in planning, organizing, and/or attending company-sponsored conferences or association-sponsored conventions. Often, executives agree to serve as members of planning committees or as speakers for sessions at such conferences. Administrative professionals become involved in ensuring that appropriate procedures are followed to prepare for the executive's leadership and participation at such conferences or conventions.

Managers tend to spend more than one third of their time in meetings each week, according to some estimates, and in many organizations as much as 15 percent of human resource budgets is spent directly on meetings. Face-to-face meetings are still seen as the primary form of communication within the office. Meetings are needed to act on business activities that affect the entire organization.

The work of administrative professionals in preparing for business meetings is crucial. Knowing appropriate procedures for setting up meetings is especially important. For the meeting to be a success, arrangements must be made for meeting rooms, reference and handout materials must be prepared, and participants must be taken care of efficiently. This chapter includes a brief discussion of parliamentary procedure and the importance of conducting effective meetings.

Executives need assistance in preparing professional presentations to complement the work of the organization. Knowing how to research for such presentations and prepare needed materials is extremely helpful.

Professional communication is also affected by the diversity of today's workforce. The need to understand cultural differences within our society and to prepare administrative professionals to handle bilingual or multilingual situations within business today is vital. The international nature of business affects the language and cultural needs of organizations.

KEY TERMS

A. Conferences and Conventions

A **conference** is defined as a formal meeting of a group of people with a common purpose. Types of conferences include company-sponsored conferences and association-sponsored conventions. In this context, the two terms conference and **convention** are treated as synonymous terms.

1. *Types of Conferences:* Conferences or conventions are sponsored by individual companies or by community, business, or professional associations.

   a. *Company-sponsored conferences:* Companies sometimes sponsor conferences for the purpose of discussing timely topics or training participants in business strategies and innovations. Such a conference might be sponsored only for company personnel for the purpose of bringing them up to date on new products, services, or research developments within the industry. Companies may also sponsor conferences for customers, stockholders, suppliers, or the community for similar purposes.

   (1) *Location:* The conference may be held on company premises or at a nearby hotel or convention center. Usually, the company prefers to have the conference at or near the corporate headquarters to facilitate the display of new products, the participation of company personnel, and training sessions that might be included.

   (2) *Leadership of the conference:* Depending upon the basic purpose of the conference, an executive within the company with responsibilities related to the conference may be appointed as the leader (conference chairperson). A committee consisting of representatives of the various divisions or departments of the company may be appointed to assist in planning and coordinating the event. Administrative support is extremely important to assist with the many arrangements that must be handled before, during, and after the conference.

   (3) *Travel to and from conferences:* Since some of the participants may be coming from other parts of the country or world, travel arrangements need to be carefully coordinated. If the conference is only for company personnel, the plan may be to obtain all travel reservations through the corporate travel department or through a local travel agency. Travel arrangements for others who have been invited to participate may also be coordinated so that appropriate lo-

cal reservations can be made to facilitate their participation. If travel expenses are to be paid, procedures and forms for reimbursement should be included.

(4) *Supportive services:* Consultation is necessary with the in-house printing or reproduction department to be sure that program booklets, handout materials, and other printed materials can be produced in house. In addition, an inquiry service might be established so that callers requesting information about the conference can receive all pertinent information from an administrative professional who is assigned this responsibility.

b. *Association-sponsored conventions:* Professional business associations sponsor numerous annual conventions primarily for the benefit of members of the association.

EXAMPLES:

Hixson, an administrative professional for AJAX Company, is a member of the International Association for Administrative Professionals (IAAP). As the president of the local chapter, Hixson will be a delegate to the IAAP International Convention in July.

McMurray, an administrative manager, is an active member of the local chapter of the professional group, Women in Management. As the secretary of the local chapter, her responsibilities include attending all chapter and board meetings as well as preparing minutes of board and chapter meetings.

(1) *Location:* Conventions are usually held in hotels and civic convention centers where adequate meeting room space, hotel rooms, and public transportation are available. Trade shows and exhibits are another feature of conventions that help participants become more up to date in their field.

(2) *Leadership of the convention:* A committee from the professional association sponsoring such a convention plans the convention. Normally, a vice president in charge of programs serves as the chair of the program planning committee. Many times a local committee composed of association members from the geographic area where the convention will be held assists with local arrangements.

- The administrative professional for an executive who is in charge of a professional convention will likely be involved in assisting with the arrangements for the convention.

- Correspondence about the convention and arrangements for attending will also be handled by the administrative professional if the executive plans to attend the convention.

(3) *Travel to and from conventions:* Executive travel to and from the convention is usually handled through the travel department or the travel agency handling company or organization business. The office professional who coordinates the travel arrangements with an agency or over the Internet must be sure that dates, times, flights, or other travel information are verified with business travelers before final reservations and arrangements are completed.

(4) *Supportive services:* A file folder should be established for any materials relating to the convention. For a large convention, a series of folders must be prepared for filing all correspondence and related materials by topic as they accumulate in the planning stages.

2. ***Planning a Convention:*** Attending a convention as a participant is relatively easy, but planning a convention for others to attend requires long hours of detailed preparation. The success of the convention depends greatly on the way procedures are handled before, during, and after the convention.

   a. *Before the convention:* Typical activities that need to be accomplished in the time period prior to the convention include the following:

      (1) *Coordinating plans with hotel or convention center:* Preliminary activities such as the following require close coordination with the hotel or convention center staff.

      - Meeting with the convention services manager of the hotel or convention center to review arrangements for the convention.
      - Reserving an adequate number of meeting rooms and exhibit space in the hotel or convention center. Most convention locations include adequate meeting space. Sometimes there are additional room and exhibit space charges.
      - Ensuring that appropriate audiovisual, projection, and computer equipment will be available for the meeting rooms. Many times there is a charge for using convention center equipment.
      - Arranging for audiovisual or video equipment and technicians to be available for recording or taping convention sessions. Make sure to inquire about service charges.
      - Arranging for computer equipment and technicians to assist with the installation and monitoring of the equipment.
      - Making preliminary arrangements for food service during the convention.
      - Reserving a block of hotel rooms for convention participants at an agreed-upon rate.

      (2) *Reviewing and coordinating plans of the convention sponsor:* The convention sponsor may have already made some preliminary decisions. These decisions need to be reviewed by the convention chairperson and program committee as program planning begins.

      - Selecting the site for the convention, unless the association has already approved the site.
      - Establishing and/or reviewing the convention budget.
      - Contacting exhibitors for the trade show if one is scheduled.
      - Arranging for hospitality rooms and other courtesies for the participants.
      - Arranging ground transportation (buses, limousines, vans) to transport participants from airport to hotel or convention site.
      - Obtaining conference favors, door prizes, and souvenirs from local merchants.

      (3) *Planning the convention program:* The program committee should meet on a regular basis to plan the program and prepare necessary convention materials.

      - Preparing preregistration materials to mail to participants, including preliminary program, registration information, and fee schedule.
      - Developing a preliminary program plan that includes sessions, timeframe, meal functions, and social activities.

- Contacting convention speakers by telephone, e-mail, fax, and/or letter confirming speaking arrangements.
- Preparing publicity for local newspapers, radio, and television coverage as well as information for online registration.
- Arranging special tours for convention participants, families, and guests.
- Contacting agents for any special entertainment that will be scheduled during the convention; arranging for performances.

(4) *Preparing convention publications and information packets:* Of particular importance is the preparation of informational materials to include in the convention packet to be distributed to each participant at the start of the convention. Here are some of the tasks the program committee must perform to get ready for the convention:

- Designing a printed convention program and handbook.
- Monitoring the publication of the proceedings of the convention if the proceedings are distributed as part of the registration packet at the convention.
- Assembling convention registration packets that include publications, nametags, information about the city and/or tours available, and tickets for meal and social functions.

b. *During the convention:* Other activities such as the following need to be accomplished during the convention.

(1) *Receiving participant registration:* The hotel or convention center designates a specific area available as a registration area. The following tasks are usually handled by members of a registration committee:

- Setting up and staffing the convention registration area.
- Handing out special packets of convention materials to guest speakers as they arrive.
- Setting up and staffing an information desk for distributing information about the community, available tours, restaurants, theatre performances, and other local sights and activities.
- Finalizing the number of people attending each meal function.

(2) *Checking in speakers and exhibitors:* The program planning committee provides special assistance to guest speakers and exhibitors with tasks like these:

- Making arrangements for speakers to be met at the airport and transported to the convention site.
- Checking in all exhibitors and issuing exhibit spaces assigned.
- Checking to see that presentation equipment (projection, audiovisual, and computer) is in place prior to each convention session.
- Presenting special folders to hosts, hostesses, chairs, and recorders for the various convention sessions.

c. *After the convention:* Once the convention is over, follow-up activities may require the assistance of one or more administrative professionals.

(1) *Completing the financial reporting for the convention:* All income derived from registration fees, exhibitors' fees, and sponsors needs to be deposited and

a final accounting of all income and expenses prepared. Some of the accounting tasks that need to be taken care of immediately include the following:

- Completing the bank deposits for the convention.
- Preparing checks for honorariums and expenses for guest speakers.
- Preparing checks for payment of all convention expenses (e.g., hotel or convention center costs, expenses incurred by committee members).
- Preparing a financial statement for the entire convention.

(2) *Preparing follow-up correspondence:* Administrative professionals are particularly skilled in helping with the preparation of follow-up correspondence through:

- Sending thank-you letters to all speakers, exhibitors, and hotel and/or convention center personnel who were involved with the convention.
- Sending thank-you letters or memorandums to all who assisted with the convention: registration workers, hosts, hostesses, chairs for sessions, recorders, members of the planning committee, and so on.
- Tabulating responses to the convention session evaluations. Utilizing optical mark sense forms improves the accuracy and timeliness of recording and disseminating this information.

(3) *Designing and preparing follow-up publications:* Many professional associations follow-up conventions with special publications and updating of convention files. The following follow-up tasks need to be completed:

- Monitoring the publication of the convention proceedings.
- Distributing copies of the proceedings to speakers and participants if the proceedings were prepared after the convention.
- Creating a reference file of all procedures used and suggestions for the next convention.

The items listed in this section are not listed in any particular order of priority. Within each category, priorities should be established and deadlines set for required activities when actually planning and carrying through a convention program.

Check Point—Section A

Directions: For each question, circle the correct answer.

A–1. Smythe, the administrative manager, tells you that she will be planning next year's convention of the International Technology Association to be held in Albuquerque. Which one of the following should you do first to help with preliminary planning?

A) Make arrangements for speakers to be met at the airport

B) Make arrangements for Smythe's lodging and air reservations

C) Reserve a block of rooms at the hotel for attendees

D) Develop a checklist of activities that will need to be accomplished before the program is finalized

A–2. One of the planning activities that needs to be accomplished before a convention is

A) placing audiovisual equipment in meeting rooms where needed for program sessions
B) finalizing the number of people who will be attending each meal function
C) monitoring publication of the convention program and proceedings
D) creating a reference file for the next convention

A–3. You are the administrative assistant for Lopez, who is the program chair for this year's American Management Association seminar for administrative professionals. During the conference, you are likely to be responsible for

A) setting up and supervising the conference registration desk
B) preparing checks for honorariums and expenses for guest speakers
C) reserving adequate meeting-room space with projection and audiovisual equipment needed
D) creating a reference file with suggestions for next year's seminar

B. Meetings

Managers spend more than one third of their time in meetings each week, and many organizations spend up to 15 percent of their human resource budgets directly on meetings. Technological and administrative changes that have been enveloping business in recent years have necessitated people's efforts to communicate in small and large groups to meet the objectives of the organization. The typical business cannot survive without meetings.

1. *Planning and Organizing Meetings:* Meetings tend to be organized either as **informal** or **formal meetings.**

   a. *Informal meetings:* Usually, an informal meeting involves an informal discussion by a small number of people (two to five) to discuss a particular business matter. Normally, a specific business issue or concern brings these people together for the meeting. The meeting can be scheduled in one person's office or in a nearby conference room.

   (1) *Committee meeting:* The people who are meeting may be members of a **committee** and must meet to further the work of the committee.

   EXAMPLE: *The Computer Advisory Committee will meet on Thursday from 9 to 10:30 A.M. to discuss the utilization of computers for administrative support.*

   (a) *Standing committee:* Members of a **standing committee** are appointed for a definite term (e.g., one or two years). The standing committee has definite objectives assigned for which it is responsible during the term.

   EXAMPLE: *Bryson serves on the Program Committee for the Maywood Business Women's Association. As a member of this committee, she is working with three other members to establish a schedule of programs for this year's monthly meetings.*

   (b) *Ad hoc committee:* An **ad hoc committee** is formed to investigate a particular event or problem that has occurred within the organization. The committee has a temporary appointment and will serve until a report is prepared and presented to the standing committee or management.

EXAMPLE: *The ABC Company has a standing committee, the Computer Selection Committee, whose primary goal is to select a new computer network for the company. An ad hoc committee has been formed that will investigate how the major departments in the company plan to use computers and various software programs in their operations. The ad hoc committee will report back to the Computer Selection Committee.*

(2) *Office meeting:* Sometimes problems arise in the day-to-day operation of an office that require two or three people to meet to discuss the problems. A department manager may find it necessary or helpful to ask two or three employees to come into his or her office to discuss a business matter.

b. *Formal meetings:* A more formal meeting would definitely have to be planned in advance so that participants in the meeting would be aware of the meeting and know the agenda items that would be presented and discussed at the meeting. Formal meetings are usually held in conference rooms or special meeting rooms. All types of conferencing (teleconference, videoconference, computer conference, or data conference) can be arranged through a national or an international communications network, depending on the needs of the organization. People who are separated by great distances still can participate in business discussions and decision making.

(1) *In-house meeting:* A formal meeting might be held in-house on company premises. A meeting or conference room would be reserved, and all people who need to attend would be notified in advance. The purpose of the meeting is typically of a more formal nature.

EXAMPLES:

The Board of Directors is planning to hold its next meeting on Wednesday, May 15, from 3 to 5 P.M. in the Sullivan Room.

The XYZ Corporation is inviting all of the regional marketing representatives to attend a one-day sales meeting at the corporate headquarters on April 4.

The in-house meeting may be for company personnel only, or it may be for outside professionals, depending on the purpose of the meeting.

EXAMPLE: *The XYZ Corporation is sponsoring a one-day office systems seminar for administrative professionals from the northern Ohio region. The purpose is to demonstrate the latest office systems that XYZ Corporation is ready to begin marketing.*

(2) *Out-of-town meetings:* Business travel to out-of-town meetings is very common for business executives. If the corporation has numerous branch offices, this is one way for the executive to monitor business operations at different sites. If the scheduling for the meeting has to come from the executive's office, the administrative professional must be sure that all reservations for travel and meetings have been arranged.

EXAMPLE: *White-Bourke, vice president for operations, just told Brennan, her administrative assistant, that she will be traveling to Montreal on June 3 and 4 to meet with the operations people in the North American-Canadian region. Brennan will need to make whatever travel, lodging, and meeting room reservations are necessary.*

(3) *Conferencing:* A relatively new way of communicating with other professionals is **conferencing.** The use of telephone and computer systems creates the networks necessary in order to conference with others without having to leave the office.

    (a) *Teleconference:* A formal **teleconference** might be set up so that several business executives from different geographic locations can "meet" through telephone communications. Instead of having to travel to a particular site for the meeting, the conferees can "meet" by speaking with others directly from their own offices. Teleconferences can be enhanced with group communication software (e.g., e-mail, e-calendar, groupware, or electronic blackboard). **Audio conference** is another term for teleconference.

        EXAMPLE: *Stevens made an appointment with Richards (New York office), Pourmand and Garcia (Atlanta office), and Clifton (San Francisco office) for a teleconference on Monday morning from 10 to 11 A.M. She wants to share some marketing strategies that the company is trying to promote. Stevens will be able to communicate through the telephone network and an electronic blackboard so that the statistics and graphs she presents from her location will be transmitted to each of the other three locations. A monitor for viewing is required at receiving sites. In this way, other participants will receive all pertinent information and find it easier to view the presentation and to participate in the ensuing discussion. Stevens, Richards, Pourmand, Garcia, and Clifton can participate by viewing the presentation on the monitor and using the telephone handset or speakerphone for discussion. Pourmand and Garcia could meet at one location in Atlanta and participate through the telephone speakerphone and visual input on a monitor. All participants entering data to be viewed on monitors by others must have electronic blackboards available at their sites.*

    (b) *Videoconference:* Another type of formal conference is the **videoconference,** which is really an extension of teleconferencing. Again, an appointment must be set up for the scheduled date and time. Participants are able to view one another on closed-circuit television. Slow scan (freeze frames) as well as full-motion video is possible. The videoconference closely approximates a face-to-face conference. Hard copies of visuals and data are transmitted through intelligent copiers or fax (facsimile) equipment.

    (c) *Computer conference:* Participants in a **computer conference** use computer terminals to transmit information to other members of the group. The response may be simultaneous or on a delayed basis, so participants do not have to participate with one another at the same time. Information or messages may be stored for later responses. All records produced, documents transmitted, and written comments are stored in the computer. This type of conference, as a form of electronic mail, may be accomplished on a national or an international network.

    (d) *Data conference:* The objective of a **data conference** is for two or more participants to have access to a document simultaneously for review and editing.

        EXAMPLE: *Kelfe (Chicago headquarters) along with Donaldson and Smyth (Wisconsin branch) use conferencing software to view a proposed budget spreadsheet. The purpose of the meeting is to modify the proposed budget according to anticipated projections and finalize these changes during the meeting. All three participants can view the results of the modifications so that discussion and final consensus can be achieved during the meeting.*

2. ***Arranging Meetings:*** Informal and formal meetings will run smoothly only if all necessary arrangements for the meetings are completed ahead of time. The busy executive has no time to worry at the last moment about what room is reserved, where the handouts are, or whether people were notified.

   a. *Selecting date and time:* The first thing to do is to select a date and time that are convenient for those people who must attend the meeting. This may mean checking each person's schedule to find alternative times so that, when each person has responded, the best possible time can be chosen. It is more efficient to access the electronic calendar for each person, determine the best possible time for the meeting, and immediately schedule the meeting. Electronic calendars can be set up so that others can view the calendar (read only).

   b. *Notifying participants of meeting:* Of course, no meeting can take place without participants being present; therefore, each person needs to be notified of the meeting date, time, and location.

      (1) *Telephone call:* The administrative assistant should telephone each participant to let him or her know as soon as possible the meeting date, time, and place and to ask participants to record this information on their calendars immediately. Voice mail enables the administrative assistant to leave a complete message for each participant.

      (2) *Electronic mail:* If a computer network is available, a memorandum can be transmitted to the participants by e-mail with information about the meeting date, time, and place and to ask them to put this meeting on their calendars immediately. In addition, the message can alert the participants of specific agenda items or information to bring with them.

      (3) *Follow-up letter or memorandum:* Depending on the availability of electronic mail within the organization, a written notice of the meeting and a confirmation of the date, and location should be sent to each participant. Knowing the agenda ahead of time is extremely helpful to those attending the meeting.

      (4) *Telephone follow-up:* If a response is required from a participant and none is received, the administrative assistant should follow-up by telephone to see whether the person will be able to attend the meeting.

   c. *Notifying the executive of those attending:* Once responses are received from all who should attend the meeting, let the person presiding over the meeting know exactly who will be present. This is a double check to ensure that everyone who needs to be present has been invited.

   d. *Preparing materials for a meeting:* Copies of materials to be distributed during the meeting should be prepared ahead of time. When participants are notified of the meeting, they should also be asked for any materials that need to be prepared or copied for the meeting.

   e. *Preparing an agenda:* An **agenda** is a list of items of business to be presented and/or discussed during the meeting. Copies of the agenda and accompanying discussion materials should be prepared and disseminated to each participant prior to the meeting. Also, extra copies of the agenda should be available at the beginning of the meeting for anyone who did not receive a copy ahead of time. A typical order of business is as follows:

- Call to order by presiding officer
- Attendance
- Announcement of quorum
- Reading of minutes of previous meeting
- Approval of minutes
- Reports of officers
- Reports of standing committees
- Reports of special committees
- Old (or unfinished) business
- New business
- Appointment of committees
- Nominations and elections (when required)
- Date of next meeting
- Adjournment

See Figure 5–1 for sample agenda.

f. *Taking notes at the meeting:* The committee secretary takes notes during the meeting so that a complete set of minutes may be prepared. If an executive is the secretary for the meeting, the executive's administrative assistant may be called on to take complete notes during the meeting.

g. *Noting meeting dates on the executive's calendar:* After the meeting is over, the administrative assistant needs to be informed of important dates for future meetings. These dates should be recorded immediately on appropriate office calendars.

h. *Preparing the room for the next meeting:* After the meeting has been adjourned, the meeting room should be left in proper order for any other meetings that follow. This includes arrangement of tables and chairs, collection of extra handout materials, and disposal of waste paper.

i. *Transcribing notes:* The meeting notes should be transcribed as soon as possible so that no important details resulting from the meeting are forgotten or ignored.

j. *Sending minutes or meeting report:* After the minutes or meeting report has been prepared, the administrative assistant should send one copy to each of the participants for review. A participant may respond within a given time with any corrections or revisions in the minutes. The administrative assistant can then prepare a final draft to be submitted for approval at the next meeting.

3. **Conducting Meetings:** Executives participate or preside over many meetings as a part of their work routine. In addition to planning and organizing meetings, conducting meetings in an expeditious manner is vital. The meeting time should be used effectively so that each participant perceives that the order of business is handled efficiently. The use of parliamentary procedures establishes a definite routine for conducting a meeting in an efficient, orderly manner.

FIGURE 5–1   Sample Agenda

INFORMATION SYSTEMS PROFESSIONALS
Board of Directors Meeting

Parker-Hyatt Hotel
Denver, Colorado

Boulder Room
Wednesday, November 19, 200X
11:30 A.M.

AGENDA

1. Call to Order: Rosella Dietz, President

2. Secretary's Report: Minutes of October Meeting

3. Treasurer's Report

4. Standing Committee Reports

   • Program Committee: Eleanor Wentkowski

   • Scholarship Committee: Maurice Thomas

   • Bylaws Committee: Theresa Gutierrez

5. President's Report

6. Old Business

7. New Business

   • Theme for 200X Professional Development Seminar

   • Representation at ISP International Convention

8. Adjournment (1:30 P.M.)

Note: A salad luncheon will be served during the meeting.

a. *Effective use of meeting time:* A number of techniques can be applied to permit meeting time to be used as effectively as possible. Here are only a few of the more important ones:

(1) *Time frame for the meeting:* A definite time frame should be established for the meeting at the time that it is scheduled so that participants know the amount of time to plan for. This time frame should be announced to the participants ahead of time so that they know how much time must be set aside for the meeting.

EXAMPLE: *The monthly staff meeting is always scheduled for Wednesday afternoon from 1 to 2:30 P.M. Having this time already scheduled on calendars means that those who attend will not allow any other conflicts during this time frame.*

(2) *Distribution of an agenda and handout materials:* If possible, the agenda and supportive handout materials should be distributed at least one or two days prior to the meeting to give people sufficient time to review these materials and prepare for the meeting. Too often people arrive at a meeting and are

given insufficient time to look through the "stack" of supportive materials needed to make effective decisions for voting on items of business.

(3) *Promptness in starting meetings:* People appreciate the courtesy of starting meetings on time. A meeting scheduled for 9 A.M. should start at that time. As a general rule, people do not expect a meeting to start on time; but if starting on time becomes the general rule, people will be prompt in getting to meetings.

(4) *Agenda items:* A meeting agenda helps to organize the order of business and keep the participants on target. An item that is not on the agenda should not be discussed at this meeting. If a new item needs to be added to the agenda, the group must decide whether to accept it for this meeting or leave it for the next meeting.

- Routine items on the agenda (e.g., reading of secretary's minutes and treasurer's report) should be handled quickly since there usually will be minor revisions in wording and few questions asked.

- Taking care of routine items quickly will leave more time to present and discuss other agenda items, which are the primary reasons for the meeting.

(5) *Summary of important points:* During a meeting the chairperson should act as a facilitator, taking time to summarize key points that are made so that everyone understands the importance or meaning of a particular action taken.

(6) *Closing the meeting:* When the business itemized on the agenda has been acted upon, the meeting should be adjourned promptly. A meeting might be scheduled for two hours. If the business can be taken care of in less time, people will appreciate having those extra minutes to return to their offices to handle tasks that need attention.

b. *Application of proper parliamentary procedures:* Conducting formal meetings requires the direct application of **parliamentary procedures** so that meetings are conducted efficiently and orderly. Some have defined parliamentary law as "common sense used in a gracious manner." *Robert's Rules of Order* (first published in 1876) has been revised numerous times over the past 128 years and still serves as the basis for acceptable parliamentary procedures followed in formal meetings. The parliamentarian (someone appointed who is familiar with parliamentary procedures) is responsible for ensuring that the meeting is conducted according to these rules. A copy of *Robert's Rules of Order* should be on hand for reference.

(1) *Basic principles of parliamentary procedures:* For a group of people to arrive at group decisions in an efficient and orderly manner, these basic principles of parliamentary procedures must be followed:

- Courtesy and justice must be accorded to all who are participating in the meeting.

- Only one topic is considered at one time. (This is the reason that the meeting agenda is so important.)

- The minority opinion must be heard; every person has an equal opportunity to be heard.

- The majority will prevail; a majority vote will result in the passing of a motion.

(2) *Conducting the meeting using parliamentary procedures:* Each item of business to be presented during the meeting for action by the group must be introduced to the group in the form of a *motion*. A motion must be made by a voting member who has secured the floor by being recognized by the presiding officer for the meeting. The motion must receive a second by another voting member. Ex officio members have the right to participate in discussions of agenda items, but they have no vote when a motion is being considered.

(a) *Types of motions:* Items of business are presented, one by one, to the group in the form of motions. Once a motion has been made and seconded, the item can be discussed thoroughly. There are five different types of motions: main motions, subsidiary motions, incidental motions, privileged motions, and unclassified motions.

- *Main motions:* A **main motion** is a motion that states an item of business. The main motion has the lowest precedence in rank among all types of motions. In other words, other motions that impact the main motion must be acted on before the main motion is finalized. The main motion must be seconded and is subject to discussion, debate, and amendment. The motion may be reconsidered or have a subsidiary motion attached to it. A majority vote is necessary to pass the motion.

  EXAMPLE:

  Watson: "I move that we accept the report of the Special Committee on Human Resource Development."

  Roth: "I second the motion."

- *Subsidiary motions:* A **subsidiary motion** may assist, modify, or dispose of the main motion. A subsidiary motion supersedes the main motion and must be acted on before the group returns to the main motion. The following subsidiary motions may be applied:
  - To table a motion (to lay the item and motion aside until later)
  - To call for the vote
  - To refer the motion to a specific committee for further consideration
  - To amend a main motion
  - To postpone action on a motion indefinitely

- *Incidental motions:* Motions that arise from pending questions are called **incidental motions.** They may be introduced at any time and must be decided before the question to which the incidental motion pertains is decided. Here are the incidental motions that may be used:
  - To suspend a rule temporarily
  - To close nominations
  - To reopen nominations
  - To withdraw or modify a motion
  - To rise to a point of order
  - To appeal to a decision of the chair

- *Privileged motions:* These motions are called **convenience motions** since they affect the comfort of the members of the group that is meeting. **Privileged motions** have precedence over all other motions. Typical privileged motions include the following:

- To call for orders of the day
- To bring up a question of privilege or an urgent matter, such as noise or discomfort
- To take a recess
- To adjourn
- To set the next meeting time

- *Unclassified motions:* Other motions that are appropriate but cannot be classified in the other four categories include the following:

  - To take a motion from the table
  - To reconsider a motion
  - To rescind decision on a motion

(b) *Quorum:* The bylaws of the organization usually specify the number of voting members who must be present in order for business to be transacted at a meeting of the organization. The required number of voting members who must be present to transact business is called a **quorum.** Members who are designated ex officio may participate in the discussion of motions, but they cannot vote on motions.

4. *Preparing Minutes of Meetings:* The minutes of a meeting are the official report of the meeting. The purpose of **minutes** is to summarize the business that has been transacted, reports that have been presented and discussed, and any other significant events occurring at the meeting.

   a. *Preliminary writing:* The notes from the meeting need to be transcribed in the format desired by the organization. Using the agenda as a guide serves as an outline of the items discussed at the meeting. Complete information—including motions, committee reports, and announcements—must be included in the minutes. See Figure 5–2 for an example of minutes.

   b. *Approval by presiding officer:* The presiding officer should approve the preliminary draft of the minutes before they are finalized, copied, and distributed.

   c. *Distribution of minutes:* The minutes need to be distributed before the next meeting so that group members can review them for accuracy and comment or make note of any minor changes or revisions. One of the first agenda items for the next meeting will be the approval of the minutes from the previous meeting.

Minutes are the official record of the meeting. Therefore, the secretary must provide accurate minutes so that the official proceedings are correctly filed.

5. *Preparing Resolutions and Petitions:* A formal expression of an entire group's appreciation, congratulations, or sympathy may be communicated as a **resolution.** A formal statement of reasons for introducing and asking for a specific action to be taken is called a **petition.** The petition is a formal expression from the people who sign the petition.

   a. *Resolution:* A resolution is a formal statement from an entire group or organization. Preparation of a resolution will require the following steps:

      (1) *Advance preparation:* The resolution must be prepared in advance by a resolutions committee appointed for that purpose. The presiding officer of the group (chairperson or president), the executive board, or the committee then must review the resolution.

FIGURE 5–2   Minutes of Meeting

VALLEYVIEW, INC.
Property Owners' Association
Board of Directors Meeting ⇓2

ValleyView Conference Room
March 10, 200X ⇓2

PRESENT: (10) C. Albergetti, T. Brock, J. Carpenter, M. Dollman, F. Hardanger, L. James, A. Longsman, M. Planters, M. Rintamaki, S. Tillman ⇓2

ABSENT: (2) ⇓2

The ValleyView Property Owners' Association monthly meeting of the Board of Directors was held on Wednesday, March 10, 200X in the ValleyView Conference Room. President Brock called the meeting to order at 7:30 P.M. ⇓2

The secretary circulated minutes from the February 8 meeting. A. Longsman moved and J. Carpenter seconded the motion that the February minutes be approved. Motion carried. ⇓2

Grounds Committee ⇓2

The planting and maintenance contract was granted to B&W Lawn-Garden Care. The contract is for April 1, 200X, through October 31, 200X. The schedule for this year is as follows: ⇓2

April 1	Plant spring flower beds
	Begin lawn grooming and mowing
April 30	Plant pine and maple trees ⇓2

Recreation Committee ⇓2

Thus far, the spring schedule of events is as follows: ⇓2

April 4	Spring Showers Picnic	Community Hall
May 10	Eagle River Cruise	Pier 3–Marina
May 30	Memorial Weekend Picnic	Hopkins Park ⇓2

F. Hardanger moved and M. Planters seconded the motion that "Detailed information regarding the social events be included in the ValleyView Bulletin." The motion carried unanimously. ⇓2

The President announced that the next meeting of the Board of Directors is scheduled for Wednesday, April 11, at 7:30 P.M. in the ValleyView Conference Room. ⇓2

No additional business was brought before the Board of Directors. It was moved and seconded that the meeting be adjourned. ⇓2

Respectfully submitted, ⇓4

Lois R. James, Secretary

Note: No reference initials are shown here because these minutes were prepared by the secretary of the organization. Notations for desired spacing are inserted: ⇓2 = 2 Enters; ⇓4 Enters.

(2) *Presentation of resolution:* The resolution may be presented orally or in writing at the meeting. However, the most effective way of presenting such an expression is in writing.

(3) *Final form:* After the meeting, the resolution must be prepared in final form, signed, and included as a part of the official proceedings of the meeting. Since the language used in the resolution is formal, the rationale for the resolution is introduced with the word *WHEREAS* preceding each reason given. The final paragraphs that state the official action to be taken are introduced by the word *RESOLVED*. If more than one action is to be taken, *RESOLVED FURTHER* is keyed in all capitals and followed by a comma and a capital letter. See Figure 5–3 for an example of a resolution.

b. *Petition:* A petition (a formal statement signed by those who are eligible to sign such a petition) asks that some specific action be taken. The petition is a formal expression only from those who sign the petition.

(1) *Advance preparation:* The petition must be prepared in advance with an adequate number of signature lines.

(2) *Circulation of petition:* The petition needs to be circulated so that the required number of signatures may be obtained. Typically, petitions are hand carried by individuals who are in support and who ask others to sign the petition.

(3) *Presentation:* Once the required number of signatures has been obtained, the petition may be presented orally and in writing at the meeting. The written

FIGURE 5–3 Sample Resolution

RESOLUTION
Adopted November 28, 200X

WHEREAS, Patricia A. MacDonald CPS has been a member of Kishwaukee Chapter, International Association of Administrative Professionals, for twenty-five years, and

WHEREAS, Ms. MacDonald has contributed significantly to the professional activities of the Chapter, having served as Secretary, First Vice President, and President, and encouraged members to become certified as Certified Professional Secretaries and Certified Administrative Professionals, and

WHEREAS, Ms. MacDonald is retiring from her position as Executive Assistant for Dr. S. R. Kuhlson, Vice President for Field Operations, Rockville Industries, Inc., where she has been employed for thirty-three years, therefore be it

RESOLVED, That the members of Kishwaukee Chapter, International Association of Administrative Professionals, go on record as expressing their sincere appreciation of Patricia A. MacDonald's many contributions to the Chapter; and be it

RESOLVED FURTHER, That the members of Kishwaukee Chapter sincerely congratulate Patricia A. MacDonald CPS on her retirement as an administrative professional and wish her happiness in her retirement years.

_____   _____
Secretary   President

FIGURE 5–4   Sample of Petition

PETITION FOR REZONING TOWNSHIP AREA

The undersigned, who are registered voters of Lexington Township, request that the Township Board of Commissioners present the following petition at the Annual Township Meeting to be held on March 18, 200X:

To see if the Township will vote to amend the Zoning Bylaws of Lexington Township by changing the zoning designation of the land described on the attachment, commonly known as the Roosevelt property, from Residential (Single-Family Dwellings) to Residential (Multiple-Family Dwellings) to allow construction of townhomes (four buildings with five townhomes each) by Erickson & Palmetto Construction.

The land proposed to be rezoned consists of an approximately five-acre site bounded northwesterly by Brigham Drive, easterly by land now or formerly owned by Westerman & Sons, Inc., southeasterly by land now or formerly owned by R. J. Platt, and westerly by land now or formerly owned by Gonzalez & Mason.

The plan for the development of the townhomes dated January 15, 200X, is submitted herewith.

No.	PRINT NAME	SIGNATURE	ADDRESS	TELEPHONE
1				
2				
3				
4				
5				

---

petition with signatures affixed is the official document. Further action by the group is discussed once the petition has been presented at a formal meeting.

A petition is often used to change or alter a previous action taken by the group. For example, perhaps a change in a zoning law needs to be considered or a previous decision made by the group needs to be changed. See Figure 5–4 for an example of a petition.

Check Point—Section B

Directions: For each question, circle the correct answer.

B–1. With technology affecting organizational change within business today, there will be

    A) more emphasis on individual participation in meeting organizational objectives

    B) more emphasis on small- or large-group participation and communication within the firm

    C) more formal meetings rather than informal meetings within the organization

    D) less opportunity for small- and large-group communication

B–2. Your executive has just told you that a special meeting of the executive committee needs to be scheduled for next Monday afternoon at 2

P.M. Which one of the following should be the *first* thing you do?

A) Send a memorandum to each member of the committee notifying each one of the meeting

B) e-Mail each member of the committee telling each one of the meeting and the location

C) Review materials needed for the meeting with your executive

D) Prepare the handout materials for the meeting

B–3. One of the basic principles of parliamentary procedure is that

A) more than one topic can be considered at one time

B) the majority must be heard

C) the minority will prevail

D) all participants must be treated courteously

C. Professional Presentations

Administrative professionals often become involved with assisting executives and managers who are guest speakers at seminars, conferences, in-service meetings, and other types of events. Because of expertise gained in a professional field, top-level managers may be invited to share their experiences or their research in a formal presentation to peers, colleagues, or other professionals. When a presentation is prepared, techniques similar to those used to prepare a written report are followed, especially in the planning stage. In fact, many presentations are developed from projects, reports, or articles previously developed or written by the presenter.

1. *Preliminary Planning for the Presentation:* First of all, answers to a number of questions will help the speaker analyze the situation and decide how to proceed with the task of preparing the presentation. Here are some of the questions to ask the sponsor or planner of the event:

   - Who is the primary audience—the people who will be listening to the presentation?
   - What is the proposed topic—if the sponsoring organization has already selected the topic?
   - What topic would be appropriate for this group—if the speaker has the option of selecting the topic?
   - How long should the presentation be?
   - Will there be time for a short question-and-answer session at the end?
   - What multimedia technology will be available for the presentation as well as for preparing ancillary materials?

   Once these questions have been answered, researching the topic can begin.

2. *Preparing the Presentation:* The actual writing of the material for the presentation begins as soon as background research on the topic has been completed. Administrative professionals are particularly helpful in conducting information searches once the topic has been decided. Organization of information into an outline and later into written text, if needed, is an important part of the writing phase.

   a. *Developing the presentation materials:* Depending upon the nature of the presentation, the following materials may be created: an outline of the presentation, actual text of the presentation (if complete text is required), visuals, and related handout materials.

      (1) *Presentation outline:* Many speakers use outlines as they speak to remind themselves of important points in their presentation. The sequential order of

the outline helps the speaker to quickly move from point to point without hesitation. The majority of presentations do not require a completely written text script—unless the presentation is based on a research project or a formal manuscript. Typed or printed outlines (and sometimes notes) are sufficient for most presenters.

(a) *Topical outline:* A topical outline directs the speaker from point to point with a brief listing of nouns rather than lengthy phrases or sentences. The speaker must rely heavily on memory during the presentation.

(b) *Phrase outline:* More extensive than a topical outline, the phrase outline contains more information related to each point. Only essential words are included, however.

(c) *Sentence outline:* Key sentences are included to prompt the speaker to expand on these ideas. A sentence outline includes the most complete information.

No matter which type of outline is adapted, details or facts that might be forgotten easily by the speaker should be noted on the outline.

EXAMPLE: *If the speaker highlights population trends in the United States and compares these trends with the number of employed persons in the country, it is a good idea to include these numbers on the outline—near the topic, phrase, or sentence used.*

(2) *Content of the presentation:* The outline becomes the basis for expanding information into complete text for the presentation. Developing the content of the presentation is really a three-step process:

- First, tell the listeners what you are going to say (introduction).
- Next, tell the listeners what you are talking about (body of presentation).
- And last, tell them what you have just said (conclusion and closing).

(a) *Introduction:* The way a speaker begins the presentation sets the stage for what follows. Here are some pointers to remember as the introduction is being planned:

- Capture the listeners' attention
- Get the listeners involved in the topic
- Establish your credibility as a speaker for this topic
- Preview the main points to be presented

The introduction is fairly short and to the point but very important in gaining the attention of the audience and moving on to the main points of the topic.

(b) *Body of presentation:* The body should focus on only a few main points, possibly two to four. Each of these main points should be developed with adequate details being given. Main ideas can be structured according to the following elements:

- Time (chronology)
- Components (products or regions)
- Importance (most to least)

- Criteria (comparisons and contrasts)
- Problems and solutions
- Pros and cons

A good idea when you are preparing a presentation is to prepare more material than you think you will need. Having a reserve of additional information helps the speaker provide as much information as possible in the time allotted.

(c) *Concluding remarks and closing:* A presenter's closing comments will probably be remembered more than some of the content of the presentation. Too many speakers "rush" to finish. They really should be using the time to summarize the main points made during the presentation and close with some courteous and meaningful comments. Remarks like "Well, that's it!" or "That's all the information I have" leave the audience wondering what the main points of the presentation were. A closing comment like "I hope that each of you will return to your offices with at least one new idea about [the topic] to try tomorrow" will leave the audience members coming up with useful ideas.

(3) *Format for the presentation:* If the entire text of the presentation needs to be made available (as is the case when a research paper is to be read by the speaker), the administrative professional must prepare the text for easy reading at the podium. The text should be arranged neatly on the page and be free of format or typographical errors. Here are some techniques that are often used to prepare printed copy of a presentation.

(a) *Spacing:* The text should be double-spaced with a triple-space between paragraphs. One-inch side margins should be sufficient as well as one-inch top and bottom margins.

(b) *Type font and size:* When using word processing software, at least a 12- or 14-point font should be used for ease of reading. A larger typeface will create images that will be much easier to read from a distance. The speaker who has trouble with bifocals or lighting conditions will especially have an easier time reading larger type.

(c) *Accuracy of printed text:* Be sure that the printed text is accurate with all revisions or corrections made. An undetected typographical error in the text may cause a serious distraction for the speaker as he or she is presenting.

b. *Preparing handout materials:* The speaker may want to share some sample handout materials with the audience. The administrative professional should make sure that these materials are prepared ahead of time and arranged so that the speaker can integrate them with the presentation. When manuscripts are being read (such as research presentations), the handout material may be an exact copy of the presentation. Copies should be available in quantity for the speaker to distribute either at the beginning of or at the close of the presentation. If the speaker prefers to have the audience follow along, copies should be distributed at the beginning of the session.

c. *Preparing visual aids:* Presentations of factual information are greatly enhanced by the use of visuals to complement the verbal or written presentation. Visual aids take the attention off the speaker and onto the topic. Some types of visual aids that are designed to accompany the presentation, such as computer visuals and transparencies, need to be planned and prepared ahead of time. The administrative professional should work in cooperation with the speaker to determine exactly what information should be included on visual aids. These media should be ready for review ahead of time so that the speaker can use them in practicing for the presentation or can indicate what changes need to be made.

(1) *Computer visuals:* Presentation software programs are often used to prepare computer visuals and handouts. The following types of materials can be prepared with this software:

(a) *Content outline:* An outline of the presentation can be created by using a template (sometimes called a "Wizard") provided with the software. The first section contains information that will go on a title slide, such as the title of the presentation along with the presenter's name and affiliation. The remaining outline text appears on the slide set and reflects information keyed in by the user when prompted. Some people prefer to prepare the slides first and then work with the content sequence. The sequence of the visuals can be easily changed even after the slideshow has been created.

(b) *Templates for creating slides:* Templates are typically provided in the presentation software program to assist in preparing slides that vary in design. A basic color scheme and background for the entire presentation can be chosen. Varying designs for individual slides can also be applied to add variety to slides. Design templates add character and mood to a presentation and project an image. Be careful when selecting a template. You want to make the best impression on your audience by choosing an appropriate template design.

Slide layouts are another element of slide design. They must be selected for individual slides. Slide layouts determine the placement of the objects on a slide. Here are some examples of typical slide layouts the user may choose from:

- Bulleted list of items
- Textual material with graph, chart, illustration, or photograph inserted
- Items listed in two columns

(c) *Multimedia effects:* Animation can be added to the slides so that lines of text move onto the screen by coming into view from either side or from the top or bottom.

- Illustrations (graphic objects) can also show movement by entering and exiting the screen. This type of animation is called "text builds."
- Sound is another multimedia effect that can be inserted into the slide from a software library.
- Short clips from videotaped recordings can be added.

Once slides have been created, they can be sequenced in any order desired for the presentation. Slide transitions that will control the movement of each slide onto and off of the screen can be applied to the entire presentation.

(d) *Handouts with notes:* When the multimedia presentation is ready for use, handouts of the slideshow can be prepared so that conference participants will be able to follow the presentation with copies of the visuals. One of the options available is to have miniature copies of three slides down the left side of a sheet of paper, with room at the right for notes to be written during the presentation.

Note this word of caution: Beware of including too much material on slides and then giving out the hard copy of the presentation and handouts *before* your presentation. Your audience may ignore you and read your speech and handouts while you are presenting.

(e) *Speaker's notes:* Another option available to the presenter is to compose a set of speaker's notes for each of the slides in the presentation. These notes are only meant for the speaker's use and can be keyed in for printing out on the same sheet as a copy of the appropriate visual. If the presenter decides to rearrange the order of the slides, the speaker's notes are included with the appropriate slide (see Figure 5–5).

(2) *Techniques for effective slide layout:* The use of presentation software enables speakers to develop effective slides to complement professional engagements.

(a) *"Do's" to put into practice:* Decisions on slide layout depend on the information to be included as well as the way that information is displayed on the electronic slides. Here are a few "do's" to keep in mind when developing slides:

- Select a slide layout that is appropriate for the text to be keyed on the slide.
- Use illustrations on selected slides as part of the design.
- Use animation to have specific items appear on the screen one at a time.
- Choose a background design and colors that make the text easy to read.

(b) *"Don'ts" to keep in mind:* As electronic slides are being developed, you should keep in mind a number of "don'ts" so that the slides are designed and used most effectively. Here are a few to remember as new slides are created:

- Don't put too many words on a slide, or you will be tempted to read the slide content to the audience.
- Don't use sounds or animation that distract the listeners.
- Don't use dark colors that make it difficult to read the words as they are projected on the screen.
- Don't forget to carefully proofread the text on each slide.

Presentation software provides a unique opportunity to be creative and innovative in designing interesting presentations. This multimedia approach requires that the presenter have a computer and projection equipment that are compatible with software used for preparing the multimedia presentation. Today's widespread use of presentation software enables speakers to have professional-looking electronic visuals to accompany presentations. The audience is left with a more positive impression of the speaker and the presentation. The use of new technologies is increasing while use of older technologies is decreasing or disappearing.

FIGURE 5–5   Computer Visuals with Speaker's Notes

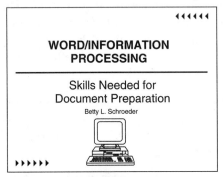

◀◀◀◀◀◀

**WORD/INFORMATION
PROCESSING**

Skills Needed for
Document Preparation

Betty L. Schroeder

▶▶▶▶▶▶

Word processing support specialists
need to possess middle- to high-level
competence with language skills, the
computer keyboard, formatting skills,
and basic computer skills.

◀◀◀◀◀◀

Language Skills

‣ Sentence Structure
‣ Grammar
‣ Punctuation
‣ Spelling
‣ Reading Skills

▶▶▶▶▶▶

Word processing functions require a
strong basis in language skills. In
particular, sentence structure,
grammar, punctuation, and spelling are
very important. Excellent reading
skills help the word processing
specialist understand the content of
high-quality manuscripts as well as
instructional or operations manuals for
word processing programs.

◀◀◀◀◀◀

Keyboarding Skills

‣ Touch-Keyboarding Speed and
  Accuracy
‣ Alphanumeric Keyboard
‣ Multifunction Keys
‣ Ergonomic Keyboard

▶▶▶▶▶▶

Typically, large quantities of textual
material must be keyed in by the word
processing support specialist.
Keyboarding rates usually range from
65 to 95 words per minute. Touch-
keyboarding skill enables the operator
to manipulate the keyboard without
looking at the keys. Sometimes it is
necessary to look at the function keys
since most of these keys are
multifunction keys.

◀◀◀◀◀◀

Formatting Skills

‣ Knowledge of Acceptable Styles
‣ Appropriate Formatting Commands
  ‣ Setting Margins
  ‣ Headers and Footers
  ‣ Page Numbers

▶▶▶▶▶▶

Letters, memorandums, and reports
must be prepared in acceptable styles.
Formatting skills require the operator
to enter appropriate commands for
setting margins, inserting headers and
footers into the manuscript, numbering
the pages of the document
appropriately, and handling other
formatting features that affect the
placement of the text on a page.

---

(3) *Use of a document camera:* Smart podiums may be equipped with document
cameras for projecting hard copy or transparencies as visuals on a projection
screen. The **document camera** looks like an overhead projector, but it has
more sophisticated features that permit the operator to "zoom in" or "zoom
out" to enlarge or reduce certain portions of hard-copy illustrations. The original copy is placed on top of a glass cover through which light from the projection bulbs shine. The hard copy can be printed or drawn on a sheet of paper
or a page from a book or magazine. The document camera eliminates the need
for a separate overhead projector.

(4) *Overhead transparencies:* A **transparency** is an acetate sheet that contains an image burned or drawn on it that can be projected on a screen or wall. Different kinds of transparencies can be created: colored background with white or black letters or images, clear background with black or colored images, shaded transparencies, or multiple-part transparencies. Using word processing software and an ink-jet or laser printer, you can produce original copy at your desktop PC. Preparing printed or drawn copy for use in making an overhead transparency requires you to use carbon-based materials. You can also make overhead transparencies from printed copy generated from multimedia slides developed with presentation software.

(a) *Using word processing software:* The advantage of using word processing software is that the original text, clip art, and charts can be edited before viewing or preparing transparencies. The transparency can be printed on an ink-jet or laser printer. If a color printer is available, the color used in the document is printed onto the transparency. If a computer printer that can handle acetate sheets is not available, a hard copy of the material can be used on a copier to make the transparency.

- *Font sizes:* Participants who are sitting in the back of the meeting room must be able to see the visual; therefore, a larger font size should be used. When using presentation software, the typical font size ranges from 18 to 40.

- *Font styles:* The word processing font style (typeface) should also be easy to read. Font styles may be italic and/or bold, have serifs (slanted or horizontal markings) or have no serifs (sans serif), and have uniform letter strokes or light-to-distinct transitions.

Refer to Office Systems and Technology, Chapter 6, Figure 6–1, for typeface characteristics for specific type fonts.

(b) *Preparing keyed or drawn copy:* Transparencies may be prepared from original black-and-white copy run through a copier that burns images from those copies into sheets of transparency acetate.

(c) *Transparency materials:* The cost of transparency material is high (as much as 40 cents per sheet), and misspelled words or careless errors can result in a transparency being discarded. The way the material is burned on the transparency acetate will depend on the type of acetate that is being used. Transparencies may be purchased that have colored backgrounds and either white or black letters, and images will be burned into the transparencies.

Transparencies may be prepared on a number of different types of copiers. Acetate sheets are placed in the paper carrier or in a bypass tray, just as bond paper is, and run through the copier in the same way. The image is burned into the acetate, creating the reproduction of the text or drawing.

(5) *Electronic blackboards:* Another way of displaying business graphics is the **electronic blackboard,** a device used with teleconferences to transmit visuals to other locations. The electronic blackboard consists of a pressure-sensitive blackboard, microphone, and speaker at one location and a television monitor, microphone, and speaker at a second location (there may be additional locations as well). As someone writes on the blackboard, the coordinates are picked up

electronically and transmitted to the monitor at the other location(s) where an image of the blackboard is displayed. An electronic blackboard must be at all locations where text will be added for viewing on flat-panel monitors.

3. *Delivery and Follow-up:* Time spent in planning and creating a presentation will help in giving the speaker more confidence in the actual delivery of the material. Here are a few techniques that may be particularly helpful in giving a presentation:

a. *Memorization of key points:* Memorize only significant parts of the presentation, such as the introduction and the closing. This will help you stay on target with the basic content of the presentation.

b. *Thorough knowledge of topic:* Because of research conducted to gather the material, you should be familiar with the content and probably have an "expert" knowledge of the specific topic.

c. *Practice makes perfect:* Practice the presentation several times, with an eye on a timer or clock. Stay within the time limit allotted, especially if your presentation is part of a convention program.

d. *Physical facilities for speaking:* Check out the physical facilities to see what the arrangement of the room is a few hours or a day prior to your presentation. Request any changes that are absolutely necessary for you to have an effective presentation.

e. *Speaking rate:* Speak at a normal, moderate rate. Just because you have only a 20-minute presentation does not mean that you will compress what could be a longer presentation into that time period. Plan your presentation for the time given.

f. *Focus on visuals:* Spend time on each visual that you use—present details on each of the points included on the visual. Try not to read the visual to the audience. Assume that each one will read the main points that you have on each slide. Your task is to present details about those points; your knowledge of the topic comes through loud and clear as you explain your visuals.

g. *Questions from audience:* Encourage questions from the audience. When someone asks a question, it is a good idea to repeat the question because the entire audience may not have been able to hear the question. Just say, "The question is . . ." Follow with your best response but try to avoid "Yes, but . . ." types of answers. This type of a response shows that you disagree with the audience member. Perhaps you should say something like "Yes, that has been considered and may be one way to handle the situation. Another consideration is . . ."

To close your presentation after you have responded to audience questions, summarize some of the main points you focused on and leave the audience with a courteous closing thought.

Check Point—Section C

Directions: For each question, circle the correct answer.

C–1. Executives are often invited to make presentations before professional groups. Which one of the following represents a method used to prepare visuals and handouts for the audience?

A) Computer graphics software
B) Electronic blackboard

C) Presentation software
D) Electronic projection

C–2. When preparing computer visuals, an electronic slide format that includes room for an illustration as well as a short list of bullets can be selected from

A) a view of slide layouts available in the program
B) an outline of the textual content
C) clip art available in the program
D) animation features of the program

C–3. An electronic blackboard is most useful in

A) transmitting statistical information as business graphics to a distant location
B) creating transparencies to be used during a presentation
C) previewing computer visuals prepared at another location
D) developing a format to use for computer visuals

D. Communicating in the Diverse Workplace

Most businesses today are involved in international trade and commerce. With the proliferation of communication technologies, businesses around the world encounter cross-cultural experiences whether over the telephone, in conferences, or through the use of the Internet and electronic mail. No matter how one communicates (voice only, face to face, or in writing), the added dimensions of cultural differences and adapting messages to diverse audiences have become primary concerns in business communication today.

1. *Cultural Differences:* Highlighting all the cultural differences one may encounter seems an impossible task since differences also encompass gender, age, position, and other business conditions. Strategies oriented toward addressing cultural differences provide a broader basis for improved business communication. Dealing with cultural differences includes awareness, sensitivity, openness, respect, and collaboration.

   a. *Awareness:* Cultural differences are embedded in language. All other human differences are embedded in experiences. Dealing with diversity is enhanced as one becomes aware of linguistic and experiential differences. Attempt to understand the backgrounds of people as you work and communicate with them. Using the "you" attitude in communication demonstrates awareness of the importance of the other person.

   b. *Sensitivity:* To enhance understanding, one needs to listen empathically and use feedback to reinforce accurate understanding. In other words, you need to be sensitive to other people—who they are and where they are coming from.

   c. *Openness:* No matter how culturally different an individual is, he or she brings ideas and knowledge to the communication process. By being open to innovative ideas, new opportunities become possible.

   d. *Respect:* As we treat those who are like us with respect and understanding, we must extend that same respect and courtesy to those who are different. Understanding comes from openness and sensitivity toward others.

   e. *Collaboration:* As we respect and understand one another, collaborative working relationships develop. Through collaboration, the communication process produces information and knowledge, resulting in good decisions for all.

2. ***Adapting Communication to Intercultural Audiences:*** Nonverbal, oral, and written communication efforts must be adapted to people of intercultural backgrounds.

   a. *Nonverbal communication:* The importance of nonverbal behavior—body language, eye contact, facial expression, posture, gestures—is evident as we approach intercultural audiences. In addition, consideration for time, space, and territory in different cultures must be emphasized. Nonverbal messages that are sent indicate the way time and space are utilized in communicating with people of other cultures. Even when nonverbal behavior is difficult to interpret, it still conveys meaning to the receiver. People interpret physical gestures differently in different cultures. What may be an approval signal in one culture may be considered an obscene gesture in another. The following three attitudes are effective in communicating with people of other cultures:

   (1) *Being descriptive:* Using specific and concrete words to provide feedback enhances the communication process. Objective words used in descriptions will help to promote positive relationships.

   (2) *Being nonjudgmental:* Avoiding rating or evaluating behaviors during communication efforts will result in more objective viewpoints with intercultural audiences. People of other cultures will tend to be much less defensive about their practices when cultural mores are treated objectively.

   (3) *Being supportive:* A nod of the head, facial expressions, eye contact, and attention to physical proximity of others will show positive support for an intercultural audience.

   Key words in other languages—*please*, *thank you*, *yes*, *no*—will usually be more helpful than physical gestures in establishing rapport. Following the lead of the businessperson from another culture will give important clues as to differences in our cultures.

   b. *Oral messages:* Speaking a variety of languages fluently may not always be necessary since the majority of business transactions around the world are conducted in English. However, some techniques are particularly helpful if one or more business associates use English as a second language.

   - Use short sentences to express ideas. Avoid using puns, slang, and jargon because of misinterpretation of such words. [**Jargon** is defined as technical language pertinent to a specific profession or group.]

   - Observe nonverbal cues that will indicate understanding or misunderstanding of messages.

   - Smiling as you speak is perhaps the most useful form of communication in business transactions.

   - Pause frequently to check for feedback and comprehension of the message.

   - Confirm agreements with follow-up correspondence. Assistance from a translator may be very helpful to be sure that written correspondence sends the intended meaning.

   Effective oral communication is extremely important in dealing with people of other cultures. In some cultures, the oral agreement is considered stronger than a written one.

c. *Written messages:* In many cultures, formality in written communication is influential in maintaining excellent business relationships. The following techniques may be helpful in preparing appropriate written communication:

- Avoid expressions that are vague or easily misunderstood like idioms, slang, jargon, abbreviations, and contractions.
- Use sentences with fewer than 15 words and paragraphs of seven or fewer lines.
- Cite numbers in figures instead of spelling them out for ease of reading.
- Use correct grammar in writing sentences and paragraphs.
- Avoid using words that have more than one meaning.

The application of sensitivity in communication with people of varying cultures is crucial in developing and maintaining excellent business relationships. If you take the time to find out about people of other cultures, they will no doubt devote attention to you and your organization's culture.

d. *Intercultural ethics:* Sometimes business ethics used with other cultures will not be the same as those practiced in your own country. Simple questions arise concerning acceptance of gifts or payments to agents for doing business in that country. The businessperson who is faced with deciding how to handle an ethical situation will need to look for some practical solutions for continuing business dealings. Here are a few alternatives that may be considered:

- Refuse to enter into a business transaction that constitutes a breach of your own code of ethics.
- Examine the customs of other cultures to see what is considered moral and practical.
- Offer public service benefits or technical expertise in place of monetary contributions.
- Conduct business negotiations as openly as possible.

The strategies you choose to use must be legal, ethical, and needed to constitute sound business practice when dealing with people of other cultures.

3. ***Diversity in the Domestic Workplace:*** In the North American workplace as well as in the global workplace, **diversity** definitely exists. For many years people from other cultures have emigrated in large numbers to the United States and Canada to begin new lives. What has resulted is a workforce that is diverse in terms of personal characteristics, physical abilities, and employment opportunities.

a. *Diversity in personal characteristics and skills:* Employees differ in terms of numerous personal characteristics: age, race, religion, national origin, and ethnicity. These characteristics cannot be legally used in making employment decisions; rather, the competencies possessed that qualify people of diverse cultures for specific positions are the primary consideration.

b. *Diversity in physical ability:* People are diverse in terms of physical ability as well. In the United States, the physically challenged individual is somewhat protected under the Americans with Disabilities Act that has been in effect since the early 1990s. Businesses and other organizations have had to revamp physical facilities as well as internal procedures to take advantage of the expertise these people possess.

c. *Diversity in employment opportunities:* Women and minority groups complain about the **glass ceiling,** an invisible barrier to advancement to higher-level corporate positions. The word "inequality" is heard often, with men traditionally being paid more than women in the same or similar types of employment. Older employees often feel discriminated against when compared with younger employees. Even though legislation such as the Civil Rights Act of 1964 and the Equal Pay for Equal Work Act of 1972 has been passed to counteract some of these complaints, the stigma is still present. Organizations are still being sued and found guilty of inattention to employment inequalities.

The workforce will continue to be diverse. By 2005 the workforce in the United States is expected to have a large component of what are now considered minority groups (African Americans, Hispanics, Asians, and Native Americans). The projection is that women will comprise 47 percent of the workforce by 2006. Another important estimate is that by 2006 over 40 percent of the workforce will be over 45 years of age. Training and other accommodations will be needed to be sure that effective communication will assist a diverse workforce in achieving personal and organizational goals.

Check Point—Section D

Directions: For each question, circle the correct answer.

D–1. In dealing with diverse cultures, which one of the following strategies enhances our understanding by listening empathically and using feedback to reinforce accurate understanding?

    A) Awareness
    B) Collaboration
    C) Respect
    D) Sensitivity

D–2. Which one of the following techniques would be particularly helpful in communicating orally with one or more business associates who use English as a second language?

    A) Pause frequently to see if the audience needs clarification of specific points

    B) Write out numbers in words rather than use figures
    C) Pay little attention to grammar since you are primarily interested in oral communication
    D) Be ready to compromise if a question of legal ethics arises

D–3. An invisible barrier (primarily for women and minority group members) to advancement to higher-level managerial positions is the

    A) workforce discrimination
    B) collaborative efforts of upper-level management
    C) glass ceiling
    D) intercultural discrimination

For Your Review

Directions: For each question, circle the correct answer.

1. Companies sponsor conferences for company personnel for the purpose of
   A) training customers and clients in specific business strategies
   B) updating business professionals in the organization about new products or services
   C) informing community representatives about new products
   D) discussing timely topics with suppliers

2. An annual convention sponsored by a professional business association is designed primarily to benefit
   A) community representatives
   B) delegates to the convention
   C) clients of the association
   D) active members of the association

3. The program for a professional convention is planned by a/an
   A) administrative professional for an executive who is involved with the convention
   B) local committee of business professionals responsible for arrangements
   C) committee chaired by a vice president of the professional association
   D) office professional who coordinates travel arrangements for the organization

4. Which one of the following activities needs to be accomplished before the convention begins?
   A) Setting up and staffing an information desk for distributing litera-
   ture about the community, available tours, and restaurants
   B) Reserving an adequate amount of exhibit space and number of meeting rooms
   C) Completing the bank deposits for the convention
   D) Sending thank-you letters to all speakers and exhibitors

5. The financial reporting for the convention includes
   A) sending follow-up correspondence to all who assisted with the convention
   B) distributing copies of the proceedings to speakers and participants
   C) developing a reference file of all procedures used before, during, and after the convention
   D) preparing checks for honorariums and expenses for guest speakers

6. The primary reason for a committee to meet is to
   A) achieve one or more specific objectives assigned to the committee
   B) further the work assigned to the committee
   C) serve until a report is presented to the organization
   D) investigate a particular event or problem that has occurred

7. A standing committee is appointed for a definite term and assigned
   A) a particular problem to study and investigate
   B) temporary responsibility to solve a specific problem

C) specific goals to achieve during the term served

D) day-to-day operations to supervise

8. People who are separated by great distances may participate in business discussions and decision making through

A) conferencing
B) in-house meetings
C) out-of-town meetings
D) intranet collaboration

9. A response is required from each participant for this month's meeting of the Technology Development Committee, but none is received from Swedberg. Which kind of follow-up would be best for Kowalski, the administrative assistant, to conduct?

A) Kowalski should notify the committee chair that Swedberg has not responded
B) Kowalski should send a letter to Swedberg including the agenda for the meeting
C) Kowalski should telephone to see if Swedberg plans to attend
D) Swedberg's name should be removed from the attendance list

10. Items of business to be presented and discussed during a meeting are included in

A) a resolution
B) a petition
C) minutes
D) an agenda

11. The application of parliamentary procedures in conducting meetings establishes the

A) time frame for the meeting
B) timely distribution of an agenda and handout materials
C) routine for conducting an efficient, orderly meeting
D) promptness in starting the meeting at the appointed time

12. An item of business that is not on the agenda

A) should not be discussed at the meeting

B) must be approved by the group before being added to the agenda
C) can be added to the agenda after being announced
D) should be left for the next meeting's agenda

13. Sweeney made a motion that the board approve the purchase of the Wolters building on Eastside Drive for a new records center. Jessup seconded the motion. The motion made is a

A) main motion
B) subsidiary motion
C) incidental motion
D) privileged motion

14. After a lengthy discussion about the purchase of the Wolters building, the presiding officer Rasmussen stopped the discussion. There appeared to be a number of funding questions still to be considered. Charleston tabled the motion, which means that the original motion

A) was denied
B) needs to be amended
C) was voted upon
D) was set aside until a future meeting

15. The required number of voting members who must be present to transact business is called a

A) resolution
B) quorum
C) petition
D) majority

16. A formal statement of reasons for requesting a group to take specific action on a business item signed by a required number of those eligible to sign is called a/an

A) resolution
B) incidental motion
C) petition
D) main motion

17. Because of her experience with ergonomic office design, Mallory has been asked to make a presentation on the principles of Feng Shui, a Chinese philosophy applied in ergonomic de-

signs, at an upcoming seminar hosted by the Society for Environmental Systems. Mallory states to one of her co-workers that she really does not know very much about Feng Shui. The writing of her presentation should take place after she has

A) created a set of electronic slides to accompany her presentation
B) developed a topical outline of the presentation content
C) conducted information searches on the topic
D) decided on the sequential order of the presentation

18. If a speaker plans to highlight statistical information in a presentation, those numbers should be highlighted on the

A) text script of the presentation
B) introduction of the presentation to catch the audience's attention
C) concluding remarks as part of the summation
D) outline for the presentation

19. A professional presentation that includes visual aids as a complement to the verbal presentation

A) is cost effective for a minimum number of people in the audience
B) will place more attention on the topic than the speaker
C) enables the speaker to modify the content during the presentation
D) requires handout materials that pertain to the presentation

20. In creating a set of electronic slides to accompany a presentation, Ramirez should perform which one of the following tasks first?

A) Select a basic color scheme and background available in the software
B) Select the slide layout for each major point in the outline
C) Sequence the slides in the order desired
D) Review the animation that is available for integration into the slides

21. Which one of the following is the best reason for distributing a handout at the close of the presentation?

A) The material is on slides so the audience can follow along easily
B) Speaker's notes project on the screen for ease in following the presentation
C) Too many words on each slide will influence the speaker to "read" the slides to the audience
D) The audience will be more interested in listening to what the speaker is saying

22. A hard-copy illustration on paper or in a book can be enlarged for projection on the screen by using a

A) transparency acetate
B) document camera
C) microform
D) presentation software's Wizard

23. Using the "you" attitude when communicating with a person of another culture demonstrates to that person your

A) ability to listen empathically
B) openness to innovative ideas
C) awareness of the other person's importance
D) willingness to collaborate with the other person

24. Which one of the following relates to an attitude that is effective in communicating with a person of another culture?

A) Evaluating the other person's behavior during the discussion
B) Receiving feedback during the discussion
C) Looking around the room occasionally to see what other business associates are doing
D) Paying attention to the personal and public space preferred by the other person

25. If one or more business associates use English as a second language, a technique that may be helpful is to

A) check for feedback at the end of the conversation

B) use jargon so technical terms can be interpreted easier

C) observe the nonverbal cues communicated by the business associate

D) confirm agreements verbally rather than in written form.

Solutions

Solutions to Check Point—Section A

Answer	Refer to:
A–1. (D)	[A-2-a]
A–2. (C)	[A-2-a]
A–3. (A)	[A-2-b]

Solutions to Check Point—Section B

Answer	Refer to:
B–1. (B)	[B]
B–2. (B)	[B-2-b (2)]
B–3. (D)	[B-3-b (1)]

Solutions to Check Point—Section C

Answer	Refer to:
C–1. (C)	[C-2-c (1)]
C–2. (A)	[C-2-c (1) (b)]
C–3. (A)	[C-2-c (5)]

Solutions to Check Point—Section D

	Answer	Refer to:
D–1.	(D)	[D-1-B]
D–2.	(A)	[D-2-b]
D–3.	(C)	[D-3-c]

Solutions to For Your Review

	Answer	Refer to:
1.	(B)	[A-1-a]
2.	(D)	[A-1-b]
3.	(C)	[A-1-b (2)]
4.	(B)	[A-2-a (1)]
5.	(D)	[A-2-c (1)]
6.	(B)	[B-1-a (1)]
7.	(C)	[B-1-a (1) (a)]
8.	(A)	[B-1-b and B-1-b (3)]
9.	(C)	[B-2-b (4)]
10.	(D)	[B-2-e]
11.	(C)	[B-3]
12.	(B)	[B-3-a (4)]
13.	(A)	[B-3-b (2) (a)]
14.	(D)	[B-3-b (2) (a)]
15.	(B)	[B-3-b (2) (b)]
16.	(C)	[B-5-b]
17.	(C)	[C-2]
18.	(D)	[C-2-a (1)]
19.	(B)	[C-2-c]

20. (A)   [C-2-c (1) (b)]

21. (D)   [C-2-c (1) (d)]

22. (B)   [C-2-c (3)]

23. (C)   [D-1-a]

24. (D)   [D-2-a]

25. (C)   [D-2-b]

Chapter 6

Research and Reference Materials

OVERVIEW

As more responsibilities are assigned to administrative professionals, the process of researching informational references is becoming more important. Researching information requires a degree of knowledge about the subject or topic, organizational skills, and time to search through libraries, computer files, or the Internet. Knowing exactly where to go to find adequate and accurate information for a research report or speech can be challenging. The administrative professional must be prepared to spend considerable time "digging" for sources of information.

Research procedures that have proved helpful include discussing the purpose of the research with the person for whom the work is being done *before* actually beginning to search for information. This is one way to determine the basic objectives of the research before embarking on the project. Sometimes interviews with experts will be necessary to obtain primary data; at other times, book, periodical, or Internet references will be sufficient. No matter what procedures are used, detailed records of all persons interviewed, references read and consulted, and other useful reference materials need to be kept to develop a complete bibliography of works consulted and cited.

Research facilities such as libraries, in-house research services, and computer search and information services should be utilized in conducting research. In addition, business and professional associations as well as community organizations can also be very helpful.

The list of reference materials included in this chapter is meant to serve as a starting point for researching information under particular headings and becoming familiar with various kinds of references. As new publications relating to the categories included in this chapter are discovered, the administrative professional should add the information so that an up-to-date list of reference materials can be maintained.

KEY TERMS

Almanac, 169
Archive, 168
Dewey Decimal
    classification system, 166
Dictionary, 174
Directories, 170
Encyclopedias, 175
Etiquette references, 175
Fact book, 169

GPO Access, 171
Index, 177
Information banks, 168
Interview guide, 164
Library of Congress
    classification system, 166
Library consortiums, 166
Official Airline Guides
    (OAGs), 179

Parliamentary procedures,
    178
Primary sources, 163
Public library, 165
Secondary sources, 163
Thesaurus, 178
Word book, 179
Writing style manuals, 180

A. Research Procedures

The role of the administrative professional is constantly changing to include more administrative responsibility in the challenging task of researching and locating information. Such a task demands a high level of organizational skill and ingenuity in gathering accurate information for reports, speeches, and other types of written materials. The research process may be a routine part of the job or the responsibility of a team of people. The kinds of procedures used in collecting the information needed will, of course, directly reflect on the quality of the report or speech produced. Here are some guidelines for developing procedures for researching business information.

1. *Understanding Purposes of Research:* Before embarking on any type of research, an administrative professional must know the purpose of the research: what the outcome will be and who will make use of the results of the research. Here are some questions that need to be answered before proceeding with the research:

   - How will the information be presented—as a report? or as a speech?
   - Who will be the primary audience?
   - Is there a secondary audience?
   - What kind of information is needed—articles written and published by professionals? or primary data and results reported in research studies?

2. *Listing Possible Information Sources:* Any investigation should begin with a list of all the possible sources of information that might be used.

   a. *Facilities:* Facilities, such as libraries, business associations, or community organizations, that will be helpful in finding the kinds of information sought need to be identified.

   b. *Types of references:* Identifying specific books, documents, or other types of information that are desired gives the researcher a start in finding reputable sources.

   c. *Personal contacts:* If primary research data will be collected through interviews, developing a list of people to interview along with their addresses, telephone numbers, and e-mail addresses will help with initial contacts.

   d. *Computer searches:* Online computer searches may help gather some of the types of information needed. Such a search may take place in a library or research center that has access to a database(s) or other libraries.

e. *Internet searches:* Specific information about a particular company or organization, its products or services, or a specific industry may be obtained through Internet Web site searches. In addition, the Internet permits access to articles that have appeared in daily newspapers, magazines, or journals, either in abstract or full-text form.

3. ***Determining Special Research Costs:*** An estimate of the cost will enable the background research to stay within budget limits. These costs may include travel to and from research facilities and libraries, telephone service, online computer searches, copying and printing costs, and additional office support.

4. ***Making Appointments for Research:*** A time-saver in performing research functions is to make appointments ahead of time with individuals (inside or outside the organization) who are in a position to provide the kinds of information sought. Other people (librarians, business executives, research specialists, community leaders) may be busy on their jobs as well, and a formal appointment will ensure an hour or two of their individual attention in responding to research queries.

5. ***Keeping Complete Records of Research Information:*** As the research continues, a written record should be maintained showing primary and secondary sources of information, complete sets of notes from both primary and secondary sources, interview schedules, and transcribed interview tapes. **Primary sources,** such as surveys and interviews you have conducted, yield actual data for you to analyze. **Secondary sources** are published and unpublished documents written by others who have studied the topic. Both primary and secondary information will be essential later as the final draft of the report or presentation is written.

a. *Preparing a bibliography:* A record of each reference used or cited needs to be maintained manually on a 3- by 5-inch card or electronically using a productivity package. The following kinds of information need to be included in a bibliographic entry:

- Author's name (if any)
- Title of book, article, or other reference
- Name of publishing company or agency
- Place of publication
- Date of publication
- Exact page reference(s)
- Web address (if available on Internet)
- Access (retrieval) date for Web/Internet information

The following information should be recorded to help you locate specific books but is not needed for the bibliographic entry:

- ISBN number of publication
- Library of Congress classification number
- Dewey Decimal System classification number

When the administrative professional uses computer application software for recording bibliographic entries, the specific directions for the bibliography tool within the application program need to be followed.

Bibliography cards prepared manually should be numbered, starting with the number 1, and filed alphabetically in a card file. Any bibliography or reference list created must be in alphabetical order. Any missing information such as author's name or publication date not found in the reference needs to be noted.

b. *Taking appropriate reading notes:* Reading notes should be complete so that all information about the original reference is readily available as the writing begins. Using a notebook computer or index cards, notes can be recorded electronically or manually.

(1) *Electronic procedures for taking notes:* Application software may be used to record research notes for writing reports. The following procedures may be helpful as notes and other information are recorded for later use.

- First, determine a system for note taking. A simple process is to create a folder with the research topic as the name. Each bibliographic entry plus notes should be saved as a separate file (document) in the topic folder.

- Word processing and other types of software permit the keying in or voice input of notes and the storing of these notes on disk for later access.

- Later, electronic bookmarks or other notations can be inserted to help locate specific facts or data easily.

- Follow the procedures for bibliographic entries given in the operating instructions for the software so the entries are correct.

(2) *Manual procedures for taking notes:* Here are some specific procedures to follow in recording accurate notes from various references:

- Write on only one side of a note card (preferably a 4- by 6-inch or 5- by 8-inch card so that there is sufficient room for more writing).

- If one particular reference refers to more than one subject, place the notes pertaining to each subject on a separate card. Identify the source of the material on each card with the code number from the bibliography card. Complete bibliographic information should be in the bibliography file.

- File the note cards in a card file alphabetically by author name (if known) or title of article or book (if author name is not known) so that they will not become lost.

c. *Duplicating materials for later reference:* Often, microfilm or microfiche is used to locate needed materials. One advantage of these methods is the ability to print copies of those pages with data that may be referred to later during the writing process. Copyright laws need to be observed carefully whenever copyrighted articles, theses, and other research information are referenced. For research purposes, one copy of copyrighted material may be copied for personal use.

d. *Recording interview information:* Interviews with people within or outside the organization will yield primary data to include in research. When interviews are conducted, following steps such as these will ensure that each interview is conducted in a concise yet complete and consistent manner.

(1) *Using interview guides:* A planned **interview guide** will include the questions that need to be asked during the interview. In some cases, it is an excellent idea to send a copy of this guide to the interviewee ahead of time so that he or she will have an opportunity to think about the questions and prepare some of the responses before the interview takes place.

(2) *Taking notes during the interview:* During the interview, taking notes should not be distracting for the interviewee. If you use a written form of shorthand or have a form where responses can be checked (yes/no) or circled (1–499, 500–999, 1,000–2,000), you should be able to take the notes quickly as the interviewee responds to specific questions while still maintaining eye contact and interjecting additional questions.

(3) *Recording the interview:* If the interview is to be recorded for later replay, transcription, and analysis, the interviewee should be asked for permission to do so before the interview begins. Sometimes people do not wish their responses to be recorded, especially if the topic tends to be a sensitive one.

(4) *Preparing a transcript:* A transcript of the interview (questions and responses) prepared from a recorded tape or notes taken during the interview should be submitted to the interviewee for review to ensure the accuracy of the transcribed information.

Check Point—Section A

Directions: For each question, circle the correct answer.

A–1. In conducting meaningful research, an administrative assistant must first know

    A) all possible sources of information
    B) the purpose of the research
    C) the names of individuals to contact for interviews
    D) the types of records to access

A–2. Which one of the following represents information that needs to be included on a bibliography card?

    A) The researcher's name
    B) Date of first access to the article
    C) Publisher of the article
    D) Additional references that might be helpful

A–3. Copying a published article that is stored on microfiche requires that the researcher

    A) observe copyright laws carefully
    B) return the microfiche to its jacket as soon as possible
    C) obtain permission before making a copy of the article
    D) use a microfiche reader to produce any printed copies needed

B. Research Facilities

One of the first research steps is to identify the types of facilities that may have information relevant to the research topic. Libraries, local chambers of commerce, business and professional associations, and local businesses may be helpful. In addition, various U.S. Government departments have excellent libraries, with qualified professional librarians in charge. Some agencies have law or medical libraries as well. Many of these organizations now have Internet sites that permit public access to information from their holdings.

1. *Libraries:* Library services are available primarily through public, company, government, and college or university libraries. A **public library** may be an excellent source for general topic information. Many companies and organizations, however, have established their own libraries so that collections of library references specific to their own industry may be used more easily. Of course, a nearby university library may be

one of the most extensive libraries in the area. Private collections housed in a university library or archive may provide valuable information for research as well. Today many public and university libraries are part of **library consortiums** with online services available that link one library with all others in the network. References that are part of one library's holdings may be borrowed by someone at another library within the consortium.

a. *Classification systems:* Libraries use two standardized classification systems: the **Dewey Decimal classification system** and the **Library of Congress classification system**. All published books are assigned numbers for these two systems, which appear near the copyright date in the book's front pages.

   (1) *Dewey Decimal classification system:* This system is based on the premise that all knowledge can be classified into ten primary groupings:

000	General Works
100	Philosophy
200	Religion
300	Social Science
400	Philology
500	Pure Science
600	Applied Science or Useful Arts
700	Arts Recreation
800	Literature
900	History

   Main subjects are identified by the hundreds 000 to 900. Subgroups are assigned numbers 00 to 99 or 0 to 9 if there are two subgroups.

   EXAMPLES:

   Mary Ellen Guffey, Business Communication: Process and Product, *4th ed., South-Western, 2003: 651.7 (6 = Applied Science and Useful Arts; rest of code applies to business writing, English language, business communication)*

   Courtland L. Bovée, John V. Thill, and Barbara E. Schatzman, Business Communication Today, *7th ed., Prentice Hall, 2003: 658.4'5 (6 = Applied Science and Useful Arts; rest of code applies to business communication, communication in organizations)*

   (2) *Library of Congress classification system:* This system, developed in the early 1900s, provides for 21 major areas of knowledge:

A	General Works
B	Philosophy, Psychology, and Religion
C–F	History
G	Geography, Anthropology, and Recreation
H	Social Sciences
J	Political Science
K	Law
L	Education
M	Music
N	Fine Arts
P	Language and Literature
Q	Science
R	Medicine

S   Agriculture
T   Technology
U   Military Science
V   Naval Science
Z   Bibliography and Library Science

The number assigned consists of an alphanumeric code, with the first two letters representing the major classification group and the numbers representing subdivisions.

EXAMPLES:

Mary Ellen Guffey, Business Communication: Process and Product, *4th ed., South-Western, 2003: HF5718.3 .G838 2002 (H = Social Sciences)*

Courtland L. Bovée, John V. Thill, and Barbara E. Schatzman, Business Communication Today, *7th ed., Prentice Hall, 2003: HF5718. B66 2002 (H = Social Sciences)*

Each year the Library of Congress adds or modifies more than 7,000 classification numbers to account for new knowledge or current events.

b. *Vertical file service:* A valuable library reference is the list of pamphlets, booklets, and leaflets that are available in vertical files within the library but are not indexed in the card catalog. The list of references may be computerized for easy access by the user.

c. *Reference collections:* Libraries house special collections, which are either publicly or privately owned. Information contained in each collection may be accessed, but often all research work must be done on the premises. All documents, books, and references in the collection are kept in the library at all times and must be signed out by the researcher. Collections such as these give the researcher an opportunity to view manuscripts, reports, and other materials that might not otherwise be available for public viewing. Special permission may be necessary for the researcher to make copies of some of the materials.

d. *Interlibrary networks:* Interlibrary communication networks or consortiums have been established in many areas to enable people to access information stored in more than one library. With a computer system, it is possible to inquire on a terminal in one library about specific books or references that are available in other libraries cooperating in the library consortium. Within two to four days, if the reference is available, any books not available in the local library can be received as a loan from another library. Copies of published articles needed for research can also be obtained through such a network.

e. *Computer information banks or databases:* Many organizations subscribe to computerized information databases available within a particular profession or field. In the company library, a terminal is available to access the database to obtain abstracts of research studies, court cases, or other materials available through the database.

EXAMPLE: *The Heist Information Bank is a comprehensive data bank for marketing practices in colleges and universities. The system's database includes hundreds of articles accumulated from past issues of* Education Marketing.

f. *Library micrographics centers:* Libraries have research studies, dissertations, and other references stored on microforms that may be accessed on the premises only.

If copies are needed of particular pages or articles, a reader-printer may be used to produce copies. Other types of audiovisual materials may also be available on cassettes, videotapes, and DVDs, such as a copy of a speech made by the president of a university.

2. ***In-House Research Services:*** Within the organization, several in-house research services may be maintained. Each of these research operations would provide professional assistance in finding needed information.

   a. *Research department:* Organizations that are heavily involved in researching information find it valuable to have a research department to assist administrative professionals and other business associates in finding needed information.

   b. *Information banks and services:* Many organizations subscribe to **information banks** within a particular profession or field. Terminals connect the company to the information source so that individuals can access abstracts of information needed or copies of entire documents.

   c. *Business archives:* An **archive** is a collection of documents of historical value to an organization. Businesses, governments, and universities have established archives so that researchers are able to access information that is protected through a high level of security. The research needs to be done on the premises since the research materials have historical or administrative value and are not allowed to be removed from the premises.

3. ***Business and Professional Associations:*** Specific information relating to a particular profession may be available through a recognized professional organization. Many of these associations have Web sites on the Internet. These sites typically contain information such as the history of the association, membership, publications available, and general information about the profession. Contacting the association by e-mailing, telephoning, or writing can yield additional information to help with research. By examining the publications of the professional group, an administrative professional may update knowledge of current happenings in the field. Such sources are particularly helpful in researching technological developments in the field.

4. ***Community Organizations:*** Business information may be obtained from organizations such as the local chamber of commerce or the municipal government. Service clubs, such as Rotary, Kiwanis, or Lions, may also be able to help, depending on the subject of the research. In preparing a speech to be given before a community organization, the executive may ask the administrative professional to research the group to find out more about the audience. Many community organizations are developing Web sites that are helpful in providing general information about the organization, community, or geographic area. Often, links to Web sites of other organizations within the area are provided.

Check Point—Section B

Directions: For each question, circle the correct answer.

B–1. The library classification system that is based on the premise that all knowledge can be classified into ten primary groups is known as the

A) Library of Congress classification system
B) Dewey Decimal system
C) interlibrary loan system
D) in-house research service

B–2. Martinez's responsibility as a paralegal for Bailey & Swift, a Chicago law firm, is to research past court cases to obtain information relative to present cases for the preparation of briefs and other legal documents. A subscription service that is available for this purpose is referred to as a/an

A) in-house research service
B) records center
C) business archive
D) computer information bank

B–3. Businesses, government agencies, and universities have organized business documents and collections that have historical value into

A) in-house research services
B) computer information banks
C) active records storage
D) archives

C. Information References

Depending on the topic being researched, many different types of information references are available for researching various types of business information. The following list represents samples of references that are currently available. However, the sources that are included are considered major ones that the administrative professional should be aware of and be able to use in conducting needed research.

1. *Almanacs and Fact Books:* An **almanac** is a book or publication, usually published on an annual basis, that includes factual information about international and national events of the year. An almanac can also be called a **fact book.**

   CIA World Factbook, Central Intelligence Agency, *www.odci.gov/cia/publications/factbook/* updated annually.

   Encyclopedia Britannica Almanac 2003, 1st ed. (Encyclopedia Britannica Books), March 6, 2003.

   Guinness World Records 2004 (Guinness World Records Editors), published annually.

   The New York Public Library Desk Reference, 4th ed., Paul Forgis, ed. (Hyperion Press), December 2002.

   The New York Times 2003 Almanac, John W. Wright, ed. (Penguin USA), November 2002.

   Time Almanac 2003: With Information Please 2003, 1st ed., Borgna Brunner, ed. (Time, Inc., Home Entertainment), formerly *Information Please Almanac.*

   The World Almanac and Book of Facts 2004, Ken Park, ed. (World Almanac), December 2003, published annually.

2. *Biographical Indexes and Dictionaries:* These publications highlight the achievements of noted individuals who contributed to their professions, to government, or to the country. The publishers' Web sites typically include descriptions of each publication.

   G. & C. Merriam Company, Springfield, Massachusetts (*www.m-w.com*)
   Merriam-Webster's Biographical Dictionary
   Merriam-Webster's Pocket Biographical Dictionary

   The H. W. Wilson Company, New York (*www.hwwilson.com*)
   Biography Index
   Biography Reference Bank
   Current Biography Illustrated
   Wilson Biographies Plus Illustrated

   Houghton Mifflin Publishing Co., Inc., Boston (*www.houghtonmifflinbooks.com*)
   The Houghton Mifflin Dictionary of Biography

Marquis Who's Who, Inc., Chicago, Illinois (*www.marquiswhoswho.com*)
Who Was Who in America
Who's Who in America
Who's Who on the Web
Who's Who in 20th Century America

Oxford University Press, Oxford, England (*www.oup.com*)
Oxford Dictionary of National Biography
American National Biography Online

3. ***Book and Periodical Directories and Indexes:*** **Directories** provide listings of companies, associations, organizations, individuals, or products in a systematic way—alphabetically, geographically, or in subject arrangements in index form.

The H. W. Wilson Company, New York (*www.hwwilson.com*)

WilsonWeb Periodical Databases (with searching by key words, title of book or article):
Applied Science and Technology Index
Book Review Digest Plus
Wilson Business Full Text

Book Review Digest: Published monthly and available on CD-ROM and in print, the digest contains excerpts from and citations to reviews of more than 8,000 books per year. Coverage includes 109 publications.

Business Periodicals Index: Published annually, this index has a subject index to over 600 periodicals in finance, insurance, banking, accounting, marketing, information processing, and other business-related subjects.

Cumulative Book Index: Published monthly, this index lists most of the books published in the United States from 1928 to the present. The books are arranged alphabetically by author, title, and subject.

Index to Legal Periodicals: Published annually, this index includes references to articles on various law-related topics. Both subject and specific case name indexes to articles are included.

Reader's Guide Full Text, Mega Edition: With daily updates, searchable full text is available for articles published as far back as 1994. An index of other published articles as far back as 1983 and in-depth abstracts of published articles as far back as 1983 are also included.

Reader's Guide to Periodical Literature: This guide is published semimonthly and includes indexing of more than 300 periodicals.

Gale Group—Thomson Learning, Detroit (*www.galegroup.com*)

Directory of Publications and Broadcast Media: This media directory contains thousands of listings for radio and television stations and cable companies. Print media entries provide address; phone, fax, and e-mail addresses; and key personnel. Broadcast media entries provide address; phone, fax, and e-mail addresses; key personnel; and owner information.

R. R. Bowker Company, New York (*www.booksinprint.com*)

Books in Print: Published annually, this directory contains over 4.7 million book titles, over 600,000 full-text reviews, and 7,000 author biographies.

McRae's Blue Book Company

McRae's Blue Book, a directory of manufacturers by product.

4. ***Business, Governmental, and Professional Directories and Publications:*** In addition to book and periodical directories, listings of members of professional associations, governmental directories and records, and business directories and publications are extremely helpful in locating appropriate sources of information.

   a. *Professional associations:* A large number of professional associations maintain Web sites to provide basic information about the association, membership, and publications. Here is a sample of professional associations with their respective Web site addresses:

   American Bar Association (www.abanet.org)
Legal and professional resources, membership information, law student resources, general public resources, and publications are highlighted at the ABA Web site.

   American Dental Association (www.ada.org)
The ADA Web site provides information about the history and mission of the ADA, conferences, health news, directories, products, services, and membership.

   American Medical Association (www.ama-assn.org)
AMA's Web site includes medical news, multimedia highlights of conferences, information about upcoming events, and newsletters.

   Association of Records Managers and Administrators (www.arma.org)
The ARMA Web site includes information about seminars, upcoming events, and publications.

   International Association for Administrative Professionals (www.iaap-hq.org)
This Web site provides information about IAAP, membership information, local chapters, publications, and professional certification programs.

   b. *Governmental directories, records, and information:* The U.S. Government produces a wealth of information daily. The official, published electronic version of public information is available through **GPO Access** (www.access.gpo.gov/). The information available at this Web site can be used without restriction, unless otherwise noted.

   This free service is funded by the Federal Depository Library Program and has grown out of Public Law 103–40, The Government Printing Office Electronic Information Enhancement Act of 1993. The following categories of free services are now available:

   • *Government information databases:* This service includes free online use of over 2,200 databases of Federal information in over 80 applications. *GPO Access* databases include:

     The Federal Register
     The Code of Federal Regulations
     Congressional Record
     Congressional Bills

   • *Permanent public access:* Permanent access is provided to the public for government information products residing on *GPO Access* servers. Public access to official government information products disseminated through the Federal Depository Library Program must be maintained permanently in regional depository libraries and by depository libraries not served by a regional library.

- *Tools to locate government information:* A number of useful, free tools are available to assist the public in finding government information:
  - ✓ Finding and ordering products available for sale through the Superintendent of Documents.
  - ✓ Exploring links to free, official Federal information available electronically.
  - ✓ Searching more than 1,350 official U.S. Federal agency and military Internet sites using key words.
- *Collections of government information available through the Federal Depository Libraries:* Searches can be conducted for information available in Federal depository library collections.
- *Federal agency files available for download:* Over 7,500 individual Federal agency files, in a variety of formats, are available for free download from the Federal Bulletin Board, providing the public with free, immediate, and self-service access to Federal information in electronic form.
- *User support:* The *GPO Access* Web site also provides contact information for trained specialists who are available on a daily basis to answer questions on GPO's electronic products and services.
- *Biennial Report to Congress on the Status of GPO Access*

c. *Business directories and publications:* Many times business research involves the use of published directories and research publications available through private business sources. Here are a few prominent business directories that are available:

Resourcelinks Business Directory (*www.resourcelinks.net*)
This Web site contains state directories for businesses and services and resource centers for comprehensive information. Searches by business name or type may be conducted.

Standard & Poor's Register of Corporations, Directors, and Executives, United States and Canada (Standard and Poor's, New York) (*www.standardandpoors.com*)

A set of three volumes is published annually. Cumulative supplements are published every April, July, and October.

Volume 1: The Corporation Directory

Over 55,000 corporations are listed alphabetically. Information included for each corporation: full corporate name, headquarters address, telephone number, names and titles of officers, directors, and principals; description of products and services.

Volume 2: Register of Directors and Executives

Over 70,000 officers, directors, and executives of more than 55,000 corporations are listed. Biographical information is given for all who are listed in the Register. The index is arranged alphabetically by corporate name and executive's name.

Volume 3: Special Indices

The following color-coded index sections are included in this volume:

- Standard Industrial Classification Index
- Standard Industrial Classification Codes
- Geographical Index
- Corporate Family Indices

- Obituary Section
- New Individual Additions
- New Company Additions

Thomas Register of American Manufacturers, (Thomas Publication Company, New York) (*www.thomasregister.com*)
The Thomas Register features a directory of over 173,000 U.S. and Canadian manufacturers, manufacturing information, product lines and addresses. Information on manufacturers' names and products is available on CD-ROM, DVD-ROM, in print, or online.

5. ***Business Newspapers and Periodicals:*** Current business information is available in numerous newspapers and periodicals published in the United States. Online editions of many of these publications are also available, many times on a subscription basis. Here is an annotated list of some of the more prominent publications:

Barron's, published weekly (Dow Jones & Company, Inc., New York) (*www.barrons.com*): National business and financial news is presented in articles on investments, industries, trends, and other business topics; stock and bond prices are included; online subscription is available.

Business Week, published weekly (McGraw-Hill Book Company, New York) (*www.businessweek.com*): Articles on specialized business topics present the important business indicators, the investment outlook, and current business developments; online subscription is available.

ComputerWorld, published weekly (ComputerWorld, Inc.) (*www.computerworld.com*): The publication includes business-focused technology news and analyses for information technology leaders. Featured white papers provide up-to-date technological news.

Forbes, published semimonthly (Forbes, Inc., New York) (*www.forbes.com*): Special features include the Forbes 500—America's Leading Companies and the Forbes International 500 Survey. The publication includes articles on business administration, new developments in business, and business outlooks.

Fortune, published 28 times per year (Time, Inc., New York) (*www.fortune.com*): This publication is known for the famous *Fortune* lists of the largest corporations (the Fortune 500, the Fortune 100, the 100 Best to Work For). *Fortune* also publishes special sections on business automation, communications, computer technology, and other current topics two or three times per year.

Harvard Business Review, published bimonthly (Graduate School of Business Administration, Harvard University, Boston) (*www.harvardbusinessonline.hbsp.harvard.edu*): This periodical is one of the outstanding business administration journals published today. The articles are written primarily for the practitioner in the field; online subscription is available.

InfoWorld, published weekly (InfoWorld Media Group, Inc.) (*www.infoworld.com*): The publication includes articles about current developments in information management and technology to help the business user function with personal computers and other information processing technology; online subscription is available.

The New York Times, published daily (The New York Times Company, Inc., New York) (*www.nytimes.com*): This newspaper is very well known for its current business news and coverage of daily business events; online subscription is available.

Wall Street Journal, published daily, Monday–Friday (Dow Jones & Company, Inc., New York) (*www.online.wsj.com*): This newspaper features business and financial news, articles on corporate strategies and events, and stock and bond prices on the various exchanges; online subscription is available.

6. **Dictionaries:** As a reference book, a **dictionary** has a very important function. Here are some of the more commonly used general and specialty dictionaries.

    a. *General dictionaries:* Administrative professionals use general dictionaries for help in finding the correct spelling of a term, the correct meaning and usage of a word or expression, and the correct syllabication of the word. Unabridged dictionaries can be especially helpful since they are the most complete dictionaries and are not based on a larger work.

        G. & C. Merriam-Webster, Springfield, Massachusetts (*www.m-w.com*)

           Merrian-Webster's Collegiate Dictionary

           Merriam-Webster's Desk Dictionary

           Merriam-Webster's Pocket Dictionary

           Webster's New International Dictionary, Unabridged

        Houghton-Mifflin Publishing Co., Inc., Boston (*www.houghtonmifflinbooks.com*)

           The American Heritage College Dictionary

           The American Heritage Dictionary of the English Language

           The American Heritage Dictionary for Learners of English

        Oxford University Press, Oxford, England (*www.oup.com*)

           Oxford English Dictionary (online, CD-ROM, and print editions available)

           Oxford Reference Online: (a database of 100 well-known dictionaries and reference books plus an encyclopedia)

        Random House, New York (*www.randomhouse.com*)

           The Random House Webster's Collegiate Dictionary

    b. *Specialty dictionaries:* Some professional dictionaries include the terminology most pertinent to a specific professional field. Others are designed to provide research assistance in finding specific types of information.

        G. & C. Merriam Webster, Springfield, Massachusetts (*www.m-w.com*)

           Webster's Geographical Dictionary

           Webster's Pocket Geographical Dictionary

           Merriam-Webster's Dictionary of Synonyms

           Merriam-Webster's Pocket Guide to Synonyms

           Merriam-Webster's Dictionary of Synonyms and Antonyms

           Merriam-Webster's Medical Dictionary

        Houghton-Mifflin Publishing Co., Inc., Boston, Massachusetts (*www.houghtonmifflinbooks.com*)

           Medical Dictionary: A Concise and Up-to-Date Guide to Medical Terms

        John Wiley & Sons, Inc., New York (*www.wiley.com*)

           Quick Medical Terminology: A Self-Teaching Guide

           Webster's New World Medical Dictionary

MedicineNet.com (*www.medicinenet.com*)
> *MedTerms Medical Dictionary* (online encyclopedic medical dictionary)

Simon & Schuster, New York (*www.simonsays.com*)
> *Webster's New World Dictionary*

c. *Other professional dictionaries:* Business organizations sometimes develop professional dictionaries with specialized terminology for a specific field.

Barron's, Dow Jones & Company, Inc., New York (*www.barronseduc.com*)
> *Barron's Finance and Investment Handbook*
> *Canadian Dictionary of Finance and Investment Terms*
> *Dictionary of Business Terms*
> *Dictionary of Finance and Investment Terms*
> *Dictionary of International Investment Terms*

Foreign-language dictionaries are particularly helpful to administrative professionals who must translate correspondence and reports or look up foreign words and phrases. Such dictionaries list words or phrases in two ways, for example, French to English in one section and English to French in another section.

7. *Encyclopedias:* As a general rule, a set of **encyclopedias** is designed as one or more general reference books on a wide variety of topics. Some encyclopedias are designed to provide very detailed information, while others may be directed toward children's use or people within a particular profession. Many encyclopedias have annual supplements available that describe key highlights and events of the past year. Here is a sample list of some encyclopedias available today:

Encyclopaedia Brittanica, Brittanica Centre, Chicago (*www.brittanica.com*)
> *Encyclopaedia Brittanica*
> *2004 Britannica Software Reference*

Funk & Wagnalls, New York (*www.funkandwagnalls.com*)
> *Funk & Wagnalls New Encyclopedia*

Gale Group, Detroit, Michigan (*www.galegroup.com*)
> *Encyclopedia of Associations: International Organizations*
> *Encyclopedia of Associations: National Organizations of the U.S.*
> *Encyclopedia of Associations: Regional, State, and Local Organizations*

Grolier, Danbury, Connecticut (*www.grolier.com*)
> *The Encyclopedia Americana*

World Book, Chicago (*www.worldbook.com*)
> *The World Book Encyclopedia*

8. *Etiquette References:* Current **etiquette references** focus on conventional requirements of social behavior and conduct as established for specific occasions. Some of the more well-known references are listed here:

Pachter, Barbara, and Susan Magee, *When the Little Things Count . . . and They Always Count: 601 Essential Things that Everyone in Business Needs to Know*, Marlowe & Company, 2001.

Post, Peggy, *Emily Post's Etiquette*, 16th ed., HarperCollins Publishers, New York, 1997.

Post, Peggy, *Everyday Etiquette*, Harper Paperbacks, New York, 1999.

Post, Peggy, and Peter Post, *The Etiquette Advantage in Business: Personal Skills for Professional Success*, HarperResource, 1999.

Segaloff, Nat, *The Everything Etiquette Book*, Adams Media Corporation, Holbrook, Massachusetts, 1998.

Tuckerman, Nancy, and Nancy Dunnan, *The Amy Vanderbilt Complete Book of Etiquette*, Doubleday, New York, 1995.

9. ***Financial Services References:*** Subscription services are available to the financial community that will give the latest information on stock prices, industry developments, legislative changes affecting organizations, and other pertinent business and financial information.

The Conference Board, Inc., New York (*www.conference-board.org*)
> *Business Cycle Indicators, Straight Talk, Across the Board, Consumer Confidence Survey, The Conference Board Newsletter.* A not-for-profit organization that creates and disseminates information about management and the marketplace to help businesses strengthen their performance. Management research and networking opportunities build on the knowledge and experience shared by executives in more than 3,000 companies in 65 countries.

Dun & Bradstreet Corporation, New York (*www.dnb.com/us/*)
> Global provider of company credit reports and profiles, risk evaluation reports, and sales and marketing solutions. Divisions: Market Data Retrieval, Small Business Solutions. Regional Offices: Australia, Czech Republic, Dun & Bradstreet Canada, Dun & Bradstreet Israel, Dun & Bradstreet UK, Ireland, and Latin America.

Moody's Investors Service, New York (*www.moodys.com*)
> *Mergent Manuals (formerly Moody's Manuals): Bank & Finance, Industrial, International, Municipal and Government, OTC Industrial, OTC Unlisted, Public Utilities, Transportation.* Annual with weekly or twice-weekly news issues. Summarizes information found in annual reports and news services and includes income statements.
> *Mergent Bond Record (formerly Moody's Bond Record):* Monthly publication that covers bond issues and gives the user information on market position and statistical background.
> *Mergent Online:* Database of statistics and information on more than 21,000 U.S. and international companies. Includes information on long-term debt issues of each company and a snapshot of each issue with ratings. Updated weekly.

Standard & Poor's Corporation, New York (*www.standardandpoors.com*):
> *Standard and Poor's Corporation/Bond Guide.* Monthly.
> *Standard and Poor's CreditWeek.* Weekly.
> *Standard and Poor's Net Advantage.* Database of statistics and articles. Includes *Bond Guide, Corporation Records, Dividend Record, Earnings Guide, Industry Surveys, Mutual Fund Reports, The Outlook, Standard & Poor's Register, Stock Guide,* and *Standard & Poor's Stock Reports.* Updated weekly.

Standard and Poor's Daily News: Financial information and business news on more than 12,000 publicly owned companies in which there is any degree of investor interest. The database is a major source of financial information for competitive analysis and investing.

Standard and Poor's Corporation, *Standard and Poor's Guide to Technology Stocks*, 1st edition, McGraw-Hill Trade, April 18, 2002.

10. ***Mailing and Shipping Publications:*** Changes in postage rates, directions for using ZIP + 4 Codes, and shipping information will be applied more easily if the references located at the Web site *www.usps.com* for the U.S. Postal Service are used.

   At the Web site, clicking on "All Products and Services" brings up an alphabetical list of postal products and services. Then, clicking on "Publications" will bring up an entire list of postal manuals and guides that can be accessed as needed. Here are a few of the information services that are especially helpful:

   > *Guide to Mailing for Businesses and Organizations*
   > *International Mail Manual*
   > *ZIP Code* (to look up actual ZIP Codes)
   > *ZIP + 4* (information about ZIP + 4 Codes)

   Bullinger's Postal and Shippers Guide for the United States and Canada, Bullinger's Guides, Inc., Westwood, New Jersey (published annually).

   Dun & Bradstreet Exporters' Encyclopedia, Dun & Bradstreet, Inc., New York (latest edition).

11. ***Newsletters and Reports:*** Some organizations publish weekly or monthly newsletters or reports that present relevant, up-to-date information on new developments in particular business-related areas. Professional organizations often publish newsletters for members.

   Kiplinger Washington Letter, published weekly (Kiplinger Washington Editors, Inc., Washington, D.C.): A letter service that covers developments and trends in business and government.

   John Naisbitt's Trend Letter, published twice monthly (John Naisbitt's Trend Letter, Inc., Washington, D.C.): An authoritative report on forces transforming the economy, business, technology, society, and the world from 1982 to present.

12. ***Newspaper Indexes:*** To make it easier for people to research particular topics or subjects that appear in the daily newspapers, some of the larger newspapers in the country have established a printed **index** to the newspaper issues.

   The New York Times Index, published semimonthly (New York Times, New York) (*www.nytimes.com*): This index provides a subject index valuable to researchers in many fields of study. Included in the index are brief abstracts of articles found in the *New York Times* newspaper, along with date, column number, and page where the entire article may be found.

   Wall Street Journal Index (Dow Jones & Company, Inc., New York) (*www.online.wsj.com*): This published index includes reference to every news item published in the *Wall Street Journal*.

13. ***Office Administration Reference Books:*** The administrative professional will find a wide variety of reference books dealing with office administration extremely helpful. Here is a representative list of some of the reference books available:

   Clark, James L., and Lyn Clark, *How 10: A Handbook for Office Workers*, 10th ed., Thompson/South-Western, Cincinnati, 2004 (workbook also available).

Editors of the American Heritage Dictionaries, *New Office Professional's Handbook: How to Survive and Thrive in Today's Office Environment*, 4th ed., Houghton Mifflin Company, Boston, 2001.

House, Clifford R., and Kathie S. Sigler, *Multimedia Reference for Writers*, Thomson/South-Western, Cincinnati, 1996.

House, Clifford R., and Kathie S. Sigler, *Reference Manual for the Office*, South-Western Educational Publishing, Cincinnati, 1994.

Jaderstrom, Susan, Leonard Kruk, Joanne Miller, and Susan Fenner, *International Association of Administrative Professionals® Complete Office Handbook*, 3rd ed., Random House Reference, New York, 2002.

Sabin, William A., *The Gregg Reference Manual*, 9th ed., McGraw-Hill Book Company, Inc., New York, 2003.

14. ***Parliamentary Procedures:*** Appropriate conduct of business meetings will depend on the application of **parliamentary procedures** by the people involved. These references should serve as excellent guides for conducting meetings.

Jones, Ossie Garfield, *Parliamentary Procedure at a Glance*, Viking Press, New York, 1990.

Robert, Henry M. III, William J. Evans, Daniel H. Honemann, and Thomas J. Balch, *Robert's Rules of Order Newly Revised*, Perseus Publishing, 2000.

Robert McConnell Productions, *Webster's New World Robert's Rules of Order Simplified and Applied*, Webster's New World, 2001.

15. ***Quotations:*** The administrative professional who assists the executive in preparing speeches or other presentations may find these references helpful in locating appropriate quotations to interject in presentations.

Bartlett, John, and Justin Kaplan, eds., *Bartlett's Familiar Quotations*, 17th ed., Little Brown & Company, New York, 2002.

Cook, John, *The Book of Positive Quotations*, Gramercy, 1999.

Knowles, Elizabeth, ed., *The Oxford Dictionary of Quotations*, Getty Center for Education in the Arts, 1999.

The Princeton Language Institute, *21st Century Dictionary of Quotations*, Dell Publishing, 1993.

Strumpf, Michael, *Webster's Dictionary of Quotations*, Random House, New York, 2003.

16. ***Thesauri:*** A **thesaurus** is a lexicon (dictionary) of similar words or information that focuses on synonyms and antonyms. Here are some thesauri that are used frequently:

Hickok, Ralph, *Roget's II: The New Thesaurus*, Houghton Mifflin Publishing Company, Boston, 2003.

Kipfer, Barbara Ann, *Roget International Thesaurus Indexed Edition*, Harper-Collins, 2001.

Morehead, Philip D., ed., *The New American Roget's College Thesaurus: In Dictionary Form*, 3rd ed., Signet, 2002.

Webster's New World, *Webster's New World Thesaurus*, 3rd ed., Simon & Schuster, New York, 2003.

17. ***Travel and Transportation Guides:*** Current editions of travel and transportation guides, atlases, and road maps are available through bookstores, automobile associations, motor clubs, oil companies, and the World Wide Web. A listing of some of the most commonly used travel and transportation guides, including the ***Official Airline Guides,*** is shown here.

Rand McNally, Chicago (*www.randmcnally.com*)
   Answer Atlas: Rand McNally World Atlas Series
   Rand McNally World Atlas Quick Reference
   The Road Atlas 2004
   United States Maps
   International Maps

American Hotel and Lodging Association (*www.ahma.com*)
   Directory of Hotel and Lodging Companies, by subscription; digital directory is available.

The New York Times Company, Inc., New York
   The New York Times Atlas of the World
      "Destination Guides" available at *(www.nytimes.com)*.

Official Airline Guides, Oak Brook, Illinois (*www.oag.com*)
   OAG Express (annual subscription)
   OAGflights.com (annual subscription)
   OAG Executive Flight Guide™ North America with OAG club membership
   OAG Executive Flight Guide™ Europe, Africa, and Middle East with OAG club membership
   OAG Executive Flight Guide™ Latin America and Caribbean with OAG club membership
   OAG Executive Flight Guide™ Asia and Pacific with OAG club membership
   OAG Flight Guide® North America, monthly or semimonthly with OAG club membership
   OAG Flight Guide® Worldwide with OAG club membership
   OAG Flight Planner™ for Windows® includes *OAGflights.com* and OAG club membership
   OAG Flight Planner™ Online includes *OAGflights.com* and OAG club membership
   OAG Official Travel Planner™
   OAG Official Travel Planner™ for Windows® includes *OAGflights.com* and OAG club membership
   OAG Official Travel Planner™ Online includes *OAGflights.com* and OAG club membership

Internet travel sites such as *www.mapquest.com* and *www.randmcnally.com* may also be accessed for road maps, driving instructions, trip planners, and other travel information.

18. ***Word Books:*** The availability of at least one word book is very important to the administrative professional who uses a computer with word processing software or dictation-transcription systems. A **word book** presents an alphabetical list of the

most frequently used words and indicates the spelling, syllabication, and recommended hyphenation.

Perry, Devern J., *South-Western Spelling Reference*, 5th ed., South-Western Educational Publishing, Cincinnati, 2000.

Leslie, Louis A., Charles E. Zoubek, and G. A. Condon, *20,000+ Words*, McGraw-Hill Book Company, New York (latest edition).

19. ***Writing Style Manuals:*** References like **writing style manuals** provide the administrative professional with assistance in preparing formal reports that require documentation (footnotes, endnotes, or in-text citations and bibliographies). Here are some of the most commonly used style manuals in business today:

The Chicago Manual of Style, 15th ed., The University of Chicago Press, Chicago, 2003.

Gibaldi, Joseph, *MLA Handbook for Writers of Research Papers*, 6th ed., The Modern Language Association of America, New York, 2003.

Martin, Paul, *The Wall Street Journal Essential Guide to Business Style and Usage*, Wall Street Journal Books, 2003.

Publication Manual of the American Psychological Association, 5th ed., American Psychological Association, Washington, D.C., 2001.

Strunk, William, Jr., and E. B. White, *The Elements of Style*, 4th ed., Allyn & Bacon, New York, 2000.

Check Point—Section C

Directions: For each question, circle the correct answer.

C–1. If you are looking for a new book titled *Business Technology for the Year 2010* and you know the publisher but not the author, which one of the following sources would help you locate the name of the author?

    A) *Ayer's Directory of Publications*
    B) *Webster's Biographical Dictionary*
    C) *Books in Print*
    D) *Reader's Guide to Periodical Literature*

C–2. Which one of the following information references would help you find out more about a point of order in a meeting?

    A) *The Book of Positive Quotations*
    B) *Robert's Rules of Order*

    C) *How 10: A Handbook for Office Workers*
    D) The Web site *www.usps.com*

C–3. Which one of the following information references would be the most helpful if you wanted to find other words that would mean the same as the word *cognizant*?

    A) *Parliamentary Procedure at a Glance*
    B) *Roget's II: The New Thesaurus*
    C) *The Book of Positive Quotations*
    D) *Wall Street Journal Index*

D. Evaluating Information References

In researching specific topics or subjects, the office professional needs to evaluate the content as well as the source for that information in judging whether its use will be beneficial to the work in progress. Of particular concern is information found on the World Wide Web that may not have passed editorial scrutiny as other types of publications (periodical articles or books) go through before printing. The following guidelines can be applied to information gained through research to help the administrative professional determine its value to a particular writing project.

1. ***The Author or Institution:*** Each reference should be examined to see how the material originated—who the author is or the institution where the information was gathered. Some of the types of information to look for include the following:

    - Name(s) of author(s)
    - Biographical information about each author
    - Information about the institution where the research or project took place
    - Other sources of information that include the author's name(s) or the institution's name
    - Reference lists and/or bibliographies included with the article or book
    - Publication or copyright date

2. ***Currency of Information:*** Another factor to consider is the recency of the information. Current, up-to-date information will typically have the most relevance to the topic unless the research is for historical purposes. Here are some features of the publication that should be considered:

    - Date of publication or date on the Web page(s) indicating when the material was changed, updated, or copyrighted
    - Date of last update of information; indication of frequency of updates
    - Outdated information included in the material

3. ***The Intended Audience:*** The researcher should consider the intended audience when examining an informational reference. The reference may be designed for a specific group of people, such as one of the following:

    - The general public
    - Researchers
    - Business practitioners
    - Members of a professional organization
    - Others, such as children or parents

4. ***Accurate and Objective Content:*** The purpose of the information may be to inform, persuade, or entertain the audience. The content should be examined carefully to determine whether any of the following is present:

    - Purpose of the information
    - Biases apparent in the content
    - Brief overview or in-depth analysis
    - Properly cited facts and statistics
    - Clearly stated opinions

The content of a report or speech will always be strengthened by the inclusion of information gathered from a variety of credible sources. Information is a valuable resource when used carefully to support creative ideas and developments. The administrative professional often has the important responsibility of collecting information from a variety of sources, ensuring that the originators of that information are properly cited within the writing, and assisting the executive in preparing business documents that enhance the image of the organization.

Check Point—Section D

Directions: For each question, circle the correct answer.

D–1. The content of a source of information found on the World Wide Web and the Internet needs to be evaluated because the

   A) reference may not have faced editorial review as evident with other types of publications
   B) general public usually asks for the results of such an evaluation
   C) user may be searching for creative references
   D) originators of the information may be cited in a number of different sources

D–2. Which one of the following items relating to an information source found at a Web site would pose a serious problem in deciding to cite the information as a reference?

   A) Copyright date is identified at the end of the Web site
   B) Links to other Web sites are included in the article
   C) A dot-com organization originated the information
   D) The article does not appear to have an author

D–3. A report's content will be strengthened if

   A) the author is cited in more than one publication
   B) the publication or copyright date is not available at the site
   C) information from several sources is included
   D) biased articles are used to support the writer's opinion

For Your Review

Directions: For each question, circle the correct answer.

1. Before embarking on any type of research, an administrative professional must know
   A) what types of articles or other references are needed
   B) facilities available for research
   C) the purpose of the research
   D) personal contacts that will be necessary to locate information

2. Specific information about a particular company or industry can best be found by searching
   A) Internet Web sites
   B) libraries
   C) published books and articles
   D) personal contacts

3. Estimating the cost of doing research is necessary to
   A) keep accurate records of research information
   B) make appointments for conducting primary research
   C) conduct Internet searches to get specific types of information
   D) stay within budget limits for the research to be conducted

4. Which one of the following research activities will yield primary data?
   A) A research study conducted by two professors in a nearby university
   B) An interview with a business professional in the field
   C) A book on the topic authored by two business practitioners
   D) An article appearing in the latest issue of *Business Week Online*

5. Which one of the following types of information is required in a bibliographic entry?
   A) ISBN number of the publication
   B) Library of Congress classification number code
   C) Web address for an Internet reference
   D) Dewey Decimal System classification number code

6. To assist in locating specific facts or data already obtained through researching a topic,
   A) electronic bookmarks can be inserted at key points
   B) all the notes for one subject or topic can be placed in a folder
   C) multiple copies of the written notes need to be prepared
   D) develop an interview guide

7. One specific reference refers to more than one topic so you have notes for each subtopic. Where is the best place for you to record these notes?
   A) Place notes for each subtopic on the same cards
   B) Keep the note cards and the information for the bibliographic entries in the same file
   C) Record the notes for each subtopic on separate note cards
   D) Make a duplicate copy of the notes for each subtopic

8. A library consortium is a
   A) public library with special collections of references
   B) college or university library which also has an archive
   C) network of libraries that permits sharing of reference holdings
   D) library network of business archives for a specific industry

9. Abstracts of research studies, court cases, and other types of professional references may be accessed through computerized databases known as
   A) reference collections
   B) information banks
   C) business archives
   D) in-house research services

10. The high level of security maintained in archives is shown by the policy that
    A) references must be used only on the premises
    B) a professional association needs to maintain the archive
    C) an industry-specific research department is established
    D) references can be checked out for only one day at a time

11. When a topic is being researched for a report and/or presentation,
    A) one specific information reference should provide the majority of information used
    B) primary information comes from information references
    C) an in-house research department should conduct the research
    D) different types of information references should be accessed

12. A publication that includes factual information about international and national events of the year is a/an
    A) biographical index
    B) periodical directory
    C) almanac
    D) business directory

13. A publisher's Web site can be a helpful information source for a

A) description of publications pertinent to a particular topic
B) description of a specific publication of that company
C) listing of all books in print
D) directory of companies and associations in a specific industry

14. Which one of the following information sources would be best for a list of published articles that pertain to the use of automated teller machines (ATMs) in the banking industry?
    A) *Applied Science and Technology Index*
    B) *Book Review Digest*
    C) *Cumulative Book Index*
    D) *Business Periodicals Index*

15. A professional association's Web site will most likely include information about
    A) specific publications of the association
    B) books published and in print for the current year
    C) *GPO Access* and government publications
    D) online information databases available

16. You have just heard about a Congressional bill concerning the establishment of ergonomic standards affecting the responsibilities of the Occupational Safety and Health Administration. Which one of the following information references will help you locate the most current legislation?
    A) Federal Depository Library Program
    B) Biennial Report to Congress
    C) GPO Access Web site to government information databases
    D) Federal Bulletin Board

17. The Web site that provides access to directories for businesses and services in all 50 states in the United States is the
    A) *Standard and Poor's Corporation Directory*
    B) *Thomas Register of American Manufacturers*

C)   *Fortune* magazine

D)   Resourcelinks Business Directory

18. Which one of the following information sources provides the most up-to-date information technology news?

A)   *Harvard Business Review*

B)   *ComputerWorld*

C)   *Wall Street Journal*

D)   *Business Week Online*

19. Specialty foreign-language dictionaries are especially helpful to administrative professionals who need to

A)   look up meanings of technical terms used in English

B)   locate more details about a specific topic

C)   translate business correspondence from one language to another

D)   find out the syllabication and hyphenation of a word in English

20. You are planning business travel to Portugal to see if your company should form a business association with a local partner. Which one of these references would no doubt help you identify acceptable social behaviors for your international travel?

A)   Moody's Investors Service *Mergent Manuals*

B)   *Kiplinger Washington Letter*

C)   *How 10: A Handbook for Office Workers* (by James L. and Lyn Clark)

D)   *The Etiquette Advantage in Business* (by Peggy and Peter Post)

21. Access to the Web site *www.usps.com* helps the administrative professional locate

A)   ZIP + 4 Codes for mailing in the United States

B)   *Wall Street Journal* articles on technological developments in business

C)   information from the *Congressional Record*

D)   a general reference manual for office professionals

22. Internet travel sites like *www.mapquest. com* allow access to

A)   airline tickets for all major air flights

B)   cultural and etiquette references for international travel

C)   driving instructions from one city to another in the United States

D)   hotel reservations for a domestic business trip

23. Which one of the following characteristics of an Internet reference would cause the researcher to question the value of the information in the article?

A)   A reference list is included with the article

B)   A publication date is not shown in the article

C)   The information came from research sponsored by Harvard University

D)   The co-authors' names are included at the Web site

24. The currency of the information found at a Web site could be determined most easily in which of the following situations?

A)   The date of the last update, February 20, 2003, is included

B)   Statistical information from the year 1995 to the year 2000 is included in the article

C)   A copyright or publication date does not appear on the article

D)   How frequently the Web site is updated is not indicated

25. An administrative professional has the responsibility for collecting information from different sources and

A)   limiting the number of sources cited in a report

B)   providing a brief overview of each source used

C)   explaining biases found in specific sources

D)   citing the originators of that information properly

Solutions

Solutions to Check Point—Section A

Answer	Refer to:
A–1. (B)	[A-1]
A–2. (C)	[A-5-a]
A–3. (A)	[A-5-c]

Solutions to Check Point—Section B

Answer	Refer to:
B–1. (B)	[B-1-a (1)]
B–2. (D)	[B-2-b]
B–3. (D)	[B-2-c]

Solutions to Check Point—Section C

Answer	Refer to:
C–1. (C)	[C-3]
C–2. (B)	[C-14]
C–3. (B)	[C-16]

Solutions to Check Point—Section D

	Answer	Refer to:
D–1.	(A)	[D]
D–2.	(D)	[D-1]
D–3.	(C)	[D-4]

Solutions to For Your Review

	Answer	Refer to:
1.	(C)	[A-1]
2.	(A)	[A-2-e]
3.	(D)	[A-3]
4.	(B)	[A-5]
5.	(C)	[A-5-a]
6.	(A)	[A-5-b (1)]
7.	(C)	[A-5-b (2)]
8.	(C)	[B-1]
9.	(B)	[B-1-e]
10.	(A)	[B-2-c]
11.	(D)	[C]
12.	(C)	[C-1]
13.	(B)	[C-2]
14.	(D)	[C-3]
15.	(A)	[C-4-a]
16.	(C)	[C-4-b]
17.	(D)	[C-4-c]
18.	(B)	[C-5]
19.	(C)	[C-6-c]

20. (D)   [C-8]

21. (A)   [C-10]

22. (C)   [C-17]

23. (B)   [D-1]

24. (A)   [D-2]

25. (D)   [D-4]

Chapter 7

Composing and Editing Written Communication

OVERVIEW

Business communication, both oral and written, is the lifeblood of any organization. In your position as an administrative professional, the use of excellent communication skills will have a tremendous effect on your relationships with executives, co-workers, organization leaders, and customers. Skill development in composing and editing written communication for later reference and review is the main focus of this chapter. Many of these guidelines, however, are applicable to oral communication as well.

A written message must be complete, coherent, and logical so that the receiver will be able to understand the sender's intended meaning of the message. The receiver has limited opportunity to ask questions if ideas presented are not clear. Improper word choice, sentence and paragraph construction, and parallelism affect the presentation of clear, understandable messages. Language must be used that will evoke clear mental images as the message is being read.

Proofreading and editing are crucial elements in the writing process. Some writers spend a great amount of time and effort researching and writing, then neglect to revise the draft with the reader in mind. Editing software is especially helpful when two or more people, sometimes in different locations, are involved in the editing phase. The end result needs to be the "perfect" document, one to be proud of.

KEY TERMS

A. Effective Word Selection

Words selected for use in the message must be appropriate for the situation. Words with the right denotative meaning (literal meaning) and connotative meaning (feeling or impression conveyed) must be selected. The key to effective word selection is to use specific nouns, action verbs, and descriptive adjectives and adverbs.

1. *Positive Language:* Business writing needs to be positive. People react to positivism by wanting to read, to think, and to act.

    a. *Focus on the reader:* Messages should be written from the reader's viewpoint. Direct the message to the reader. Focus on the use of pronouns such as *you* and *your* rather than *I* or *me*. This is often called the "you" view or the "you" approach.

        (1) Express what has been done in a positive manner. What has already been accomplished should be the focus rather than what should have been done or what cannot be done.

        (2) Emphasize the reader's interest in the subject of the message.

        (3) Compliment the receiver of the message, if appropriate to the situation.

    b. *Limited use of negative expressions:* Messages should limit the use of negative expressions. A letter or memorandum should not be written in a moment of anger.

        (1) Avoid using the word *not* or contractions containing *not*.

        EXAMPLE:

        Positive: *Remember to call us the next time you need help with your office décor.*

        Avoid: *Don't forget to call us for help with your office décor.*

        (2) Avoid using negative expressions that tend to express doubt or sorrow or unnecessarily accuse the reader. Words like *regret*, *unfortunately*, *apologize*, *neglected*, and *failed* have negative connotations.

        EXAMPLE:

        Negative: *You failed to enclose a check to pay for the order.*

        Revision: *Please send a check to pay for the order by June 15.*

2. *Tone:* The manner in which a certain attitude is expressed is referred to as **tone.** What you choose to say and how you say it determine the tone of your writing. More effective business writing conveys a tone that is friendly, conversational, businesslike, objective, and personalized. Tone, together with style, creates an overall impression with the reader.

3. *Familiar Words:* In conversation and writing during a typical business day, most people use only 1,000 to 1,500 words out of the more than 700,000 words in our language. Most words in the English language are unfamiliar to many of us.

    a. *Synonyms:* Use commonly known synonyms for unfamiliar words.

b. *Technical words:* Avoid confusing unfamiliar words with technical words. When writing to a member of the same profession, technical words may be used without an explanation. However, the same terms may need to be explained when writing to a person outside the profession.

c. *English equivalents:* The English equivalents for foreign expressions may be used. Use foreign expressions only when these expressions fit the topic or the receiver's cultural background.

d. *Jargon:* Refrain from using jargon in business writing. **Jargon** is defined as technical language pertinent to a specific profession or group.

e. *Acronyms:* Spell out acronyms when first used in a document, followed by the acronym in parentheses. An **acronym** is a word formed with the initials of words in a set phrase or name. After the complete name and acronym have been presented, just the acronym can be used in succeeding references.

EXAMPLE: *The American Management Association (AMA) is a professional organization for people employed in management positions. The AMA also offers membership to college and university professors of business.*

f. *Slang:* Avoid using slang expressions because the intended meaning may not be conveyed to the receiver. **Slang,** a form of jargon, is defined as expressions that are idiomatic (peculiar to a particular language) that cannot be translated literally into another language.

EXAMPLES:

beat around the bush	*to evade the issue*
put up with	*to tolerate*

4. ***Concrete Language:*** Being precise and specific in writing is very important. The use of words and terms with meanings that people generally agree on helps to make language more precise. Some words are too general to effectively convey a message. **Concrete language** refers to the use of words and terms that are precise in meaning. **Abstract language** refers to the quality of language where meanings can be interpreted differently by different people, even in the same type of situation.

a. A word or phrase may be added to an abstract word to define it more precisely.

EXAMPLE: *building*

The Sears Tower is the tallest building in Chicago, Illinois.

b. The abstract term may be explained within the sentence.

EXAMPLE: *application*

You may use application software to prepare a business letter.

You may use word processing software to prepare a business letter.

(Word processing refers to the specific software application.)

c. The most specific, concrete word possible should be used when it is important to the meaning of the message.

EXAMPLE: *building*

bank, restaurant, library

d. Short, simple words convey the meaning much more directly and more clearly than do long, complex words. Of course, choose the word most appropriate to the reader.

EXAMPLES:

Short, Simple Words	Long, Complex Words
later	subsequent
people	professionals
car, truck, bus	vehicle
use	application

5. **Active Words:** Active words denote *action by a performer*, whereas passive words emphasize *inaction or waiting for something to happen.* The use of active verbs, descriptive adjectives, and descriptive adverbs will create more action in your writing.

a. *Active verbs:* Verbs denote the action that is taking place. An action verb conveys a precise meaning, which is what is needed in business writing. Such verbs convey the degree of precision in the action being expressed.

EXAMPLES:

Active Verbs	Passive Verbs
speaks	is conversing
writes	is composing
participates	will be meeting

b. *Active and passive voice:* When the performer of the task is emphasized, we are writing in active voice. When the action being taken is emphasized rather than the performer of the action, we are writing in passive voice.

EXAMPLE:

Active Voice

Meyers placed the order for the new computers needed in the marketing department. The emphasis in this sentence is on who *placed the order (the performer).*

Passive Voice

The order for the new computers in the marketing department was placed by Meyers.
The emphasis in this sentence is on what *happened to the order.*

In business writing, a combination of sentences using both active and passive voice is needed. Sometimes you need to emphasize the performer of the task; at other times, what actually occurred, rather than the performer, is more important.

c. *Descriptive adjectives:* Adjectives are used to describe nouns or pronouns used as subjects or objects of sentences and to support active verbs. Descriptive adjectives are sometimes called key words or **descriptors.** As descriptors, adjectives may be precise or imprecise in the way they describe nouns or pronouns.

EXAMPLES:

Imprecise Descriptors

good   better   best   fine   real

Precise Descriptors

A <u>cellular</u> telephone is a <u>sophisticated</u> <u>communication</u> system with such <u>digital</u> functions as <u>text</u> messaging, <u>web</u> browsers, and <u>electronic</u> games.

d. *Descriptive adverbs:* Adverbs modify verbs, adjectives, or other adverbs. Adverbs, too, need to be descriptive so that precise meanings are conveyed to the reader.

EXAMPLES:

Imprecise Descriptors

>   *nearly   well   fairly   barely   likely*

Precise Descriptors

>   *neatly   courteously   concisely   frequently*

Mervin <u>politely</u> asked for a <u>neatly</u> prepared report.

The use of active words will make your communication more meaningful to the receiver. Here are two examples of how exact information can be more helpful:

EXAMPLE:

Imprecise: Come in <u>early</u> tomorrow morning, and Smith will see you.

Precise: Come in <u>at 9:15</u> tomorrow morning, and Smith will see you.

6. ***Contemporary Words and Expressions:*** The selection of contemporary words and expressions makes your writing more relevant.

EXAMPLES:

>   *word processing   modular work space*
>   *hard copy   soft copy*
>   *Windows 2003 operating system*

7. ***Confusing Words:*** Effective word selection comes with practice. Some words in the English language are confusing and often used incorrectly. A review of some of these confusing words is presented here.

a. *Accept* and *except: Accept* means to receive or approve of; *except* means not to include.

EXAMPLES:

I accept your apology.

I have everyone's time card except yours.

b. *Advise* and *advice: Advise* is a verb meaning to make a recommendation; *advice* is a noun meaning counsel.

EXAMPLES:

My manager advised me to sit for the CPS exam.

I think using that reference is good advice.

c. *All ready* and *already*: *All ready* is an adjective phrase meaning everyone or everything is prepared; *already* is an adverb meaning before.

EXAMPLES:

The executives are all ready for the communications seminar.

Dr. Pascal already responded to the invitation.

d. *Among* and *between*: *Among* refers to more than two; *between* refers to only two. The word *and* should always be used between the choices.

EXAMPLES:

Poor communication causes dissatisfaction among employees.

Between you and me, I did receive my raise.

e. *Awhile* and *a while*: *Awhile* is an adverb meaning for some period of time; *while* is a noun referring to an indefinite period of time.

EXAMPLES:

Can you stay awhile?
(adverb modifying <u>stay</u>*)*

Can you stay for a while?
(noun—object of the preposition for*)*

f. *Bad* and *badly*: *Bad* is the adjective; *badly* is the adverb. *Badly* is used after linking verbs when emphasis is on the verb. However, *bad* is the preferred adjective form after linking verbs.

EXAMPLES:

The stock maneuver looks bad.
(adjective modifying the subject maneuver*)*

Since the accident, Sutherland limps badly.
(adverb describing the verb limps*)*

Thompson feels badly about the sale.
Thompson feels bad about the sale.
(Many people object to the use of badly *as the adjective after a linking verb; therefore, it is best to use* bad.*)*

g. *Complement* and *compliment*: Both words can be used as a noun or a verb. *Complement* means finished or fitting together. *Compliment* is used when referring to praise.

EXAMPLES:

The new wall hangings complement *the furniture.*
(The word complement *means fit together.)*

I must compliment *Douglas on his choice in wall hangings.*
(The word compliment *means praise.)*

h. *Effect* and *affect*: *Effect* is a noun meaning result; *affect* is a verb meaning influence.

EXAMPLES:

The effects of telecommunications have had a great impact in the last several years.
(effects = subject of the sentence)

The weather affected our plans.
(affected = verb)

i. *Good* and *well*: *Good* is an adjective; *well* is either an adjective or an adverb. The most common error is using the adjective *good* in place of the adverb *well*. *Good* and *well* are both used as predicate adjectives with the verb *feel*; however, the connotation is different.

EXAMPLES:

Everyone had a good time at the department party.
(adjective modifying the noun time*)*

All is well with the new couple.
(adjective modifying the subject all*)*

After the hurricane, the cleanup went well.
(adverb modifying the verb went*)*

Johnson does not feel well.
(adverb modifying the verb does feel *and referring to Johnson's health)*

Eckels felt good about building the addition.
(adjective modifying Eckels and referring to Eckels' mental feeling—happiness)

j. *Lay* and *lie*: *Lay* is a verb meaning to put or place; it requires an object. *Lie* is a verb meaning to recline; it does not require an object.

The principal parts of *lay* are *lay, laid, laid.*
The principal parts of *lie* are *lie, lay, lain.*

EXAMPLES:

I do not know where I laid my folder.
*(*folder *is the direct object of the verb* laid*)*

Grandpa should lie down for a rest.
*(*should lie *is the verb)*

k. *Lose* and *loose*: *Lose* is a verb meaning misplace; *loose* is an adjective meaning not tight or a verb meaning let go.

EXAMPLES:

Don't lose my place.
The dress is too loose.
Martin loosened the dog's collar.

l. *Most* and *almost*: *Most* is an adjective meaning large in number; *almost* is an adverb meaning nearly.

EXAMPLES:

Most administrative professionals sitting for the CPS exam take a review course.
(adjective modifying the subject professionals*—meaning the majority and referring to large in number)*

Her writing almost meets our specifications.
(adverb modifying meets*)*

m. *Proceed* and *precede*: *Proceed* means to continue; *precede* means to go before.

EXAMPLES:

We must proceed with our plans.
Learning the concepts precedes lab application.

n. *Principal* and *principle: Principal* is a noun or adjective meaning first in importance; *principle* is a noun meaning rule or basis for conduct.

EXAMPLES:

The new principal is planning major revisions.
To adhere to one's principles is important.

o. *Real* and *really: Real* is an adjective meaning actual or true; *really* is an adverb meaning indeed.

EXAMPLES:

The real way to make progress is to work hard.
Everyone is really working hard at the office.

p. *Set* and *sit:* Both *set* and *sit* are verbs. *Set* means to place and requires an object; *sit* refers to remaining in position and does not take an object.

EXAMPLES:

Please set my papers in the red in-basket.
(Set "what?" my papers
"where?" in the red in-basket)
Please sit down on the couch.

q. *Site, cite,* and *sight: Site* is a noun meaning location. *Cite* is a verb meaning quote or recognize. *Sight* is a noun meaning vision.

EXAMPLES:

The new office site has a beautiful view.
Wells cited many abuses of the policy.
James' sight was impaired because of the injury.

r. *Stationary* and *stationery: Stationary* is an adjective that means fixed or placed in a specific location. *Stationery* refers to letterheads, envelopes, and other business papers designed for preparing the correspondence of a specific organization.

EXAMPLES:

The receptionist's desk has been placed in a stationary location near the front entrance.
Douglas needs to place an order for stationery for our new company.

s. *Their, there,* and *they're: Their* is the possessive form of *they. There* is an adverb. *They're* is a contraction for *they are.*

EXAMPLES:

Their automobile was severely damaged.
(their—plural possessive pronoun)

Put the plant over there.
(there—adverb)

They're going to the theater for the performance.
(They're—*contraction for* they are)

t. *Then* and *than: Then* means at that time and is an adverb; *than* is a conjunction usually used in comparisons.

EXAMPLES:

Call me this afternoon. We can then set a time.
I like the Model 1850 better than the new one.

u. *To, too,* and *two: To* is a preposition. *Too* is an adverb meaning *also* or *very. Two* is the number.

EXAMPLES:

Please bring the car to the garage for repair.
The steak was too rare.
We have two external drives with our computer.

v. *Who, which,* and *that:* The relative pronoun *who* is used when referring to a person and often introduces a restrictive clause. A **restrictive clause** is one that is necessary to the completeness of the sentence and does not require commas.

EXAMPLE:

Administrative professionals who use word processing software encounter less frustration when editing business writing.
(who use word processing software *refers to administrative professionals, adds meaning, and does not require commas*)

The relative pronoun *which* refers to a thing or a place and often introduces a nonrestrictive clause. A **nonrestrictive clause** is one that does not add meaning to the sentence, may be considered parenthetical, and is set off by commas.

EXAMPLE:

This manual, which was written by the information systems manager, is very easy to follow.
(which was written by the information systems manager *refers to manual; it is a nonrestrictive clause that is not required to complete the meaning of the sentence and requires commas*)

Another relative pronoun, *that,* is used to refer to a thing or a place and typically introduces a restrictive clause.

EXAMPLE:

This is software that can be learned quickly.
(that can be learned quickly *is a restrictive clause referring to software, is necessary to complete the meaning of the sentence, and does not require commas*)

8. *Unbiased Language:* If caution is not used, bias can creep into writing very easily. Equal treatment must be given to everyone (men and women, members of minority groups, and jobholders). Sometimes people become stereotyped into particular jobs or positions, even though both men and women can be effective jobholders. Here are some basic guidelines that may be followed so that bias-free language will be used in all business writing.

a. *Gender-free language:* Language in business writing must be free of gender bias.

(1) Whenever people are referred to in general, gender-free words and phrases should be used instead of masculine or feminine words.

EXAMPLES:

manpower	*peoplepower*
manhours	*working hours*

Here are some ways in which these changes in word usage can be achieved:

- Sentences may be reworded to remove unneeded pronouns.
- The number can be changed from singular to plural.
- Masculine pronouns can be replaced with *s/he*, *she* or *he*, *her* or *his*, *one*, or *you* to decrease the use of gender-biased language.

A variety of these techniques may be used to avoid monotonous, repetitious writing or difficulty in reading the material.

EXAMPLE:

Each administrative professional needs to complete her report by the end of the week.

Instead, say:

Each administrative professional needs a complete report on file by the end of the week.

(2) Men and women should be referred to as equals, and references to them should be phrased consistently. You should use the person's full name in the first reference to that person; then, you may use the first name, the last name, or an appropriate pronoun in later references.

EXAMPLE:

Erin O'Grady was recently appointed the chairperson of the awards committee. Erin has been with the company since 1998.

Erin O'Grady was recently appointed the chairperson of the awards committee. She has been with the company since 1998.

(3) Avoid unnecessary labels and stereotypes in business writing.

EXAMPLES:

female executive = executive
just like a man or just like a woman (this phrase should not be used)
male nurse = nurse

(4) The words *man* or *woman* should not be used as a prefix or suffix in job titles.

EXAMPLES:

chairman	*chairperson*
chairwoman	*chair*
	presiding officer
foreman	*supervisor*

(5) When referring to people by gender, parallel language should be used.

EXAMPLES:

the ladies and the men	*man and wife*
should be	should be
the women and the men	*husband and wife*
or	
ladies and gentlemen	

(6) When referring to people by name, parallel language must be used in expressing their names.

EXAMPLE:

Please telephone one of our marketing representatives, either Bill Gray *or* Mrs. Brown*, with the description of the cabinet.*

Instead, say:

Please telephone one of our marketing representatives, either Bill Gray *or* Muriel Brown*, with the description of the cabinet.*

(7) General expressions used should refer to both men and women. Use generic titles or descriptions for both women and men.

EXAMPLES:

male secretary	*secretary*
female executive	*executive*
male programmer	*programmer*

b. *Racially or ethnically unbiased language:* Equal treatment of people within certain racial or ethnic groups is a necessity in business writing so that the audience will not be offended by the words used.

(1) Qualifiers may be used to reinforce racial or ethnic stereotypes. Do not add information that suggests that a person is an exception to a racial or ethnic norm.

EXAMPLE:

Schultz, an employee from Germany, has very good spelling skills.

(Does this sentence imply that Germans, as a general rule, have difficulty with spelling?)

(2) The identification of racial or ethnic origin should not appear in the writing unless it is pertinent to the message being conveyed.

EXAMPLE:

Gonzalez has contributed some fine examples of etiquette appropriate in conducting business in Hispanic cultures.

In proofreading and editing, watch for bias that is sometimes implied in context.

c. *Job-related language:* In business writing, the types of jobs held by people should not be stereotyped. Examples should be used of both men and women in positions that might easily be stereotyped.

EXAMPLES:

Shirley Stone, an administrative assistant in the financial department, is responsible for the drafting of all research reports. (Are all administrative assistants female?)

Glenn Baker, an administrative assistant in the loan department, supervises the five part-time employees.

Check Point—Section A

Directions: For each question, circle the correct answer.

A–1. Which one of the following statements best reflects a positive message?

   A) I apologize for not contacting you sooner.
   B) I have mailed the material by air express.
   C) If further information is needed, do not hesitate to fax your request.
   D) Please contact us if you decide to pursue this alternative.

A–2. Which one of the following techniques would demonstrate that concrete language is being used?

   A) Avoiding short, simple words
   B) Having industry-specific language dominate the writing

   C) Having specific words with precise meanings dominate the writing
   D) Using acronyms to eliminate unnecessary wording

A–3. Which one of the following statements uses unbiased language in expressing an idea?

   A) As a result of the new policy, every administrative professional on our staff must use her vacation time before December 1.
   B) C. R. Adams, our top salesman, reported that sales for May had increased 7 percent.
   C) Everyone in the audience gave the speaker a standing ovation.
   D) The young male attorney prepared a brief that was highly regarded by his peers.

B. Effective Sentence and Paragraph Construction

Sentences and paragraphs need to be constructed carefully to be effective in meaning. In business writing, the number of words in a sentence should not exceed 20 words (two printed lines of text). Most paragraphs include three to five sentences.

1. *Constructing Effective Sentences:* A sentence is a complete thought expressed in words that are understandable. A sentence must have a subject and a predicate.

   a. *Errors in sentence construction:* Common sentence errors are incomplete sentences (fragments), run-on sentences, and comma-splice sentences.

      (1) *Incomplete sentence:* An incomplete sentence is one that is missing a subject or a verb (predicate) and is considered a sentence **fragment** (only part of a

sentence or thought). Incomplete sentences occur frequently in speech; therefore, these sentences often appear in written documents. An incomplete sentence can be corrected in one of these ways:

(a) *Supplying the missing words:* Many times incomplete sentences follow complete sentences to which the sentence thoughts are related. It is important to watch for incomplete sentences and supply the missing subject or verb.

EXAMPLE:

The new chairs for the communications center were delivered today. Believe they are adjustable.
(The subject in the second sentence is missing. The sentence might be corrected to read: *I believe they are adjustable.*)

(b) *Connecting the incomplete sentence to another sentence:* Sometimes it is more convenient to connect the incomplete sentence to another related sentence.

EXAMPLE:

The report was sent to the finance department yesterday. The report on building expansion.
(The verb in the second sentence is missing.)

Corrected sentence:

The report on building expansion was sent to the finance department yesterday.

(c) *Dropping the sentence:* Many times incomplete sentences are explanatory phrases or clauses that are not necessary to the meaning of the sentence and can be dropped from the written material.

(2) *Run-on sentences:* Running two or more complete sentences together, with no punctuation between them, creates a run-on sentence. These sentences can be rewritten into two separate sentences or connected with correct punctuation.

(a) *Two separate sentences:* Because of the length of a run-on sentence, it is sometimes best to separate it into two separate sentences. Also, a well-written document needs sentences that vary in length.

EXAMPLE:

A four-year degree in business administration is required for the new position because it is a supervisory position in the administrative services department that is the department responsible for information processing.

Corrected:

A four-year degree in business administration is required for the new position. It is a supervisory position in the administrative services department responsible for information processing.

(b) *Correct punctuation for run-on sentences:* Two complete sentences connected with punctuation and a conjunction create a **compound sentence.**

If the run-on sentence does not have a conjunction, a semicolon is to be used between the two sentences. If the run-on sentence has a conjunction, a comma is used between the two sentences.

EXAMPLE:

Run-on sentence:

Bryant and Cappilari formed a partnership several years ago their success is based on the mutual respect they have for each other.

Corrected with punctuation:

Bryant and Cappilari formed a partnership several years ago; their success is based on the mutual respect they have for each other.

Corrected with punctuation and conjunction:

Bryant and Cappilari formed a partnership several years ago, and their success is based on the mutual respect they have for each other.

(3) *Comma-splice sentences:* Sometimes two complete sentences are joined by only a comma instead of a stronger mark of punctuation like the semicolon. When a comma is used in this way, the error is called a comma splice.

EXAMPLE:

The memorandum is being replaced with an e-mail message, both of these types of communication require the writer to focus only on one topic.

Corrected:

The memorandum is being replaced with an e-mail message; both of these types of communication require the writer to focus only on one topic.

or

The memorandum is being replaced with an e-mail message, but both of these types of communication require the writer to focus only on one topic. (comma and conjunction)

Sometimes a conjunctive adverb like *however, therefore,* or *thus* precedes the second sentence. The sentence should be punctuated like this:

The memorandum is being replaced with an e-mail message; however, both of these types of communication require the writer to focus only on one topic. (semicolon because there is no conjunction; the word *however* is an introductory word in the second sentence)

b. *Types of sentences written:* The types of sentences written should be varied, which will add interest to a message. A combination of simple, compound, complex, and compound-complex sentences also affects emphasis or tone.

(1) *Simple sentences:* Each sentence must have a subject and a verb and may have modifiers—adjectives, adverbs, or complements. A **complement** consists of additional words that help complete the meaning of the sentence.

EXAMPLE:

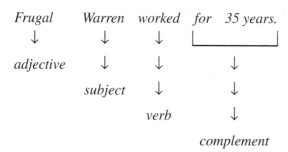

(2) *Compound sentences:* A compound sentence consists of two independent clauses joined by a comma and a conjunction (*and*, *but*, *or*, *nor*) or a semicolon. Sometimes a conjunctive adverb such as *however* or *therefore* begins the second sentence. An independent clause conveys a complete thought and can stand alone as a sentence.

EXAMPLE:

Sales increased in June (independent clause), *but* (comma and conjunction) *the vice president of marketing expected a greater increase in July* (independent clause).

Sales increased in June (independent clause); (semicolon, no conjunction) *the vice president of marketing expected an even greater increase in July* (independent clause).

Sales increased in June (independent clause); (semicolon, no conjunction) *however,* (conjunctive adverb beginning second sentence, comma follows) *the vice president of marketing expected an even greater increase in July.*

(3) *Complex sentences:* A **complex sentence** consists of one independent clause and one or more dependent clauses. An independent clause is a complete thought, but a dependent clause is incomplete and cannot stand alone as a sentence. Dependent clauses begin with a connecting word showing their subordinate relationship. The connecting word is either a relative pronoun (*who*, *which*, *that*) or a subordinate conjunction (*if*, *because*, *when*, *since*).

(4) *Compound-complex sentences:* A **compound-complex sentence** consists of two or more independent clauses and one or more dependent clauses. Compound-complex sentences should be used sparingly.

EXAMPLE:

As far as Harrison determined (dependent clause), *no problem existed with the local area network in the accounting department* (independent clause).

When the dependent clause appears at the beginning of a sentence, as in the preceding example, a comma always separates the dependent clause from the independent clause. However, when the dependent clause follows the independent clause, no comma is required because the main idea of the sentence continues through the dependent clause.

EXAMPLE:

No problem existed in the local area network in the accounting department as far as Harrison could determine.

c. *Length of sentences:* Typically, sentences in business writing should average from 15 to 20 words. A combination of short, medium, and long sentences will keep the reading interesting. A sentence that exceeds 35 to 40 words should be rewritten into two or more sentences.

d. *Connectives:* Sentences (independent clauses) should be joined when the ideas presented in the first sentence continue in the second sentence. The expression of related ideas within these sentences needs to be evident to the reader.

EXAMPLE:

The administrative professional reviews each document before it leaves the office; this is an important responsibility.
(two independent clauses, no conjunction—use semicolon between)

e. *Sentence formats:* Some ideas are better stated as questions than as statements. A clause or a phrase may begin a sentence, which adds variety to the format. Certain words may be in bold, underlined, or italicized.

EXAMPLES:

Question:
Are you aware of the importance of interviewing candidates carefully?

Statement:
Our interviewing techniques include a set of questions to ask each candidate.

Beginning with a clause:
When a candidate comes in for an interview, we administer a vocabulary test.

Beginning with a phrase:
With the change in legislation, we must be extremely careful in asking each candidate specific questions.

2. ***Organized Paragraphs:*** A paragraph represents the writer's thoughts on a specific portion of a subject. The entire document represents the writer's thoughts on the entire subject. Therefore, a skilled writer needs to logically organize separate thoughts or ideas about a subject before attempting to create paragraphs.

a. *Writing approach for paragraphs:* Groups of related sentences are formed into paragraphs, with each paragraph having at least one central idea or theme. When the idea changes, the writer should begin a new paragraph. Paragraphs within a document are written with either a deductive approach or an inductive approach.

(1) *Deductive approach:* When the **deductive approach** is used, the organization of paragraphs within the message is *direct*. The main idea is stated in the first paragraph, followed by supporting details and a closing paragraph.

(2) *Inductive approach:* The organization of paragraphs when the **inductive approach** is used is *indirect*. This means that the supporting details are presented first, primarily to act as a buffer while the situation is explained in the message. Later in the message, the main idea of the message is presented, followed by closing comments.

b. *Paragraph composition:* Even though paragraphs will vary in length and purpose, most paragraphs consist of three types of statements: overview statement, supporting statement, and detail statement. One main idea is presented in each paragraph, with detailed information to support that idea.

(1) *Overview statement:* Many paragraphs contain a topic sentence at the beginning, which provides an overview of what is to follow. Such a sentence can be a rephrasing of previous material when the paragraph is an expansion on a previous point. Sometimes an overview statement comes at the end of a paragraph summarizing what was presented in the paragraph.

(2) *Supporting statement:* A supporting statement within the paragraph presents the ideas or opinions the writer has on the particular point made.

(3) *Detail statement:* Good writing consists mainly of detail statements that present facts about the topic. Generalizations and opinions are best supported by accurate facts.

Business writing manuals always advise that an outline be prepared prior to writing. When writing skills are being developed or improved, the outline is usually written on paper. As writers become more skillful with their writing, some choose to mentally organize their thoughts. However, many writers consistently produce a paper sketch of the topic before writing. It is important to recognize when this step is required to produce logical, clearly written, and complete material.

3. *Criteria for Effective Sentences and Paragraphs:* To be effective, sentences and paragraphs need to be constructed with several qualities in mind: coherence, emphasis, unity, conciseness, variety, clarity, and accuracy.

a. *Coherence:* Thoughts are coherent if the writing shows consistency in style, word choice, and word usage. Coherence means that the sentences and paragraphs are constructed so each word contributes to the sentence, each sentence contributes to the meaning of the paragraph, and each paragraph contributes to the entire message. The following techniques can help the writer maintain cohesion in business writing:

(1) *Stress on words:* Coherence is shown by emphasizing certain aspects of the message, that is, placing special stress on a particular word or thought. Repeating a word from the preceding sentence emphasizes that thought. Sometimes specific ideas need to be stressed equally. Comparing or contrasting to show similarities or differences is another way to stress specific points. Here are some other ways of placing stress on specific words or thoughts:

- Present information in rank order to emphasize importance, with the most important item first.
- Underline or italicize specific words for emphasis.
- Place specific words or phrases in bold.
- Change the format; consider using a bulleted list.
- Use a different size or style of type.

You need to be selective in stressing words or phrases so the reader will easily see the words you are emphasizing.

    (2) *Word choice and usage:* Sentences are directly linked when writing techniques like the following are used:

- Use a pronoun to represent a noun from the preceding sentence in order to avoid redundancy.

- Begin sentences with connecting words (conjunctive adverbs) like *however*, *therefore*, or *also*. Connecting words imply continuations of the same topic.

- Use words that are commonly found together:

        state . . . federal

        employer . . . employee

        graduate . . . undergraduate

        winter . . . spring . . . summer

    (3) *Parallelism:* Ideas that are equal in thought should be stated in identical grammatical form. Violations of parallel construction lead to misinterpretation and awkward sentence formats.

EXAMPLE:

The purpose of the meeting is <u>to organize</u> our plan for a new networked system and <u>implementing</u> procedures for writing the proposal.

(The words that are underlined are not parallel.)

The purpose of the meeting is <u>to organize</u> our plan for a new networked system and <u>to implement</u> procedures for writing the proposal.

(The underlined words are parallel.)

b. *Emphasis:* Emphasis is a very important part of developing coherence in writing; the two criteria—coherence and emphasis—are closely related. **Emphasis** means that greater importance is attached to a particular fact or idea.

    (1) *Word choice and order:* Key information should be placed at the beginning of sentences or messages so that the reader will be sure to see it. Selecting words that relate precisely to the idea being conveyed permits the writer to emphasize the idea correctly.

    (2) *Balance:* Items of equal value should be emphasized equally in the writing.

    (3) *Restatement:* Sometimes a fact or detail needs to be restated in different words so that the reader will be more likely to pay attention to that fact.

EXAMPLE:

Setting up appropriate procedures for accepting work is important and will save time for the busy office professional. In other words, a log-in procedure will enable you to organize the work in less time.

    (4) *Format:* Sometimes the format is changed within a document to add emphasis to specific details. Within the body of a letter, a statistical table might be included to emphasize facts that would otherwise be obscured in the body of the message. Type sizes and styles help to vary the format as well.

c. *Unity:* The term **unity** suggests that a coherent flow of ideas exists throughout a written work—within sentences, within paragraphs, and between paragraphs.

(1) *Detailed information:* Factual information to support the main ideas is included within the paragraphs. If a direct approach is used, the main idea of the message is presented first, followed by more details. With a more indirect approach, the details are presented first to support the main idea, which is presented later in the message.

(2) *Connectives:* Conjunctions and other connecting words are used to form relationships between and among words and sentences.

(3) *Repetition:* Sometimes key ideas are summarized at the end of the message to emphasize their importance and also to serve as reminders to the reader.

d. *Conciseness:* Business writing needs to be concise because a busy executive will usually look briefly at the first page of a document to determine the main idea being presented and to decide whether to read further. **Conciseness** is defined as writing in a brief but comprehensive manner; in other words, as few words as possible are used to express the information presented. In preparing communication that is concise, you must first identify the main purpose of the correspondence and plan your approach.

(1) *Planning:* Determining what you are going to write will result in more concise writing. Plan what needs to be said, keeping in mind that the communication must be clear. What is not required is stating the obvious.

(2) *Revising:* In the revision stage, when reviewing the communication from the reader's viewpoint, look for short, simple sentences and active voice. Using a conversational style will also lead to more concise writing.

e. *Variety in writing:* In order to maintain a reader's interest in what you are attempting to say, use techniques that will enhance the message you are conveying. The use of synonyms helps to vary the word usage and the choice of words. Individual sentences may be constructed in different ways. Entire messages may need to be varied in cases where the same letter is being sent to a number of different people—remember to keep the reader's perspective in mind.

(1) *Word usage:* A **thesaurus** is a reference that is helpful in determining other words that have the same meaning as the one being conveyed in the message. Look for synonyms to add variety to the writing. Thesauri, spelling checks, and grammar checks are helpful writing tools available in word processing software packages.

EXAMPLES OF SYNONYMS:

Action: performance, movement, operation, task

Record: account, minutes, diary, journal, proceedings

(2) *Sentences:* The use of a combination of simple, compound, and complex sentences, and occasionally a compound-complex sentence, will help to vary the sentence construction. Using a combination of short, medium, and long sentences keeps the reader interested in the message. Sentences should normally average about 15 to 20 words.

(3) *Messages:* To make the writing interesting to both the writer and the reader, messages need to be written so that they are appropriate for the person receiving them and the purpose for which they are intended. Variable information needs to be inserted so that each message is personalized.

EXAMPLE: *In word/information processing, form letters and form paragraphs are used to express the same messages to a number of different people. Even though the basic message can stay the same, paragraphs or other variable information pertinent only to one person can be inserted to personalize the message. The receiver feels that the message was written personally, even though the basic message is standard to all recipients.*

f. *Clarity:* Any message needs to be written in a clear, accurate manner. Knowing the purpose of the message first will help you accomplish clarity in your writing. Combining clarity with the use of the "you" approach will help to direct the message to the reader.

  (1) *Purposes:* Writers find that outlining is a helpful technique before they begin writing. By identifying the reasons for writing a message, the writer should be able to focus on those points first rather than "going off on tangents."

  (2) *Review:* Once the message has been written, set the material aside for a short time. Rereading it later helps the writer be more objective about the writing and may help to achieve a greater degree of clarity. Another technique is to have a co-worker read the material to see whether the message is clear and understandable.

Administrative professionals and executives need to work together to read and react to one another's writing. Such a critique can be a very helpful strategy in improving written messages distributed from the office. This is especially important in cases where the writing deals with sensitive issues.

g. *Accuracy:* Any type of business writing should be accurate in terms of message, format, and language.

  (1) *Message:* The message should contain accurate, detailed, and complete information. Specific references to information sources are extremely important, especially if the reader needs to know the credibility of the material. The message should present the information in a logical, sequential manner so that the reader can follow the accuracy of the message.

  (2) *Format:* The message should be produced with accurate document format. The margins should "frame" the writing so that the appearance is pleasing to the eye. Also, information can be placed in tables within the document to enhance the presentation of key points. The administrative professional plays an important role in ensuring that the document format is determined *before* the message is prepared and the writing style fits.

  (3) *Language:* A message must be written with grammatically correct language. Poor English and inaccurate punctuation affect the reader's impression of the message as well as the company. The typical reaction to poorly written messages is that the firm probably produces an inferior product or service as well.

4. ***Development of Goodwill:*** Each message conveyed from one organization to another has the capacity for creating goodwill between the organizations. **Goodwill** develops when people work together, within the organization or with others outside the organization, creating a positive, clear, and courteous communication climate.

a. *Considerateness:* To create goodwill, the communication needs to express consideration for the other person. In other words, the writer must think of the receiver of the message and the effect the message will have on that person. A genuine interest in the reader must be emphasized in the communication.

EXAMPLES:

A message of welcome to the new administrative professional is a warm, considerate step for the office staff to take.

When an employee has been out of the office because of illness, a "welcome back" message helps bridge the gap for that person—that first day back to the office requires adjustment for all.

b. *Empathy:* The "you" approach in business writing helps to create empathy in writing. The writer must be able to see the difficulty or problem from the reader's point of view. **Empathy** refers to understanding the feelings or emotions of another person. It is important to know the difference between *sympathy* (feeling sorry for another person) and *empathy* (understanding the emotions and feelings of another person).

EXAMPLE:

Moving to a new location has not been an easy task for you and your family, and I want to be as helpful as I can with the transition.

c. *Courtesy:* Concern for the reader will help you deliver a courteous message. Words like *please* and *thank you* come naturally when you consider the best interests of others. The best tone your letter can produce is a natural one. A technique that often shows courtesy is the inclusion of the reader's name within the correspondence; it gives the reader the feeling of importance.

EXAMPLE: *Please send us your report as soon as it is convenient for you. Your writing is always of the highest quality, so I know only minor revisions may be necessary. Thank you for your willingness to help us with this report.*

d. *Sincerity:* Genuine sincerity is an expression of confidence and trust shown in other people. In some business writing, confidentiality in withholding certain facts is extremely important. Sincere writing eliminates excessive humility, flattery, or overstatement of information.

EXAMPLE:

We know that you will be able to give us the information we need because of your expertise in this area. We want to assure you, however, that your responses to our questions will be held in confidence and analyzed as part of the aggregate response from the sample.

e. *Respect:* Effective business communication requires that respect be shown for the company represented, for products or services being provided, and for the reader of the message. The use of tact, consideration, and courtesy is very important in business writing if you want the reader to respond in a positive way. Respect needs to be shown not only for the person but for the person's position within the firm as well.

EXAMPLE:

We are very eager to have you try our latest product—SmartLabel—because we think you will find it more adaptable to your needs than other labeling software on the market. Some software may not be compatible with the latest versions of

word processing software. Ours is! Your experience as an administrative profes-
sional will enable you to give us an honest evaluation of this new product.

The development of goodwill among people and organizations is very important in today's business world, and administrative professionals can do much to further goodwill through attention to considerateness, empathy, courtesy, sincerity, and respect in effective written communication.

Check Point—Section B

Directions: For each question, circle the correct answer.

B–1. "After you have charted the information, you should save the graph and import it into the Word document." This sentence is a

A) simple sentence
B) compound sentence
C) complex sentence
D) compound-complex sentence

B–2. In business writing, effective sentences should

A) average about 20 words
B) be joined when the thought continues to enhance clarity
C) be simple sentences
D) have an independent clause and a dependent clause

B–3. Which one of the following statements best reflects empathy toward the reader?

A) I apologize for not contacting you sooner.
B) I have sent the order by Federal Express so you should have it by Monday.
C) If further information is needed, do not hesitate to fax your request.
D) I know you are anxious to get your new product—CAPSTONE—into production as soon as you receive this shipment of supplies.

C. Proofreading and Editing

An important responsibility for most administrative professionals is checking and revising the final draft of a written document before sending it to the receiver. The process of producing a business document that will make a favorable impression requires the application of language, proofreading, and editing skills by everyone involved in the writing and editing phases. Tying these skills together results in a document that has a clear, concise, and courteous tone.

1. ***Proofreading Techniques:*** Proofreading is the process of checking a soft or hard copy of a document for spelling, punctuation, and formatting accuracy. The procedure for proofreading soft copy depends on the proofreader's responsibility and authority. If the proofreader is to flag only necessary corrections, then proofreading marks may be inserted within the hard-copy document or word processing commands inserted in the soft copy to mark changes or insert editorial comments.

   a. *Proofreading for typographical errors:* When using word processing software, an initial step is to use a spelling check to detect obvious typographical errors. However, even a spelling check can miss some types of errors. Reading the hard-copy text backward can be helpful because the proofreader must concentrate on each word separately as spelling is being checked. Neither of these methods should be used for checking content. For example, if the word *to* were typed as *so*, the spelling error would go undetected unless an error in grammar is noted.

b. *Proofreading by office professionals:* Because proofreading is so important, many firms have proofreading or editing specialists. Before a document is released, someone other than the originator, copy editor, or word processing specialist reviews it. In many cases, two people do the proofreading, one reading the material aloud from the writer's copy and another checking the final document. Administrative professionals working together within a firm can also adopt this technique. Someone who was not involved in preparing the document should proofread the original document. The one who reads from the writer's copy could be someone who was involved in the document preparation.

c. *Proofreading techniques:* Whether proofreading is done alone or others are assigned to do the proofreading, the following techniques should be used:

(1) *Reading the copy:* When proofreading, read the copy slowly and concentrate on the material.

(2) *Aligning copy:* Use a ruler or a straight-edge to follow the line of print on hard copy. This is particularly helpful with statistical copy. The ruler is also helpful in making sure that a line of text is not skipped in reading. Scrolling one line at a time when proofreading soft copy ensures that a line is not omitted during proofreading.

(3) *Proofreading vertically:* If the material is in table form and was keyed horizontally in columns, proofread the copy vertically. This is particularly helpful when proofreading alone.

(4) *Counting entries:* If there are lines of entries that can be counted, count the number of entries in the original and compare that with the number of entries keyed in the final document.

(5) *Delaying final proofreading:* If time permits, do not proofread the final draft immediately after keying the material. If you wait for an hour or more, errors are more likely to be found. The longer the wait, the better—the proofreader will be more objective in making judgments about errors.

d. *Proofreading symbols:* When proofreading hard-copy text, the proofreading symbols illustrated in Figure 7–1 should be used. Proofreading marks on a hard copy should be inserted with a colored pen for ease of reading and editing. Once the document has been proofread, appropriate editing changes need to be made and the revised document saved.

2. ***Editing:*** The term editing has traditionally been associated with preparing documents for publication. Administrative professionals in all types of offices have been performing editing and copyediting functions, but the task has often been referred to incorrectly as proofreading, another important skill. It is important to recognize the difference between these sets of skills. **Copyediting** is the revision of a draft or a document for consistency, conciseness, and grammatical accuracy. Revisions are marked manually within the body of the document using proofreading and copyediting symbols (Figures 7–1 and 7–2a) or indicated with software tools such as track changes (see Figure 7–2b).

FIGURE 7–1 Proofreading and Copyediting Symbols

Meaning	Symbol	Example	Final Edited Copy
Transpose	∿	chnage the letters around	change the letters around
Delete	ℓ	to take something out	to take out
Close up	⌒	to bring to gether	to bring together
Insert	∧	the insert symbol a caret	the insert symbol is a caret
Space	#	insert aspace	insert a space
Paragraph	¶	Using the symbol means to begin a new paragraph.¶A new thought means a new paragraph.	Using the symbol means to begin a new paragraph. A new thought means a new paragraph.
Move left	⊏	Align the material to the left.	Align the material to the left.
Move right	⊐	Align the material to the right.	Align the material to the right.
Spelling or spell out	sp or ◯	When a word is spelled incorectly, write sp in a circle above the misspelled word. When an abbrev is to be spelled out, circle the word.	When a word is spelled incorrectly, write sp in a circle above the misspelled word. When an abbreviation is to be spelled out, circle the word.
Capital letters	≡ or CAPS	underline all letters that are to be capital letters or write the letters CAPS in the margin.	Underline ALL letters that are to be capital letters OR write the letters CAPS in the margin.
Lower case	/ or lc	Draw a line through letters that should be Lower Case Letters OR write the letters lc in the margin.	Draw a line through letters that should be lower case letters OR write the letters lc in the margin.
Let stand	- - - or stet	Keep it the original way. Writing stet in the margin also means "let it stand."	Keep it the original way. Writing stet in the margin also means " let it stand."
Insertion of punctuation	⌃ ⌄ ⌄⌄	When a comma needs to be inserted use the caret symbol but dont use it for an apostrophe or quotation marks. Use the inverse caret.	When a comma needs to be inserted, use the caret symbol but don't use it for an apostrophe or quotation marks. Use the inverse caret.

FIGURE 7–2a   Editing of Paragraph Text—Manual Procedures

Body of Report   Based on your research questions, decide on the themes to be
included within the body of the report. If you have ③ research questions, then you
will have ③ sections, one for each of the ③ themes.

Use a descriptive First-Level Heading for each of the three
themes. Use a phrase rather than the entire research question.
divide each section into at least two subsections with a Second-
Level Heading for each of the subsections. Be sure that these
headings are descriptive of the content within that particular section or
subsection. Present detailed information and data on each of
the three themes, documenting the sources of information with
parenthetic citations. Use the apa style for these citations. Be
sure to write only in ③rd person.

lc

CAPS

Be sure that each paragraphs have a topic sentences and that all the
sentences in each paragraph relate to the topic of that paragraph. If you find
that you have topics different in one paragraph, you may want to divide the
paragraph or revise it. Be sure that each paragraph is a reasonable length.
keep your sentences within the twenty 20-word limit. Try to end each section
with a summary statement about that theme.

The edited copy is returned to the writer for revision and verification. After all revisions have been made and the document is prepared in final form, the administrative professional will proofread the document for typographical accuracy.

a. *Preparing copy for editing:* Copy to be edited can be prepared in rough-draft format. These guidelines for keying rough-draft copy should be followed:

(1) *Side margins:* Side margins should be a 1-inch minimum; 1¼ inches would be even better.

(2) *Spacing:* Double or triple spacing should be used so corrections can be inserted easily. Never single-space printed rough-draft copy.

(3) *Paragraphs:* If the rough draft is double spaced, indent paragraphs so that a new paragraph can easily be identified. An alternative is to quadruple-space between paragraphs if triple spacing is used for the document and to triple-space between paragraphs if double spacing is used for the document.

(4) *Readability of copy:* Even though this is a rough-draft copy, neatness should be maintained. When using word processing, format codes such as hyphenation or page breaks are not included. These codes are included before printing the final copy. Page numbers are always helpful in keeping rough-draft pages in order. Readability is the key factor. Rough-draft copy will be read for revision, and reading is easier if the copy is neatly keyed.

FIGURE 7–2b   Editing of Paragraph—Software Tools

Body of Report   Based on your research questions, decide on the themes

to be included within the body of the report. If you have **three** research

questions, then you will have **three** sections, one for each of the **three** themes.

   Use a descriptive first-level heading for each of the three themes. Use a phrase

rather than the entire research question. Divide each section into at least two

subsections with a second-level heading for each of the subsections. Be sure

that these headings are descriptive of the content within that **particular** section

or subsection. Present detailed information and data on each of the three themes,

documenting the sources of information with parenthetic citations. Use the **APA**

style for these citations. Be sure to write only in **third** person.

   Be sure that **each** paragraph has a topic sentence and that all the sentences

in each paragraph relate to the topic of that paragraph. If you find that you have

different **topics** in one paragraph, you may want to divide the paragraph or revise it.

Be sure that each paragraph is a reasonable length. Keep your sentences within the

20-word limit. Try to end each section with a summary statement about that theme.

Deleted: 3
Deleted: 3
Deleted: 3
Comment: Lower case letters should be used.
Deleted: F
Formatted: Right: 0"
Deleted: L
Deleted: H
Deleted: d
Deleted: ,
Deleted: S
Deleted: L
Deleted: H
Deleted: Insert the word particular
Deleted: ae
Deleted: Insert paragraph here
Deleted: Insert comma after themes.
Deleted: Insert space
Deleted: Capital letters for APA
Deleted: apa
Deleted: 3rd
Deleted: Indent: Left 0", First line: 0.5"
Deleted: your
Deleted: s
Deleted: ve
Deleted: s
Deleted: topics
Deleted:
Deleted:
Deleted: k
Deleted: twenty

   b. *Basic editing skills:* An administrative professional needs to develop a strong background in language skills, especially grammatical construction and punctuation. Copyediting requires grammar, punctuation, spelling, and composition skills as well as the ability to maintain consistency in both format and language usage throughout the document. These skills are the underpinnings of the editing process when reading a document for completeness and accuracy.

   (1) *Grammar skills:* Because of the complexity of the English language as well as changes in grammar rules, a current English handbook should be available and used by every administrative professional. Through review and practice, an administrative professional maintains and updates writing and editing skills.

   (2) *Punctuation skills:* A periodic brush up on punctuation skills is also vitally important.

   (3) *Spelling skills:* Spelling can be improved by using the dictionary, a word book, or a software spelling/grammar tool and by concentrating on vocabulary

building. The jargon of the technical field must be learned. When entering a new career field, new terminology can be learned by adding one word to a vocabulary list every day. This technique can also be used for regular vocabulary expansion. The words should be used in daily communication; periodically, give yourself a spelling test on the words you have learned.

(4) *Composition skills:* Composition is the ability to accurately tie grammar, punctuation, and spelling together into a written communiqué. A well-written document is one that is understood (clear), is stated in as few words as necessary (concise), and appeals to the reader (empathy). To develop effective communication skills, much practice is required and the reader (or receiver) needs to evaluate the writing.

(a) *Reading for content:* When reading the copy for content, put yourself in the reader's position. The aim of all communication is to produce a document that will appeal to and communicate with the reader while maintaining the company's objective. Sometimes reading for content can best be accomplished by reading aloud. Also, when someone else (a coworker) reads the document for content, that person should evaluate the document from the receiver's perspective.

(b) *Checking accuracy of content:* Someone other than the author of the document should be reading for accuracy. Usually, an author reads what he or she wants to say, not what has been written.

When a written document is seen for the first time, the reader will be more eager to examine the entire document if the content, format, and appearance of the document are familiar and attractively displayed. People are more comfortable when a document has a neat, attractive appearance.

3. ***Editing for Organization:*** All written documents should be clearly and logically written whether by an individual or a writing team. The topic and the purpose of the document should be well understood by the writers as well as the copy editor. The approach used to develop the document should be identified and an outline developed to aid in the writing and editing of the textual material. First, there must be an open dialogue among those who are writing the document. As the copy editor becomes more involved in the final appraisal, joint communication among writers and the copy editor is a necessity.

a. *Communication among team writers:* Members of a writing team may have been assembled to develop a collaborative document. **Collaboration** means that the members of a team work together to accomplish a specific goal or task. The team members each have a vested interest in the outcome of the project. Individual expertise possessed by team members is invaluable for the completion of the project. The team members may be situated at the same location, in different regions of the country, or in another country; but they still need to be able to communicate quickly with each other in person or electronically.

(1) *Development of team Web site:* A custom Web site with features that help a team work together can be created. Only team members specified by a systems administrator and activated by a systems technician have access to this Web site. The Web site provides services and information needed by the team: electronic mail, a chat room, document files, directions, and announcements. Each user will be given the uniform resource locator (URL) for the team Web site and instructions for communicating with the other team members.

(2) *Types of collaborative communication:* Writing, decision making, problem solving, and presentations are the primary types of collaborative communications that are needed in business today. Team members may be involved in composing different parts of the document to share with the other team members. In return, each one has an opportunity to critique, revise, and edit the content written by all other team members. One person on the team needs to take the lead in compiling all of the suggested revisions into a revised draft to be routed to the other members of the team for review and edit. If the team members are in the same location, they can meet in person and share ideas. However, the development of a Web site for team members, whether in the same location or not, will be a more efficient way of enabling team members from the same or various locations to work together and contribute toward the development of the document.

b. *Communication between writer(s) and copy editor:* Open communication between the writer(s) and copy editor is very important. The communication needs to be clearly explained. If the communication exchange takes place on the telephone, one person needs to be a listener while the other is speaking. Then, the roles will reverse. However, this dialogue takes place online more often today. Online communication through document comments and the ability to ask and respond to questions enables the collaborators to accept or reject proposed edits. Such an information exchange will help in making sure that the topic and purpose of the document are well understood.

c. *The writing approach:* The copy editor needs to know whether the document was written in the direct approach (the deductive approach) or the indirect approach (the inductive approach). Letters, memoranda, and short reports can use either approach, depending on the content of the document and the anticipated reaction by the reader.

(1) *Direct approach:* This approach explains the main point immediately and then presents the facts to support the main point.

(a) *Good or routine news:* The direct approach is used when the material conveys positive or routine news.

(b) *Analytical reports:* Analytical reports follow the direct approach. With an analytical report, it is important to establish goals. These goals include a statement of the problem and the purpose of the report, which are included at the beginning of the report under the subheadings *Statement of the Problem* and *Purpose*.

(2) *Indirect approach:* This approach presents the facts before the whole picture is presented. If the reader needs supporting evidence, the indirect approach provides a complete explanation so the main point will be viewed with an open mind.

(a) *Negative news:* Material that conveys negative news should follow the indirect approach.

(b) *Persuasive writing:* When the material in the document needs to overcome the feelings and emotions of the reader, the indirect approach should be used.

d. *Outline:* The outline used by the writer for organizing his or her thoughts can also be used by the copy editor. However, some writers prefer that the communication between the writer and the copy editor be used by the copy editor to develop an outline to follow for editing. This method allows for a possible different approach to the subject. Utilizing this method typically requires more time. If the copy editor approaches the topic differently, the writer and editor will need time to work out these differences.

4. ***Editing for Completeness and Content Accuracy:*** The four basic rules of copyediting that an administrative professional must keep in mind when editing for completeness and content accuracy are looking it up, checking and double-checking, being consistent, and maintaining the author's writing style.

   a. *Looking it up:* When in doubt, look up the punctuation rule, the correct spelling, or the grammar rule. Reference manuals are the office professional's "right hand" and should be used without hesitation while copyediting.

   b. *Checking and double-checking:* The administrative professional who edits the material can never assume that the facts and/or structure are correct. The copy editor's job is to check everything for accuracy. Checking and double-checking means being inquisitive as well as discriminating. An administrative professional will not remain in that position for long if the excuse "Well, that's exactly what you wrote" is used.

   EXAMPLES:

   > *When a document indicates facts and figures, check the accuracy of the figures.*
   > *If a word seems to be incorrectly used, question its meaning in this situation.*
   > *When a specific reference does not seem accurate, check the original source.*

   c. *Being consistent:* It is obvious that excellent grammar and punctuation skills will be important for copyediting. However, these skills must be matched with the skill of being observant. A copy editor must be observant of inconsistencies such as the following:

   - Transpositions of letters and/or words (e.g., rec*ie*ve instead of rec*ei*ve; or *the document final* instead of *the final document*)
   - Information that appears to be left out of the draft
   - Incomplete sentences in the document
   - Repetitive use of information

   EXAMPLE:

   > *When reference is made to a conference in Dallas on the first page of a report, and later Houston is mentioned as the conference site, this discrepancy must be detected by the copy editor.*

   d. *Maintaining the author's writing style:* The document is the writer's, and the writing style of the writer must be maintained. This skill develops as the writer and copy editor work together over a period of time. However, it can be developed more quickly if an effort is made to identify the writing characteristics peculiar to the writer. Of course, this does not mean that a copy editor should allow incorrect writing habits to continue. A tactful conference between the writer and copy editor can help identify those writing characteristics that the writer will want help in changing. There may be certain characteristics that the author may not allow to be changed; these writing characteristics are to remain in the material as the author's style.

   e. *Document format:* The visual impact of a document makes an instant impression on the reader even before the material is read. Using specific formatting guidelines will help to give any document a professional appearance.

(1) *Envelope format:* The two envelope styles are the OCR style and the conventional style. The position of the address in relation to bar codes on the envelope is another important consideration.

(2) *Letter format:* The three most common letter styles are block letter style, modified block letter style, and simplified letter style. The style used depends on individual or business preference. When the reader encounters a style that is familiar and is properly used, the reader develops confidence in the writer. Also, one must decide on the punctuation style to be used after the salutation and the complimentary closing (open or mixed).

(3) *Other document formats:* All business documents have guidelines to follow. This is true of preprinted forms as well as original material such as a memorandum or a report. Even rough-draft copy has guidelines to be followed which enable the writer to edit the material more easily.

Refer to Chapter 9 for details on formatting documents.

f. *Document appearance:* With modern technology, administrative professionals have the advantage of using word processing to produce business documents. A neat, attractive appearance means proper spacing of the document; clear, dark print; and a nonglossy paper for ease of reading. Preparing the original document carefully will help to create that perfect look. Ink-jet and laser printing creates clear, neat images on the hard copy.

Using proofreading techniques to "catch" typographical errors is very important. Spelling and grammar checks will help to locate obvious errors, but actual proofreading of the document copy will help in detecting errors that spelling checks will overlook. As text is keyed in, obvious errors in spelling or grammar are indicated with colored wavy lines under the words in question. These lines signal "spots" where decisions are needed in the text. Some office professionals like to key in the text, with little consideration for checking spelling and grammar at that time, and then come back to carefully proofread and edit the text.

5. *Use of Editing Software:* Software suites that include word processing, database, spreadsheet, and presentation programs typically include a number of time-saving editing tools. With the text stored on magnetic media, revisions can easily be made. With stored text, it is a simple matter to change the order of the material, reword sentences, insert new text, or delete unneeded text.

a. *Spell check tools:* All productivity software (e.g., word processing, spreadsheet, database management system, and presentation graphics) includes a spell check feature that will quickly scan the document for spelling errors.

(1) *Activating the spell check feature:* When the spell check is activated, the software scans the soft-copy document for words it does not recognize—words that are *not* in the spell check dictionary, such as proper names. The spell check feature can check spelling as the text is keyed in, giving an almost-instantaneous response to a possible misspelling.

(a) The unrecognized word is highlighted on the screen so that the proofreader can verify the spelling of the word.

(b) If the word is correct, the proofreader ignores the suggested spellings and activates the command to continue the spell check.

(c) If the word is incorrect, the proofreader can correct the word immediately before continuing the spell check function. A spell check also gives the proofreader possible spellings from which to choose.

(2) *Adding words to the electronic dictionary:* Spell check programs allow the proofreader the option of adding new words to the electronic dictionary before continuing. Names and other frequently used technical terms should be added.

(3) *Creating or adding custom dictionaries:* Custom dictionaries with industry-specific terms can also be added to the electronic dictionary. Medical, legal, or construction terms are some of the types of custom dictionaries that may be purchased from a third-party company. Another option is to create a custom dictionary including terms that are used most often in documents and correspondence within the company.

(4) *Highlighting words appearing twice:* Some spell check programs highlight words that appear twice (e.g., the last word in a sentence and the first word in the next sentence). This helps the proofreader to check to see whether the sentence structure should be edited.

b. *Grammar check tools:* Word processing programs also include grammar checks. The spell check and grammar check tools typically run simultaneously. If the sentence structure is considered grammatically incorrect, the grammar check tool highlights that portion of the sentence in question. These tools may correct improper word usage.

EXAMPLE:

Madison keyed in the following sentence:

> *Their should be a meeting on . . .*

The grammar check tool in the word processing software highlights their should be *as an alert so Madison can make a decision as the text is being keyed in. Some grammar tools automatically change* their *to* there.

c. *Software editing tools:* Some of the ways in which software editing tools available with word processing and other software programs are helpful is in highlighting text changes, tracking changes in text, and collaborative writing.

(1) *Highlighting text:* When editing, sometimes deleted or added words need to be highlighted so that the writer recognizes the major changes that are suggested by another person. This method is often used when legal documents or minutes of meetings have been corrected. Two ways of highlighting deleted or added words are **strikethrough** and **shading.**

(a) *Strikethrough and double strikethrough:* The strikethrough feature is used to highlight words that have been deleted from the text. By invoking the word processing command, a line is drawn through each letter or word that should be changed. If the word has already been keyed, the strikethrough can be added by highlighting the word and then invoking the strikethrough command.

EXAMPLE:

The text needs to be ~~edited~~ changed to reflect ~~current~~ up-to-date procedures.

Another form of highlighting is **double strikethrough.** A double line is drawn through each letter or word that is being highlighted for change.

EXAMPLE:

Our ~~primary~~ main concern is to prepare business ~~correspondence~~ letters that will complement ~~the~~ our sales and marketing ~~plan~~ efforts.

Highlighting changes in this way enables the writer to see exactly what types of changes the editor is suggesting. Then, the decision can be made to accept or reject each change quite easily.

(b) *Shading text:* Through shading, any new words or sections that have been added to the document are easily highlighted. If the section has already been keyed, shading can be added by highlighting the section and then invoking the shading command. Both shading and highlighting can be used to show the complete revision. An entire section of text can be shaded to alert the reader to carefully check this part.

EXAMPLE:

Our ~~primary~~ main concern is to prepare business ~~correspondence~~ letters that will complement ~~the~~ our sales and marketing ~~plan~~ efforts.

Our main concern is to prepare business letters that will complement our sales and marketing efforts.

(2) *Tracking changes in text:* Another word processing feature that is especially helpful in editing is **track changes.** When this feature is activated, you are able to perform editing functions (delete, insert, or move text), and the software notes these changes so the writer of the text can see exactly what editing changes are being recommended. The original text is not deleted or changed, except as noted within the text or in comments appearing in the margin. The writer has the option of accepting or rejecting each change that is suggested (see Figure 7–3).

(3) *Collaborative editing:* Any time more than one person is involved in the editing of a document, collaboration must take place. Each person should have the opportunity to indicate changes in the document so that the other person can consider the benefit of the suggestions made. In addition, each person may accept or reject suggested revisions. A final draft needs to incorporate all revisions deemed necessary by the writers and copy editor.

EXAMPLE: *Marquez in the New York City offices and Del Rossi, a Milan, Italy, business associate, are collaborating on developing an advertising campaign for a new product. Their joint presentation will be presented to the organization's Advertising Council for approval next month. In the meantime, they are connected electronically to a specific Web site, e-mail, chat room, and document file. Davison, the advertising manager for the company, is located in the Philadelphia headquarters and reviews and critiques their progress on a day-to-day basis.*

Once the written materials have been developed, Marquez and Del Rossi will collaborate on the development of the electronic presentation to the Council. Because of the nature of the materials prepared, they should be able to make the presentation jointly from their various locations using videoconferencing technology.

Figure 7–3 shows an example of an edited document using track changes.

The process of editing written material is much easier when the editing features in the word processing software program are fully utilized. This is especially true when writer and editor do not have the opportunity to work face to face on editing a document. Often the writer will send textual material as an attachment to an e-mail message so that the editor can read through the material and electronically note suggested revisions on the manuscript itself. The writer then reviews the suggestions to see how these proposed changes will enhance the document content.

6. *Copyediting Style Sheet:* The saying "practice makes perfect" is apropos in the development of copyediting skills. When a long document must be edited, a style sheet is a very helpful tool. The function of the style sheet is to assist the copy editor in remembering all the formatting points the author is expected to follow as well as any editing decisions made while reading the material. The style sheet helps the copy editor maintain consistency throughout the document.

The headings of a style sheet will vary to meet individual needs. An administrative professional who assists in editing articles for publication developed the style sheet illustrated in Figure 7–4. Figure 7–5 illustrates how the style sheet is used to note consistencies in writing.

FIGURE 7–3   Track Changes in Text

THE KEY TO BUYMANSHIP

Economic theory assumes that **all** consumers have all the information required about the products they **need to purchase**. Can the automobile buyer **who buys a new vehicle every one to three years** make an even-handed deal with a salesperson who sees dozens of customers a day? Can the consumer select the correct remedy at the **very** best price without comparative prices being available? The basic question still remains: "**Can** rational decisions **be made** without information?"

Deleted: buy
Deleted: once-every-three years
Deleted: Is it possible to make

Government Regulation

Legislation has been proposed| for regulations to have businesses make available price lists for various services performed. These services would be divided into categories so consumers could specifically see the cost of various components that are purchased.

Comment: Perhaps you could find specific legislation to cite here.
Comment: Good idea! I will check publications to see what I can find.

Product Pricing Information

The Federal Trade Commission contends|that package prices are costing consumers more than they are willing to pay. The trend in government regulation of trade appears to

Comment: You need to cite a secondary source here.
Deleted: and refusal to advertise prices that are not required by law

FIGURE 7–4   Editing Style Sheet

SPELLING	PUNCTUATION	REFERENCES	FORMAT NOTATIONS	OTHER NOTATIONS
NUMBERS	CAPITALIZATION	FACTS	WEB SITES	ATTACHMENTS

FIGURE 7–5   Editing Style Sheet for Editing Text for Article[1]

Spelling	Punctuation	References	Format Notations	Other Notations
1. year-round 2. follow-up meeting 3. boss' office	1. Comma before or or and in series 2. Single quotes within double quotes 3. Semicolon in series when comma already used 4. success—that (dash)	Adela Margrave SPHR, co-author with Robert Gorden, *The Complete Idiot's Guide to Performance Appraisals* (Alpha Books, 2001)	***Steps*** Bold Enumerated Step 1: Step 2:	***Book Title*** Italics ***Web Site*** (Italics)

Numbers	Capitalization	Facts	Web Sites	Attachments
1. 20 years 2. 10-year career coach 3. 12 years 4. $5,000 5. 10 administrative assistants 6. seventh in salary 7. 30 seconds	1. Barbara Abrahamsen CPS 2. Omaha, Nebraska 3. Corporate Diversified Services Inc. 4. Diana Hodges CPS 5. Savannah, Georgia 6. Savannah Electric and Power Co.	Article includes interviews with Barbara Abrahamsen CPS and Diana Hodges CPS	Julie Jansen, Stamford, Connecticut (www.juliejensen.net)	"Tips for Getting the Compensation You Deserve" by Liz Hughes, vice president of OfficeTeam Sidebar: "Don't Get Emotional" by Karen Fritscher-Porter

[1]*Karen Fritscher-Porter, "Positive Performance Appraisals," OfficePro 63(7), October, 2003, pp. 7–12.*

7. *Copyediting Symbols:* To make manual copyediting easier, the symbols illustrated in Figure 7–1 are used. When copyediting manually, these symbols are made within the body of the document. When these editing symbols are written with a colored pencil or pen, they stand out from the printed text. Also, each symbol must be written clearly to aid the writer and administrative professional when the text is reread for verification and prepared in final form.

Composing drafts of documents and editing these drafts comprise an extremely important part of the writing process. Administrative professionals need to perfect their writing, proofreading, and editing skills in order to assist with the preparation of well-written business documents.

Check Point—Section C

Directions: For each question, circle the correct answer.

C–1. When proofreading a business document,
- A) check tables by reading vertically if the material was keyed in horizontally or vice versa
- B) do so immediately while the content is still fresh
- C) page down a screen at a time on soft copy to make sure material is not skipped
- D) read slowly for content while checking for typographical errors

C–2. When editing a business document, the main purpose is a well-written document that
- A) adheres to correct document format
- B) applies correct grammar and punctuation rules
- C) adjusts the writing style from an editor's perspective
- D) is clear, concise, and appeals to the reader while maintaining the writer's objective.

C–3. A copyediting style sheet is a useful tool that
- A) is helpful in maintaining the editor's writing style
- B) should be used when any document is edited
- C) helps to maintain consistency when editing long documents
- D) should have only three areas of concentration for comments

For Your Review

Directions: For each question, circle the correct answer.

1. Business messages need to be written
   A) from the writer's viewpoint
   B) with first-person pronouns like *I* or *me*
   C) from the reader's viewpoint
   D) with a focus on a goal that cannot be achieved

2. Which one of the following statements emphasizes the reader's interest in the message?
   A) Won't you consider becoming an active sponsor of the program?
   B) You have always been a strong supporter of the Special Olympics.
   C) Last year you were contacted about contributing time or money to the program.
   D) We would appreciate your quick response to our request.

3. What you decide to say and how you say it determine the
   A) tone of your business message
   B) style of your business writing
   C) jargon used in your business writing
   D) concreteness of the words you use

4. When you wish to use a foreign expression, you need to be certain that the expression
   A) does not need additional explanation
   B) fits the receiver's cultural background
   C) will be understood by the receiver
   D) will continue to be written in the foreign language

5. Technical language that pertains to a specific professional field is known as
   A) slang
   B) concrete language
   C) acronyms
   D) jargon

6. The difficulty when trying to include slang expressions into business writing is to convey the
   A) sender's intended meaning
   B) meaning of technical language used
   C) tone of the message
   D) message using abstract words

7. Which one of the following expressions is able to be translated literally into another language?
   A) Moore-Longley is expected to cut the mustard within the first few weeks on the job.
   B) Pull up a chair and join us.
   C) Langford was promoted recently to the top position.
   D) Daylight savings time requires us to fall back one hour in October and spring forward one hour in the spring.

8. Select the sentence that is written in active voice.
   A) November 15 is the date for the next AMA professional seminar.
   B) Peterson approved Wolanski's request to attend the AMA professional seminar next month.

C) The AMA professional seminar is scheduled for November 15 in Chicago.

D) Wolanski's participation in the AMA professional seminar on November 15 has been approved.

9. Which one of the following statements illustrates the use of contemporary expressions?

A) Business correspondence can be prepared much faster with up-to-date technology.

B) Typewritten copies of the business documents in the file are available for review.

C) Documents are printed and stored for editing purposes.

D) Today's business information systems require the use of integrated software tools to prepare business documents.

10. Select the statement that includes correct word usage.

A) In your report you can use all of these references except the one by Brody.

B) Your list of references is already to be finalized.

C) Ms. Stevenson has all ready contributed her time to this special event.

D) Your report includes a bibliography for all references accept the one by Brody.

11. Which one of the following sentences uses words correctly?

A) Letterheads and other types of business stationary may be ordered from Central Stores.

B) Plants and other greenery placed between the modular units create a stationery divider between work areas.

C) A conventional executive desk will be placed in a stationary location near the window.

D) To order business stationary, contact R-S Printers at their Web site.

12. Gender-free language is evident in which one of the following sentences?

A) The flight attendant responded to his passengers' questions about the flight delay.

B) Each evening the cleaning woman tidied up the office and vacuumed the carpet.

C) Each administrative professional agreed to review the proposal for salary increases.

D) During the holiday season, a special black-tie dinner is planned for the corporate executives and their wives.

13. *The modular units for the new office are being shipped. Delivery date December 10.* This sentence includes a

A) run-on sentence
B) comma-splice sentence
C) simple sentence
D) sentence fragment

14. *Hunter is an administrative professional with 15 years of experience with the same firm she has just decided to become an entrepreneur.* How would you classify this sentence?

A) simple sentence
B) run-on sentence
C) complex sentence
D) comma-splice sentence

15. A compound sentence consists of two independent clauses joined with a

A) comma and a conjunction
B) comma
C) conjunction
D) semicolon and a conjunction

16. *A business letter is external communication from one organization to another, electronic mail is both internal and external communication.* This sentence is classified as a

A) run-on sentence
B) sentence fragment
C) comma-splice sentence
D) complex sentence

17. The deductive writing approach requires that the
    A) first paragraph includes supporting details for the message
    B) main idea of the message is identified in the first paragraph
    C) first paragraph serves as a buffer
    D) main idea is presented later in the message

18. Coherence in writing is shown by placing special stress on specific words or thoughts. One way of doing this is to
    A) use a pronoun as a substitute for a preceding noun
    B) use words that are commonly found together
    C) write ideas that are equal in thought in parallel form
    D) change the format to a bulleted list of details

19. Placing greater importance on a specific idea or fact is known as
    A) coherence
    B) emphasis
    C) unity
    D) conciseness

20. Applying the "you" approach in documents helps to create
    A) sympathy in business writing
    B) goodwill between the two organizations
    C) empathy in business writing
    D) clarity in expressing key ideas

21. Checking a soft or hard copy of a document for spelling and punctuation accuracy is called
    A) editing
    B) collaborating
    C) proofreading
    D) copyediting

22. The proofreading symbol in this notation (the garden secret) means
    A) the words are transposed
    B) the words should be deleted

C) punctuation needs to be inserted
D) the words need to be capitalized

23. Which one of the following situations best exemplifies collaboration?
    A) The writer uses the direct approach to write a document so that the main idea is presented first.
    B) An administrative professional asks a co-worker to proofread a document just keyed in and to comment on the accuracy of the content.
    C) One team member writes the document and then routes it to the other four team members for their critique and ideas for revision.
    D) A team Web site is established so the five team members (in different locations) can connect through e-mail, a chat room, and document exchange.

24. Collaborative communication enables documents to be developed as a result of writing team members
    A) being in the same location so joint writing can take place
    B) sharing their expertise in producing a document
    C) critiquing a document written by one member of the team
    D) in-person dialoguing between the team members and the copy editor

25. The software editing tool that permits an editor to comment on possible editing changes and that creates explanatory notes so the writer can see both the original copy and suggested revisions is
    A) copyediting
    B) highlighting
    C) track changes
    D) accessing a team Web site

Solutions

Solutions to Check Point—Section A

Answer	*Refer to:*
A–1. (D)	[A-1-a]
A–2. (C)	[A-4-c]
A–3. (C)	[A-8-a (1)]

Solutions to Check Point—Section B

Answer	*Refer to:*
B–1. (C)	[B-1-b (3)]
B–2. (A)	[B, B-1-c]
B–3. (D)	[B-4-b]

Solutions to Check Point—Section C

Answer	*Refer to:*
C–1. (A)	[C-1-c (3)]
C–2. (D)	[C-2-b (4)]
C–3. (C)	[C-6]

Solutions to For Your Review

Answer	Refer to:
1. (C)	[A-1-a]
2. (B)	[A-1-a (2)]
3. (A)	[A-2]
4. (B)	[A-3-c]
5. (D)	[A-3-d]
6. (A)	[A-3-f]
7. (C)	[A-3-f and A-4]
8. (B)	[A–5-b]
9. (D)	[A-6]
10. (A)	[A-7-a]
11. (C)	[A-7-r]
12. (C)	[A-8-a]
13. (D)	[B-1-a (1)]
14. (B)	[B-1-a (2)]
15. (A)	[B-1-a (2) (b)]
16. (C)	[B-1-a (3)]
17. (B)	[B-2-a (1)]
18. (D)	[B-3-a (1)]
19. (B)	[B-3-b]
20. (C)	[B-4-b]
21. (C)	[C-1]
22. (A)	[C-1-d]
23. (D)	[C-3-a (1)]
24. (B)	[C-3-a (2)]
25. (C)	[C-5-c (2)]

Chapter 8

Writing Business Documents

OVERVIEW

As an administrative professional, you have the responsibility of developing clearly written messages. Many executives rely on administrative professionals to handle the majority of the office correspondence as well as to critique the executive's writing. Realizing this, the administrative professional must understand that written communication is more than just stating those facts that an executive believes are important.

Writing what you have to communicate is *encoding* the message in words that you want the receiver to interpret and clearly understand. That message may be delivered to the receiver through a variety of written channels such as an office memorandum, a letter, a formal report, or an electronic mail message, to mention only a few. The selection of a channel is important in persuading the receiver to read the entire message and interpret its intended meaning.

Message interpretation requires the receiver to *decode* the message. As a writer, your responsibility is to strive to have the decoded message convey the intended meaning and understanding of your encoded message. A means for assessing whether this has been accomplished is to seek a response (feedback) from the receiver.

Communicating is more than stating what is important to you. Consideration must be given to all aspects of the communication process—the sender, the channel, the receiver, the feedback—or the written message may result in weak and ineffective communication.

KEY TERMS

Analytical report, 253
Appendix, 262
Bibliography, 262
Buffer, 234
Chronological style, 253

Coding, 258
Data collection, 254
Deductive approach, 231
Direct approach, 231
External report, 252

Findings, 259
Glossary, 262
Goodwill, 230
Horizontal report, 252
Index, 263

229

A. Business Letters

The business letter is *external* communication used most often for corresponding with others outside the organization. The sender uses the letter as a means to inform the receiver of business news and events, to persuade the receiver to take some specific action, and/or to create goodwill between individuals and organizations. Business letters written from the reader's viewpoint apply the "you" approach.

1. *Positive Letters:* Of course, the most pleasant type of letter to write or receive is the *positive* or *favorable* letter—the letter that says "yes" or otherwise presents good news to the reader. The main purpose of the positive letter is to transmit needed information that will please the receiver.

   a. *Types of positive letters:* Positive or favorable letters are written for a variety of reasons. Here are some of the more typical types of positive correspondence.

      (1) *Order for goods or services:* Especially in small companies or in situations where a purchase order is not used in ordering goods or services, a letter will initiate such an order. Complete information identifying the exact purchase needs to be included in the letter, such as the following:

         • Name of item(s) or service(s)

         • Descriptions: order numbers, quantities, sizes, or type of service requested

         • Price per item or unit (if known)

         • Total price of items ordered

         • Shipping information, including means of shipping preferred and shipping costs

      (2) *Letter granting refund or adjustment:* The claim should be described briefly and the exact refund or adjustment explained. Such information as purchase order or invoice numbers must be included in the letter.

      (3) *Response to inquiry for information:* Frequently, letters are received that request certain types of information. The direct approach enables the writer to provide responses to those questions asked.

         EXAMPLE: *Inquiries might include requests for information about a subscription to a new information processing magazine, an application for a new credit account, or a new training program available for administrative professionals.*

      (4) *Goodwill message:* The primary purpose of some correspondence is to generate **goodwill** (a favorable attitude and feeling) toward you and your organization from others with whom you conduct business. A goodwill message can express sympathy, thanks, or congratulations.

EXAMPLES:

Sympathy: *A letter to Jacoby, one of the firm's clients, expresses condolence on the death of her husband.*

Thanks: *A letter thanks Robinson, a business consultant, for presenting the seminar, "Communication Techniques for Administrative Professionals," at the January meeting of the local chapter of the International Association for Administrative Professionals™.*

Congratulations: *A letter congratulates Moore-Young on being promoted to manager of the new Kendall Trust Company branch office.*

b. *Writing approach:* The **direct approach,** also called the **deductive approach,** is used in writing positive letters. When correspondence carries good news, the main idea is presented immediately. Why begin with details when you know the reader is most interested in hearing the good news first? Then, you can follow up with facts and details and close the message with a positive, forward-looking statement. When applying the direct approach in writing a positive letter, you assume that the receiver will be receptive to your message because it contains only positive news.

(1) *Opening paragraph:* Since goodwill is created in the very first paragraph, begin with a general statement of the main point of the message. With the direct approach, you immediately provide the reader with the information he or she wishes to receive.

EXAMPLE:

Our network manager, Mr. Randy Dailey, will be glad to speak to your trainee group on Tuesday, December 4. Mr. Dailey will meet with your group in Conference Room B from 1:30 to 3 P.M.

The opening paragraph says "yes" immediately, indicating a favorable response.

(2) *Body paragraphs:* In the next one or two paragraphs, the necessary details should be fully explained. The reader needs to understand any conditions or other details relating to the message.

EXAMPLE:

From your suggestions, he plans to discuss shared resources, viruses, and system demands. Please review these areas with the trainees prior to December 4. Following his presentation, the trainees will have an opportunity to participate in a short question-and-answer session.

This body paragraph covers the details of the presentation. If more extensive details are needed, you may have additional paragraphs.

(3) *Closing paragraph:* The message should close with a general positive statement or a request for action (a courteous request). If you need the receiver to act by a certain date, this deadline should be included as well as any special reasons for needing this information by that date. You should include contact information (telephone number and e-mail address) so the receiver knows exactly how and when to get in touch with you in case additional questions arise.

FIGURE 8–1   Example of Positive or Favorable Letter

Dear Ms. Stanley:

Our network manager, Mr. Randy Dailey, will be glad to speak to your trainee group on Tuesday, December 4. Mr. Dailey will meet with your group in Conference Room B from 1:30 to 3 P.M.

From your suggestions, he plans to discuss shared resources, viruses, and system demands. Please review these areas with the trainees prior to December 4. Following his presentation, the trainees will have an opportunity to participate in a short question-and-answer session.

Please confirm with Mr. Dailey the number of trainees who will be involved in this session. Exchanging information with talented trainees just entering the field of information technology is always exciting. If you have any questions about the session, please contact me at extension 4135.

Sincerely,

EXAMPLE:

Please confirm with Mr. Dailey the number of trainees who will be involved in this session. Exchanging information with talented trainees just entering the field of information technology is always exciting. If you have any questions about the session, please contact me at extension 4135.

The closing paragraph includes a positive note about working with talented trainees and indicates whom the receiver should contact if any questions arise.

Figure 8–1 illustrates the complete example of the positive or favorable letter.

2. ***Routine or Neutral Letters:*** The primary purpose of the routine letter is to exchange day-to-day information. Routine or neutral letters are written more often than any other type of letter. The routine nature of these letters results in a favorable reception to the content.

  a. *Types of routine letters:* Primarily, routine correspondence includes either requests for information or responses to information requests received. Following are some typical types of routine or neutral letters.

   (1) *Request for information:* A simple request for information can be stated precisely and sometimes briefly.

   EXAMPLE: *A letter requests a vendor to send pricing information for a new computer system just being marketed.*

   (2) *Response to information request:* Sometimes inquiries are received that need to be answered within a short period of time.

   EXAMPLE: *An inquiry is made about appropriate procedures to use in securing an automobile loan from the credit union.*

  b. *Writing approach:* The direct (deductive) approach is also applied when writing routine or neutral correspondence. The reader of the message is expected to be receptive to the information contained in the letter.

   (1) *Opening paragraph:* The main point of the message is presented in the first paragraph. The reader knows immediately what this letter is about.

EXAMPLE:

Would you please give me your opinion on the storage problem that exists with our outdoor storage?

This opening sentence is a direct request for advice and information.

(2) *Body paragraphs:* Factual information should follow in the body paragraphs so that the reader understands the need for the information.

EXAMPLE:

We have an option to purchase a two-year supply of steel moldings. A decision to expand operations means the factory warehouse is needed for other manufacturing materials. Our production manager suggested that the steel moldings could be stockpiled outdoors.

This body paragraph follows up with factual information.

My concern with stockpiling outdoors is the effect of rust and pitting. I understand that your company has used this method of storage for a number of years with much success. In your opinion, what risk might we experience if these steel moldings are exposed to weather conditions for possibly up to two years?

This additional body paragraph identifies major concerns and makes the actual inquiry.

(3) *Closing paragraph:* A summarizing statement in the closing paragraph emphasizes the main point of the message or requests some type of action, sometimes according to a specific deadline. The writer should also include contact information (e.g., telephone number and e-mail address) so that the receiver can provide a response using a more convenient channel.

EXAMPLE:

I would appreciate any advice you can offer about outdoor storage. At our June 15 meeting, we will make a final decision on the steel molding purchase. Could I hear from you before that date? You may telephone me at 815-989-2300, extension 45, or by e-mail at <u>ststone@mhmfg.com</u>.

This closing paragraph asks for action and sets a timeline for a reply. The receiver also has information to help with either a telephone or an e-mail response.

Figure 8–2 shows the complete example of the routine or neutral letter.

3. *Negative Letters:* When correspondence conveys a "no" response or some other form of bad news, you should use the **indirect approach.** This approach may also be referred to as the **inductive approach** and is used when the sender is uncertain about how receptive the receiver will be to the information that is presented. Many times the reader is more likely to take the action you hope she or he will take and is more willing to accept the bad news if the details are presented first. Otherwise, the facts may not even be read. Some feel that the bad news should be placed within a paragraph in the middle of the letter. If this approach is used, you must be very careful that the news you are relaying to the reader is clear. Of course, you will want to close the message with a forward-looking comment that can be positive for both you and the reader. The negative letter is also referred to as an *unfavorable* letter.

FIGURE 8–2   Example of Routine Letter or Neutral Letter

Dear Mr. Boyce:

Would you please give me your opinion on the storage problem that exists with our outdoor storage?

We have an option to purchase a two-year supply of steel moldings. A decision to expand operations means the factory warehouse is needed for other manufacturing materials. Our production manager suggested that the steel moldings could be stockpiled outdoors.

My concern with stockpiling outdoors is the effect of rust and pitting. I understand that your company has used this method of storage for a number of years with much success. In your opinion, what risk might we experience if these steel moldings are exposed to weather conditions for possibly up to two years?

I would appreciate any advice you can offer about outdoor storage. At our June 15 meeting, we will make a final decision on the steel molding purchase. Could I hear from you before that date? You may telephone me at 815-989-2300, extension 45, or by e-mail at *ststone@mhmfg.com.*

Sincerely,

a. *Types of negative letters:* Many different types of business situations require letters that say "no" or include a refusal. Here are a few types of negative letters that may be written.

   (1) *Refusal to send information:* You may receive an inquiry for some information that is not readily available or cannot be released. In this case, a refusal letter must be written in a polite, courteous manner so that the reader will not be offended.

   (2) *Refusal to give assistance:* A request asking for help with a particular problem might be received. You may feel that you are not the right person to ask or do not have the time to adequately carry out the request. Perhaps your organization cannot respond favorably to the request at this time.

   (3) *Problem with order for goods or services:* An order that has been received may not be able to be filled at this time. Perhaps the inventory is low, and the order will not be filled until the inventory is replenished. A letter will need to be sent explaining the delay in shipment.

   (4) *Refusal to grant particular action:* Perhaps you are unable to grant the particular action requested by the sender. In cases where you will be unable to grant a claim or extension of time, a refusal letter must be written.

b. *Writing approach:* The indirect, or inductive, approach is recommended for negative letters.

   (1) *Buffer paragraph:* Since the facts need to be read and understood *before* the bad news is communicated, a beginning paragraph setting the stage may be necessary. Such a paragraph is called a **buffer.** The sender must be careful not to be too wordy, or the reader will begin to read between the lines, assume the news, and not read the important part of the letter—the facts.

   EXAMPLE:

   You can count on a large, interested readership for the article you are writing about the importance of sales letters in business.

This paragraph illustrates a buffer beginning, yet it is not too lengthy.

(2) *Rationale for refusal:* Following the opening paragraph, the first body paragraph needs to explain the reasons for the refusal. The facts must be put into perspective from two viewpoints:

(a) The philosophy of the business, reflecting the goals of the organization

(b) The reader's viewpoint, realizing the wants and concerns of the reader

This is where the balancing act comes into play. By carefully outlining these two viewpoints, the message can be developed in an honest approach while never losing sight of the reader's wants and concerns. The message needs to be delivered in a tactful, understanding manner.

EXAMPLE:

Our company depends on effective sales letters to interest new clients. Through the years, we have tested our letters extensively to find the most effective sales techniques for the written message. Our writers are continually revising, conducting test mailings, and comparing returns. The best letters used by Appleton Enterprises represent a considerable investment in both time and money.

This paragraph presents reasons based on company policy. However, company policy is an internal matter and should not be used as a reason in external communication. Also, reasons given should be logical so there is no need for an apology.

(3) *The "bad news":* Once the reasons for the decision have been given, the refusal or other "bad news" is presented.

EXAMPLE:

Because of this time and research effort, several companies have expressed interest in using our material. Therefore, we decided to copyright all of our sales letters and confine them to company use. Should we release them for publication, we would incur the same expense once again because their effectiveness for us would be decreased.

This paragraph implies "no." Yet, this explanation is written clearly enough so that the reader understands that the letters cannot be used as examples in the article.

(4) *Closing paragraph:* The ending of the letter will ask for action on the part of the reader and/or present a forward look if the news is unfavorable. Since you are hoping to continue correspondence with the reader, you will want a pleasant closing for your message. Avoid being apologetic. If the facts are well thought out and logically presented, no apology will be necessary.

EXAMPLE:

I am enclosing two bulletins and a bibliography we have found helpful in developing our letters. You may also find the material helpful as you prepare your article. I look forward to reading your article in the Writer's Guide *when it is published.*

This letter closes on a positive note, stating interest in reading the article when it is published. In addition, reference materials are being sent to the reader in an effort to help even though the letters cannot be shared.

FIGURE 8–3 Example of Negative Letter

> Dear Ms. Brothers:
>
> You can count on a large, interested readership for the article you are writing about the importance of sales letters in business.
>
> Our company depends on effective sales letters to interest new clients. Through the years, we have tested our letters extensively to find the most effective techniques for the written message. Our writers are continually revising, conducting test mailings, and comparing returns. The best letters used by Appleton Enterprises represent a considerable investment in both time and money.
>
> Because of this time and research effort, several companies have expressed interest in using our material. However, we decided to copyright all of our sales letters and confine them to company use. Should we release them for publication, we would incur the same expense once again because their effectiveness for us would be decreased.
>
> I am enclosing two bulletins and a bibliography we have found helpful in developing our letters. You may also find the material helpful as you prepare your article. I look forward to reading your article in the *Writer's Guide* when it is published.
>
> Sincerely,

In writing a negative or unfavorable letter, you must take the time to write a tactful, courteous letter with the reader's feelings in mind. If the letter discusses a particularly sensitive issue, set it aside for a short time before carefully proofreading and editing it. Then, reread it and revise it so that the message is clear and will be interpreted correctly by the reader. Alternatively, have a co-worker read the letter for clarity, empathy, sincerity, and goodwill.

Figure 8–3 shows the complete example of the negative letter.

4. ***Combination Letters:*** When you can say "yes" to the reader for only part of what is requested, the message should begin with the positive response, followed by details that support both the positive and negative responses. The "no" response needs to be clearly stated, with the letter ending on a positive note.

   a. *Types of combination letters:* Letters that contain both a positive and a negative response may be written for a variety of reasons. Here are a few examples of how the combination letter might be used:

      (1) *Partial order being filled:* Perhaps only part of a sales order can be filled at this time. The combination letter must identify the part of the order that can be filled, followed by reference to the part of the order that cannot be filled.

      (2) *Partial response to information request:* A request for information may include some questions to be answered as well as questions that need replies from other departments or individuals.

   b. *Writing approach:* When you are writing a combination letter, you should begin with the positive aspect of the message.

      (1) *Opening paragraph:* Begin the first paragraph with the positive or "yes" response to the original message. Be careful not to lead the reader into thinking the "yes" is a total response.

EXAMPLE:

Your four rose bushes should arrive by May 20, just in time for spring planting. They were shipped via AR Express, one of our most reliable shipping companies.

The opening paragraph says "yes," making it clear which part of the request is positive—four rose bushes shipped.

(2) *Body paragraphs:* Follow the "yes" statement with details supporting both the positive and the negative aspects of the message. The presentation of these details needs to be logical. It should be clear to the reader which facts relate to the positive part of the message and which ones relate to the negative part of the message.

EXAMPLE:

You will be more than happy with the blossoms these rose bushes yield. These bushes should be planted in a sunny area, keeping the ground moist with evening waterings. For your climate, rose mounds or cones are needed for winter protection.

Facts relating to the good news are presented in this paragraph and are separated from the facts in the following paragraph, which carries the bad news.

The peach trees you ordered normally bloom in April, a time when the Illinois climate varies between 35 and 50 degrees. These peach trees would almost certainly bloom before the last freeze of the winter season. For trees that bloom after the danger of frost in your area, we recommend the Ambrosia. This peach tree produces peaches similar to those of the trees you ordered. The Ambrosia blooms in late May; details are presented in the enclosed brochure.

This paragraph advises that the item ordered is not the best choice, and facts about the tree ordered are compared with facts about an alternative choice so that the reader can decide what action to take. A brochure is enclosed with more detailed information to help the reader make an appropriate decision.

(3) *Closing paragraph:* The letter should close with a positive, forward-looking request for action on the part of the reader. The "no" response to the reader must be clearly stated. Contact information such as a telephone number and an e-mail address is also helpful to the reader who has additional questions about the situation.

EXAMPLE:

Just indicate your instructions on the enclosed postcard or, if you would like a quicker response, call me at 815-245-3390. If we hear from you prior to May 1, we can change your order to the Ambrosia for the same price. Also, you would still be able to plant your trees to take advantage of this season's growth and have them in bloom next year.

Figure 8–4 is the complete example of the combination letter.

5. ***Persuasive Letters:*** A persuasive letter presents positive information to the reader, but the nature of the information is more complex. The writer requests that the

FIGURE 8–4   Example of Combination Letter

Dear Ms. Wieland:

Your four rose bushes should arrive by May 20, just in time for spring planting. They were shipped via AR Express, one of our most reliable shipping companies.

You will be more than happy with the blossoms these rose bushes yield. These bushes should be planted in a sunny area, keeping the ground moist with evening waterings. For your climate, rose mounds or cones are needed for winter protection.

The peach trees you ordered normally bloom in April, a time when the Illinois climate varies between 35 and 50 degrees. These peach trees would almost certainly bloom before the last freeze of the winter season. For trees that bloom after the danger of frost in your area, we recommend the Ambrosia. This peach tree produces peaches similar to those of the trees you ordered. The Ambrosia blooms in late May; details are presented in the enclosed brochure.

Just indicate your instructions on the enclosed postcard or, if you would like a quicker response, call me at 815-245-3390. If we hear from you prior to May 1, we can change your order to the Ambrosia for the same price. Also, you would still be able to plant your trees to take advantage of this season's growth and have them in bloom next year.

Cordially yours,

receiver take some action. However, the writer has the task of providing enough justification for the action that the receiver will be motivated to take.

a. *Types of persuasive letters:* Letters that are persuasive in nature may be used for a number of different reasons. Here are some typical types of persuasive communication that might be written.

   (1) *Special requests for assistance:* Community agencies or nonprofit organizations may engage in fundraising activities. Requests for assistance may be sent to names on mailing lists to encourage contributions.

   (2) *Special requests for information:* People who are engaged in research may make special requests to persons known in a field to help with certain types of information. Such a request must persuade the receiver to cooperate and assist with the study.

   (3) *Marketing goods, services, or ideas:* The marketing or sales letter attempts to interest the receiver in a new product, service, or idea. Such a persuasive letter must be written with the receiver in mind so that the new product or service would appeal to that age group, a person in that particular position, or a person with specific types of needs.

b. *Writing approach:* The approach used most often in writing the persuasive letter is the A-I-D-A (*attention-interest-desire-action*) approach.

   (1) *Opening paragraph:* The opening paragraph must get the reader's *attention*. This may be accomplished by appealing to the reader's responsibilities, interests, or problems. Sometimes, beginning with a question is helpful in gaining the reader's attention.

   EXAMPLE:

   May we have your help again this year? Thanks to your very generous donations in the past, we have been able to keep our Oaken Acres Animal

Shelter open. This holiday season we need your thoughtfulness and kindness once again.

This paragraph begins with a question and then introduces the reader to the problem to, hopefully, get the reader's attention.

(2) *Body paragraphs:* You need to emphasize the reasons why the reader should respond positively to the request. Describe the details of your request by using words that peak the reader's *interest* and help the reader identify with the positive benefits of responding favorably to your request. You want the reader to react positively to your message.

EXAMPLE:

The animals we house at the shelter must be kept warm, clean, and fed through the winter months. Here are some of the ways in which we use your contributions:

- *Homes are provided for many stray dogs and cats until they are adopted.*
- *Veterinarian care is provided for hurt, sick, or abused animals.*
- *Programs on responsible pet care are made available to the general public.*
- *Visits with the animals at the senior citizens retirement centers are very therapeutic and bring much happiness to the residents.*

As a result of reading this detailed follow-up, the interested reader will want to help. Thus, the reader's *desire* to help will no doubt result in a contribution.

(3) *Closing paragraph:* In the closing paragraph, explain to the reader what *action* should be taken. In a courteous manner, appeal to the reader's interest in helping solve the problem.

EXAMPLE:

Please use the enclosed self-addressed envelope to send your contribution today. Your holiday donation will show your continued love and concern for animals and those who benefit from the shelter's service to the community.

Figure 8–5 is the complete example of the persuasive letter.

6. ***Merged Letters:*** Correspondence with some identical parts may be sent to more than one person or company for a specific purpose. Perhaps a person has not paid a bill within the first 60 days, and a form letter prepared for this situation will be sent to each person who still owes a bill. The word processing mail-merge feature can create the main document (a letter) that will be combined with the variable information from a data source that must be inserted on each letter. Merged letters may be of these three types: personalized repetitive letters, letters with variable information, and letters created from standard form paragraphs.

a. *Personalized repetitive letters:* The same letter may be written and sent to a list of different people. One of the benefits of word processing is the opportunity to personalize these repetitive letters with the recipient's address and an appropriate salutation (greeting). Each letter will appear as if it has been individually prepared for the receiver. In addition, the letter may contain a personalized message for the recipient—a postscript on some messages or the use of the person's name in the body of the message. Here is a typical message that is intended for a large group of people.

FIGURE 8–5   Example of Persuasive Letter

Dear Ms. Rodriguez:

May we have your help again this year? Thanks to your very generous donations in the past, we have been able to keep our Oaken Acres Animal Shelter open. This holiday season we need your thoughtfulness and kindness once again.

The animals we house at the shelter must be kept warm, clean, and fed through the winter months. Here are some of the ways in which we use your contributions:

- Homes are provided for many stray dogs and cats until they are adopted.
- Veterinarian care is provided for hurt, sick, or abused animals.
- Programs on responsible pet care are made available to the general public.
- Visits with the animals at the senior citizens retirement centers are very therapeutic and bring much happiness to the residents.

Please use the enclosed self-addressed envelope to send your contribution today. Your holiday donation will show your continued love and concern for animals and those who benefit from the shelter's service to the community.

Sincerely yours,

EXAMPLE:

Every year Royal Travel serves hundreds of Milwaukee area residents who wish to escape from the winter snows and bask in the sunny climate of Florida for the winter.

We have groups leaving Milwaukee during the first week of every month from December through March so vacationers can spend from two to four weeks at their favorite vacation spot. Our service allows you to "leave the flying to us"; let us arrange your flight, ground transportation, and lodging accommodations, if needed.

Our next vacation group leaves from Milwaukee on January 4 for sunny Florida. Won't you let us help you plan your winter vacation in Florida?

(1) *Use of personal names:* The inside address, the salutation, and perhaps a reference within the body of the message require personal information about the receiver—first name, last name, and address. The content of the letter should be kept as standard as possible, with very few changes from letter to letter.

EXAMPLE:

Inside Address:

> *Mr. and Mrs. Robert Stevens*
> *433 West Wisconsin Avenue*
> *Milwaukee, WI 53215-4312*

Salutation:

> *Dear Mr. and Mrs. Stevens:*

Reference in Letter:

> *Every year Royal Travel serves hundreds of Milwaukee area residents like* Robert and Mary Stevens *who wish to escape from the winter snows and bask in the sunny climate of Florida for the winter.*

Note: The rest of the message would stay the same.

(2) *Use of postscripts:* When a number of repetitive letters are being prepared, a postscript can easily be added to some letters to personalize the message. Here is an example of a postscript that might be added to the foregoing example.

EXAMPLE:

P.S. Robert and Mary, we are looking forward to the possibility of having you with us again this year. Didn't we have fun last year? By the way, be sure to ask for the 10 percent discount available to those who have traveled with us before.

b. *Letters with variable information:* A repetitive letter may have variable information as well as constant information. Constant information is the wording that will stay exactly the same on every letter produced. Variable information is any text that must be inserted to complete the message; this information will change on each letter produced. The letter used in the preceding example may be changed to include variable information.

EXAMPLE:

Variable information—Letter 1

Name and Address:	*Mr. and Mrs. Robert Stevens*
	433 West Wisconsin Avenue
	Milwaukee, WI 53215-4312

(1) Departure Site:	*Milwaukee*
(2) Destination:	*Florida*
(3) Departure Date:	*January 4*

Variable Information—Letter 2

Name and Address:	*Dr. George P. Hendricks*
	5554 North Michigan Avenue
	Chicago, IL 60656-1047
(1) Departure Site:	*Chicago*
(2) Destination:	*Arizona*
(3) Departure Date:	*January 10*

Every year Royal Travel serves hundreds of (1) area residents who wish to escape from the winter snows and bask in the sunny climate of (2) for the winter.

We have groups leaving (1) during the first week of every month from December through March so vacationers can spend from two to four weeks at their favorite vacation spot. Our service allows you to "leave the flying to us"; let us arrange your flight, ground transportation, and lodging accommodations if needed.

Our next vacation group leaves from (1) on (3) for sunny (2). Won't you let us help you plan your winter vacation in (2)?

Two methods are used in word processing for the preparation of letters with variable information: the use of mail-merge fields for keying in variable information or the use of data sources (databases) to create records of variable information to merge with form letters and other types of forms.

(1) *Use of mail-merge fields:* The form letter (the main document) is recorded as a word processing document with appropriate merge fields indicated at the "spots" where variables should be keyed. The insertion of each variable is a

manual operation, prompted by the merge field that has been created. Once a variable has been keyed and inserted into the document, the administrative professional can continue the automatic operation to the next "spot" where variable information needs to be inserted.

(2) *Data sources for database:* A complete record of data sources (variable information) may be available in the form of a database. In word processing, this is usually referred to as a mail-merge function, which requires the preparation of a **main document** (the form letter) and a database (the variables). This database of information can include the following types of information for each person on the mailing list:

- Personal or professional title
- Last name
- First name or initial
- Middle name or initial
- Home street address
- Home city
- Home state
- Home ZIP Code
- Home telephone number
- Business street address
- Business city
- Business state
- Business ZIP Code
- Business telephone number
- E-mail address
- Any other variable information that might be pertinent

When the form letter is prepared, merge fields are inserted at the points where variable information will be inserted into the merged letter. These merge fields are prompts that ask for specific information from the database. In the final preparation of the letter, the form letter is merged with appropriate information from the database.

c. *Letters from form paragraphs:* Business organizations use many kinds of form paragraphs to create form letters. Some form paragraphs say "yes" while others say "no" or persuade. A series of form paragraphs pertaining to particular situations can be stored so that the administrative professional can recall only those paragraphs that are appropriate for a given situation. The result is a personalized letter for each recipient.

EXAMPLE:

Form Paragraphs

(1) Every year Royal Travel serves hundreds of (1) area residents who wish to escape from the winter snows and bask in the sunny climate of (2) for the winter.

(2) Every year Royal Travel serves hundreds of (1) businesses that wish to schedule conferences in other parts of the country. Getting away from the winter snows and spending time in a sunny climate may appeal to you and your business associates.

(3) We have groups leaving (1) during the first week of every month from December through March so they can spend from two to four weeks at their favorite vacation spot. Our service allows you to "leave the flying to us"; let us arrange your flight, ground transportation, and lodging accommodations if needed.

(4) We can schedule a group tour, if you wish, at any time during the month and at any time of the year. Special rates are available, depending on the length of your conference. Our service allows you to "leave the flying to us"; let us arrange any flight, ground transportation, lodging, or meeting accommodations your organization may require.

(5) Our next vacation group leaves from (1) on (3) for sunny (2). Won't you let us help you plan your winter vacation in (2)?

(6) Please contact our local representative, (4), at (5) to obtain more details on our conference service to business organizations in the area. Try us—you'll like us!

The merged letter in Figure 8–6 combines form paragraphs (2), (4), and (6).

FIGURE 8–6   Example of Merged Letter

October 25, 200X

Robert Jensen & Associates
5430 North Michigan Avenue
Chicago, IL 60656-1274

Dear *Mr. Jensen*:

Every year Royal Travel serves hundreds of *Chicago* businesses that wish to schedule conferences in other parts of the country. Getting away from the winter snows and spending time in a sunny climate may appeal to you and your business associates.

We can schedule a group tour, if you wish, at any time during the month and at any time of the year. Special rates are available, depending on the length of your conference. Our service allows you to "leave the flying to us"; let us arrange any flight, ground transportation, lodging, or meeting accommodations your organization may require.

Please contact our local representative, *C.S. Moore*, at *(312) 555-2300* to obtain more details on our conference service to business organizations in the area. Try us—you'll like us!

Sincerely,

Paulette S. Bronson
General Manager

Note: The underlined information represents the variable information that would be entered either manually or from the data source.

The more routine, repetitive letters are designed as form letters and prepared using word processing software, the more time the administrative professional will have for customized work. Any time that a letter must be prepared more than once with identical information, a mail-merge procedure should be considered.

Check Point—Section A

Directions: For each question, circle the correct answer.

A–1. Which one of the following examples would be considered a favorable letter?

A) Letter of explanation with an anticipated shipping date
B) Request for information
C) Letter marketing a new product
D) Response to an inquiry for information

A–2. When the direct writing approach is used for a business letter, the first paragraph

A) is a buffer paragraph that sets the stage for the details that follow
B) is written to get the reader's attention
C) begins with a general statement of the main point of the message

D) begins with the facts so that the reader immediately knows the reasons for the answer

A–3. When a negative letter needs to be written,

A) company policy should be used as a rationale for the refusal
B) reasons for the refusal should be clearly presented in the first paragraph followed by a goodwill paragraph
C) the refusal should be clearly stated in the first paragraph and immediately followed by the rationale
D) the first paragraph should set the stage so that the rationale for the refusal (presented in the body paragraphs) is read

B. Memoranda and Short Reports

Within an organization, a very common form of communication is the memorandum, which is *internal* correspondence sent from one office to another. Because memoranda are correspondence between people who know each other and work together, the tendency is to be informal. An electronic mail message is a specific type of memorandum, which is used for both internal and external communication. Short or informal reports can also be written as memoranda.

1. *Memoranda:* A common medium for corresponding within the firm is the memorandum. The memo (as it is often called) can always be used for communication whenever the sender and the receiver of the message work for the same organization. Just as with business letters, memoranda can be prepared that are favorable, unfavorable, or persuasive in nature.

    a. *Favorable memoranda:* When writing a memorandum that is favorable in nature, the same principles that are used for writing favorable business letters can be applied.

        (1) *Types of favorable memoranda:* Here are some of the more common types of favorable memoranda that may be written.

(a) *Request for information:* The memo is written to present a request for explanatory information.

(b) *Response to information request:* The memo may be written as a reply to a previous request for specific information.

(c) *Request for assistance:* The memo may be a request for help in locating specific information from the files or records.

(d) *Directives:* The memo may issue a directive from management with complete instructions for performance of a particular assignment.

(2) *Writing approach:* The direct (deductive) approach is used in writing favorable memoranda. Each memorandum should include information pertaining to only one topic or objective. The style of writing may vary somewhat depending on the purpose of the memorandum. The receiver is expected to be receptive to the message in a favorable memorandum.

(a) *Opening paragraph:* The main idea (subject) of the message should be presented in the opening paragraph. Begin the memorandum with a statement of the general objective.

EXAMPLE:

The attached list of clients who have utilized our services at least once in the last six months will give you the information you requested for your semiannual report.

(b) *Body paragraphs:* Follow the general opening paragraph with detailed information supporting the ideas presented in the memo. Otherwise, it can become difficult to determine under what subject or name the memo will be filed for later reference.

EXAMPLE:

The alphabetical list is sequenced according to the product or service provided. We have also included the name of the branch office serving each client. The list is updated every two weeks.

(c) *Closing paragraph:* A closing comment or statement is required to summarize or give an opinion or recommendation. In addition, an offer to help further provides a courteous closing to the message.

EXAMPLE:

Please let me know if you still need additional client information for your report. You may reach me by telephone at extension 6859 or by responding to this e-mail message.

Figure 8–7 shows a complete illustration of this favorable memorandum.

b. *Unfavorable memoranda:* Memoranda that are unfavorable in nature and carry a "no" response should be written using the *indirect*, or *inductive*, approach. The position and status of the sender and the receiver of the message should also be considered very carefully so that lines of authority are observed in the tone and style of the memorandum. Techniques similar to those used in writing negative letters should be used.

FIGURE 8–7   Example of Favorable Memorandum

January 23, 200X

TO: Dr. Chris McMahon

FROM: Robert Hanrahan

SUBJECT: CLIENT LIST FOR SEMIANNUAL REPORT

The attached list of clients who have utilized our services at least once in the last six months will give you the information you requested for your semiannual report.

The alphabetical list is sequenced according to the product or service provided. We have also included the name of the branch office serving each client. The list is updated every two weeks.

Please let me know if you still need additional client information for your report. You may reach me by telephone at extension 6859 or by responding to this e-mail message.

Attachment

(1) *Types of unfavorable memoranda:* Here are some of the most common reasons for writing unfavorable memoranda:

  (a) *Refusal of information request:* You may receive a request for information that is confidential in nature and cannot be released or for information that is not available to you. Reasons should be given in the memorandum explaining why you cannot supply the requested information.

  (b) *Refusal to give assistance:* You may be asked for your help, but you may need to consult with your superior to see whether you will be permitted to help. When you need to refuse, you should do it in a courteous way, perhaps suggesting an alternative.

  (c) *Performance evaluation:* A memorandum that explains an unfavorable performance evaluation should be handled with care. The contents of the memorandum should be explained in person as well as in written form so that the individual being evaluated has an opportunity to question or discuss aspects of the evaluation with the supervisor.

(2) *Writing approach:* The indirect, or inductive, approach is recommended for unfavorable memoranda. The writing style used will depend on the position of the person who is receiving the memorandum as well as the nature of the message being presented. The receiver is not expected to be receptive to this type of message.

  (a) *Opening paragraph:* The beginning paragraph acts like a buffer in setting the stage for the explanation that follows. A brief introduction to the nature of the memorandum should be stated clearly.

  EXAMPLE:

  The interviews for the three finalists for the new position as information services manager have been completed. We were especially fortunate to have you as one of the finalists. Your ten years of experience with our organization have been invaluable to us.

(b) *Rationale for refusal:* The basic reasons for having to refuse to assist, refuse to give information, or say "no" should be explained briefly and clearly. The details must be presented so that the views of the organization as well as the reader are considered important.

EXAMPLE:

Just as we were considering our final decision, President Lowell Ramirez announced that we will have to delay our decision for six months. We need to see first how our services are faring in today's economy.

(c) *The negative news:* The refusal or other bad news should be clearly stated so that the recipient will fully understand the message.

EXAMPLE:

Therefore, we are not selecting a new information services manager at this time.

(d) *Options:* Following the refusal, you may present available options: make a referral, offer a substitute, or suggest an alternative procedure. Offering an option is called *refusing with recourse.*

EXAMPLE:

When our "hiring freeze" is lifted, we will contact you to see if you are still interested in being considered for the position.

(e) *Closing paragraph:* The ending of the memorandum may ask for some further action on the part of the receiver or present an alternative that might be considered. Contact information should be included so that the receiver can respond more directly to the sender.

EXAMPLE:

In the meantime, if you have any questions about our promotion policy, please call me at extension 3651 for an appointment. I will be glad to respond to any question you may have.

Figure 8–8 illustrates the complete unfavorable memorandum.

c. *Persuasive memoranda:* An approach similar to that used for persuasive letters should be used in writing memoranda that are persuasive in nature. The *attention-interest-desire-action* approach should be used to develop a message that results in some positive action taken by the receiver.

(1) *Types of persuasive memoranda:* Usually, a persuasive memorandum is designed to get someone else to act or to do something for you. Here are some typical reasons for writing persuasive memoranda.

(a) *Special request for information:* You may need some information for a research project you are working on. A special request to someone in charge of organizational records may provide you with needed information to complete your research.

(b) *Special request for assistance:* Sometimes administrative professionals need help in handling a particularly difficult problem. A special request in the form of a memorandum would be needed in situations where a brief explanation of the problem would help the person decide whether to help or to assign someone else to help.

FIGURE 8–8   Example of Unfavorable Memorandum

September 10, 200X

     TO: Samuel Scott

  FROM: Dorothy M. Presley
              Human Resources Manager

SUBJECT: INFORMATION SERVICES MANAGER POSITION

The interviews for the three finalists for the new position as information services manager have been completed. We were especially fortunate to have you as one of the finalists. Your ten years of experience with our organization have been invaluable to us.

Just as we were considering our final decision, President Lowell Ramirez announced that we will have to delay our decision for six months. We need to see first how our services are faring in today's economy.

Therefore, we are not selecting a new information services manager at this time. When our "hiring freeze" is lifted, we will contact you to see if you are still interested in being considered for the position.

In the meantime, if you have any questions about our promotion policy, please call me at extension 3651 for an appointment. I will be glad to respond to any question you may have.

     (c) *Selling a service or idea:* An offer to help another person within the organization, through a service or an idea, should be put into writing so that the receiver will have time to consider the importance of the offer to help with particular tasks. A serious offer such as this requires time so that the recipient of the message can consider alternatives.

  (2) *Writing approach:* The writing approach used for persuasive letters will also be used for writing persuasive memoranda. The primary objective of the memorandum is to encourage someone within the organization to act positively toward a request that is being made.

     (a) *Opening paragraph:* The opening paragraph of the memorandum must get the reader's attention. Sometimes an opening question will appeal to the reader's interest.

     (b) *Body paragraphs:* The rationale for a positive reaction to the request needs to be presented next. You need to emphasize the reasons why the reader should respond favorably to your request, and you need to provide details so that the reader completely understands your request.

     (c) *Closing paragraph:* End the memorandum with a courteous request that a certain action be taken. In this paragraph, you need to appeal to the reader's interest in helping to solve the problem or act in a specific way.

  2. ***Informal or Short Reports:*** Another form of internal communication is the informal or short report. This type of report is used to transmit meaningful information to other people within the organization. Perhaps the most important aspect of the report, besides its content, is the fact that it is *informal* and *short*. Typically, an informal report

is no more than four to seven pages. In fact, the fewer pages the better; the busy executive will look at the first page of such a report and will need to be persuaded through the message to read further.

a. *Types of informal, short reports:* The informal or short report can present business information in a number of ways. Some of the more common types of reports include the following.

   (1) *Proposal:* Designing new office procedures or planning for new equipment may necessitate the development of a proposal to present to management. A **proposal** is a plan that includes information such as *what* the new development is, *why* it is important to the continued efficient operation of the business, *how* it will be used, and *how much* implementation will cost. A short report should give enough information to management so that the decision can be made whether to continue with the plan.

   (2) *Feasibility study:* An analysis of business systems and procedures obtained through a feasibility study may be presented to management as an informal or short report. An explanation of the procedures used as well as the results will provide management with a summary of the research highlights.

   (3) *Progress report:* Sometimes an administrative professional is called upon to prepare a **progress report** that outlines steps already completed in a project and others that still need to be completed. The format for an informal or short report is very appropriate for this type of report, sometimes referred to as a *work-in-progress report.*

   Any business report can be written as an informal, short report. In fact, most reports are written in this form.

b. *Acceptable formats:* Basically, the three formats used for informal or short reports are the memorandum (sent within the organization), letter (sent outside the organization), and manuscript (both internal and external).

c. *Writing approach:* The direct, or deductive, approach is often used in writing an informal or short report. Some managers prefer to present results or solutions first, followed by the detailed information relating to those results. The inductive approach is popular, too, especially for persuasive reports.

   (1) *Personal style:* The writing style may be personal and conversational, with limited self-reference. Writing in the first or second person is acceptable if it is not overused.

   (2) *Presentation of information and analysis:* Depending on the problem pursued, both basic information and detailed analysis may be included in the report. Attention should be focused on brevity, however, since this is a short report (four to seven pages). The data analysis, if any, need not be as detailed as in a more formal report. A limited number of tables and charts may be used to support findings.

   (3) *Supplementary information:* The report itself, without supplementary parts like appendices and bibliographies, may be the most important to the reader. Sometimes the informal or short report includes only the highlights or outline of events that were studied, with a final notation that if the reader wishes access to more detailed bibliographic information or appendices, a request should be made.

Check Point—Section B

Directions: For each question, circle the correct answer.

B–1. Kim, the vice president of operations, needs to communicate a new company directive with complete instructions for finishing a project. Which form of communication is best?

A) Combination letter
B) Favorable memorandum
C) e-Mail
D) Formal report

B–2. Which type of communication is best for a performance evaluation that stipulates the need for skill improvement?

A) e-Mail
B) Negative letter
C) Informal/short report
D) Unfavorable memorandum

B–3. A three-page informal report recommending that the need for a new records system must be communicated to several administrators within the organization is called a

A) feasibility study
B) progress study
C) proposal
D) technical report

C. Electronic Mail

Electronic mail (e-mail) is becoming a typical way of transmitting informal communication both internally and externally in a very effective manner. Networked organizations are finding that effective use of electronic mail has improved the dissemination of information and, consequently, decision making. Here are some of the advantages of e-mail messaging:

- An e-mail message is focused, short, and to the point.
- The message is transmitted immediately over the network.
- The cost of communicating decreases through the use of e-mail.
- e-Mail provides a relatively easy method for sending and receiving information.

1. *Fundamentals of Writing e-Mail Messages:* As an informal means of communication, an e-mail message should deal with one topic, the subject of the message. The fundamentals of effective business writing are applied in preparing short messages that concentrate on the four Cs: conciseness, correctness, completeness, and courtesy.

    a. *Conciseness:* An e-mail message presents only the information that is pertinent at that point in time. Sentence structure affects the reader's understanding. Typically, short, simple sentences are used in e-mail communication. More detailed information about the subject can follow in a memorandum, a short report, or a business letter.

    b. *Correctness:* Any facts or detailed information presented in the e-mail message must be accurate. The writer must not misrepresent the intended meaning of the message by being too concise and possibly omitting important information. Also, the use of spelling and grammar checks will eliminate the possibility of making simple word or keyboarding errors.

    c. *Completeness:* Before invoking the *send* command, read the e-mail message carefully to make sure that it accurately conveys your message and that any important documents are attached. You must be concise, yet complete. Sometimes there is a very fine line between being concise and being complete.

    d. *Courtesy:* With the ease in composing and sending e-mail messages, it becomes easy to be too curt and too much to the point. The reader's perspective, the "you" approach, is as important in e-mail messages as it is in any other business communication.

2. ***Subject of the Message:*** Since the purpose of e-mail is to enhance rapid communication, the recipient needs to know the topic of the e-mail before opening the message. Because of the fear of viruses, some people will not even open an e-mail message without knowing the subject, even though they know the sender. A descriptive subject line of three to five words is important for all business e-mail.

EXAMPLE:

IAAP International Convention *is a much more descriptive subject line than just* Convention.

3. ***The Message:*** The message of the e-mail should be concisely written with special attention to correctness, completeness, and courtesy shown to the receiver.

   a. *Salutation:* Include a greeting, either formal or informal, to begin the message. The greeting is followed by either a colon (formal), a comma (informal), or an exclamation point (for emphasis).

   EXAMPLES:

   Greetings, Ben: Hi, Joe!

   Dear Nancy,   Dear Mr. Lawrence:

   b. *Message:* The same principles applied to writing favorable, unfavorable, and persuasive memorandum messages can be applied to the writing of e-mail messages. Only one topic (subject) should be covered in an e-mail message. Complete information about the topic needs to be included in the message. Use complete sentences of no more than 20 words to express your thoughts and ideas. Paragraphs should be three to five sentences for ease of reading.

   Figure 8–9 shows an example of an entire electronic mail message.

FIGURE 8–9   Example of Electronic Mail Message

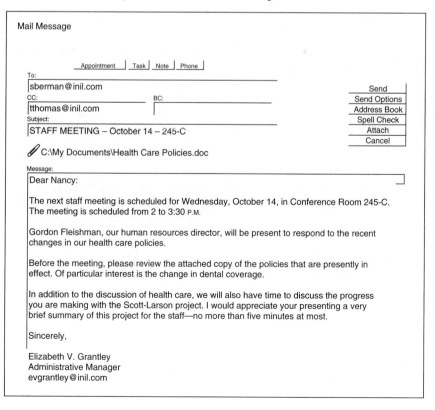

Check Point—Section C

Directions: For each question, circle the correct answer.

C–1. Electronic mail is best used for
  A) external communication to a keynote speaker confirming the details of the program
  B) external and internal communication regarding the new automated teller bank location
  C) internal communication regarding several new company procedures
  D) internal and external communication that is focused, short, and to the point

C–2. To enhance the effectiveness of e-mail communication, the recipient first needs to know the
  A) subject of the e-mail message
  B) sender of the message
  C) action required of the recipient
  D) deadline being imposed

C–3. An e-mail message should accommodate
  A) all details related to a specific topic
  B) the writer's point of view
  C) information related to one specific topic or subject
  D) action desired of the receiver

D. Business Reports

The primary purpose of the business report is to transmit meaningful data to one or more persons who need the information for decision-making purposes. A business report may be oral or written. (The concentration in this chapter is on the written report.)

1. *Types of Reports:* Reports are classified according to type of text or data material, time interval, informational flow, context, function, and message style.

   a. *Textual material:* Reports that include primarily text material (words) are referred to as **narrative reports.** Reports that include primarily numerical data are referred to as **statistical reports.**

   b. *Time interval:* Reports known as **scheduled reports** are issued at regular, stated intervals—weekly, monthly, or quarterly. Progress reports may be prepared during a project to report on its status. **Special reports** may be prepared on demand that concern unusual or nonroutine requests for information.

   c. *Informational flow:* A **vertical report** may be prepared for someone at a higher level within the organizational structure of the company or for someone at a lower level. A **horizontal report** is communication at the same administrative level and may be distributed from department to department or division to division within the organization. An **external report** is one that will be disseminated outside the organization. Sometimes these reports are called *radial reports*, which are reports that cut across levels of authority or move both inside and outside an organization.

   d. *Context:* **Nontechnical reports** convey information to people who do not have backgrounds in a given subject area. In writing such a report, an effort is made to refrain from using technical language. **Technical reports** are designed for conveying information to professionals within the field who will understand the specialized vocabulary and terminology included in the report.

e. *Function:* Reports may be informational or analytical in nature.

   (1) *Informational report:* Facts are presented in an organized, structured manner within an **informational report.** Sometimes the report is prepared using a standardized format, such as in the case of an inspection report or an accident report.

   (2) *Analytical report:* In addition to presenting basic information and facts, the **analytical report** presents primary data and provides an analysis and interpretation. A thorough analysis of the findings will lead to the development of conclusions and recommendations based on the data presented.

f. *Message style:* A report may be prepared in **chronological style** (according to the sequence in which events occurred), **logical style** (according to patterns of reasoning), or **psychological style** (according to the receiver's needs).

2. ***Planning, Designing, and Conducting Research:*** Prior to doing the actual research for a report, it is necessary to plan exactly what the research will entail. The research can involve the study of a problem, a trend, or an issue. When a *problem* is researched, the result is a preferred solution from several alternatives. A *trend* examines a topic over a specific period of time. An *issue* has no resolution as yet and must be examined in terms of different points of view. The report is the *result* of the research. Therefore, if care is exercised in planning the research study, the information required in the final report will be collected in a systematic manner.

   a. *Definition of problem, trend, or issue:* First, you need to know what problem needs to be solved, trend needs to be reviewed, or issue needs to be studied. We generally refer to the topic as the problem. You must distinguish the problem from its symptoms. A clear definition of the problem, as well as any limitations, is necessary.

      (1) *Research questions:* Specific research questions need to be answered through the study being conducted.

      (2) *Subproblems:* The topic might be further defined into at least three subproblem areas that become the themes for the study.

      (3) *Preliminary research:* To become familiar with the problem, find out how the organization has been involved in this type of problem solving. Research other types of background information that will help you plan the report. This phase includes the review of related literature that presents current, practical information from business.

      (4) *Limitation of the study:* Usually, the general topic of the report must be narrowed so that a particular problem, trend, or issue can be pursued. Some typical questions to ask in narrowing the topic include the following:

         • *What* do you want to do?
         • *Why* is this important?
         • *When* will the study take place?
         • *Where* will the study take place?
         • *Who* are the people (the sample or population) being studied? (This is relevant if people are involved.)

      (5) *Scope of the study:* Another consideration in defining the topic is to determine exactly what will be studied and what will *not* be studied.

(6) *Identification of factors or variables:* Key elements of the research are independent variables, dependent variables, and other factors affecting the design of the study and report. The identification of these elements tends to give structure to the study (and the future report). Such factors as employee attitudes, work flow, and technology help to frame the focus of the study and specific themes related to the problem.

The topic must be defined before the subsequent steps in the process may be effectively pursued. The rest of the report format depends on the data that need to be collected and analyzed.

b. *Collecting data:* Once the problem has been defined and approved by superiors, the collection of research data may begin. **Data collection** is the accumulation of data or facts from primary and secondary sources to analyze the problem thoroughly and evaluate possible solutions to the problem.

(1) *Secondary sources:* A review of previous research enables you to gain valuable background information relating to the topic of your study. **Secondary research** is an investigation to gather information that others have written and prepared as the basis for primary research.

(a) *Prior research:* A review of prior research will show what research has already been done. This information is valuable to you in determining the direction your research should go, especially in terms of new directions.

(b) *Related themes:* You may find related themes that also need to be considered in your research, including some not previously considered.

(c) *Justification for need:* A review of prior research and literature pertaining to the problem should lead to the supportive information needed to justify this particular research study or report.

(d) *Supporting evidence:* Sometimes you need supportive information for procedures you choose to use or actions you hope to take to solve a problem. If someone has already used a particular procedure, this could support your use of the same procedure in a different research setting.

Secondary research data may be obtained from company publications, general reference books, government documents, periodicals, information banks and databases, research studies, and other types of reports. The Internet and World Wide Web provide access to a multitude of secondary references that may be helpful in obtaining current data and information. However, Internet and WWW sources tend to be less reliable at times because of the scarcity of information about each source (i.e., publication or copyright date or author names are sometimes missing).

(2) *Primary sources:* When you gather the original information to use as current data in a report, you are conducting **primary research.** Three types of primary research are typically conducted: experimental, observational, and survey research.

(a) *Experimental research:* The purpose of experimental research is to determine whether a change in one factor or variable causes a change in another factor or variable. The research design must ensure that any change that results is due to the factor in question.

(b) *Observational research:* The purpose of observational research is to see or observe the actions or results of individual or group activities. Such research may be conducted in person by actually spending time in the research location observing people's behavior. An intermediary process, such as videotaping or filming a work process for later review and analysis, is another method of collecting observations.

(c) *Survey research:* In survey research, the primary purpose is to determine opinions, beliefs, or reactions to specific work situations. The types of questions asked could range from questions about an actual work process to questions concerning the environment, technology used, or opinions about the future. A survey can be administered either in written form (a questionnaire) or oral form (an interview) to an entire population or a sample drawn from a large population.

(3) *Data collection procedures:* Procedures used in collecting valid and reliable data must be planned and carefully monitored. Care in using sampling techniques and developing questionnaires will help to increase the validity and reliability of collected data. Valid research procedures measure what they are intended to measure. Reliable data are data that are consistently and accurately measured.

(a) *Questionnaire:* Factual data, attitudes, and opinions may be obtained through the use of a questionnaire. A *questionnaire* is a written form that includes all questions to be answered, with space allowed for providing the answers on the form or on an additional answer form. The use of optical mark recognition (OMR) response forms (mark sensing) will improve the speed and accuracy of data input for analysis. Specific techniques should be used in developing items for a questionnaire. Here is a sampling of some of these techniques.

- The items must be worded in a parallel manner so that they will be accurately interpreted.
- Only one response should be obtained per item; ask only one question per item.
- Responses to the questions should not be influenced by the way the question is written. The statement or question should be stated as objectively and nonjudgmentally as possible.
- Only items that pertain to the research problem should be included.
- Items must be written so that answers are bias free.
- The format used for each statement or question will help in making it relatively easy for the respondent to quickly and easily answer.
- The items should be sequenced in a logical, coherent order. All items pertaining to a particular subproblem or theme might be placed in the same section.

The questionnaire should be designed in such a way that the data will be collected in the order in which results will be presented in the report. The tabulation and evaluation of the data will always appear in the same sequence.

Questionnaires may be administered through the U.S. Postal Service, Web sites, or electronic mail. A letter or e-mail message will explain the need for the research to each person in the sample. Written directions will be given for completing the questionnaire items, and the deadline for return of the completed questionnaire will be indicated.

When mailing a questionnaire, a self-addressed envelope should be included for ease in returning completed questionnaires. Responses to questions on Web sites are automatically submitted when completed. Responses to an e-mail questionnaire can be returned by e-mail to the sender when completed.

(b) *Personal interview:* Another technique that is used to obtain responses to open-ended questions is the **personal interview.** An interview allows you to obtain responses to questions in person. An interview schedule will indicate the actual interviews set up along with the open-ended questions to be asked. It is important to make an appointment ahead of time with each interviewee to be sure that the respondent sets aside adequate time to respond to the questions. If numerous interviews are being conducted, each should be conducted in exactly the same way, with the questions being asked in the same sequence. Individual responses need to be recorded in writing or taped for further analysis. The personal interview has the advantage of providing the opportunity for a more in-depth response than the mail questionnaire.

(c) *Telephone interview:* The telephone can be an important research tool as well. An interview can be conducted over the telephone, asking the respondents the same questions that would be asked in a mail questionnaire or a personal interview. The telephone interview must be designed so little time is needed to administer it. Sometimes the data are keyed directly into a computer as the respondent answers the questions. In questions with subquestions (or branches), the computer can be programmed to skip to the next appropriate question.

EXAMPLE:

If the question is this:

Do you believe that the open plan has contributed to better communication in the office?

Yes _____   No _____

If you answer "yes," skip to Questions 15–18.

The interviewer asks the respondent the question. If the respondent answers "yes," then the computer will immediately branch to Question 15 when the interviewer enters the "yes" answer on the keyboard.

The telephone interview is still not as effective as the personal interview. A relatively small number of questions can be included in the telephone interview compared with the personal interview, but, of course, the personal interview is more expensive.

(4) *Question format:* The format of the question plays an important role in data analysis. Select a format that makes data analysis easy. Question formats can be closed, open, or scaled.

(a) *Closed format:* The closed- question format provides the respondent with a choice of answers. Choices can be as simple as "Yes, No, Don't know" or "Agree, Disagree, No opinion." Sometimes the closed question requires a selection from a list.

EXAMPLES:

Current Occupation (please check)

_____	*Student*
_____	*Blue-collar worker*
_____	*White-collar worker*
_____	*Professional*
_____	*Unemployed*
_____	*Retired*
_____	*Other: _____*

Household Income—Combined (please check)

_____	*Below $10,000*
_____	*$10,000–24,999*
_____	*$25,000–39,999*
_____	*$40,000–59,999*
_____	*$60,000–74,999*
_____	*$75,000 and over*

The respondents are to circle or check their responses. Sometimes it is important to clarify the choice so that the respondent understands what the category means. For current occupation, it may be helpful to provide a definition of blue-collar worker, white-collar worker, and professional. Notice in all cases that a choice for alternative answers (Other, $75,000 and over) is provided.

(b) *Open format:* The open-question format, sometimes called the open-ended question, requires the respondent to provide an answer. No choices are provided. With open questions, data analysis may be more difficult because of the variety of responses. Two respondents may use different terminology but in fact provide similar answers. Many open questions can be made into closed questions. If open questions are used, provide enough space for the respondent's answer.

EXAMPLE:

What advice would you give a recent high school graduate about becoming an administrative professional?

_____

_____

(c) *Scaled format:* Rating scales allow the respondent to rank a list of items or to respond according to a continuum. The scaled format also complements data analysis.

EXAMPLES:

Please rank the job characteristics in order of importance to you. Use 1 for most important, 2 for second most important, and so on, until you have ranked all the items. Two blank lines have been provided for you to write in other important job characteristics.

_____	*Challenge*
_____	*Interaction with people*
_____	*Job responsibility*
_____	*Salary*
_____	*Task variety*

_____

_____

For each job characteristic, please circle the degree to which the characteristic is important to you.

CHALLENGE

1	*2*	*3*	*4*	*5*
Unimportant		*Moderately Important*		*Very Important*

INTERACTION WITH PEOPLE

1	*2*	*3*	*4*	*5*
Unimportant		*Moderately Important*		*Very Important*

c. *Analyzing data:* The next step is to analyze, evaluate, and interpret the data that have been collected. Data are really nothing until this phase of the research; this is the step that gives meaning to the data.

   (1) *Data organization:* Once the data are collected, they need to be organized for further evaluation and interpretation. Some of the data organization should have occurred during the development of the questionnaire, at least in the grouping of categories of questions on the questionnaire.

   (a) *Data classification:* Data need to be classified into appropriate groups. These groups should be meaningful so that results of the data analysis will have meaning.

   (b) *Data editing:* Data must be examined carefully for missing or inaccurate data. A respondent may not have followed the directions carefully enough in completing the questionnaire or survey. If there are missing data, you can use specific procedures in handling the response, depending on the computer program you are using to assist in the data analysis. In some cases, you will want to eliminate the respondents' answers to the entire questionnaire if there is too much inconsistency in responding.

   (c) *Data coding:* If data are to be entered and analyzed by a computer program, the data coding procedure is very important. **Coding** means that a number is assigned to each response classification.

(d) *Data tabulation:* The number of responses in each classification for each statement or question will need to be counted. Frequency distributions are created from the data. The counting can be done manually or by the computer.

(e) *Statistical analysis:* Statistics can be generated that will result in percentages, measures of central tendency, and measures of dispersion.

  • *Percentages:* Percentages are ratios that show a relationship between two or more response classifications; percentages are presented as a base of 100.

  • *Measures of central tendency:* These statistics measure the center value of a data distribution.

    Mean: The arithmetic average or *mean* of a group of responses is obtained by computing the sum of all the responses and dividing by the number of responses.

    Median: The *median* is the midpoint in a distribution of responses.

    Mode: The response that occurs the most frequently in a distribution of responses is the *mode*.

  • *Measures of dispersion:* These values show the variation of the data in a distribution.

    Range: The difference between the value of the highest response and the value of the lowest response in a distribution is called the *range*.

    Standard deviation: The *standard deviation* is a measure of the degree of scattering of a frequency distribution about its arithmetic mean.

(2) *Data evaluation and interpretation:* The summary statistics that have been computed can be used to make specific inferences from the data about the problem that was defined earlier. Any inferences made about the population (even though you might have only used a sample) are based on the accuracy, significance, and relationships shown in the data. During this stage, meaning is derived from the data, and you must use logical reasoning in order to develop any conclusions based on the data. The result of the data evaluation and interpretation is the development of *findings* (or facts) and *conclusions* (generalizations) derived from the study.

d. *Reporting findings and drawing conclusions:* The findings are usually reported immediately following the research data presentation that supports the findings. In the data analysis, the narrative sequence includes the presentation and explanation of the data within the paragraphs, followed by the statistical table representing the supportive evidence. A complete set of findings and conclusions derived from these findings are usually presented in a summary chapter or section of the report.

(1) *Findings:* The majority of a report discusses primary research data from which findings are derived about the population or sample studied. The **findings** are usually summarized immediately following the presentation of the data as a capstone to the data analysis section of the report. The findings (or key findings) may also be summarized in the final chapter (or section) of the report if there is a section for such a summary.

(2) *Conclusions:* An informational report merely presents facts resulting from secondary sources to the reader that may be useful in further study or review. However, your research may involve the preparation of an analytical report that requires the collection of primary data that were subsequently analyzed. Conclusions are generalizations about the population or sample that are drawn as a result of the data analysis. Such conclusions *must* be based only on the data that were analyzed; no proof exists for any other inferences. If you find significant differences between two sets of data, reporting the significance is a finding. A conclusion drawn from the finding can present an explanation of what this finding means to the entire population.

(3) *Recommendations:* The conclusions drawn as a result of the findings form the basis for recommendations that may result in further research and study, new materials to be developed, or training programs to be designed. Sometimes there are implications for organizations that should be considered as well, even though the exact consequences might not be known. Implications might include the need for additional professional staff, changes in business systems utilized, or developmental plans for the organization.

e. *Organizing the report:* Developing the final written report will depend most on how well the report plan is organized. The sequence of the report must be decided, whether the report will be inductively or deductively written. In addition, the outline for each report section needs to be determined.

(1) *Inductive organization:* Inductive writing leads from specific to general. This is the most prominent plan used for formal reports. The report includes the following major sections:

> Introduction to the problem or topic
> > Background information
> > Statement of the problem or topic
> > Importance of the study
> > Definitions of terms
>
> Presentation of major themes of the study
> > Identification of subproblems (themes)
> > Supporting data analysis
>
> Findings
>
> Conclusions
>
> Recommendations
>
> Works cited or referenced

An inductively organized report enables the reader to see in detail what the entire research study entailed.

(2) *Deductive organization:* Deductive writing begins with a presentation of general information, followed by the more specific information obtained through the research. A report developed in this way includes the following major sections:

> Conclusions
>
> Recommendations

> Statement of the problem or topic
>> Background information
>> Importance of the study
>> Definition of terms
>
> Research procedures applied in the study
>
> Data analysis
>
> Findings
>
> Summary
>
> Works cited or referenced

When reviewing a deductively written report, the reader can become familiar with the conclusions and recommendations first before delving into the intricate details of the report itself.

(3) *Other types of organization:* Sometimes a report will be presented chronologically because of the importance of a particular time frame or specific trends. Such a report might be divided into phases or sections based on certain periods of time. Reports might also be presented that highlight activities or functions affecting different aspects of the organization (e.g., sales according to geographic regions).

The report should be planned in such a way as to develop an outline of the major report headings that will be used. This outline serves as a guideline for the writer and eventually will become the table of contents (with the addition of subheadings inserted as the writing goes along). The writer needs to be consistent in outlining, using appropriate outline symbols and sequences.

f. *Writing the report:* The final step in the research process is the actual writing of the report itself. Whether formal or informal style is used to write the report depends on the situation and the needs of people for whom the report is being prepared. A formal, impersonal style may be used for longer reports written primarily for people at the executive level within the organization or for other organizations. A more impersonal, less formal style may be used when memorandum reports or letter reports are prepared. In this section, we have emphasized the long, formal report, which may have three primary sections: preliminary parts, body of the report, and supplementary parts.

(1) *Preliminary parts:* These parts are included prior to the main body of the report and help to provide the kind of organization needed in the report.

(a) *Letter or memorandum of transmittal:* Sometimes a letter or memorandum must accompany a report as a brief introduction to the report. The transmittal correspondence begins with a general introduction to the report and may present a brief summary of some of the findings and conclusions. Its purpose is to motivate the receiver to read the attached report.

(b) *Title page:* The information on the title page includes the title of the report; the name and position of the writer and department or division; the organization's name and address, if the report is external; and the date.

(c) *Authorization form:* The person authorizing the research must sign an authorization form prior to the start of the research. This form immediately follows the title page.

(d) *Table of contents:* Every report should have a table of contents that indicates the major subdivisions of the report along with page references.

(e) *Table of figures:* All figures and illustrations included in the body of the report should be listed in a table of figures along with the specific page references.

(f) *Abstract:* Sometimes an abstract is requested to precede the report. This abstract is usually 300 to 500 words in length and provides a brief summary of the conduct of the study and the reporting of the data, findings, and conclusions of the study.

(g) *Executive summary:* A brief but comprehensive overview of a report's main points gives the reader a quick look at the contents of the entire report. An executive summary is similar to an abstract and is usually organized in the same way as the report. A rather short business report may have a one-page executive summary whereas a longer report may have a two- or three-page executive summary. The main purpose is to encourage the reader to find the time to examine the entire report or at least selected sections.

(2) *Body of the report:* The report is usually subdivided into the introduction, data analysis and findings, and summary of conclusions and recommendations.

(a) *Introduction:* The main purpose of the introduction is to present the reader with a statement of the problem of the study, research questions, hypotheses, limitations of the study, rationale for the study or report (with supporting information), definitions of terms used, and procedures used in the study.

(b) *Data analysis and findings:* In this section, the complete data analysis must be presented. Each finding must be presented and explained in terms of the statistical analysis that was conducted. These statistical analyses are normally presented in tables accompanied by an appropriate narrative.

(c) *Conclusions and recommendations:* The summary provides an overview of the study and a look at the complete set of findings or selected findings, if appropriate. In addition, conclusions derived from the findings are included in this section, as are recommendations that can be drawn directly from the conclusions.

(3) *Supplementary parts:* The last section of the report includes the bibliography or works cited, glossary, appendix (or appendices), and index.

(a) *Bibliography:* An alphabetical list of all information sources used for the report, including sources for citations included in the report, is called a **bibliography.**

(b) *Works cited:* A **works cited** or **references** list is an alphabetical list of all references that were directly cited within the body of the report.

(c) *Glossary:* The **glossary** is an alphabetical list of terms defined for the reader.

(d) *Appendix or appendices:* Supplementary research material, such as a sample questionnaire, sample letters written to respondents, and detailed data analysis not included in the body of the report, are usually included in the **appendix.**

(e) *Index:* An alphabetical list of names and subjects, called an **index,** included at the end of the report contains page references to quickly find specific information contained in the report.

The business report is a very important business document and must be prepared with care so that it will be functional in assisting in the decision-making process. (For more information on business report formats, see Chapter 9.)

Check Point—Section D

Directions: For each question, circle the correct answer.

D–1. In planning a report that will require both primary and secondary research, the first task is to

A) conduct primary research in order to become familiar with the problem

B) define the problem that needs to be solved

C) develop a questionnaire to gather factual data

D) identify the variables of the study

D–2. Harris was asked to study the behavior of administrative professionals on the job and recommend to the office manager how individual assignments could be changed. Which research method would be the *best* to use?

A) Experimental research

B) Observational research

C) Secondary research

D) Survey research

D–3. An alphabetical list of all references directly cited within the body of the report is called

A) an appendix

B) a glossary

C) an index

D) works cited

For Your Review

Directions: For each question, circle the correct answer.

1. A business letter's primary purpose is to
   A) provide information from the writer's point of view
   B) inform, persuade, and/or create goodwill with the receiver
   C) transmit positive or favorable information that will please the receiver
   D) communicate internally within an organization

2. Which one of the following situations would prompt the writing of a positive or favorable letter?
   A) A request for information about a new cleaning service being offered by a company
   B) A response to a request for information about a new product
   C) A refusal to be a guest speaker at a community function
   D) Granting an adjustment to a customer's balance

3. When a positive business letter is written, the letter begins with
   A) the main idea in the first paragraph
   B) facts and details about the main idea of the message
   C) a forward-looking statement
   D) a compliment to the receiver for being receptive to the message

4. Routine or neutral correspondence is written
   A) with an inductive approach
   B) so that the first paragraph serves as a buffer
   C) more often than any other type of letter

D) with detailed information presented in the first paragraph

5. The body paragraphs of a routine response to an information request need to include
   A) information that serves as a buffer
   B) summarizing statement that reflects the main point of the message
   C) any specific deadlines to keep in mind
   D) factual information responding to the request

6. A letter that refuses to grant a particular request opens with the
   A) main point of the message
   B) facts and details of the situation
   C) "bad news"
   D) reasons for the refusal

7. The reasons for the refusal of an internal request need to be explained based upon the
   A) business's philosophy and policies
   B) viewpoint of the sender
   C) sender's apology for the refusal
   D) lack of resources

8. When you give a positive response to the reader for part of a request, the message should begin with the
   A) details that support the positive response
   B) negative response
   C) details that support the negative response
   D) positive response

9. To motivate action by the receiver, a persuasive letter requires the writer to

    A) purchase a new product or service
    B) provide reasons for the action the receiver should take
    C) seek the receiver's interest first; then get his or her attention
    D) identify positive and negative effects of responding to the request

10. The word processing mail-merge feature may be used to create a

    A) mailing list of names and addresses
    B) data source with variable information
    C) main document (a letter) with constant information
    D) personalized greeting for a select group of recipients

11. Each memorandum that is written should pertain to

    A) any topics that need consideration at this time
    B) only one topic or objective
    C) the receiver's point of view
    D) favorable topics to be discussed

12. Which one of the following memoranda would need to be written using the inductive approach?

    A) A response to a request for confidential information that cannot be released
    B) A request for information about a new product
    C) A request for assistance in locating specific information from the records
    D) A directive from management with instructions for setting up a specific database

13. The negative news contained in a memorandum should be clearly stated so that

    A) the sender gives a complete apology
    B) the receiver is aware of other options
    C) no further action is required of the receiver

    D) the receiver will understand the "no" in the message

14. A memorandum written for which one of the following situations needs to be persuasive in nature?

    A) A response to a request for confidential information that cannot be released at this time
    B) A management directive with instructions for preparing a progress report for a specific team project
    C) A request for assistance in solving a specific problem
    D) A response to a request for information from a supplier

15. An administrative project is underway and is scheduled for completion in January. Morrison, an administrative professional assigned to the team, has been asked to prepare an interim report outlining the steps already completed and those yet to be accomplished. This type of report is called a

    A) proposal
    B) progress report
    C) feasibility report
    D) formal report

16. Use of electronic mail decreases the

    A) effectiveness of sending and receiving information
    B) amount of information that can be transmitted at one time
    C) conciseness of the message that is being sent
    D) cost of communicating through a network

17. When an e-mail message is prepared, the sender should remember to

    A) read the message carefully before sending
    B) send copies of any additional documents with another e-mail message
    C) write from the sender's viewpoint using pronouns like *I* or *we*
    D) keep the subject line to one or two words, if possible

18. Some recipients will not open an e-mail message without knowing the subject because of the possibility of
    A) negative responses
    B) inaccurate e-mail addresses
    C) viruses
    D) long subject lines

19. A business report that primarily includes numerical data is referred to as a
    A) narrative report
    B) statistical report
    C) technical report
    D) progress report

20. The purpose of a technical report is to
    A) present primary data and an analysis and interpretation of that data
    B) present factual information in an organized, structured manner
    C) present the report's message according to a sequence of events
    D) convey specialized information to business professionals within a specific field

21. Researching a problem results in a/an
    A) preferred solution from several alternatives
    B) historical perspective about the topic
    C) study of different points of view about a topic
    D) examination of a topic over a definite period of time

22. One of the first steps in conducting business research is to
    A) review related literature pertaining to the specific research questions
    B) broaden the study to include three separate topics
    C) identify factors or variables to be studied
    D) write specific research questions about the topic that will become the themes for the study

23. Research studies and professional articles that have already been published or disseminated are known as
    A) primary sources
    B) secondary sources
    C) primary research
    D) observational research

24. In the collection of primary data by means of a survey, care needs to be taken in
    A) interviewing people who will respond to the survey
    B) detecting changes in factors or variables over a period of time
    C) developing a survey instrument that will yield valid and reliable data
    D) observing the behaviors of individuals as they perform certain work tasks

25. A letter of transmittal that accompanies a report includes
    A) a summary of procedures for conducting the research
    B) one or more recommendations based on the results of the research
    C) a general introduction to the attached report
    D) a works cited list of references

Solutions

Solutions To Check Point—Section A

Answer	Refer to:
A–1. (D)	[A-1-a (3)]
A–2. (C)	[A-1-b (1)]
A–3. (D)	[A-3-b (1)]

Solutions To Check Point—Section B

Answer	Refer to:
B–1. (B)	[B-1-a (1) (d)]
B–2. (D)	[B-1-b (1) (c)]
B–3. (C)	[B-2-a (1)]

Solutions To Check Point—Section C

Answer	Refer to:
C–1. (D)	[C]
C–2. (A)	[C-2]
C–3. (C)	[C-3-b]

Solutions To Check Point—Section D

Answer	Refer to:
D–1. (B)	[D-2 and D-2-a]
D–2. (B)	[D-2-b (2) (b)]
D–3. (D)	[D-2-f (3) (b)]

Solutions to For Your Review

Answer	Refer to:
1. (B)	[A]
2. (D)	[A-1-a (2)]
3. (A)	[A-1-b (1)]
4. (C)	[A-2]
5. (D)	[A-2-b (2)]
6. (B)	[A-3-b (1)]
7. (A)	[A-3-b (2) (a)]
8. (D)	[A-4-b (1)]
9. (B)	[A-5]
10. (C)	[A-6-a and A-6-b]
11. (B)	[B-1-a (2)]
12. (A)	[B-1-b (1) (a)]
13. (D)	[B-1-b (2) (c)]
14. (C)	[B-1-c (1) (b)]
15. (B)	[B-2-a (3)]
16. (D)	[C]
17. (A)	[C-1-c]
18. (C)	[C-2]
19. (B)	[D-1-a]

20.   (D)   [D-1-d]

21.   (A)   [D-2]

22.   (D)   [D-2-a (1)]

23.   (B)   [D-2-b (1)]

24.   (C)   [D-2-b (2) (c) and D-2-b (3)]

25.   (C)   [D-2-f (1) (a)]

Chapter 9

Producing Documents in Final Format

OVERVIEW

Once the document content has been developed, attention turns to format, the key to an attractive appearance for a business document. Such format factors as vertical and horizontal placement, spacing, and document style determine the usability of a particular document. Without proper application of these factors, a printed document may be unusable. Therefore, attention to document formatting must receive high priority when preparing final drafts.

The first impression any document makes on the reader depends on the visual quality of the document. In the discussion of various document formats, appropriate style will be emphasized and examples shown to demonstrate how each format is applied.

Administrative professionals must make many judgments with regard to document format in the course of the workday. The application of fundamental knowledge related to document format will result in more effective document production.

KEY TERMS

A. Business Letters

A very important document created in business today is the business letter. The format used when preparing a letter will help to create attractive, well-placed copy that will be positively received.

1. ***Format of Business Letter:*** Proper placement of a letter printed on an 8½- by 11-inch sheet of letterhead or bond paper can be determined by using the Letter Placement Table (Figure 9–1). Once the approximate length of the body of the letter has been determined, the table can be used to decide the left and right margins, where the date should be keyed in, and the number of Enters between the date and the inside address.

   Note: Office professionals need to adopt acceptable formats for business use. Software defaults can be changed to other settings, turned off, or overridden.

   a. *Date line:* The most accepted style for the current date is the month spelled in full followed by the day and the year.

   EXAMPLE:

   > *October 5, 200X*
   >
   > *Not*
   >
   > *10/05/200X*

   Europeans would interpret the date 10/05/200X as May 10, 200X.

   Other styles may be used in correspondence with U.S. government agencies or businesses in foreign countries. The international standard format for the date is

   5 October 200X   13 December 200X

   Typical placement for the date line is two inches from the top edge of the paper or two lines below the letterhead.

   b. *Inside address:* The name of the person to whom the letter will be sent, along with the person's complete address, is called the **inside address**. Use the Letter Placement Table (Figure 9–1) for correct spacing between the date line and the inside address.

FIGURE 9–1   Letter Placement Table (Using Letterhead)

Number of Words in Body of Letter	Left and Right Margins	Date Line	Number of Enters Between Date and Inside Address*	Inches Between Date and Inside Address
Up to 100 words (short)	1½–2″	2″ from top edge; 2 lines below letterhead	6–10	1–1½″
100–200 words (average)	1–1½″		4–7	½–1″
Over 200 words (long)	1″		3–5	½–1″
Over 300 words (2-page)	1″		3–5	½–1″

*6 lines = 1 inch; the number of Enters indicates how many times you need to press Enter to get to a specific point (i.e., seven Enters would leave six blank spaces, and you would key in text on the seventh line).

1. *Titles:* A title should precede all individual names. Titles include Mr., Ms., Honorable, Dr., and so on. Current business practice is to always use *Ms.* as the courtesy title for women unless the woman prefers *Mrs.* or *Miss.*

2. *State:* In the inside address, the state should be abbreviated using the two-letter state abbreviation followed by the ZIP + 4 Code. On the envelope, the two-letter state abbreviation is required for optical scanning of the address by the U.S. Postal Service.

A business letter should be addressed to an individual or an organization and should have a complete mailing address: a street address, post office box, city, state, and ZIP + 4 Code.

EXAMPLES:

Inside Addresses

Mr. Terry Addams
567 Wills Drive
Rockford, IL 61108-1917

Ms. Martha Boes
Human Resources Department
Colonial Brothers, Inc.
1111 Railway Blvd.
Clifton, NJ 00186-0500

Harrington Bank
PO Box 345
Butternut, WI 54514-9345

Honorable T. M. Carr
Carr & Carr Ltd.
1435 Morgan Drive, Suite 4
Newberry, MI 49868-1222

c. *Attention line (optional):* When a letter is addressed to a company, an **attention line** may be included to direct the letter to a specific individual within the company. The attention line is keyed in a double-space (two Enters) after the inside address or as the second line in the inside address. The word *attention* may or may not be followed by a colon, may be in all capital letters or begin with an initial capital, and may or may not be underlined.

EXAMPLES:

Harrington Bank
PO Box 345
Butternut, WI 54514-9345

ATTENTION: Ms. Amy Miles

or

Attention Ms. Amy Miles

Harrington Bank
Attention Ms. Amy Miles
PO Box 345
Butternut, WI 54514-9345

If both an attention line and a subject line are in the letter, use the same style for each.

d. *Salutation:* The greeting to the receiver is called the **salutation**. The salutation begins with *Dear* when addressed to a person and is followed by either the person's title and last name only (formal) or just the person's first name (informal). If the letter is addressed to an organization, proper salutations are *Ladies and Gentlemen, Dear Sir or Madam,* and *Dear,* followed by use of a title within a department.

EXAMPLES:

> *Dear Ms. Miles*   *Dear Amy*
>
> *Ladies and Gentlemen*   *Dear Sales Manager*

The salutation is included in block and modified block letter styles and is keyed a double-space (two Enters) after the previous notation (either the inside address or attention line).

EXAMPLE:

> *Ms. Martha Boes*
> *Human Resources Department*
> *Colonial Brothers, Inc.*
> *1111 Railway Blvd.*
> *Clifton, NJ 00186–0500* ↓2 Enters
>
> *Dear Ms. Boes*

e. *Subject line (optional):* The **subject line**, if used, tells in a descriptive phrase what the letter is about and typically appears a double-space (two Enters) after the salutation. The word *subject* may or may not be followed by a colon, may be in all capital letters or only in initial caps, and may or may not be underlined. If both a subject line and an attention line are in the letter, use the same style for each.

EXAMPLES:

Subject Lines

> *SUBJECT: INVOICE NO. 9874—NANCE IMPLEMENTS*
>
> *Subject Invoice No. 9874—Nance Implements*
>
> *Subject Approval of Contract for Roadwork*
>
> *Subject: Approval of Contract for Roadwork*

Subject Line with Salutation

> *Dear Ms. Miles* ↓2 Enters
>
> *SUBJECT: INVOICE NO. 9874—NANCE IMPLEMENTS*

f. *Body of the letter:* The detailed information included in the letter is called the **body** of the letter. Body paragraphs in a business letter are single-spaced with double-spacing between the paragraphs. A letter should have at least two paragraphs; three is the most common number of paragraphs.

Paragraphs may begin at the left margin or may be indented one-half inch (one standard tab) or more, depending on the letter style used. The first paragraph begins a double-space after the previous notation (either salutation or subject line).

g. *Complimentary closing:* The closing of the letter is keyed a double-space (two Enters) after the last line in the body of the letter. Only the first word of the complimentary closing is capitalized. The **complimentary closing** should be in agreement with the salutation (formal or informal). The most common complimentary closings are as follows:

Formal	Yours very truly	Very truly yours
	Cordially	Cordially yours
Informal	Truly yours	Yours truly
Formal/	Sincerely	Sincerely yours
Informal		

The complimentary closings *Respectfully* and *Respectfully yours* are usually used when the letter has been addressed to individuals holding important positions in government (president, governor, or legislative members), military (general, captain), and religious organizations (pope, pastor, or board members).

h.   *Signature line:* The name of the person sending the letter is keyed in four Enters (leaving three blank lines) after the complimentary closing. Only the writer's name need be used in the signature line, exactly as the writer signs his or her name. If it is difficult to identify the individual as male or female by the signature line, a title (Mr., Ms.) should be included with the name. If a woman wishes to be addressed by her title (Ms., Mrs., or Miss), this title should be included with the name. The title can be keyed in before the name or after the name. Any other title that the person holds may be included with the signature line. A visual balance should always be maintained when titles are included with the signature line.

EXAMPLES:

Mr. T. M. Johnson

T. M. Johnson, Ms.

Ms. Terry M. Johnson, CPS

T. M. Johnson (Ms.)

Theresa M. Johnson
Human Resources Director

i.   *Reference initials:* **Reference initials** include the initials of the administrative professional who prepared the letter and may also include the writer's initials. These initials are keyed in a double-space (two Enters) after the signature line. The most common style today is the use of the administrative professional's initials only. If the writer's initials are used, they are keyed in first, followed by a slash or colon and the administrative professional's initials.

EXAMPLES:

rji	*administrative professional's initials only*
TJ/ri	*writer's initials followed by administrative professional's initials*
TMJ:rji	*writer's initials followed by administrative professional's initials*

j.   *Enclosure notation:* If material is enclosed with the letter, an **enclosure notation** should be keyed in two Enters (a double-space) after the reference initials at the left margin. (See Section A-1-k for proper order when both copy and enclosure notations are included in the letter.) The word *enclosure* or *attachment* may be abbreviated or keyed in full.

EXAMPLES:

One enclosure or attachment

> *Enc.*
>
> *Enclosure*
>
> *Attach.*
>
> *Attachment*

Two or more enclosures or attachments

> *Encs.*
>
> *Enclosures*
>
> *Encs.: 2*
>
> *Encs—Prints*
>
> > *Order Blank*
>
> *Attachments 2*

The enclosure notation may be on a line by itself, or it may be followed by the number of enclosures contained within the letter or a listing of the enclosures. If additional information follows the enclosure notation, a space, a colon, a slash, or a dash should be keyed between the word *enclosure* or *attachment* and the additional information.

k.   *Copy notation:* A **copy notation** is used on the letter only when a copy is being sent to one or more persons. The notation is keyed in two Enters (a double-space) below the reference initials at the left margin. However, if there is also an enclosure notation, the copy notation comes before the enclosure notation if the person being sent a copy is *not* receiving the enclosure. If copies of the enclosure are also being sent to the person receiving the copy, the copy notation is keyed in a double-space after the enclosure notation. The word *copy* is abbreviated *c* in the notation and is followed by a blank space, a colon, or a slash and then the person's name and title and/or company name.

(1) The copy notation can be in lowercase or capital letters, but there are never any periods.

(2) If several people are receiving copies, the names are listed under one another, but the first name is the only one preceded by the notation.

(3) The copy notation appears on all copies: the original, the copies, and the file copy.

Before the letters are presented for signature, the copies are identified with a check mark next to the name of the person who is to receive that copy. Copy markings are as follows:

•   Placing a check mark next to the name

•   Underlining the name

•   Highlighting the name with a marker

EXAMPLES:

> *c Betty Appleton, Apex Corporation*

> C: B. Appleton, Apex Corporation
> <u>Martha Thornton</u>, Martin Engineering

> c/Betty Appleton, Apex Corporation
> ✓Martha Thornton, Martin Engineering

l. *Blind copy notation:* When a copy of the letter is sent to another person and the recipient of the letter need not be aware of this, a **blind copy notation** is placed on the copies of the letter—but not on the original copy. The notation *bc* followed by the name of the person is placed two Enters (a double-space) below the last notation on the copies at the left margin.

EXAMPLE:

> c Betty Appleton, Apex Manufacturing
> Martha Thornton, Martin Engineering↓2

> bc George Ramos, ABC Publishing

m. *Line spacing:* The paragraphs in the body of the letter are single-spaced with double-spacing between paragraphs. Spacing between the date line and inside address depends on the length of the letter (see Figure 9–1). Minimum spacing between the complimentary closing and signature line is four Enters (three blank lines).

n. *Special notations:* All special notations such as CONFIDENTIAL, PERSONAL, CERTIFIED, REGISTERED, and SPECIAL DELIVERY are keyed in a double-space below the date line at the left margin and in all capital letters. The spacing between the special notation and the inside address will vary according to the length of the letter (see Figure 9–1).

EXAMPLES:

> May 6, 200X↓2 Enters

> CERTIFIED MAIL↓4 Enters Minimum

> Mr. Terry Addams
> 367 Wills Drive
> Rockford, IL 61108-1917

> May 6, 200X↓2 Enters

> CONFIDENTIAL↓4 Enters Minimum

> Honorable T. M. Carr
> Carr & Carr Ltd.
> 1435 Morgan Drive, Suite 4
> Newberry, MI 49868-1222

Sometimes a copy of a letter is faxed to the recipient, with the original copy being mailed. A fax notation could be placed on the original copy of the letter with the same placement as a special notation.

EXAMPLE:

> May 6, 200X↓2 Enters

> FAX 302-555-0505↓4 Enters to Inside Address

2. ***Letter Styles:*** Letter styles commonly used in business today are the block style, the modified block style, and the simplified style. Acceptable formats for these three

FIGURE 9–2   Block Letter Style with Open Punctuation

	Transformation Dynamics
	125 Broadway, P.O. Box 2001 *Batavia, IL 60510-2001*
	Telephone 631-878-2700 *Fax 631-878-2702*
Date Line	April 14, 200X ⃰4 Enters
Inside Address	Mrs. Marline Walsh, Manager Lewis Medical Clinic 3619 Parkview Lane Montclair, NJ 07915-0913 ⃰2
Salutation	Dear Ms. Walsh ⃰2
Body of Letter	Many organizations have adopted the Block Letter Style with open punctuation. The primary reason is efficiency. Once the margins are set, the administrative professional can quickly key in the letter because all lines of the letter begin at the left margin. Also, there is no worry about making sure you have the correct punctuation after the salutation and complimentary closing. No punctuation mark follows either the salutation or complimentary closing when using the open punctuation style. ⃰2
	Attention to the following spacing guidelines will help you create an attractive business letter: ⃰2
	➢ The paragraphs are always single-spaced, with double-spacing between the paragraphs. ⃰2
	➢ There is double-spacing between all parts of the letter except between the date line and the inside address and between the complimentary closing and the signature line. ⃰2
	➢ The spacing between the date line and the inside address is a minimum of three blank lines (four Enters). However, the spacing could be as many as ten blank lines for a short letter with the date line two inches from the top edge. ⃰2
	➢ The spacing between the complimentary closing and signature line is three blank lines (four Enters). ⃰2
	This letter illustrates the Block Letter Style with open punctuation. Remember, a letter prepared in this style can also apply mixed punctuation style—a colon after the salutation and a comma after the complimentary closing. ⃰2
Complimentary Closing	Sincerely yours ⃰4
Signature Line/ Title	Dr. Diane M. Graf CPS Transformation Facilitator
Reference Initials	bls

styles are outlined in the following section. Within the paragraphs of the illustration for each style, the format is discussed in detail. Punctuation styles are also explained, and the punctuation style used for each illustrated letter style is discussed within the paragraphs of the illustration.

a. *Block letter style:* All lines of the **block letter style** begin at the left margin. This letter style is considered to be very efficient. Figure 9–2 shows an example of a letter prepared in block style.

b. *Modified block letter style:* The distinguishing characteristics of **modified block letter style** are the placement of the date line, complimentary closing, and signa-

FIGURE 9–3   Modified Block Letter Style with Blocked Paragraphs and Mixed Punctuation

Transformation Dynamics
125 Broadway, P.O. Box 2001
Batavia, IL 60510-2001

Telephone 631-878-2700
Fax 631-878-2702

September 10, 200X ↓4 Enters

Mrs. Marline Walsh, Director
Lewis Medical Clinic
3619 Parkview Lane
Montclair, NJ 07915-0913 ↓2

Dear Marline: ↓2

SUBJECT: MODIFIED BLOCK LETTER STYLE ↓2

Many businesses still prefer the appearance of Modified Block Letter Style. Some choose to use mixed punctuation with this letter style, and others prefer to use open punctuation. Either punctuation style is appropriate. This sample letter illustrates Modified Block Letter Style with mixed punctuation. ↓2

With this letter style, the administrative professional may key in the current date either beginning at the center point of the writing line or so the date ends at the right margin. In this illustration, the date line begins at the center point. All other letter parts begin at the left margin unless paragraphs are indented (see Figure 9–4). ↓2

With mixed punctuation style, a colon (:) is keyed after the salutation and a comma (,) after the complimentary closing. In business writing, a comma is never used after the salutation. With mixed punctuation, the colon is used after the salutation whether you are using a formal or an informal salutation. In this letter, the salutation and complimentary closing are informal. ↓2

The spacing of the Modified Block Letter Style follows the same guidelines as the Block Letter Style. Because of your current needs, Marline, I am sending you a copy of our Office Style Manual which has just been published. ↓2

Yours truly, ↓4

Dr. Diane M. Graf CPS
Transformation Facilitator ↓2

DMG:bls ↓2

Enclosure: Office Style Manual

ture line. A letter prepared in modified block letter style may have blocked or indented paragraphs.

(1) The date line is centered or may end at the right margin.

(2) The complimentary closing and signature line begin at the center point of the line of writing.

(3) Paragraphs may be blocked (beginning at the left margin) or indented one standard tab (½ inch minimum).

(4) All other parts of the letter begin at the left margin.

Figure 9–3 shows an example of a business letter prepared in modified block style with blocked paragraphs and mixed punctuation. Figure 9–4 also shows an

FIGURE 9–4   Modified Block Letter Style with Indented Paragraphs and Open Punctuation

Transformation Dynamics
Telephone 631-878-2700
Fax 631-878-2702

125 Broadway, P.O. Box 2001
Batavia, IL 60510-2001

September 10, 200X

Ms. Marline Walsh
Administrative Manager
Lewis Medical Clinic
3619 Parkview Lane
Montclair, NJ 07915-0913 ↓2

Dear Marline ↓2

    Again, I am using a Modified Block Letter Style, but this time the paragraphs are indented. Paragraphs typically are indented one standard tab (½ inch), but I have chosen to indent the paragraphs two standard tabs (1 inch). Some feel that this allows enough space to emphasize the beginning of each paragraph. The maximum paragraph indentation usually does not exceed 1½ inches (three standard tabs). ↓2

    Also with this letter style, the current date ends at the right margin. In this example, the right margin is justified, since I am using Times New Roman, a proportional font. A ragged right margin is more appropriate when you use a font that is monospaced. The complimentary closing and typed signature line will begin at the center point of the line of writing. ↓2

    This letter is average length. The date for this letter was keyed in two lines below the letterhead (2¼ inches from the top edge of the paper). Four Enters (three blank lines) were keyed in between the date and the inside address. ↓2

    After you peruse the material I sent you last week, Marline, please call me if you have any questions. Otherwise, I look forward to seeing you at the regional conference in Chicago in November. ↓2

    Sincerely ↓4

    Dr. Diane M. Graf CPS
    Transformation Facilitator ↓2

DMG/bls

example of a business letter prepared in modified block letter style, but with indented paragraphs and open punctuation.

c. *Simplified letter style:* Another letter style that is similar to the block letter style is referred to as the **simplified letter style**. This letter style is considered the most efficient though perhaps not as widely used as the block and modified block styles. All lines of the letter begin at the left margin. The distinguishing characteristics of this letter style affect the salutation, the subject line, and the closing lines.

(1) The salutation is omitted from this letter style. Instead, three Enters (two blank lines) follow the inside address.

    (2) A subject line is required in this style, keyed in all capital letters below the inside address. The word SUBJECT is omitted from the subject line.

    (3) After the subject line, there are three Enters (two blank lines) to the first paragraph of the letter.

    (4) The complimentary closing is omitted. After the last paragraph of the letter, there are four Enters (three blank lines) before the signature line.

    (5) The signature line is keyed in all capital letters.

Figure 9–5 shows an example of a business letter prepared in simplified letter style. This letter style is particularly applicable in situations where it is difficult to address the letter to a specific person or where the letter needs to be addressed to a committee or a department.

3. ***Punctuation Styles:*** Two basic punctuation styles are used in business correspondence today: open punctuation and mixed punctuation. Open punctuation is considered the more efficient style.

    a. *Open punctuation:* No punctuation is keyed in after the salutation or the complimentary closing. Therefore, we say that **open punctuation** is being used after these two letter parts (see Figures 9–2 and 9–4).

    b. *Mixed punctuation:* Punctuation is keyed in after the salutation and the complimentary closing.

        (1) *After the salutation:* A colon (:) is used in both a formal and an informal salutation. In business writing, there is never a comma after the salutation. Even an informal salutation such as *Dear Ted* is followed by a colon.

        Note: A comma appears after the salutation only in personal letters, but not business letters.

        (2) *After the complimentary closing:* In mixed punctuation, a comma (,) follows the complimentary closing. Because two different punctuation marks are used, this punctuation style is referred to as **mixed punctuation** (see Figure 9–3).

In Figures 9–2, 9–3, 9–4, and 9–5, some letters have open punctuation and others have mixed punctuation. Block and modified block letter styles can have either punctuation style. Simplified letter style does not include a salutation or complimentary closing.

4. ***Second Page of Letter:*** The second page of a business letter is printed on plain bond paper of the same quality as the letterhead. Because multiple pages of a letter are not stapled together, a heading is required beginning on the second page. This heading consists of three lines: the name of the addressee, the date, and the page number. If the letter is addressed to a company, the company name is the addressee. For the page number, also use the word *Page* for clarity.

    a. *Block style:* If the letter is prepared in block style, each line of the second-page heading begins at the left margin. The first line can begin either ½ inch (line 4) or 1 inch (line 7) from the top edge of the paper. The heading is single-spaced. After the last line of the heading, triple-space (two blank lines) to continue the letter on the second page. Block style is also used for the second page of a simplified letter format. A third page of a letter would have the same type of heading. An example of the second-page heading using block letter style is shown in Figure 9–6.

FIGURE 9–5   Simplified Letter Style

Transformation Dynamics
Telephone 631-878-2700
Fax 631-878-2702

125 Broadway, P.O. Box 2001
Batavia, IL 60510-2001

September 18, 200X ⇓4 Enters

Ms. Marline Walsh
Administrative Manager
Lewis Medical Clinic
3619 Parkview Lane
Montclair, NJ 07915-0913 ⇓3

SIMPLIFIED LETTER STYLE FORMAT ⇓3

The Simplified Letter Style was introduced in the 1950s by the Administrative Management Society, then known as the National Office Management Association. The purpose of adopting the simplified style was for efficiency in creating a business letter with a crisp, neat appearance. Here are the primary features of the Simplified Letter Style: ⇓2

- To maintain keyboarding efficiency, the Block Letter Style format was adopted. Every line begins at the left margin. The date line is keyed in two inches from the top edge or two lines below the letterhead. There are always four Enters (three blank lines) between the date and the inside address. ⇓2

- To be more efficient, the salutation is omitted. Immediately after the inside address, a subject line is keyed in all capital letters—without the word SUBJECT. There are three Enters (two blank lines) between the inside address and the subject line and three Enters between the subject line and the first paragraph. ⇓2

- After the last paragraph, the complimentary closing is omitted. Four Enters are keyed in after the last paragraph. The signature line is keyed in all capital letters. ⇓2

- Any enumerations or bulleted items within the letter begin as close as possible to the left margin; each one is treated as a new paragraph. ⇓2

- A copy notation, if needed, begins with c/ followed by the names of people who are to receive copies of the letter. ⇓2

Over the years, many businesses have adopted this letter style. The features of the Simplified Letter Style should be reviewed and considered as a possible style for future use. ⇓4

DR. DIANE M. GRAF CPS ⇓2

bls ⇓2

c/Melissa Thompson CPS

FIGURE 9–6   Second-Page Heading—Block Style

4 or 7 Enters (0.5 to 1 inch)

Person's Name
Page 2
Date ⇓3 Enters

as we had hoped before the end of the year. Will you please
let us know what your wishes are by Wednesday, December 3, so
that we can proceed.

FIGURE 9–7   Second-Page Heading—Modified Block Style

```
        4 or 7 Enters (0.5 to 1 inch)

    Person's Name                Date                Page 2
    Department ⇓3 Enters



    as we had hoped before the end of the year. Will you please
    let us know what your wishes are by Wednesday, December 3, so
    that we can proceed.
```

b. *Modified block style:* If the letter is prepared in modified block style, the addressee's name is keyed in at the left margin, the date in the center, and the page number at the right margin, all on the same line. The heading may be keyed in either ½ inch (line 4) or 1 inch (line 7) from the top edge of the page. Triple-space after the heading to continue the letter. An example of the second-page heading using modified block letter style is shown in Figure 9–7.

c. *Word processing headings:* Word processing software provides a header feature. The header allows the user to key the information once for automatic placement at the top of the second and succeeding pages. The page number automatically increments when the appropriate page number command is used with the header. To allow enough space at the top of the page, the top margin will need to be changed from 1 inch to at least 1½ inches for the second and succeeding pages.

Check Point—Section A

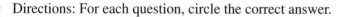

Directions: For each question, circle the correct answer.

A–1. The address to whom a business letter will be mailed is called the

A) inside address
B) salutation
C) body of the letter
D) letterhead

A–2. If the letter contains both an attention line and a subject line, the attention line

A) is keyed a double-space after the inside address, with the subject line immediately following
B) may be underlined while the subject line is keyed in all capitals

C) should follow the same style as the subject line: both all caps, initial caps, and/or underscored
D) immediately follows the subject line, which is keyed a double-space after the inside address

A–3. A letter with all lines beginning at the left margin, including the salutation and complimentary closing, is prepared in

A) modified block letter style
B) block letter style
C) simplified letter style
D) indented letter style

B. Envelopes

The two standard envelope sizes are No. 10 (9½ by 4⅛ inches) and No. 6¾ (6½ by 3⅝ inches). Three styles are used in addressing envelopes: conventional style, addressing for optical character recognition, and labels. Envelope and label addresses are computer generated using word processing software.

1. ***Conventional Style:*** When printing an address on either a No. 10 or a No. 6¾ envelope, follow these procedures.

    a. *Addressing the envelope:* The address on a No. 10 (large) business envelope begins 4 inches from the left edge of the envelope and 2¼ inches (14 Enters) from the top edge of the envelope. On a No. 6¾ (small) business envelope, the address would be keyed or printed 2 inches from the left edge of the envelope and 2 inches (12 Enters) from the top edge of the envelope. The U.S. Postal Service prefers that envelope addresses be no more than four lines. The following procedures are based on U.S. Postal Service requirements for addressing business envelopes.

    - Use block style for the address.
    - Single-space the address.
    - Key all words in the address in all capital letters. The word processing software formats the address in single-spacing. When proportional spacing is used, such as a Times Roman font, use two spaces between words for ease in reading.
    - Do not use punctuation marks anywhere in the address.
    - Use the two-letter state abbreviation for optical scanning by postal equipment.
    - Use the ZIP + 4 Code.

    EXAMPLES OF ENVELOPE ADDRESSES:

    <u>*United States Addresses*</u>

    MR TERRY ADDAMS
    567 WILLS DRIVE
    ROCKFORD IL 61108-1917

    MS MARTHA BOES
    COLONIAL BROTHERS INC
    1111 RAILWAY BLVD
    CLIFTON NJ 00186-0500

    HARRINGTON BANK
    PO BOX 345
    BUTTERNUT WI 54514-9345

    HONORABLE T M CARR
    CARR & CARR LTD
    1435 MORGAN DRIVE STE 4
    NEWBERRY MI 49868-1222

    <u>*Puerto Rico Addresses*</u>

    MS MARIA GONZALEZ
    URB LAS GLADIOLAS
    255 CALLE ALAMOS
    SAN JUAN PR 00926-1295

DR JOSE SANTIAGO
URB ROYAL OAK
448 CALLE 4
BAYAMON PR 00961-0242

Some areas in Puerto Rico do not have street names. The word CALLE means "street" and should be placed before the name of the street. The urbanization name (URB) refers to the name of an area or residential development within a city.

Virgin Islands Addresses

MR JOHN SHEPHERD
408 SUNSET LANE
ST THOMAS VI 00802-1222

MS ROSA MAYANELO
RR 2 BOX 419
KINGSHILL VI 00650-9802

b. *Special mailing notations:* Notations such as *Personal, Confidential,* or *Please forward* should be keyed below the return address on the third line. Special mailing notations such as *Registered, Special Delivery,* or *Certified Mail* should be keyed in all capital letters in the upper right corner of the envelope, just under the postage block.

Figure 9–8 shows an address properly keyed or printed on a No. 10 envelope with special mailing notations. A small envelope would be prepared in a similar fashion.

2. **OCR Requirements:** The U.S. Postal Service uses optical character recognition (OCR) equipment to process volumes of mail. The following guidelines have been developed so that mail can be OCR-readable.

a. *The OCR-read area:* The entire address should be located within an imaginary rectangle, which is the OCR-read area, formed by the following boundaries:

- One inch from the left edge
- One inch from the right edge

FIGURE 9–8   No. 10 Business Envelope with Special Notations

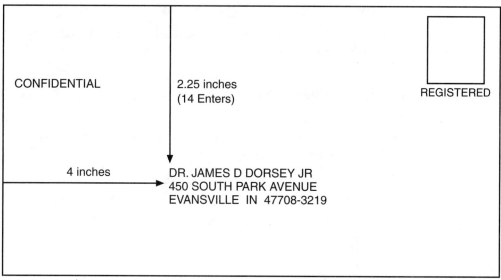

Note: On a No. 6¹/4 (small) business envelope, the address would be keyed in two inches from the left edge and down two inches (12 Enters) from the top edge. Special notations would have identical placement as on a large envelope.

FIGURE 9–9   No. 10 Business Envelope Addressed for OCR Requirements

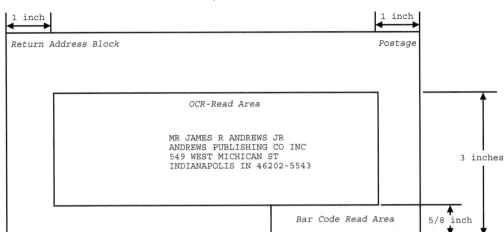

- Bottom margin of ⅝ inch
- Three inches from the bottom edge

Within the OCR-read area, the entire space below the top line of the address block should be used to print only the address. Boxes, advertising, or computer punch holes should not be placed within this area. See Figure 9–9 to see how these boundaries are formed.

b.   *Preparing the address:* The address should have a uniform left margin and be legible. Here are some general guidelines the U.S. Postal Service recommends.

(1)   *The address format:* The address should not exceed these four lines of printing:

- The name of the recipient (top line)
- Attention line or company name (second line)
- Delivery address, including unit, apartment, office, or suite numbers (third line)
- City, two-letter state abbreviation, and ZIP + 4 Code (fourth line)

The entire address must always be visible. The ZIP + 4 Code may be placed on the fifth line, depending on the space available.

(2)   *The window envelope:* If a window envelope is used, the entire address must have at least a ¼-inch clearance between the edge of the window and all sides of the address.

(3)   *International addresses:* Mail addressed to someone in a foreign country must be addressed in this way:

Line 1: NAME OF ADDRESSEE (caps)

Line 2: STREET ADDRESS or P.O. BOX NUMBER (caps)

Line 3: CITY NAME (PROVINCE, STATE, COUNTY, and POSTAL CODE) (caps)

Line 4: COUNTRY NAME (caps)

The lines are single-spaced, and all words are typed in capitals as shown.

EXAMPLES:

Canada

The location of the country name and the postal code are interchangeable. Either one may be placed on the last line, and the other one should be placed after the city.

MS DOROTHY H. CHATTEAU
2341 CLEAR LAKE DRIVE
OTTAWA ON K1A 0B1
CANADA

or

MS DOROTHY H. CHATTEAU
2341 CLEAR LAKE DRIVE
OTTAWA ON CANADA
K1A 0B1

England

MS DOROTHY H. CHATTEAU
2341 BUCKINGHAM DRIVE
LONDON WIP 6HQ
ENGLAND

France

MONSIEUR PIERRE LAFAYETTE
33, BOULEVARD DES FRANCES
75002 PARIS
FRANCE

The person's name might appear with the surname preceding the first name in all capitals like this:

Monsieur LAFAYETTE Pierre
33, BOULEVARD DES FRANCES
75002 PARIS
FRANCE

c. *Type for OCR reading:* Cyrillic, italic, artistic, and script-like fonts cannot be read by OCR equipment. Characters or numbers should not touch or overlap within a word or the ZIP + 4 Code. The point size for characters or numbers should be no smaller than 10 point.

d. *Spacing:* Attention to vertical spacing and line spacing will result in an address that can be read by OCR equipment. Here are the main guidelines to follow:

(1) All capital letters are required for the address when the line spacing is eight lines per inch. Preferred spacing is six lines per inch (typical vertical spacing).

(2) The space between words should be one to two character spaces.

(3) The space between the last character of the two-letter state abbreviation and the first digit of the ZIP + 4 Code can be one to five character spaces.

Additional information about OCR requirements may be obtained from the U.S. Postal Service.

3. ***Computer-Generated Mailing Labels:*** Addresses for mailing labels are generated using word processing or database software. The amount of space for the address is confined to the label. The address style used could be conventional, OCR, or label. Label-making equipment compatible with word processing software is also common in today's electronic office. When labels are required for a large mailing list, a data file needs to be created so that labels can be prepared whenever needed. Laser printers prepare mailing labels on sheets of pressure-sensitive labels fed through the sheet feeder.

   a. *Creating address files:* A file must be created for all addresses in a specific mailing list or directory. A file includes a record for each addressee with the necessary variable address data in fields. Each field should reference only one variable; this provides the most flexible use of the address variables. Here is an example of addressee data (fields) for one record:

   EXAMPLE:

Data Field	*Addressee Data*
Title	*MS*
First Name	*MARLENE*
Last Name	*KITTLESON*
Position	*ADMINISTRATIVE MANAGER*
Department	*INFORMATION SYSTEMS*
Company	*ABBOTT REGAL INC*
Address	*325 LINCOLN HIGHWAY*
City	*BATAVIA*
State	*IL*
ZIP Code	*60510–2301*

   Database software programs include label commands to print labels from the address file. Reference only those data fields that you want to print in the address block.

   b. *Word processing software:* Word processing software with a text-merge function is used to prepare mailing labels, too. Either envelopes or labels can be produced for a mailing list.

   (1) A data file is created with all addresses in the mailing list. A record is prepared for each addressee (from only one addressee to many), including data fields like the ones previously shown.

   (2) A primary file is created for the document (one mailing label or a sheet of mailing labels). The user can choose to print one mailing label or a group of mailing labels for an entire address directory.

   (3) The user can also choose to prepare return addresses, if needed, for the mailing envelopes as well.

   Database and word processing software programs enable the administrative professional to create data files that can be used for mailings to customers and clients. Such files will need to be updated as customer or client addresses change, but the convenience of having directories on file and being able to prepare mailing labels as needed will ease the stress involved in preparing special mailings.

Check Point—Section B

Directions: For each question, circle the correct answer.

B–1. When keying an address on a standard business envelope,

  A) the five-digit ZIP Code is sufficient

  B) punctuation marks should be used after any abbreviated word

  C) the name of the state should be written in full

  D) all words are to be keyed in capital letters

B–2. Where should special mailing notations, such as REGISTERED and CERTIFIED, be placed on a business envelope?

  A) In the lower-left corner

  B) In the upper-left corner, a double-space after the return address

  C) In the upper-right corner, a double-space under the postage block

  D) A double-space above the first line of the mailing address

B–3. To process large volumes of mail, the U.S. Postal Service uses

  A) magnetic ink character recognition (MICR)

  B) optical character recognition (OCR)

  C) point-of-sale (POS) terminals

  D) express mail

C. Memoranda

Memoranda are used for correspondence between individuals, departments, and branch offices of the same organization. Usually, a heading is printed on the memorandum form, and the side margins are determined by this heading. When you do not have a memorandum form, the top and side margins must be set to produce visual appeal.

1. *Format of a Memorandum:* The general appearance of a memorandum depends on the format that is used for the entire message.

    a. *Top margin and heading:* The top margin for a memorandum varies from 1 to 2 inches. The most common is 1½ inches. The word *MEMORANDUM (or MEMO)* is usually centered horizontally in all capital letters. Another variation is to key in the heading in initial caps and use underlining or boldface—but not both.

    b. *Side margins:* The left and right margins of the memorandum will vary depending on the length of the memorandum. A long memorandum would have the narrowest margin and the longest line of print (1-inch left and right margins). A short memorandum would have the widest margin and the shortest line of print (2-inch left and right margins). However, the left margin may be aligned with preprinted guide words on forms normally used for memorandums.

    c. *Guide words:* A memorandum begins with guide words for DATE, TO, FROM, and SUBJECT. The arrangement of these guide words varies, depending on the writer's preference. These **guide words** are keyed in at the top of the page a double-space below a heading at the left margin or centered (MEMO or MEMORANDUM). There should be a double-space between guide words.

      The guide words may be a part of a memorandum template selected from a variety of available styles. An administrative professional would then key in the variable information aligned at the first tab after the longest guide word (SUBJECT).

There should be at least two spaces after the colon that follows a guide word. Various styles are acceptable for the guide words:

(1) Align guide words at the left and variable information after the longest guide word (SUBJECT or MEMO TO).

EXAMPLE — Align Left Side; All Capital Letters:

DATE: February 4, 200X
TO: Leon Dresser
FROM: Mary-Louise Westcott
SUBJECT: REQUEST FOR PROFESSIONAL LEAVE

(2) Align guide words on the colons, and key in all variable information at the first tab after the colon to the right of the longest guide word.

EXAMPLE — Colons Aligned; Initial Caps:

To: Leon Dresser
From: Mary-Louise Westcott
Subject: Request for Professional Leave
Date: February 4, 200X

(3) Key in guide words in all capital letters or initial caps only (see examples 2 and 4).

(4) Include titles or departments.

EXAMPLE — Left Alignment; Guide Words and Subject Line In All Caps; Names and Titles; Date Aligned At Right:

TO: Leon Dresser   DATE: March 22, 200X
*   IT Director*

FROM: Mary-Louise Westcott
*   IT Manager*

SUBJECT: REQUEST FOR PROFESSIONAL LEAVE

(5) Place DATE as the first guide word, the fourth guide word, *or* on the same line as the guide word TO but to the right (see previous examples).

(6) Include three or four descriptive words as the subject so that the reader knows what the memorandum is about.

EXAMPLE — Colons Aligned; Guide Words In All caps; Names and Titles; Subject Line and Date to Right:

TO: Leon Dresser   SUBJECT: Request for
*   IT Director   Professional Leave*

FROM: Mary L. Westcott   DATE: March 22, 200X
*   IT Manager*

d. *Body paragraphs:* After the guide words, double- or triple-space to the body of the memorandum. Paragraphs are single-spaced with double-spacing between. Block style is used for all memoranda.

e. *Reference initials:* Reference initials are also included on a memorandum and are keyed in a double-space after the last paragraph at the left margin. Formats for reference initials are included in Section A-1-i.

Figure 9–10 illustrates a memorandum using these basic style guidelines.

FIGURE 9–10   Memorandum Style

MEMORANDUM

August 2, 200X ↓2 Enters

    TO: Ms. Geri Rankowski CPS/CAP
              General Manager, Operations ↓2

  FROM: Darla M. Roxbury
              President ↓2

SUBJECT: PREPARATION FOR AUGUST BOARD MEETING ↓3

      Our next board meeting is scheduled for Tuesday, August 19, and is a particularly important one. Sang Lee, manager of Asian Operations, will be here that week for individual meetings with managers of our different divisions and for the board meeting. ↓2

      Sang plans to spend Monday, August 18, with you and me going over details for the new blending of the Asian Operations with the North American and European ventures. We need to review products and services being offered through all of our operations. ↓2

      Can we begin our meeting on Monday with an 8 A.M. breakfast in the Executive Dining Room followed by a general meeting in Conference Room B? I would like you to share with us, too, the excellent presentation you made to the Board of Directors last week. I have invited the other general managers to join us for this meeting. ↓2

      ri

---

2. ***Using Word Processing Templates:*** Word processing software programs include templates for memorandum forms where only the variable information and the message need to be inserted. Even the date is automatically inserted. If the memorandum is saved, be sure to key in the date rather than use the insert function. The date will remain the same as the date the memorandum was prepared and sent.

Check Point—Section C

Directions: For each question, circle the correct answer.

C–1. A correspondence format specifically designed for internal use between individuals, departments, and branch offices is the

    A) business letter
    B) memorandum
    C) news release
    D) report

C–2. Which one of the following is a characteristic of memorandum format?

    A) Indented format for body paragraphs

    B) Complimentary closing at the end of the message
    C) Subject line with descriptive words
    D) Signature line

C–3. The subject of a memorandum consists of three or four descriptive words to let the reader know

    A) the content of the memorandum
    B) how soon a response is needed
    C) information about two or more topics
    D) who is sending the message

D. Electronic Mail

Electronic mail (e-mail) is a very effective way informal communication is transmitted internally and externally. Attention needs to be paid to the format used for e-mail messages so that the receiver of the message will only need to spend a minimum amount of time reading and responding to the message.

1. *Preliminary Sections of e-Mail Format:* The preliminary sections of the e-mail format include spaces for the e-mail address of the sender of the message (FROM address), the e-mail address of the receiver of the message (TO address), the option to send copies or blind copies to other individuals, the subject of the message, and the date and time.

   a. *The FROM address:* The sender's e-mail address is already entered in the system and is placed automatically in the FROM section of the message.

   b. *The TO address:* The e-mail address of the receiver(s) is keyed in the TO section. An address consists of the person's or organization's name followed by the @ symbol and the domain name. With appropriate punctuation between addresses, multiple recipients can be listed. Only those individuals involved in the communication should receive the message. Copies should be sent only to those who need to be informed of the communication.

   c. *Copies sent to others:* The e-mail addresses of individuals not involved in the e-mail dialogue but who should be kept informed of the communication taking place are designated after the copy notation (c:).

   d. *Blind copies sent to others:* If the original recipient of the message should not know that a copy is sent to other individuals, the e-mail can be copied blind. With a blind copy, only the sender and the copy recipient are aware of the copy being sent. The e-mail address of the person to receive a blind copy is placed after the blind copy notation (bc:).

   e. *Date and time of message:* The date and time the message is sent are automatically recorded on the e-mail listing and on the e-mail message itself. This provides an up-to-date record of the message transmission.

   f. *Subject of the message:* The moment the recipient receives the e-mail message, the subject line is indicated in the listing of messages received thus far. Since the purpose of e-mail is to enhance rapid communication, the recipient sees the subject of the e-mail before opening the message. Because of the fear of viruses, some people will not even open an e-mail message without knowing what the subject is, even though they know the sender. A descriptive subject line of three to five words is important for each e-mail message.

      EXAMPLE:

      SUBJECT: Professional Development Seminar

2. **The Message Format:** The format for the message will help the receiver decode the message and interpret the meaning. Block style is used for the body paragraphs of the e-mail message. The paragraphs are single-spaced, with a double-space between paragraphs. It is very important to include multiple paragraphs in the message rather than putting the entire message in just one long paragraph.

a. *Salutation:* First, a greeting, either formal or informal, is needed to begin the message. Key in the salutation at the left margin of the first line of the message. The receiver knows immediately if he or she is meant to receive the message, and such a greeting personalizes the message.

EXAMPLES:

Hi, Duncan!

Dear Marguerita,

Greetings, Sophia:

b. *Message:* The block style will help the readability of the message. Word wrap automatically adjusts the right margin of the material. Enter two times at the end of a paragraph to leave one blank line between paragraphs. Sometimes lists of information are more easily read if they appear in bulleted form.

c. *Complimentary closing:* A complimentary closing is keyed in a double-space below the last paragraph at the left margin. A comma can follow the complimentary closing if mixed punctuation is preferred.

EXAMPLE:

Sincerely yours,

d. *Signature file:* Each e-mail message needs at least a signature line so the receiver knows for certain who is sending the message. If the FROM section of the e-mail message does not clearly identify the sender or if the person receiving the e-mail does not know the sender, a **signature file** should be inserted at the end of the message. A standard signature file can be prepared and stored to be automatically affixed to an e-mail message whenever needed. The signature file includes the sender's name, title, company name, e-mail address (if not shown elsewhere in the message), telephone number, and fax number.

EXAMPLE:

Elizabeth V. Grant
Organization Facilitator
Transformation Dynamics
evgrant@inil.com
630-879-6213

3. **Attachments:** e-Mail messages often involve the sharing of information from any variety of business documents from spreadsheets or graphs to electronic slides or copies of other business correspondence. Electronic copies of these documents can be attached to the e-mail message and sent to the receiver. The files for any **attachments** will be selected from the appropriate directory and automatically listed in the Attachment line. As with all business correspondence, only send those documents relevant to the message. Particularly long documents should be zipped so that they require less storage space.

Note: When attaching a document that has not been zipped, make sure to submit it as an "All Files" document and not as a hypertext document. The use of hypertext reformats the document.

Figure 9–11 shows an example of the format to be used for an e-mail message.

FIGURE 9–11   Format of Electronic Mail Message

```
Mail Message

                Appointment   | Task | Note | Phone |
        To:
        lneely@niu.edu
        CC:                              BC:                              Send
                                                                         Send Options
                                                                         Address Book
        Subject:                                                         Spell Check
        PROFESSIONAL SUBMISSIONS REQUESTED                               Attach
                                                                         Cancel

        Message:
        Dear ILA Member:

        I hope that you had the opportunity to see this year's issue of The Listening Professional.
        This publication has been designed as a tool for the business membership of the International
        Listening Association as well as a selling piece to entice a broader membership to the
        organization. The Listening Professional has less of a research-educational focus, yet provides
        much of that same educational information in a less formal manner.

        We are currently planning the 200X issue of The Listening Professional and would like to
        invite you to submit an article for publication. Generally, we are looking for a good combination
        of short, quick-read articles of 500 to 1,000 words or longer, more in-depth articles to give the
        publication some balance.

        Please let me know if you are interested in submitting an article for the upcoming issue. Our
        reviewers need the copy by January 31, 200X, in order to make editorial decisions by March 31.
        Please respond by e-mail to let me know of your interest in writing for our publication.

        Sincerely,

        Georgia Lee-Hanson
        Publication Director
        glee-hanson@aol.com
```

Check Point—Section D

Directions: For each question, circle the correct answer.

D–1.   Providing a salutation for an e-mail message lets the receiver know that

A)   he or she is the appropriate person to receive the message

B)   the e-mail message is a high-priority item

C)   what the topic of the message is

D)   a response to the message is needed as quickly as possible

D–2.   Which one of the following statements illustrates a characteristic of e-mail message format?

A)   An indented format is used for the body paragraphs

B)   The body of the message is usually one long paragraph

C)   Message paragraphs are single-spaced with a double-space between paragraphs

D)   No complimentary closing or signature lines are used at the end of the message

D–3.   When information contained in a previously stored business document needs to be transmitted with a message, a/an

A)   signature file is included at the end of the message

B)   attachment is included with the message

C)   format change will be necessary to include that document's information

D)   separate e-mail message must be sent with the attached document

E. Business Reports

A business report is a common means of communication *within* business firms as well as *between* business firms. Format guidelines for reports vary in office reference manuals. A short report is referred to as a memorandum report if it is internal communication and formatted as a memorandum. Similarly, a short report that is prepared for external distribution may be prepared as a letter report. However, the following guidelines are acceptable for any business report that is prepared in manuscript format.

1. *Physical Layout:* The physical layout of the format includes decisions on margins (top, bottom, right, left), how the title of the report should be keyed in, and the general spacing of paragraph text.

   a. *Margins:* Specific guidelines need to be followed for the top, bottom, left, and right margins of a report written in manuscript format. Before keying in the text of the report, the page format command should be used to change any of the default margin settings to those margins needed for the report format.

      (1) *Top margins:* The top margin on the first page is 1½ to 2 inches. The top margin on succeeding pages is 1 inch.

         (a) *First page:* The top margin on the first page of the report is 2 inches when the report is leftbound or unbound and a title is included as the first line on the page. The top margin on the first page of the report is 1½ inches when no title is included on this page. The top margin of a topbound report must be an additional ½ to 1 inch.

         (b) *Succeeding pages:* The top margin on the second page and succeeding pages is 1 inch. If the report is topbound, the top margin is 1½ to 2 inches. A descriptive **header** (with words from the title) should appear at the left margin within the top margin on each page. Use the header command to enter the words you want as the header. (The page numbering should be entered separately from the header and may be keyed in as a footer. Page numbers may be at the top or bottom right margin or in the bottom center of each page.)

      (2) *Left margin:* The left margin will vary, depending on whether the report is leftbound or unbound. If the report is leftbound, ½ inch needs to be added to the left margin.

         (a) The left margin on an unbound report is 1 inch.

         (b) The left margin on a leftbound report is 1½ inches. The centerpoint of the page is then ¼ inch to the right of the center of the page. Any centered headings must be centered between the left and right margins.

      (3) *Right margin:* On all reports, the right margin should be 1 inch.

      (4) *Bottom margin:* A bottom margin of 1 inch is needed on all pages of the report.

   b. *Title of report:* The title of the report is keyed on the first page, centered in all capital letters. If the title is excessively long, it can be keyed in inverted pyramid style on more than one line and single-spaced. The first line is the longest, and each successive line of the title must be shorter than the previous line. If a title page is prepared for the report, then no title needs to appear on the first page of the report.

c. *Line spacing and paragraphing:* With word processing, the spacing should be kept as uniform as possible.

(1) *Spacing within text:* The text of the report is usually double-spaced for ease in reading. Some short reports (one page) are single-spaced, and periodically a business may decide to single-space a longer report to conserve paper. However, it is advisable to double-space all reports unless otherwise instructed. If a report is double-spaced, no extra blank lines are needed anywhere in the report. Memorandum or letter reports are single-spaced with a double-space between paragraphs.

(2) *Paragraph indentions:* Because reports are generally double-spaced, the paragraphs must be indented ½ inch (one standard tab) to identify the beginning of each paragraph. A first-line indent of ½ inch can be set so that an automatic indent is applied when the Enter key is depressed twice to begin a new paragraph. If a report is single-spaced, the paragraphs may or may not be indented, but there must always be double-spacing between the paragraphs.

d. *Headings:* In a report, there can be as many as seven levels of headings. When using headings, the number of subtopics needed under a major division determines the number of levels of headings used.

(1) *Hierarchy of levels:* Moving from the broadest, most important level to the most specific, least important level, headings should be formatted as follows:

Centered headings:
- Level 1—All capital letters
- Level 2—Initial caps and underlined
- Level 3—Initial caps and not underlined

Side headings:
- Level 4—All capital letters
- Level 5—Initial caps and underlined
- Level 6—Initial caps and not underlined

Paragraph headings:
- Level 7—Underlined and ending in a period or a period and a dash

Headings should begin with levels 1, 2, or 3. Then, you may move down the hierarchy by skipping to the next level of heading you desire. Let's say you have three divisions and begin with a level 2 heading. The next division could be level 5, and the last division could be level 7. Heading divisions must be consistent throughout a document.

EXAMPLE:

<u>*Progress Report on Bradford-Brown Sale*</u>
(centered heading—level 2)

Preliminary Investigation of Property
(side heading—level 6)

<u>*Abstract of Title.*</u>*—The title to the property is in the name of Arthur J. Bradford, Jr., as shown in the deed . . . (paragraph heading—level 7)*

(2) *Spacing for headings:* When headings are inserted into the text for a report, consistent spacing is required for each level of heading.

- *Centered headings:* Double-space before and after a centered heading. If a side heading immediately follows a centered heading, double-space before the side heading. An introductory paragraph would help the reader make the transition from one heading to another. Always double-space after a side heading.

- *Side headings:* Double-space before a side heading, but be consistent in the spacing used. Always continue double-spacing after the side heading.

- *Paragraph headings:* A paragraph heading begins a paragraph. Therefore, there is always double-spacing before a paragraph heading. Paragraph headings are always underlined and followed by a period and two spaces or a period and a dash.

e. *Pagination:* The appropriate numbering of pages helps to keep the report organized and the pages in order.

(1) *Placement of page numbers:* The most appropriate places for a page number are at the right margin—in the upper right corner or the lower right corner—or at the bottom center. The page-numbering command automatically places the number at the same location on each page of the report within the top or bottom margin. If the top or bottom margin is 1 inch, the page number will appear ½ inch into the margin.

(2) *Style of page number:* The page number is usually keyed by itself without the word *Page* or any other notations. However, format choices are available at the page-numbering command such as *-1-*, *-2-*, and *-3-* or Roman numerals such as *i, ii,* and *iii*. Preliminary pages of the report, such as the letter or memorandum of transmittal, the table of contents, and an executive summary, are numbered with Roman numerals. The main body of the report is numbered with arabic numbers, beginning with 1.

f. *Automatic generation of supplements:* When reports or other long documents are prepared, a table of contents; a list of tables, figures, or maps (when included in the document); and a bibliography (when references are used) must be included.

Word processing software includes a feature that assists in creating the table of contents, lists, bibliography, or index from the document being prepared. This automatic feature eliminates the rekeying of headings for the table of contents; tables, figures, or map titles; bibliographic references; or index. Also, as changes are made within the document, the information contained in these document supplements changes automatically.

g. *Widow/orphan lines:* To avoid a widow or orphan line at the bottom or top of any page, you may have more than a 1-inch bottom margin. A **widow/orphan line** is one line of a paragraph by itself on a page. You must always have at least two lines of a paragraph on a page. If the widow/orphan function is turned on, the computer system will automatically make sure that two lines of a paragraph will be left at the bottom or top of a page. The widow/orphan control can be activated with the appropriate command as needed.

Figure 9–12 shows a business report in manuscript format.

FIGURE 9–12   Business Report in Manuscript Format

Key to Buymanship

THE KEY TO BUYMANSHIP

Economic theory assumes that consumers have all the information required about the products they buy. Can the once-every-three years automobile buyer make an even-handed deal with a salesperson who sees dozens of customers a day? Can the consumer select the correct remedy at the best price without comparative prices being available? The basic question still remains: "Is it possible to make rational decisions without information?"

Government Regulation

Legislation has been proposed for regulations to have businesses make available price lists for various services performed. These services would be divided into categories so consumers could specifically see the cost of various components that are purchased.

Product Pricing Information

The Federal Trade Commission contends that package prices and refusal to advertise prices that are not required by law are costing consumers more than they are willing to pay. The trend in government regulation of trade appears to be assisting consumers in the quest for information. Many "secret" pricing practices and "secret" formulas and ingredients are now going public so consumers can compare and choose based on greater foreknowledge.

Areas of Regulation

The Federal Trade Commission has pushed for more price information in many areas. For example, a number of states have passed laws permitting pharmacists to substitute less expensive generic drugs which are chemically equivalent to the expensive brand-name prescription drugs. In recent years, more than sixty bills were introduced to Congress to bring more information to consumers on food labels.

More of these types of bills are expected to be introduced in the mid-2000's. Proposed regulations would even require funeral directors to have available price lists for various services they perform.

1

2. *Documentation:* Preparing appropriate documentation of information contained in a report is very important when the report contains the results of both primary and secondary research. The use of ideas and words from original works is governed by copyright legislation. In business writing, **documentation** is defined as giving appropriate credit to information sources within the text and in bibliographic form at the end of the report. Depending on the documentation format selected, documentation typically refers to the form of reference notes (footnotes, endnotes, or in-text citations) and the source information contained in the reference list at the end of the report. A bibliography, works cited list, or reference list identifies complete information about the sources used in the preparation of the report.

   a. *Copyright protection:* The Copyright Act of 1976, which became effective January 1, 1978, and subsequent amendments influence the way in which original works of authorship may be used for reference and cited within documents.

FIGURE 9–12   *(continued)*

THE KEY TO BUYMANSHIP

Economic theory assumes that consumers have all the information required about the products they buy. Can the once-every-three years automobile buyer make an even-handed deal with a salesperson who sees dozens of customers a day? Can the consumer select the correct remedy at the best price without comparative prices being available? The basic question still remains: "Is it possible to make rational decisions without information?"

Government Regulation

Legislation has been proposed for regulations to have businesses make available price lists for various services performed. These services would be divided into categories so consumers could specifically see the cost of various components that are purchased.

Product Pricing Information

The Federal Trade Commission contends that package prices and refusal to advertise prices that are not required by la
are willing to pay. The trend in governmen
assisting consumers in the quest for

Key to Buymanship

information. Many "secret" pricing practices and "secret" formulas and ingredients are now going public so consumers can compare and choose based on greater foreknowledge.

Areas of Regulation

The Federal Trade Commission has pushed for more price information in many areas. For example, a number of states have passed laws permitting pharmacists to substitute less expensive generic drugs which are chemically equivalent to the expensive brand-name prescription drugs. In recent years, more than sixty bills were introduced to Congress to bring more information to consumers on food labels.

More of these types of bills are expected to be introduced in the mid-2000's. Proposed regulations would even require funeral directors to have available price lists for various services they perform.

Critics of the Information Boom

Many critics, however, have voiced strong concerns about the ways in which information is currently being conveyed to consumers. Even publications like *Consumer Reports* must be extremely cautious to report findings in a fair and equitable manner. Product testing and evaluation needs to be conducted using unbiased, nonjudgmental methods. The consumer has the right to accurate information about warranties in addition to acceptable price ranges

2

(1) *Types of works protected:* Almost all major nations follow the Berne copyright convention. In the United States, almost everything created after April 1, 1989, is copyrighted and protected whether a copyright notice is included with the source or not. The copyright legislation identifies the following types of original works:

- *Literary works:* novels, nonfiction prose, poetry, newspaper articles and newspapers, magazine articles and magazines, computer software, software manuals, training manuals, manuals, catalogs, brochures, advertising text, and compilations such as business directories.

- *Musical works:* songs, advertising jingles, and instrumentals.

- *Dramatic works:* plays, operas, and skits.

- *Pantomimes and choreographic works:* ballets, modern dance, jazz dance, and mime works.

- *Motion pictures and other audiovisual works:* movies, documentaries, travelogues, training films and videos, television shows, television advertising, and interactive multimedia works.

- *Sound recordings:* recordings of music, sounds, or words.

(2) *Term of copyright protection:* Three factors affect the length of time a copyright protects an original work: who created the work, when the work was created, and when it was first distributed commercially. The term for a copyrighted work created on or after January 1, 1978, is the life of the author plus 50 years. A work created by an employee within the scope of employment is owned by the employer because it is considered a "work for hire." The term for such works is 75 years from the date of first publication or 100 years from the date of creation, whichever expires first. Most published works contain a copyright notice. For works published on or after March 1, 1989, however, the use of copyright notice is optional. The fact that a work does not show a copyright does not mean that the work is not protected by copyright.

(3) *Copyrighted works on the Internet:* A simple rule to follow in using information from the Internet is this: If you did not write the original work and you want to use or reproduce it, you must ask the author (creator) for permission. The general rule of thumb today is that other people's works are copyrighted and may not be used or copied unless you have definite proof of no copyright or you have obtained the permission of the copyright holder. Just because information is posted to an Internet Web site does not mean that the information is in the public domain, which means anyone may use this information.

(4) *Fair use of copyrighted material:* An exemption exists in U.S. copyright law called "fair use." This was created to allow commentary, parody, news reporting, research, and education about copyrighted works without the permission of the author or creator. The "fair use" concept varies from country to country and has different names and limitations in other countries. For example, the term used in Canada is "fair dealing."

Facts and ideas can never be copyrighted, but the way they are expressed and structured can. A writer always has the choice to write facts in his or her own words and to give appropriate credit for information gleaned from various secondary sources.

b. *Documentation styles:* The documentation style selected for a report must be accepted by business professionals. The three most commonly used styles in business are the *American Psychological Association Style (APA)*, the *Modern Language Association Style (MLA)*, and the *Chicago Manual of Style (CMS)*. Although information used in business documents is sometimes not as heavily cited and documented as information contained in other types of research documents, the business writer should become accustomed to documenting ideas obtained from other writers and sources. Otherwise, the risk of being accused of plagiarism is great. **Plagiarism** is defined as the use of information or ideas from secondary sources by writers who intentionally refrain from including documentation giving the original author appropriate credit. When preparing a report with references, one documentation style must be selected, and that style must be applied throughout the report.

(1) *The American Psychological Association (APA) style:* Most often used and commonly accepted in business professions, the APA style features reference notes called in-text parenthetical citations, which give an abbreviated reference to each information source. A references list at the end of the report presents complete bibliographic information about each information source cited in the text of the report.

(2) *The Modern Language Association (MLA) style:* Often used in the language fields, the MLA style features in-text parenthetical citations, similar to APA style. In addition, a works cited list of references is included at the end of the report, listing complete information about each of the sources that were cited in the report.

(3) *The Chicago Manual of Style (CMS):* Documentation of information sources requires superscripts (raised numbers) identifying citations included in the body of the text and a choice of reference notes—either footnotes on each page or endnotes at the end of the report. In addition, a bibliography of all references used and cited is included at the end of the report.

c. *Types of reference notes:* Reference notes, or **reference citations** as they are sometimes called, are used to cite specific information that is quoted or paraphrased from secondary information sources. A writer has only two choices when using information from secondary sources: to directly quote from the material or to paraphrase the original author's ideas and words. In both instances, however, reference notes (citations) are needed to ensure that the originators of the information receive proper credit in the document.

- *Direct quotations:* Sometimes the writer prefers to cite a passage verbatim (word for word) from an information source. Each **direct quotation** must be placed within quotation marks and followed by a reference citation. A short quote of four or fewer lines is included in the body of the text. A longer quote of more than four lines is set off as a separate paragraph—with all lines indented one tab from the left margin but without quotation marks and followed by a reference citation.

- *Paraphrasing:* More commonly in business writing, we try to rewrite the original author's words or ideas into our own words. This is called **paraphrasing** but does not make the ideas our own. Therefore, a reference citation is still needed within the text to give the originator (author) of the ideas proper credit.

The types of reference citations that are commonly used in reports are in-text citations, footnotes, or endnotes. These citations acknowledge published and unpublished sources of information and give proper credit to the authors or publications for any passages referred to in the text of the report. Business writing is strengthened when information from various sources is integrated into the text and supported with appropriate documentation.

EXAMPLES:

Published sources: Books, periodical articles, or research reports (online or hard copy)

Unpublished sources: Theses, dissertations, television or radio programs, lectures, letters, or some World Wide Web/Internet online references

Some online material is published while other material is unpublished. A number of publishers offer online references and books for a fee.

(1) *In-text citation:* The American Psychological Association (APA) and the Modern Language Association (MLA) documentation styles use in-text citations rather than footnotes or endnotes. These citations are required so that proper credit is given to the author and/or source of the ideas included in the report. Each reference citation is shown in parentheses in the appropriate location within the body of the text.

(a) *APA style:* An in-text citation using APA style consists of the author's last name, then year of publication, followed by month and day of publication (if known) and page number(s). If the pages of the source are not numbered, then the writer numbers the paragraphs and references the paragraph number instead, i.e., par. 3. These parenthetical citations are placed appropriately within the text of the report.

EXAMPLE:

Direct quotation:

"The U.S. economy is so robust that its impact is reaching right into the heart of America's long-suffering cities" (Bernstein, 1999, October 18, p. 157).

Paraphrased sentence:

America's cities are experiencing the impact of the strength of the economy (Bernstein, 1999, October 18, p. 157).

Direct quotation:

"Readers look in the bibliography section to locate the sources of ideas mentioned in a report" (Guffey, 2003, p. 465).

Paraphrased sentence:

The bibliography contains complete references to the sources cited in a report (Guffey, 2003, p. 465).

If the information source has no author, the first major word of the title of the article or publication should be used, along with the publication date and page number (if there is one).

EXAMPLE:

Direct quotation:

"Our survey of more than 10,000 computer users also revealed that software makers fall short in satisfying consumers when compared with other service providers" (When, 2003, September, p. 12).

Paraphrased sentence:

A recent <u>Consumer Reports</u> *survey of over 10,000 computer users shows that software producers may not be meeting consumers' needs (When, 2003, September, p. 12).*

If the author's name appears within the sentence, only the publication date and the page number are necessary in the citation.

EXAMPLE:

Guffey states that in APA style an abbreviated citation appears within the text and a complete reference to the source appears in a bibliography at the end of the report (2003, p. A-44).
or

Guffey (2003, p. A-44) states that in APA style an abbreviated citation appears within the text and a complete reference to the source appears in a reference list at the end of the report.

Sometimes an article or book has two or more authors. In these cases, the last names of all authors are included in the citation or the first author's last name followed by *et al.* is used to refer to all of the authors.

EXAMPLE:

Campbell et al. (1994, p. 33) present a number of examples to help the writer develop appropriate in-text citations for either the APA style or the MLA style.

  (b) *MLA style:* The format for the MLA style includes only the author's last name and the page reference in the in-text citation. The citation is placed within parentheses, just like in the APA style, in the appropriate place in the sentence. If the author's name is included in the sentence, only the page reference is required.

       EXAMPLES: *In MLA style an abbreviated citation with the author's name and page appears in parentheses within the text and a complete reference to the source appears in a works cited bibliography at the end of the report (Guffey A-42).*

       or

       Guffey (A-42) states that in MLA style an abbreviated citation with the author's name and page appears in parentheses within the text and a complete reference to the source appears in a works cited bibliography at the end of the report.

       Figure 9–13 shows examples of reference citations.

  (2) *Source footnotes or endnotes:* The CMS style requires the use of footnotes or endnotes. A footnote or endnote gives credit to a source of information included in a report. **Footnotes** (with reference marks, superscripts, in the text) are included at the "foot" (bottom) of the page where the reference is made. **Endnotes** are also indicated in the text with superscripts but appear on a separate page at the "end" of the report. The first time the reference is referred to, the citation must have complete information about the source;

FIGURE 9–13   Examples of Reference Citations

Examples of Reference Citations	Footnotes or Endnotes Chicago Manual of Style	In-text Citation (APA Style)	In-text Citation (MLA Style)
Book with one author	[1]Julie Morgenstern, *Organizing from the Inside Out* (New York: Henry Holt and Company, LLC, 1998), 73–89.	(Morgenstern, 1998, p. 75)	(Morgenstern 75)
Book with two authors	[2]James F. Kurose and Keith W. Ross, *Computer Networking: A Top-Down Approach Featuring the Internet,* 2nd ed. (Upper Saddle River, NJ: Pearson Addison Wesley, 2002, July 17), 66.	(Kurose and Ross, 2002, July 17, p. 66)	(Kurose and Ross 66)
Book with editor only	[3]Martha H. Rader, ed., *Effective Methods of Teaching Business Education in the 21st Century,* National Business Education Yearbook, No. 41 (Reston: National Business Education Association, 2003), 85.	(Rader, 2003, p. 85)	(Rader 85)
Magazine or journal article (with author)	[4]Anya Martin, "Digging Out of the Digital Office," *OfficePro* 63, no. 6 (August/September 2003), 10–13.	(Martin, 2003, August/September, pp. 10–13)	(Martin 10–13)
Magazine or journal article (no author)	[5]"When Good Software Goes Bad," *Consumer Reports* 68, no. 9 (September 2003), 12–14.	(When, 2003, September, 12–14)	(When 12–14)
Newspaper article (with author)	[6]Rachel Osterman, "Is It Really Fair to Grade Workers on a Curve?", *The Chicago Tribune,* September 7, 2003, 5–5.	(Osterman, 2003, September 7, Sec. 5–5)	(Osterman 5–5)
Interview	[7]Diane Routhier Graf, president, Transformation Dynamics, November 15, 2003. Interview by author, Rockford, Illinois.	(Graf, 2003, November 15)	(Graf)
Electronic reference (with author)	[8]Helen Peters, "Risk, Rescue and Righteousness: How Women Prevent Themselves from Breaking Through the Glass Ceiling," *Female Executives and the Glass Ceiling,* Hagberg Consulting Group, 2003 http://www.hcgnet.com/html (September 17, 2003).	(Peters, 2003, par. 3)	(Peters par. 3)
Electronic reference (no author)	[9]"Business Netiquette International," Pearman Cooperation Alliance, April 26, 1999 http://www.bspage.com/1netiq/Netiq.html (September 17, 2003).	(Business, 1999, April 26, par. 5)	(Business par. 5)
Electronic reference (no author, no date)	[10]"International Etiquette," EffectiveMeetings.com http://www.effectivemeetings.com (September 17, 2003).	(International, no date, par. 9)	(International par. 9)

later reference to the same work can be abbreviated. The source information in the footnote or endnote includes the following:

- Name(s) of author(s)
- Name(s) of editor(s)
- Publication title—book, published article, or published report

- Publication information—name of publishing company, city, publication date, volume of publication, number of publication issue, page number(s) referenced
- Electronic reference—online source, Web site name, URL, and retrieval or access date

The format for a footnote or endnote citation is the way the reference actually appears on the printed page. The separation line, numbering, indentation, and spacing are very important considerations.

(a) *Separation line:* A 1½-inch horizontal line should separate the body of the text from the footnotes. There should be one blank space above and below this line. When you key in the footnote with word processing, the program enters the separation line before you begin the first footnote for that page.

(b) *Numbering:* Each reference must be consecutively numbered with arabic numerals. All footnotes within a report may be consecutively numbered; or, if the report is particularly lengthy, all footnotes within a particular chapter may be consecutively numbered. A reference mark (a superscript number) is inserted automatically when the footnote command is activated at the point in the text where a footnote is needed. At the same time, the complete footnote entry can be entered at the bottom of the screen.

(c) *Indentation:* Paragraph style is used most often when keying in the text for each footnote or endnote. The first line of the footnote must be indented one standard tab (½ inch). If the footnote format does not allow for this indentation, you may enter it manually before the first superscript. All other lines are flush left.

(d) *Spacing:* Footnote references should be single-spaced with a double-space between if there are two or more citations on the same page. Once you have activated the footnote or endnote command, you can adjust the format by indenting the first line of each entry and leaving a double-space (one blank line) between entries. The software will insert the separation line between the text and the footnotes automatically.

See Figure 9–13 for examples of footnotes when referenced according to the *Chicago Manual of Style*.

For additional examples of reference citations (footnotes, endnotes, or in-text citations), refer to the following:

Guffey, Mary Ellen, *Business Communication: Process and Product*, Fourth Edition (Cincinnati: Thomson South-Western, 2003), A–41 to A–46.

Lesikar, Raymond V., and Marie E. Flatley, *Basic Business Communication: Skills for Empowering the Internet Generation*, Ninth Edition (New York: McGraw-Hill/Irwin, 2002), 569–578.

Slade, Carole; William Giles Campbell; and Stephen Vaughan Ballou, *Form and Style: Theses, Reports, Term Papers* (Boston: Houghton Mifflin Company), latest edition.

(3) *Discussion footnote or endnote:* This type of reference note gives additional information that might be related indirectly to the topic.

EXAMPLE:

[1]*The verbs used by office systems researchers in submitting critical incidents were modified to conform to the original taxonomy developed by Huffman et al.*

(4) *Reference footnote or endnote:* This type of citation refers to related sources or serves as a cross-reference to other parts of the report.

EXAMPLE:

> [2] *See Figure 9–10, "Memorandum Style," 291.*

(5) *Later references to same citation:* Sometimes you need to footnote a particular source more than once in a report. You may shorten these references either by using traditional Latin abbreviations or by using the author's name and page number.

- *IBID.:* The word *ibidem* means "in the same place." This term may be used when reference is made to the immediately preceding footnote or endnote.

EXAMPLES:

> [3] *Ibid. (Reference for same page as preceding footnote)*
>
> [4] *Ibid., 334–345. (Citation for same reference as preceding footnote, but different page reference)*

- *OP. CIT.:* The words *opere citato* mean "in the work cited." This term is used when reference is made to a previous source but there are intervening references.

EXAMPLE:

> [5] *Kurose and Ross, op. cit., 44.*

- *LOC. CIT.:* The words *loco citato* mean "in the place cited." This term refers to the same page reference as the previous footnote for that source.

EXAMPLE:

> [6] *Kurose and Ross, loc. cit.*

- *Author's name and page number:* Another way of writing subsequent references to a previous source is to use the author's name and the page number.

EXAMPLE:

> [7] *Osterman, 5–5.*

(6) *Placement of endnotes:* If you choose to have the reference notes included at the end of the report as endnotes, you will make this choice before you key in the text. The endnotes remain in the same order as the notes appear in the report. This list is automatically created at the end of the report. When the reference is made, the superscripts appear in the text of the report as well as in the endnote.

The title ENDNOTES needs to be centered at the top of the endnotes page. The first line of each endnote should be indented one-half inch (one standard tab) from the left margin. The succeeding lines of an entry should be flush left. The endnotes should be single-spaced with one blank line between endnotes.

Word processing software programs have a reference feature that permits a choice of footnote or endnote format. Using this feature can save the administrative professional a great deal of formatting time, particularly if editing revisions in the text change the order of the footnotes or endnotes. These changes are then automatically revised throughout the document. The author of the report and the administrative professional should review the software format to see whether it adheres to guidelines required for the final report.

FIGURE 9–14   General Bibliography in Chicago Style (Hanging-Indent Format/Alphabetic List)

BIBLIOGRAPHY

"Business Netiquette International." Pearman Cooperation Alliance. April 26, 1999 <http://www.bspage.com/1netiq/Netiq.html> (September 17, 2003).

Graf, Diane Routhier, president, Transformation Dynamics. Interview by author. Rockford, Illinois. 15 November 2003.

"International Etiquette." EffectiveMeetings.com. <http://www.effectivemeetings.com> (September 17, 2003).

Kurose, James F., and Keith W. Ross. *Computer Networking: A Top-Down Approach Featuring the Internet,"* 2nd ed. Upper Saddle River, NJ: Pearson Addison Wesley, 2002.

Martin, Anya. "Digging Out of the Digital Office." *OfficePro* 63, no. 6 (August/September 2003): 10–13.

Morgenstern, Julie. *Organizing from the Inside Out.* New York: Henry Holt and Company, LLC, 1998.

Osterman, Rachel. "Is It Really Fair to Grade Workers on a Curve?" *The Chicago Tribune,* 7 September 2003, sec. 5, p. 5.

Peters, Helen. "Risk, Rescue and Righteousness: How Women Prevent Themselves from Breaking Through the Glass Ceiling." *Female Executives and the Glass Ceiling.* Hagberg Consulting Group. 2003 <http://www.hcgnet.com/html> (September 17, 2003).

Rader, Martha H., ed. *Effective Methods of Teaching Business Education in the 21st Century.* National Business Education Yearbook, No. 41. Reston: National Business Education Association, 2003.

"When Good Software Goes Bad." *Consumer Reports* 68, no. 9 (September 2003): 12–14.

d. *Bibliography:* A **bibliography** is a list of *all* references consulted by the author that contributed to the content of the report. The *Chicago Manual of Style* requires the inclusion of a bibliography. The bibliography is placed at the end of the report on a separate page.

(1) *Types of bibliographies:* The basic types of bibliographies that are used with reports include a general bibliography and an annotated bibliography.

(a) *General bibliography:* This type of bibliography, sometimes referred to as a *working bibliography*, includes all references used in researching the content of the report. A general bibliography includes references that were directly cited in the text as well as others that were helpful but not the basis for any of the citations (see Figure 9–14).

(b) *Annotated bibliography:* After each bibliographic entry, a brief paragraph comments on the content and value of the reference. The annotated bibliography gives basic information about each reference used in preparing the content of the report.

EXAMPLE:

[8]Martha H. Rader, ed., *Effective Methods of Teaching Business Education in the 21st Century,* National Business Education Yearbook No. 41 (Reston: National Business Education Association, 2003).

Research, teaching strategies, and suggested resources for all areas of business education. Four parts (business education perspectives, instructional concepts, business education curriculum, and organizational and professional responsibilities). Chapter authors from business education profession.

(2) *Bibliography format:* The format dictates the appearance of the bibliography. The placement of the bibliography on the page, the way the entries appear, and the spacing required are important to an attractively prepared bibliography.

(a) *Placement on page:* The placement of the bibliography depends on the documentation style being used. These directions pertain to a bibliography formatted according to the *Chicago Manual of Style*.

- The word BIBLIOGRAPHY should be centered 2 inches from the top edge of the page (line 13).
- There should be either a double-space or a triple-space after the title.
- The first line of each entry must be flush left. The second and succeeding lines are indented at least ½ inch. This type of indentation is calling **hanging indent**. The user sets the software for a hanging-indent paragraph style.
- Each entry is single-spaced with a double-space (one blank space) between entries.
- The second and succeeding pages of the bibliography continue the entries beginning 1 inch (line 7) from the top edge of the page.

(b) *Arrangement of entries:* The bibliographic entries may be listed in two different ways—in an alphabetic list or in categories of references.

- *Alphabetic list:* The entire bibliography is alphabetized and prepared as a single list of references.
- *Reference categories:* Each reference is included in the appropriate category (books, articles, research reports, electronic references, interviews, miscellaneous). Within each category, the entries are alphabetized according to the documentation style selected. Side headings highlight the different categories.

(c) *Preparation of entries:* The following procedures help to standardize the way in which the bibliographic entries are keyed:

- If the author is known, the author's last name is listed first, followed by first name.
- If the author is unknown, the title is listed first.
- Within the alphabetic sequence, if an author is listed for more than one reference, a 1-inch line is keyed instead of the author's name in the second and succeeding entries.
- Periods, rather than commas, separate the various sections of each entry.
- The title of the work should be shown exactly as it appeared in the citation; that is, the name of a periodical article is keyed in initial caps, lowercase, and enclosed in quotation marks; the name of a book is keyed in italics or underlined.

EXAMPLES:

Article: "Hold Technology in Your Palm"

Book: *The Electronic Cottage* or <u>The Electronic Cottage</u>

- In entries for periodical articles, the exact page numbers should be included.

- In entries for books or works that are used in total, the entire reference is cited rather than individual pages.

Figure 9–14 illustrates a general bibliography developed according to the *Chicago Manual of Style*. This bibliography includes all references cited and used in the preparation of a report.

Figure 9–15 is an example of a works cited bibliography following the MLA style. Only those references that are cited within a report are included in Works Cited. MLA style varies from other styles in the way words are capitalized and punctuation used within the entry. These differences are shown in the examples.

Figure 9–16 is an example of a reference list following APA style. Only references that were cited within a report are included in References. APA style varies from other styles in the way the entry is written—words capitalized, punctuation used. These differences are shown in the examples.

FIGURE 9–15 Works Cited—MLA Style (Parargraph Format/Alphabetic List)

WORKS CITED

"Business Netiquette International." Pearman Cooperation Alliance. 26 April 1999 http://www.bspage.com/1netiq/Netiq.html (September 17, 2003).

Graf, Diane Routhier, president, Transformation Dynamics. Interview by author. Rockford, Illinois. 2003, November 15.

"International Etiquette." EffectiveMeetings.com. http://www.effectivemeetings.com (September 17, 2003).

Kurose, James F., and Keith W. Ross. *Computer Networking: A Top-Down Approach Featuring the Internet.* 2nd ed. Upper Saddle River, NJ: Pearson Addison Wesley, 2003.

Martin, Anya. "Digging Out of the Digital Office." *OfficePro* 63,6 (August/September 2003): 10–13.

Morgenstern, Julie. *Organizing from the Inside Out.* New York: Henry Holt and Company, LLC, 1998.

Osterman, Rachel. "Is It Really Fair to Grade Workers on a Curve?" *The Chicago Tribune* 7 September 2003: 5–5.

Peters, Helen. "Risk, Rescue and Righteousness: How Women Prevent Themselves from Breaking Through the Glass Ceiling." *Female Executives and the Glass Ceiling.* Hagberg Consulting Group. 2003 http://www.hcgnet.com/html 17 September 2003.

Rader, Martha H., ed. *Effective Methods of Teaching Business Education in the 21st Century.* National Business Education Yearbook, No. 41. Reston: National Business Education Association, 2003.

"When Good Software Goes Bad." *Consumer Reports* 68,9 (September 2003): 12–14.

FIGURE 9–16   References—APA Style (Paragraph Format/Alphabetic List)

REFERENCES

Business netiquette international. (1999, April 26). Pearman Cooperation Alliance. Retrieved September 17, 2003, from http://www.bspage.com/1netiq/Netiq.html

International etiquette. (no date). EffectiveMeetings.com [Online] Retrieved September 17, 2003, from http://www.effectivemeetings.com

Kurose, J. F., & Ross, K. W. (2002). *Computer networking: A Top-down approach featuring the Internet.* 2nd ed. Upper Saddle River, NJ: Pearson Addison Wesley.

Martin, A. (2003, August/September). Digging out of the digital office. *OfficePro,* 63(6), 10–13.

Morgenstern, J. (1998). *Organizing from the inside out.* New York: Henry Holt and Company, LLC.

Osterman, R. (2003, September 7). Is it really fair to grade workers on a curve? *The Chicago Tribune,* p. 5–5.

Peters, H. (2003). Risk, rescue and righteousness: How women prevent themselves from breaking through the glass ceiling. *Female executives and the glass ceiling.* Hagberg Consulting Group. Retrieved September 17, 2003, from http://www.hcgnet.com/html

Rader, M. H., ed. (2003). *Effective methods of teaching business education in the 21st century.* National Business Education Yearbook, No. 41. Reston: National Business Education Association.

When good software goes bad. (2003, September). *Consumer Reports,* 68(9), 12–14.

Note: An interview is cited in the text only but does not appear in the list of references.

Check Point—Section E

Directions: For each question, circle the correct answer.

E–1. Documentation typically refers to the style in which the

    A) works cited list is prepared

    B) reference list at the end of a report is prepared

    C) reference citations appear within the text

    D) reference notes and bibliographic information appear within the report

E–2. Which one of the following is an in-text citation written in APA style?

    A) (Parkinson 25)

    B) (Stevens 2004 February 2 25)

    C) (World 225)

    D) (Williams & Parke, 2004, p. 251)

E–3. A list of all references cited by the writer in the content of the report is called a/an

    A) annotated bibliography

    B) in-text citation

    C) works cited bibliography

    D) general bibliography

F. Other Forms of Business Communication

As communication is very important in the office, there are many forms in which written communication is transmitted. Only some of the most common are presented here, along with highlights of the formats used for minutes, news releases, itineraries, outlines, abstracts, and précis.

  1. *Minutes:* The purpose of **minutes** is to summarize the events taking place during a meeting. The minutes become the official report of the meeting. Figure 9–17 shows

FIGURE 9–17 Minutes of Meeting

International Association of Administrative Professionals
Kishwaukee Chapter
Regular Meeting—Minutes
September 9, 200X—8 P.M.
Kishwaukee College, Malta, Illinois

Attendees:	Barb Anderson CPS, Pat Burch CPS, Ginny Dumdie, Ruth Hart CPS, Geri Henkel, Donna Peterson, Betty Schroeder, Pat Siebrasse CPS.
Call to Order:	President Ruth Hart called the meeting to order at 8:15 P.M., following the progressive dinner.
Secretary's Report:	Pat Burch made a motion to approve the May 15 minutes; Ginny Dumdie seconded the motion; motion passed.
Treasurer's Report:	The account balances are presently as follows: checking account, $1,569.88; savings account, $2,363.94. Last year's books were audited by Geri Henkel.
	Ginny Dumdie reported that two additional amounts need to be deposited: $37 for purchase of stamps left over from the PEP mailing and a $10 contribution toward the scholarship fund.
	The scholarships for the three winners have been forwarded to Kishwaukee College for deposit in the students' accounts to be applied to next semester's fees.

Old Business:

P.E.P. Seminar—Saturday, September 20, 200X
Best Western, DeKalb, Illinois
✓ Ginny Dumdie reported that there are 51 registrations thus far—45 paid and 6 franked.
✓ Several baskets will be prepared by members to raffle as a fundraiser. The members decided that only the minimum value of each basket should be identified on the basket. These baskets are due on the day of the seminar.
✓ A one-page information sheet about the day's events will be included in the folders along with a list of registrants.
✓ No special Friday night event is being planned.
✓ Chapter members will need to come about 7:30 A.M. to help with registration, the 50/50 raffle, the silent auction, and membership.
✓ The continental breakfast and registration begins at 8 A.M.
✓ Ruth Hart will confirm the number with the food caterer.

Great Lakes District Conference—October 3–5, 200X
Troy, Michigan
✓ Pat Burch and Pat Siebrasse will be attending; no delegate is needed because this is the last GLDC conference.
✓ The chapter will contribute items toward an Illinois basket. Suggestions were made: pins, corn candles, dreamcatcher.
✓ Pat Burch indicated that the vendor table costs $40 so the suggestion was made to perhaps share a table with another chapter.

Fashion Show/Raffle—Saturday, November 1, 200X
Chandelier Room, Northern Illinois University—11:30 A.M.
✓ Pat Siebrasse has contacted Fashion Bug and Weekender about participating and showing fashions.
✓ Geri Henkel is making contacts for large raffle items. Raffle ticket sales will begin in late September.
✓ Ruth Hart is in charge of the door prizes.
✓ Names for modeling were suggested.
✓ A sample flyer was reviewed; flyers will be mailed out mid-September.
✓ Vendor tables will be free, but vendors will need to pay for their own lunch.

New Business:
The schedule of programs for the year was reviewed.
Chapter directories were distributed. Committee assignments are identified in the booklets.
Pat Burch moved and Ginny Dumdie seconded the motion that the $15 one-time fee be waived for new members. Motion passed.

Next Meeting
The next chapter meeting will be held on Monday, October 13, at 7 P.M. at Kishwaukee College in Room A-112. The board will meet at 6 P.M. that night in the same room.

Meeting adjourned at 9:15 P.M.

Respectfully submitted,

Betty Schroeder
Secretary

an example of minutes prepared by an administrative professional. Sometimes detailed minutes are preferred; at other times, only brief coverage of topics is required. All minutes, however, should be prepared in the following way.

a.   *Heading:* The heading must contain the following types of information:

1. Name of the organization (department or division) holding the meeting

2. Date of the meeting

3. Time of the meeting

4. Location of the meeting

5. Type of meeting (regular or special)

The heading begins 1½ to 2 inches from the top edge of the page, is either centered or arranged across the line of print, and is either keyed in initial caps or in all capital letters. After the heading, double- or triple-space (two or three Enters) to the next section.

b.   *Attendance:* An alphabetical list of the names of the people (members) who attended the meeting is included in the first paragraph of the minutes. Including an alphabetical list of people (members) who are absent (or the number of people absent) is desirable but optional. Special guests at the meeting may also be identified.

c.   *Body:* Minutes are a summary of the topics discussed at the meeting. It is helpful to follow the agenda while taking minutes at a meeting. The presentation of this summary information is usually in paragraph form. The marginal format for preparing reports is followed for minutes. If headings are used, follow the same format as for reports. Minutes are usually single-spaced with double-spacing between paragraphs. However, double-spacing is also appropriate.

d.   *Motions:* For routine motions, the administrative professional can record, *It was moved and seconded that . . . .* When a motion is made where the exact wording is required, the names of those making and seconding the motion are also recorded. The recording of any motion is included in the topic paragraph pertaining to the motion. Some correctly stated motions are as follows:

EXAMPLES:

Caldwell moved and Hernandez seconded the motion that . . . .

The motion was made by M. Caldwell and seconded by R. Hernandez that . . . .

It was moved and seconded that . . . .
(This example is for routine motions only).

Note: Last names may be used when identifying people who made or seconded motions or entered into the discussion of motions. However, when two participants have the same last name, initials or first names must be used to properly identify the persons involved in the motions or discussion. In the latter case, all participants should be identified in the same way throughout the minutes.

e.   *Closing:* The complimentary closing for minutes is *Respectfully submitted.* There are three blank lines (four Enters) between the complimentary closing and the keyed signature of the secretary, the person selected by the group to take the minutes. If you are preparing the minutes for the secretary, your reference initials should follow a double-space after the typed signature at the left margin.

EXAMPLE:

*Respectfully submitted,*₁₁4 Enters (3 blank lines)

M. E. Schneider
Secretary

gmd

2. *News Release:* The **news release** is an announcement about a business event that usually needs to be prepared by an administrative professional. The urgency of the item will depend on the date of the news. From the reader's viewpoint, news is news only if it is announcing something before the fact or immediately after it happens. If you are responsible for making sure news releases get to the press in time (whether the press is in-house or the local newspapers), you should be aware of the lead time required. This is particularly true for announcement news. Typical lead time required for a news release is ten days. To find out the specific lead time for your local paper, contact the newspaper's City Desk. A news release should include these parts: heading, body, and closing symbols.

   a. *Heading:* The heading should include the fact that it is a news release, when it should be released, the company name and address, the name of a person to contact in case there are questions, a telephone number, and an e-mail address. The heading may also include the date of the release. After the heading, there should be a break indicated by underscores or asterisks across the line of print.

   b. *Body:* The body of the news release should have a title that is indicative of what is in the news. A news release is written in the direct approach. The news is presented in the first sentence. Important facts to remember for the beginning are who, what, where, when, and why. The balance of the release follows up with pertinent facts. A good news release is clearly and concisely written.

   c. *Closing symbols:* To indicate the conclusion of the release, printer's closing symbols are centered at the end. The symbol can be either three number symbols (###) or a number 30 with a hyphen before and after (-30-).

   EXAMPLES:

   ### or # # #

   -30- or - 30 -

   d. *Spacing the news release:* A few simple guidelines for spacing and margins will help the news release look very professional.

   (1) *Top margin:* The top margin can vary from ½ to 2 inches, depending on the length of the news release. If the news release is lengthy (although remember, good news is clear and concise), the top margin should be narrower to keep the release to one page.

   (2) *Side margin:* Side margins can also be adjusted to make sure that the release is one page in length. Side margins should never be narrower than 1 inch, however. You must be able to judge the length of the news release and strive to have it set up attractively on one page.

   (3) *Bottom margin:* A minimum of 1 inch is necessary as a bottom margin. However, with shorter news releases, the bottom margin is likely to be more than 1 inch.

   (4) *Heading:* Single-space lines in the heading that belong together and double-space between groups of lines. Information that needs to stand out should be

in all capital letters. For emphasis, the heading can be keyed in with one space between letters and three spaces between words, like this:

N E W S   R E L E A S E

(5) *Break line:* A blank space should appear between the heading and the break line. If you use the underscore, single-space to the underscore. If you use asterisks for the break line, double-space to the asterisks.

EXAMPLES:

<u>*N E W S   R E L E A S E*</u>   *ALFO INDUSTRIES*
1321 Manchester Court
Silver Spring, MD 20901–1321

<u>*RELEASE IMMEDIATELY*</u>   *For Further Information*
Contact Sally Mitchell
(301) 754–3214

NEWS RELEASE
RELEASE IMMEDIATELY

ALFO INDUSTRIES   *For Further Information*
1321 Manchester Court   *Contact Sally Mitchell*
Silver Spring, MD 20901–1321   *(301) 754–3214*

****

(6) *Body:* Triple-space from the break line to the title of the news release. The title should be centered and keyed in all capital letters. If the title consists of more than one line, it is to be single-spaced. Triple-space to the paragraphs. Double-space the paragraphs with standard (½ inch) paragraph indentations. If block paragraphs are used, triple-space between the paragraphs.

(7) *Closing symbols:* Triple-space after the last paragraph to the closing symbols. The closing symbols are centered on the line of print.

3. *Itinerary:* An **itinerary** is a travel plan that specifies all details concerning a business trip. Copies should be available prior to the trip for those who need to know the details of the trip—those within the organization, the traveler, and the traveler's family.

   a. *Types of information:* The itinerary typically includes the following details:
   - Departure date, time, and place
   - Type of confirmed transportation
   - Arrival date, time, and place
   - Lodging reservation(s) for each date or segment of the trip
   - Scheduled appointments and meetings
   - Complete travel information for the return trip

   b. *Parts of the itinerary:* The following guidelines will help in preparing an itinerary for the traveler to share with the organization and family (see Figure 9–18 for a sample itinerary).

      (1) *Headings:* The itinerary should be titled *Itinerary for* (insert name of business traveler). The dates of the trip can be a subheading. These lines should be centered.

FIGURE 9–18   Example of Itinerary

ITINERARY FOR MARLENE BAILEY

January 10–12, 200X

MONDAY, JANUARY 10 (Chicago to New York City)

8:20 A.M. (CST)	Leave Chicago O'Hare Airport on United Airlines Flight 208; 747; breakfast served.
9:33 A.M. (EST)	Arrive at New York LaGuardia Airport. Take limousine to Waldorf Hotel, 2021 Second Avenue, New York (212-542-6000); guaranteed hotel reservation; confirmation in trip file.
1:00 P.M.	Meeting with Roger C. Harper, Jr., President, ACF Corporation, 994 Third Avenue, New York (212-776-1420).
7:00 P.M.	Dinner-Meeting at Stewart's Restaurant, 727 Avenue of the Americas, New York, with Joyce L. Rohrson, Consultant, American Business Systems (212-325-4692).

TUESDAY, JANUARY 11 (New York City)

9:30 A.M.	The National Office Systems Conference, City Conference Center, 1004 Central Parkway, New York (212-554-4200).
9:45 A.M.	Presentation: "The Office Environment—Networking and Today's Electronic Office."
1:00 P.M.	Luncheon with Rosalyn L. Bernard, Vice President and General Manager, Wilson Automation, Inc., at the Oakdale City Club, 9250 Fifth Avenue, New York (212-347-3300).
3:00 P.M.	Tour of Advanced Business Systems, Inc., 125 Seventh Avenue, New York. Contact Person: Helen Adams, Business Systems Consultant (212-774-1550).

WEDNESDAY, JANUARY 12 (New York City to Chicago)

9:45 A.M.	Leave Waldorf Hotel by limousine for John F. Kennedy Airport.
11:55 A.M. (EST)	Leave Kennedy Airport on United Airlines Flight 648, business class; lunch served.
2:10 P.M. (CST)	Arrive at Chicago O'Hare Airport. Company limousine will meet you at baggage claim.

---

(2) *Columns of information:* Two groups of information are included on the itinerary: the dates and times of business commitments during the trip on the left and the travel and meeting information on the right.

(a) *Dates/times:* On the left side of the itinerary, the dates and specific times of flights, meetings, appointments, and any other events must be keyed in. A special notation of the time in effect for each location (e.g., CST for Central Standard Time) should be included so that there will be no misunderstandings in regard to appointment times.

(b) *Travel and meeting information:* To the right, entries give detailed information regarding reservations (transportation and/or lodging), meetings, luncheons, conferences, or other commitments. Complete information for companies (names, addresses, telephone numbers, contact people) and any other special details should be included.

(c) *Format of itinerary:* The itinerary is prepared in printed form so that it can serve as an easy-to-understand reference for the executive and others to use.

- *Margins:* Side margins should be at least 1 inch, with a top margin of 2 inches and a bottom margin of 1 inch on the first page. If the itinerary carries onto a second page, top and bottom margins of 1 inch are appropriate.

- *Spacing:* Headings should be double-spaced, with a double- or a triple-space before the body of the itinerary begins. The text material should be single-spaced with a double-space between each entry.

- *Headings:* Headings should be double-spaced and centered. The main heading should be in all capital letters, while the subheading should be entered in initial caps and may be underlined.

- *Second-page continuation:* If the itinerary is more than one page, the second-page continuation should have a header like this:

ITINERARY FOR MARLENE T. BAILEY
Page 2
January 10–12, 200X

Succeeding pages will also have a header, but the page number will change.

4. *Outline:* Sometimes a document must be in outline format, or an outline may be prepared as part of the document. An **outline** consists of key words coded in descending order, using Roman numerals, numbers, and letters of the alphabet at different levels of the outline.

   a. *Coding the outline:* The Roman numeral is considered the highest in coding sequence. In descending order, the outline adheres to the following sequence:

      (1) Roman numeral, beginning with I

      (2) Capital letters of the alphabet, A–Z

      (3) Numbers, beginning with 1

      (4) Lowercase letters of the alphabet, a–z

      (5) Numbers in parentheses, beginning with (1)

      (6) Lowercase letters of the alphabet in parentheses, (a)–(z)

      Each section starts the sequence from the beginning code, and each section should have at least two codes within the sequence. Also, when setting up the side margins for an outline, you should determine the code that will require the most space. Indent from that point so the decimal points for all codes within the sequence are aligned. All codes end with a period or parenthesis. Space twice after the period or parenthesis.

In word processing, use of the "bullets and numbering" feature for outline numbering will help you select the appropriate numbering scheme. If the text that follows each enumeration is longer than one line, the text will automatically wrap and align with the previous line.

Figure 9–19 is an example of an outline format with two major divisions (identified by Roman numerals). Division II includes the lowest sequencing. Notice that all sequencing consists of at least two codes within that sequence.

  b. *Spacing an outline:* The first consideration must be given to readability from the reader's viewpoint. Therefore, judgment on your part as to single-spacing or double-spacing the outline is important. Once the spacing format has been determined, be consistent throughout the document. When the text for an enumeration consists of more than one line, single-space that section.

    (1) If the outline consists mainly of phrases that are two or more lines in length, the outline is usually double-spaced between all points.

    (2) If the key words are short in nature, you may decide to single-space within that outline.

Spacing before the main sections (those coded with Roman numerals) is always double-spaced. Spacing after the main sections may or may not be double-spaced. In Figure 9–19, double-spacing was used for readability because of the length of the lines. The outline is still on one page.

5. **Abstract and Précis:** An **abstract** or a **précis** is a concise summary of all key points in an article or reference. Whether an abstract or a précis is used, all relevant information must be included, major conclusions must be mentioned, the original must be documented, the language must be consistent with the original, and the format must be easy to read.

  a. *Concise summary of key points:* The length of the summary will depend on the depth of the material in the original. It must be kept in mind, however, that the purpose of an abstract or précis is to summarize the key points of the original so that time is saved for the executive when reading the material.

    (1) *Abstract:* An abstract can be from one fourth to one half the length of the original material.

    (2) *Précis:* A précis is usually one third the length of the original. In writing a précis, the original material is recomposed, omitting illustrations, amplifications, or flowery language.

  b. *Relevant information:* Since the purpose of the abstract is to condense the original so that more material can be read in the same amount of time, it is not necessary for the administrative professional to spend time rewording the material. With a précis, time will be spent on recomposing the original while maintaining the author's point of view, writing style, and tone without using the author's exact words or phrases.

Both an abstract and a précis must include the key points of the original. The following writing characteristics can be used as flags to identify key points.

    (1) *Facts:* The easiest characteristics to identify are facts. Facts are usually represented in figure format. This information clearly stands out from the written word. The administrative professional must make sure that only relevant facts

FIGURE 9–19   Example of Outline

CHECKLIST FOR ERROR CHECKING[1]

I. BASIC SKILLS FOR ERROR DETECTION
   A. Spelling
      1. Use of references
         a. Dictionary
         b. Company style guide
         c. Reference manual
      2. Spell-checker program
   B. Word hyphenation
   C. Capitalization of personal and company names
      1. Letterhead
      2. Company Web page
      3. Official company logo

II. PROOFREADING TECHNIQUES
   A. Reserving time for proofreading
   B. Checking document formats
      1. Headings
      2. Spacing
      3. Paragraph structure
   C. Checking word accuracy
      1. Mistaken words
      2. Misspellings
      3. Grammatical errors
   D. Proofing content
      1. Proofreading sentences more than once
      2. Verifying figures
         a. Checking totals
         b. Checking math functions
      3. Verifying dates and days of week
      4. Reading material aloud
         a. Subject-verb agreement
         b. Pronoun-antecedent agreement
         c. Words spelled correctly but used incorrectly
   E. Proofing electronic copy
      1. Track changes
      2. Drawing toolbar with text boxes
   F. Obtaining assistance from others
      1. Proofreading technical material
      2. Final proofing

---

[1]Susan Jaderstrom and Joanne Miller, "Checklist for Error Checking," *OfficePro* 62 (7), October 2002, p. 29.

are contained in the abstract or précis and that the summary includes other key points from the original.

(2) *Listings:* Many authors list important points as 1, 2, 3, and so on. Another listing technique is to make a point without any listing notation and follow up with the word *second* when the author is making a succeeding point. The word *second* would be a flag that a point has previously been made and that there may be more to follow. The word *last* is often used to indicate a concluding point.

(3) *Headings:* Headings throughout the material should be followed for the summary. Headings are usually flags for key points to be discussed. At the end of the material within the heading, there usually will be summary statements.

(4) *Topic sentences:* Sometimes a new paragraph is a continuation of the previous paragraph, including new thoughts. When a completely new idea or concept is introduced, the paragraph normally begins with a topic sentence. This sentence can be used to identify a key point. Many paragraphs end with a summary statement, or the paragraph itself is a summary of a section.

c. *Reporting major conclusions:* Many authors conclude their writing with a summary statement, paragraph, or section. To understand the gist of the material, read the concluding summary material first. For a book, the preface should be read first.

Understanding the concluding remarks will help the administrative professional locate key points within the document. Also, these concluding points should be part of the abstract or précis.

d. *Complete documentation:* Credit must be given to the original author; therefore, it is important to include all bibliographical information on the abstract or précis.

(1) *Bibliographical information:* The following types of information need to be included with the abstract or précis:

- Title of the publication (report, book, magazine, periodical, or journal)
- Name(s) of author(s)
- Volume number, issue number, and page number(s)
- Title of article in magazine, journal, or periodical
- Date of publication
- Name of publisher and location
- Type of electronic reference (online source)
- Web address for electronic reference
- Retrieval or access date for electronic reference

(2) *Placement of bibliographical information:* Exactly where to include the bibliographical information can vary. The executive and the administrative professional should identify the format preferred and follow that format for all documentation.

(a) *Photocopies:* On photocopies, the information can be included on either the front of the first page or the back of the last page. Sometimes the information is included on the back of the first page or the bottom (at the end) of the last page.

(b) *Abstract and précis:* The abstract and précis will contain source title, author, and title of the article in the main heading of the summary. Page numbers will be included within the abstract as needed. Other bibliographical information may be included in the main heading or at the end of the summary in footnote format.

e. *Level of language consistent with original:* When summarizing the material, it is important to maintain the tone and thought of the author. Even when preparing an abstract, the thought can be altered completely by leaving out a word, punctuation mark, or key point. Also, even though a précis is a summary of the original material, it is important to maintain the author's point of view.

The following guidelines will help maintain consistent language with the original source:

(1) *Summaries within original:* Read any summary sections or paragraphs first. This helps establish the general idea of the document.

(2) *First reading:* Quickly read the entire material; do not take notes. If the material is lengthy, quickly read the first major division. This also helps establish the general idea.

(3) *Second reading:* With the second reading, look up unfamiliar words or references to unfamiliar material. With the unfamiliar clarified, you are better able to understand the material and will more accurately note only the important ideas. Following this procedure will help distinguish amplifications from key points.

(4) *Taking notes:* With the third reading, you are ready to take notes. Record only the important ideas and facts using the guidelines presented in Section F-5-b. If you are writing a précis, use your notes to summarize the material in your own words.

(5) *Rough copy:* Key in the summarized notes in rough-draft format. Remember, the purpose of an abstract or précis is to be concise yet clear!

(6) *Editing:* Compare the abstract or précis with the original for accuracy. Edit the summary by eliminating unnecessary words and making sure that the wording is clear.

(7) *Final copy:* Key in the abstract or précis in an easy-to-read format.

f. *Outline and paragraph formats:* An abstract is prepared in either an outline format or a paragraph format. Précis are typically prepared only in a paragraph format.

(1) *Abstract format:* An abstract can be prepared in outline format or in paragraph format. The decision as to whether the format should be in paragraph or outline form will depend on the executive's preference. If there is no preference, then the format is left to the administrative professional's discretion. Choose the format that you consider easiest to follow and most appropriate for the material.

(2) *Précis format:* A précis should be keyed in paragraph format.

An example of an abstract in outline form is illustrated in Figure 9–20. Figure 9–21 illustrates a précis for the same article in paragraph form.

g. *Distinguishing abstracts from précis:* For the administrative professional who needs to prepare both abstracts and précis, it will be important to indicate when the summary is an abstract and when it is a précis. This is necessary in order to determine how the information might be used in a letter, a speech, or a report. Also, it is important when the administrative professional retrieves the summary from the file later and needs to remember whether the material is a direct quote or a paraphrase.

Usually a capital P in parentheses or circled identifies the material as a précis; a capital A is used for an abstract. This code can be recorded on the front of the first page (top, right corner) or on the back of the last page (top, right corner). Whatever is decided on, however, should be consistently followed for all abstracts and précis.

FIGURE 9–20   Abstract in Outline Format

AUTHORS: Lillian H. Chaney, Ed.D., and Catherine G. Green, Ed.D., CPS   Ⓐ
TITLE: "Meeting Manners"
SOURCE: *OfficePro*, November/December 2003, Volume 63, Number 8, pp. 19–21

I. INTRODUCTION—MEETINGS
  A. Purpose of meetings
    1. Impressions of credibility, power, efficiency, and effectiveness
    2. Opportunities to acquire and disseminate information, develop skills, and make a favorable impression
  B. Employee negative attitudes about meetings
    1. Survey of 1,000 business leaders
      a. One third of time spent in meetings unproductive
      b. About 65 percent of meetings achieve intended outcomes
    2. Changing employee negative attitudes
      a. Conducting meetings properly
      b. Following correct procedures
      c. Practicing good manners

II. INTRODUCTIONS AND SEATING
  A. Introductions by meeting chairman
    1. Arriving early
    2. Introducing people, especially newcomers
    3. Greeting participants upon arrival
  B. Seating arrangements—rank rather than gender or age
    1. Position of greatest authority
      a. "Power perch"
      b. Head of a rectangular table farthest from the door
    2. Seat to right of chairman
      a. Assistant to chairman
      b. Person next in importance to chairman
      c. Administrative professional recording minutes of meeting
    3. Seat to left of chairman reserved for person next in line of authority or importance
    4. Regular attendees in remaining seats
    5. People invited to make special presentations
    6. Confrontational seating position opposite end of table from chairman

III. MEETING BEHAVIORS
  A. Responsibilities of person in charge of meeting (chairman)
    1. Select location
      a. Adequate seating
        (1) Physically disabled attendees
        (2) Audiovisual equipment
      b. Type of meeting space
        (1) Meeting with employees—a conference table in neutral territory
        (2) Informal meeting—office area
        (3) Boardroom—impression of authority or power
    2. Schedule meeting space in advance
      a. Convenient date and time
      b. Participants' preferences on dates and times
    3. Distribute agenda a few days in advance
      a. Date and location
      b. Beginning and ending times

FIGURE 9–20 *(continued)*

     c. Topics to be discussed with notations on agenda ("for discussion only," "for decision today")

     d. Statement that luncheon or refreshments will be served

   4. Avoid recapping information for late arrivals

   5. Follow parliamentary procedure (*Robert's Rules of Order* and *Jones' Parliamentary Procedure at a Glance*)

   6. Maintain control of meeting

     a. Anticipate issues that may cause conflict or disagreement

     b. Limit participants' comments to a couple of minutes

   7. Thank people who gave presentations

   8. Recognize those who contributed to success of meeting

   9. Start and end on time

  B. Proper participant behavior

   1. Arrive early; be punctual

   2. Introduce themselves to others

     a. Shake hands

     b. Visitors extend hands first

   3. Wait for chairman to be seated and indicate seating of participants

   4. Sit erectly and lean forward slightly to indicate interest

   5. Maintain appropriate eye contact with the speaker

   6. Turn off cell phones, or set them on vibration mode

   7. Thank person in charge at end of meeting

     a. Shake hands with chairman

     b. Shake hands with other participants as they leave

  C. Inappropriate participant behavior

   1. Carry on side conversations

   2. Engage in distracting behaviors

   3. Engage in activities not related to meeting

IV. REFRESHMENTS

  A. Provide when meeting is expected to exceed 1½ hours

  B. Arrange refreshments so participants can serve themselves

   1. Use a tablecloth

   2. Provide napkins, small plates, and eating utensils

   3. Furnish glasses and/or cups

   4. Provide ice for assortment of drinks

  D. Select food appropriate for time of day

   1. Avoid crunchy, greasy, or messy foods

   2. Accommodate vegetarians

   3. Have decaf and regular coffee

V. FOLLOW-UP ACTIVITIES

  A. End meeting with chairman's summary

   1. What the meeting accomplished

   2. Reminders to participants of tasks for which they volunteered or were assigned

   3. Date of next meeting

  B. Leave meeting room in good order

  C. Send summary memo to all participants indicating assignments and deadlines

  D. Send formal letters of appreciation to presenters and special contributors

  E. Arrange for preparation and distribution of minutes

  F. Review and evaluate success of meeting

FIGURE 9–21   Précis in Paragraph Format

MEETING MANNERS[1]   Ⓟ

Purposes of business meetings range from creating impressions of credibility, power, and efficiency to providing opportunities to disseminate new information and develop skills. Employees sometimes develop negative attitudes toward meetings as a survey of 1,000 business leaders shows. The respondents indicated that one third of the time spent in meetings was unproductive and only 65 percent of meetings achieve intended outcomes. Chaney and Green indicate that to change employee negative attitudes toward meetings, proper procedures and good manners need to be exhibited.

The meeting chairman should arrive early to introduce participants, especially newcomers. Seating arrangements should be based on rank rather than gender or age. The chairman should sit in the "power perch" at the head of a rectangular conference table farthest from the door. To the right of the chairman, the person next in importance to the chairman should be seated. The seat to the left of the chairman should be reserved for the person next in line of authority or importance. Participants can be seated in the remaining seats, and finally people invited to make special presentations are seated.

Chaney and Green summarized the following responsibilities of the person in charge of the meeting:

- Select the location with adequate seating and meeting space
- Schedule the meeting space in advance at a convenient date and time after obtaining participants' preferences for dates/times
- Distribute the agenda in advance; include information on the date, location, beginning and ending times, topics to be discussed, and serving of luncheon or refreshments
- Avoid recapping information for late arrivals
- Follow parliamentary procedure (*Robert's Rules of Order* and *Jones' Parliamentary Procedure at a Glance*)
- Maintain control of meeting by anticipating issues that may cause conflict and limiting participants' comments on specific issues
- Thank people who gave presentations
- Recognize those who contributed to the meeting's success
- Start and end the meeting on time

Participants should demonstrate the following behaviors during the meeting:

- Be punctual and arrive early
- Introduce themselves to others by shaking hands
- Wait for the chairman to be seated and to indicate seating assignments
- Be attentive to the speakers: sit erectly, lean forward slightly, and maintain appropriate eye contact
- Turn off cell phones, or set them on vibration mode
- Thank the person in charge at the end of the meeting, and shake hands with the chairman and other participants as they leave

Inappropriate participant behavior such as carrying on side conversations or engaging in distracting behaviors or activities not related to the meeting are very noticeable.

Refreshments should be provided when the meeting is expected to exceed 1½ hours. They should be arranged so participants can serve themselves. A tablecloth, napkins, small plates, eating utensils, glasses and/or cups, and ice for an assortment of drinks should be provided. Food appropriate for the time of day should be selected.

The meeting should end with the chairman's summary of what was accomplished during the meeting and reminders to participants of tasks to be completed. The date of the next meeting should be decided upon.

Other duties of the chairman and his/her assistants are to send a summary memo to all participants and formal letters of appreciation to presenters and special contributors. The minutes of the meeting need to be prepared and distributed. And, finally, the success of the meeting needs to be reviewed and evaluated.

Chaney and Green conclude that office professionals who chair or participate in meetings need to know that other business professionals will notice their social skills, which can be an asset in promotion decisions.

[1]Lillian H. Chaney and Catherine G. Green, "Meeting Manners," *OfficePro,* November/December 2003, Volume 63, Number 8, pp. 19–21.

h. *Using the abstract or précis:* In using the material for speeches, training sessions, or other writing, the executive would be plagiarizing if credit was not given to the original author of the reference material. Bibliographical information can be provided in a footnote, or reference to the author and source can be incorporated in the body of the summary.

When a direct quotation is included in an abstract, quotation marks are required around the verbatim words. When the ideas are paraphrased in a précis, quotation marks are not required around the material. In both cases, the original author must receive credit for the material.

Check Point—Section F

Directions: For each question, circle the correct answer.

F–1. The official report of a meeting summarizing the events that occurred during the meeting and distributed to those who attended is known as

A) an agenda
B) minutes
C) proceedings
D) a précis

F–2. An itinerary is a plan for

A) the agenda for a business meeting
B) an announcement of a special business event for the organization

C) business travel that specifies all details for the trip
D) summarizing the important points of a specific published article

F–3. An abstract is

A) a brief summary of the events that took place during a meeting
B) an announcement containing information about a business event that will take place in the near future
C) prepared in the same format as the business report it represents
D) a brief summary of the key points presented in an article or reference

For Your Review

Directions: For each question, circle the correct answer.

1. The most accepted style for the date line is
   A) 2/07/200X
   B) February 7, 200X
   C) 7 February 200X
   D) Feb. 7, 200X

2. The full name of the person to whom a letter is being sent is included in the
   A) salutation
   B) subject line
   C) signature line
   D) inside address

3. Which one of the following is the correct way to present the recipient's full name on a letter?
   A) Ms. Laura R. Garcia
   B) L. R. Garcia
   C) Laura R. Garcia
   D) Laura Robinson Garcia

4. Which one of the following is a complete inside address?
   A) Thomas J. Knowlton, Dr.
      Knowlton & Carson, Ltd.
      4513 North Carlton Place
      Columbia, SC 29207–1334
   B) Dr. Thomas J. Knowlton
      Knowlton & Carson, Ltd.
      N. Carlton Place, #4513
      Columbia, SC 29207–1334
   C) Dr. Thomas J. Knowlton
      Knowlton & Carson, Ltd.
      4513 North Carlton Place
      Columbia, SC 29207–1334

   D) Dr. T. J. Knowlton
      Knowlton & Carson, Ltd.
      4513 North Carlton Place
      Columbia, SC 29207

5. The attention line is used to
   A) direct the letter to a specific person in the organization
   B) tell the recipient what the letter concerns
   C) include the correct Zip + 4 Code
   D) indicate that a copy of the letter is being sent to someone else in the organization

6. Which one of the following would be considered an informal salutation?
   A) Dear Mr. Kincaid
   B) Dear Dr. Saribha
   C) Dear Ms. Johnsberg
   D) Dear Charles

7. Which one of the following salutations would be considered most appropriate when addressing a letter to an organization?
   A) Dear Sir
   B) Dear Ms. Milford
   C) Dear Sales Manager
   D) Dear George

8. The subject line of a letter describes
   A) detailed information about the main idea of the letter
   B) what the main idea of the letter is
   C) any deadlines for specific action to be taken by the receiver
   D) the person who needs to receive a copy of the letter

9. The paragraphs in the body of a business letter are

A) indented one standard tab
B) double-spaced with a triple-space between paragraphs
C) blocked at the left margin
D) single-spaced with a double-space between paragraphs

10. The complimentary closing of a letter needs to be in agreement (formal or informal) with the

A) inside address
B) salutation
C) subject line
D) signature line

11. Which one of the following would be considered the most appropriate as a signature line if the woman prefers use of a specific title?

A) Ms. Dana M. Cortland, CPS
B) Dana M. Cortland, CPS
C) D. M. Cortland
D) Mrs. D. M. Cortland

12. The enclosure notation on a letter should be keyed in two Enters after the

A) signature line
B) copy notation
C) reference initials
D) blind copy notation

13. Which one of the following is a characteristic of a Modified Block Letter Style?

A) The signature line is at the left margin
B) The complimentary closing is omitted in this style
C) The date line appears at the left margin
D) Body paragraphs may be indented

14. The Simplified Letter Style is characterized by the

A) indention of paragraphs
B) omission of salutation and complimentary closing
C) date line beginning at the center point
D) omission of enclosure or copy notations

15. On an envelope, the notation "Please Forward" should be keyed

A) immediately above the receiver's address
B) below the postage block
C) below the return address
D) below and to the left of the receiver's address

16. The last line of an envelope addressed to someone in a foreign country is the

A) name of the country in all capital letters
B) postal code for that location
C) city or county name
D) province name

17. If the guide words on a memorandum begin at the left margin, the variable information to be filled in after each guide word will be aligned

A) at the tab following the first guide word
B) two spaces after the colon following each guide word
C) at the closest tab following the longest guide word
D) even with the left margin for the body paragraphs

18. If the receiver of an e-mail message does not know the sender, a

A) Web address for the sender should be included
B) signature file should be inserted at the end of the message
C) salutation needs to be inserted at the beginning of the message
D) descriptive subject line helps with the meaning of the message

19. The left and right margins of a left-bound report are

A) 1 inch for each margin
B) 1½ inches for each margin
C) 1¼ inches for each margin
D) 1½ inches for left margin and 1 inch for right margin

20. If a centered heading is followed by a side heading in a report, the transition

is eased with the inclusion of an introductory paragraph

A) after the centered heading
B) after the side heading
C) before the next paragraph heading
D) before the centered heading

21. As you gather research for a report you are writing, you locate an unpublished article posted to a Web site, and you want to reproduce a large portion of the article in your report. The article contains a date (October 4, 2002) and the name of one author but no copyright notice. Which one of the following statements is correct?

A) Since there is no copyright notice on the article, you may treat the article as being in the public domain
B) Because of the recency of the article, the article is not protected by copyright legislation
C) "Fair use" permits you to reproduce the original information in your report without permission from the author
D) The article (or a portion of it) may be reproduced in your report, but you need permission from the author

22. An in-text citation for a secondary source contains which one of the following as the first word?

A) publication date
B) author's last name
C) page or paragraph reference
D) name of publisher

23. A news release is an announcement about a business event that is written with the

A) indirect approach to present a buffer before the presentation of the main ideas
B) "you" approach in presenting the information to the reader
C) direct approach to present the main ideas of the announcement first
D) persuasive approach to get the reader interested in the announcement

24. Which one of the following sequences is correct for an outline?

A) II-3-C-b(1) (b)
B) I-B-3-a(b) (3)
C) IV-A-3-b(d) (3)
D) I-B-2-a(2) (c)

25. The main purpose of an abstract or précis is to

A) condense an original source so the main points can be reviewed quickly
B) provide more detail about an original source for the reader
C) summarize the original source and provide additional references to support the information
D) provide an addendum of additional information and references as a supplement to the original source

Solutions

Solutions to Check Point—Section A

Answer	Refer to:
A–1. (A)	[A-1-b]
A–2. (C)	[A-1-c and A-1-e]
A–3. (B)	[A-2-a]

Solutions to Check Point—Section B

Answer	Refer to:
B–1. (D)	[B-1-a]
B–2. (C)	[B-1-b]
B–3. (B)	[B-2]

Solutions to Check Point—Section C

Answer	Refer to:
C–1. (B)	[C]
C–2. (C)	[C-1-c (6)]
C–3. (B)	[C-1-c (6)]

Solutions to Check Point—Section D

Answer	Refer to:
D–1. (A)	[D-2-a]
D–2. (C)	[D-2]
D–3. (B)	[D-3]

Solutions to Check Point—Section E

Answer	Refer to:
E–1. (D)	[E-2]
E–2. (D)	[E-2-c (1) (a)]
E–3. (C)	[E-2-d, Figures 9–15 and 9–16]

Solutions to Check Point—Section F

Answer	Refer to:
F–1. (B)	[F-1]
F–2. (C)	[F-3]
F–3. (D)	[F-5]

Solutions to For Your Review

Answer	Refer to:
1. (B)	[A-1-a]
2. (D)	[A-1-b]
3. (A)	[A-1-b (1)]
4. (C)	[A-1-b]
5. (A)	[A-1-c]

6.	(D)	[A-1-d]
7.	(C)	[A-1-d]
8.	(B)	[A-1-e]
9.	(D)	[A-1-f and A-1-m]
10.	(B)	[A-1-g]
11.	(A)	[A-1-h]
12.	(C)	[A-1-j]
13.	(D)	[A-2-b (3)]
14.	(B)	[A-2-c (1) and A-2-c (4)]
15.	(C)	[B-1-b]
16.	(A)	[B-2-b (3)]
17.	(C)	[C-1-c]
18.	(B)	[D-2-d]
19.	(D)	[E-1-a (2) (b) and E-1-a (3)]
20.	(A)	[E-1-d (2)]
21.	(D)	[E-2-a (3)]
22.	(B)	[E-2-c (1) (a) and E-2-c (1) (b)]
23.	(C)	[F-2-b]
24.	(D)	[F-4-a]
25.	(A)	[F-5-a and F-5-b]

Chapter 10

Information Distribution

OVERVIEW

Information is a critical asset in today's business organization, and the procedures involved in the internal and external distribution of information are of prime importance to organizations. Organizations today are even able to place a value (a price tag) on having usable information at the right time, in the right form, and at an affordable cost.

This chapter emphasizes some of the methods and procedures that administrative professionals need to be aware of and use in making decisions about information distribution. The technology involved may be mentioned, but detail is available in other chapters, as specific references will indicate.

KEY TERMS

Airmail service, 339
Bar codes, 337
Bound printed matter, 339
Certificate of mailing, 339
Certified mail, 340
Collect-on-delivery (COD) mail, 340
Express mail, 337
First-class mail, 338
Home page, 346

Insured mail, 339
International mail, 340
Intranet, 334
Library mail, 339
Mailgram, 340
Media mail, 339
Netiquette, 344
Package services, 338
Parcel post, 338
Periodicals, 338

Priority mail, 338
Registered mail, 339
Spam, 345
Special delivery, 339
Special handling, 339
Standard mail, 338
Telegram, 341
Web site, 346
Webmaster, 346
ZIP + 4 Code, 336

A. Basic Principles of Information Distribution

Information is considered a valuable resource in all types of organizations today, and successful management and distribution of information is a critical issue. Office administrators must deal with a multitude of different types of information received from sources through numerous paths and routes. A large quantity of information is distributed and stored on paper, but information transmitted electronically is becoming even more popular as business executives, managers, and other administrative professionals become more versatile with technology.

1. ***Guidelines for Information Distribution:*** Specific guidelines for establishing appropriate means of information distribution include the following:

   a. *Condition of the information:* The receiver of the information being distributed must be able to use or apply the information to tasks at hand. If the information is not in a usable condition or format, the information is of no value until it can be converted to the format required.

   EXAMPLES:

   If a summary report is required and a detailed report is received, the report is of limited value.

   If an unexpected situation requires immediate information (ad hoc [demand] report) and the information system supports only scheduled (periodic) reports for this output, the information system is not meeting the needs of the organization.

   b. *Internal and external distribution:* Procedures need to be established for both internal and external information distribution to occur without undue difficulty.

   c. *Speed of transmission:* The information being transmitted must be distributed rapidly enough that the contents are still current and applicable to the needs of the receiver. Information that is out of date or too late to be useful is of little value to the receiver.

   EXAMPLE:

   If the information needed for tomorrow morning's meeting was mailed through regular mail service rather than express mail, the information will arrive too late to be useful.

   d. *Accuracy of information:* Another essential element in the distribution of information is the importance of accuracy in information as well as the transmission of that information.

   EXAMPLES:

   As the secretary of the local IAAP chapter, Bennington has the responsibility of preparing the minutes for the monthly chapter meetings. She has just finished preparing the minutes for the September 8 chapter meeting and plans to e-mail a copy to Hart, the president, to be included in the chapter newsletter. Hart should reply, indicating that the minutes were received and adding any comments on revisions that might be necessary before the minutes are transmitted to the entire membership.

   When a multiple-page document is sent as an e-mail attachment, the receiver should reply as soon as possible, verifying that all pages of the document were received.

   e. *Distribution cost:* The volume of information to be transmitted, the urgency with which the information is needed, and the means by which the information is transmitted will be important factors in determining the distribution cost of the information.

2. ***Criteria for Selecting Information Distribution Means:*** To select the appropriate method or means to use in distributing information, administrative professionals must keep in mind these criteria:

a. *Type of information to be distributed:* The amount of information to be distributed and the type of information are important considerations in deciding which means to use in transmitting the information. If the type of information is statistical in nature, it may be presented best in a written form. If the information is more informal in nature, a brief message in the form of a telephone call or an e-mail may suffice.

b. *Speed of transmission desired:* How important is it that the information be quickly transmitted? If transmission must take place within the next few minutes, e-mail, telephone, or fax might be the answer. If the information is more informal in nature, a brief message in the form of a telephone call or an e-mail may suffice.

c. *Format of the information:* In what format is the information: written or oral? The format of the information will help in determining how to transmit the information where it is needed.

d. *Effect of peak work periods:* "Busy seasons" impact an organization's ability to handle the creation and transmission of information requests and information reporting. During peak seasons, most organizations increase the staff hours to handle information processing.

EXAMPLE:

An accounting firm has certain times of the year that are busier than others. A firm involved with the preparation of income tax returns has an increased workload from January through April 15 and typically increases the number of staff during those months.

e. *Cost of information distribution:* Information that is to be distributed immediately will tend to be more expensive to send. The use of Internet e-mail capabilities provides efficient distribution service at a lower cost between organizations networked into the World Wide Web environment.

EXAMPLE:

A legal document required immediately can be sent via express mail delivery for delivery the next day. In 2003 the cost to send a 1-ounce envelope was approximately $13.65 compared with $3.85 if sent by priority mail or $.37 for first-class postage. However, the information will no doubt be worth the extra expense since it is needed as soon as possible.

Check Point—Section A

Directions: For each question, circle the correct answer.

A–1. Computer technology facilitates many business applications today in creating a relatively new asset known as

A) capital
B) management
C) information
D) investment

A–2. The receiver of information being distributed must be able to

A) file the information for future use

B) apply the information to business tasks to be performed

C) critique the information to determine its present value

D) convert the information to a useful form

A–3. The cost of distributing information depends most on the

A) accuracy of the information being transmitted

B) application of the information to a specific task

C) nature of the information

D) means by which the information is transmitted

B. Internal Information Distribution

Decisions need to be made on the means used to distribute information within the organization. The types of information services available for internal distribution of information involve an intranet, a telephone communication system, or an interoffice mail system. The hard-copy internal distribution is typically handled through a mail distribution center or personnel assigned the responsibility of handling the mail. Specific types of internal distribution include e-mail, intranet bulletins, telephone and voice messaging, and interoffice correspondence.

1. ***The Intranet:*** The organization's internal network for electronically communicating company policies, procedures, news items, and data/information available to employees is referred to as the **intranet.** A simple intranet includes a computer with Web server software; each user's computer is linked with a Web browser to the server. Firewall software protects the intranet information from being accessed by the external public.

    a. *Electronic mail:* Many organizations have installed wide area networks (WANs) and local area networks (LANs) to facilitate the type of electronic communication that is expected to occur. When a person wants to access information stored on the network or to transmit an e-mail message, the LAN is put to use. A decision must be made as to whom the message should be sent: one person or a number of people within the organization. The basic premise of electronic mail and LANs is to make information available to people on the network quickly and effectively, thereby reducing the number of hard copies (paper) that flows through the office. Some individuals abuse the ease of transmitting information by not discriminating who should receive the document. Company procedures for e-mail use should establish appropriate guidelines.

    EXAMPLE:

    Edwards has a message about a new product to send by e-mail to department managers. She accesses the directory and locates the mailing list of all department managers. Edwards decides that the department managers can determine whether their assistants should receive the product information. She makes a conscious decision to notify only the department managers, sending the e-mail to 20 people rather than 50. This decision helps others with their own management of information.

    b. *Intranet notices:* The intranet can become an effective way to post general notices regarding company events and news. Also, having policies and procedures electronically available to employees reduces paper costs and maintains more reliable and accurate information. When a policy is changed, it only needs to be corrected on the electronic copy (soft copy). An e-mail notice to appropriate office professionals informs employees of the change; they can reference the document through the intranet.

2. ***Telephone Communication System:*** The telephone continues to be a very important way of communicating with other people within the organization. Needed information is often obtained from a quick phone call to the right destination. The primary difficulty in using the telephone is to be able to reach the desired receiver of the information.

EXAMPLE:

"Telephone tag" is a frequent occurrence, with one person phoning another only to find that the person called is not available. Leaving a message helps, but when that person calls back, perhaps the original caller is not in. Therefore, handling voice messages properly impacts effective distribution of information.

a. *Voice messages:* When the person is unavailable to answer a call, a message can be left through a voice message system. The effectiveness of this system depends on the quality of the information left in the message. Messages must be left with the idea that the individual will be able to respond directly to the information contained in the message. Voice mail is especially effective for short messages. Many voice message systems have only a short period of time (30 seconds) allotted for recording a single message. Some of the latest voice message systems permit a longer total recording time, for example, 15 minutes, no matter the number of calls received. Most systems incorporate a closing command that indicates the end of the message.

b. *Telephone messages:* An important part of appropriate interoffice communication is leaving messages that are complete and meaningful to the recipient. Information such as the following needs to be included in a telephone message:

- The date of the call
- The time of the call
- The name of the person who should receive the message
- The name and telephone number of the person who is calling, including the area code
- A brief but complete message

Telephone messages need to be complete so that the receiver can respond appropriately. The caller should plan in advance and be prepared as to what pertinent information needs to be left on the message. When the call is returned, the previous message should be referenced so that the answers provided make sense to the receiver. This saves time for both parties and enables information to be effectively and efficiently disseminated.

3. ***Interoffice Communication:*** Communication also takes place between offices or departments with hard-copy documents and through face-to-face communication.

a. *Interoffice correspondence:* Even within an organization, one important decision is to put specific information in writing, depending on business needs or inquiries being made. The format generally used is a memorandum that is written about one topic, short and to the point, and quickly transmitted through internal mail (see Chapter 9, Section C, for an example of a memorandum).

b. *Face-to-face communication:* Many times transmitting information in person is best. This is particularly helpful if the information is critical to a particular business function or if the sender (distributor) of the information is not exactly sure how the information will be received. Face-to-face communication is beneficial if there needs to be some discussion about the matter. Written interoffice correspondence, telephone calls, or electronic correspondence cannot replace the interpersonal enhancements of face-to-face conversation.

Check Point—Section B

Directions: For each question, circle the correct answer.

B–1. The basic premise of a local area network is to

A) make information quickly available to people on the network

B) increase the amount of hard-copy information flowing through the office

C) send identical messages to every employee throughout the company at the same time

D) establish guidelines for the use of e-mail throughout the organization

B–2. Which one of the following would be the most helpful practice to use in curbing "telephone tag"?

A) Leaving recorded messages with date, time, name of caller, and nature of the call

B) Sending information requests through interoffice correspondence

C) Implementing a voice-mail system

D) Installing a local area network to facilitate interoffice communication

B–3. The sender who is transmitting information of a critical nature regarding a particular business function may prefer to use which one of the following channels?

A) Electronic mail

B) Express mail service

C) Voice-mail message

D) Face-to-face communication

C. External Information Distribution

Mail services, private messenger and delivery services, and telecommunications are the primary means of externally distributing information. Cost comparisons will help determine which distribution means will be the most cost effective and provide the best service for specific types of information and documents.

1. *Mail Services:* Postal or mail services are designed to facilitate incoming communication as well as outgoing communication from the organization. Within the organization, there needs to be a mail distribution center with appropriately assigned personnel who have the responsibility of handling incoming and outgoing mail services.

a. *Use of ZIP + 4 Codes and bar codes:* To expedite mail deliveries throughout the United States, the U.S. Postal Service initiated the **ZIP + 4 Code** to enable mail to be sorted and delivered faster and more accurately. **Bar codes** imprinted on envelopes also contain ZIP Code information and enable mail to be processed more quickly.

b. *Procedures for incoming mail:* Once the day's mail has been received, several procedures must be followed so that the mail is delivered to the correct locations within the firm.

   (1) The mail must be sorted and delivered to the correct department or person. This can be accomplished in different ways: a messenger delivering the mail to each department, conveyor systems, pneumatic tubes, or electronic mail carts.

   (2) Once the mail is received within departments, administrative professionals have the responsibility of opening the mail, date and time stamping the mail, sorting it by priority, and delivering it to the manager or executive for action.

   (3) The contents of the envelopes should be examined by an administrative professional to see what additional information might be needed when the manager or executive needs to respond to the correspondence.

      (a) Mail containing checks or money must be recorded and logged. A paper trail must be created for this type of mail. Payments received must be forwarded immediately to the accounting professionals who credit such payments to specific accounts.

      (b) Files or specific records may be necessary in order to respond to the correspondence received.

      (c) Stamping the date and time on each piece of correspondence is very important. Even though a date appears on the correspondence, the date of receipt is equally important in the case of incoming mail.

c. *Procedures for outgoing mail:* Mail that is being sent from the organization must be classified and grouped according to the type and destination.

   (1) *Categories of outgoing mail:* The U.S. Postal Service classifies mail into the following categories:

      (a) *Express mail:* The fastest mail delivery service, which guarantees next-day delivery and second-day delivery, is known as **express mail.** All express mail travels by regularly scheduled airline flights. Any mailable item weighing up to 70 pounds may be sent. Express mail rates, based on the weight of the item and the distance it must travel, include insurance coverage, record of delivery, and a receipt. No discounted or bulk rates are available for express mail. The basic rate for mailing anything in the special flat-rate envelope provided by the U.S. Postal Service was $13.65 in 2003.

         Global Express Guaranteed (GXG) is an international expedited shipping option from the U.S. Postal Service and DHL Worldwide Express. This service is available from 20,000 retail locations throughout the United States to more than 200 countries and territories worldwide.

         Another way to ship to 18 European countries is through Global Express Mail™. Effective September 3, 2003, the U.S. Postal Service expanded its agreement with Royal Mail Group's Pan-European parcel delivery company, General Logistics System, to deliver mail to three more countries—Finland, Greece, and Ireland. The 2003 postal rates start at $15.50.

(b) *Priority mail:* First-class mail that weighs up to a maximum of 70 pounds and has a maximum size of no more than 108 inches in length and distance around the thickest part combined is classified as **priority mail.** An average of two or three days is required for delivery. Priority mail can be delivered to every address in the United States, all post office boxes, and military addresses.

Global Priority Mail (GPM) is an airmail service that provides a reliable, economical means of sending mail and parcels of less than 4 pounds to more than 51 countries worldwide.

(c) *First-class mail:* Personal and business correspondence, handwritten and printed messages, bills, statements of account, postcards, printed forms filled out in writing, and business reply mail not requiring the highest priority are classified as **first-class mail.** There is a minimum charge for first-class mail weighing up to 1 ounce, with an additional charge for each additional ounce or fraction of an ounce. The maximum weight allowed for first-class mail is 13 ounces. The minimum quantity for discounted rates is 500 pieces. All first-class mail must be sealed. Forwarding and return services are included. First-class mail is transported by air on a space-available basis.

(d) *Periodicals:* Publications such as newspapers, magazines, and other periodical publications whose primary purpose is transmitting information to a subscription list are included in the class of mail called **periodicals.** These publications must be published at regular intervals at least four times per year from a known office of publication. Special lower postage rates are available for publications of nonprofit organizations and classroom periodicals. Mailing must be sent in bulk lots or volume mailings.

(e) *Standard mail:* Mail matter that is not required to be sent by first-class mail or periodicals must be sent by **standard mail.** Printed matter, flyers, circulars, advertising, newsletters, bulletins, catalogs, and small parcels are included in this class. There are two subclasses of standard mail, A for mail of less than 16 ounces and B for mail of more than 1 pound. The minimum quantity of standard mail is 200 pieces or 50 pounds. All pieces in the mailing must belong to the same processing category. For example, the mailing must be all letters, all flats, or all machinable parcels. Lower rates for nonprofit organizations are available. Standard mail rates, which are bulk rates, are available only for domestic mail. Delivery of bulk mailings can sometimes be delayed up to two or three weeks.

(f) *Package services:* The class of mail intended for catalogs, merchandise, and other printed material is called **package services**. This classification of mail has the following four subclasses.

- *Parcel post:* Merchandise, books, circulars, catalogs, and other printed matter may be mailed by **parcel post.** The maximum weight of a package is 70 pounds. Bulk rates and destination entry rates are available for large quantities. A barcoded discount is also available.

- *Bound printed matter:* Advertising, promotional material, directories, or editorial material may be sent as **bound printed matter.** This type of material must be securely bound with permanent fastenings like staples, glue, or stitching. The sheets of paper used must be 90 percent imprinted with words, letters, characters, figures, or images by any process other than handwriting or typewriting. No personal correspondence can be included with this type of printed matter. Bound printed matter cannot include stationery or printed forms.

- *Media mail:* The types of materials that can be sent by **media mail** include books of at least eight pages, film, printed music, printed test materials, sound recordings, play scripts, printed educational charts, medical information, and computer-readable media. Presorted rates are available for mailing bulk quantities. The minimum mailing is 300 pieces, and barcoded discounts are available.

- *Library mail:* Qualifying institutions (libraries, universities, zoos, research institutions) can mail educational and research material by **library mail.** Presorted rates are available for bulk quantities of at least 300 pieces. Barcoded discounts are also available.

The maximum weight per piece is 15 pounds for bound printed matter and 70 pounds for parcel post, media mail, and library mail. Package services do not include free forwarding and return services. Postage discounts are available for bulk quantities that meet additional standards for volume, presort, and destination entry.

(2) *Other postal services:* Some of the additional mailing services available through the U.S. Postal Service include the following:

(a) *Airmail:* **Airmail service** is advantageous for distances greater than 250 miles. Airmail is used for international mail but is no longer vital for domestic delivery within the United States.

(b) *Special delivery/special handling:* Immediate delivery within prescribed hours and distances may be necessary. **Special delivery** includes regular postage plus an extra fee for the special delivery. **Special handling** is for unusual mail and packages sent by first-class mail, priority mail, and package services that require preferential handling. Such mail will be delivered on regularly scheduled delivery trips.

(c) *Registered mail:* Protection is given to valuable items, money, checks, jewelry, bonds, stock certificates, and important papers. All classes of mail may be sent by **registered mail,** but first-class rates must also be paid. The U.S. Postal Service will pay claims up to $25,000 regardless of the amount for which the package was registered.

(d) *Insured mail:* Mail may also be sent as **insured mail.** The insurance covers up to $500 against loss or damage. A receipt is issued to the sender. This service is available with express, first-class, priority, and standard mail as well as package services.

(e) *Certificate of mailing:* When proof is needed that an item was taken to the post office for mailing, a **certificate of mailing** may be purchased, not as proof of delivery but rather as proof of mailing.

(f) *Certified mail:* First-class mail with no dollar value of its own may be sent as **certified mail,** thus providing proof of mailing and delivery. A mailing receipt and online access to delivery information is provided.

(g) *Collect-on-delivery (COD) mail:* The seller may choose to send an item as **collect-on-delivery (COD) mail.** COD service can be obtained by paying a fee in addition to the regular postage. The seller must prepay fees and postage; the seller specifies the total COD charges (price of item shipped plus postage and COD fee) to be collected from the buyer in cash or personal check. The maximum amount collectible (insurance coverage against loss or damage) on one package is $1,000. The U.S. Postal Service maintains a delivery record.

(h) *International mail:* Postage for letters and postal cards mailed to Mexico is the same as that for letters and cards mailed within the United States. Rates for **international mail** such as Global Express Guaranteed and Global Express going to all other countries are higher, and the weights are limited. Customs declaration forms may be necessary for specific contents within parcels.

(i) *Mailgrams:* The post office that serves the ZIP Code of the addressee may receive a **mailgram,** an electronic message, forwarded from Western Union. The post office provides next-day delivery for mailgrams, along with the day's mail delivery, to any address in the United States. Mailgram services are also available for Canadian addresses.

(3) *Web tools available:* The U.S. Postal Service also has developed a number of Web tools, available at the Web site *www.usps.com,* to help individual and business users with shipping services. Here are some of the Web tools available:

(a) *Domestic rate calculator:* With this tool, the shipping cost for any package that is to be shipped domestically can be calculated. The user can determine whether express mail, priority mail, or one of the four package services will be the most cost effective.

(b) *International rate calculator:* This rate calculator will provide the shipping costs for Global Express Guaranteed™, Global Express Mail™, Global Priority Mail™, Airmail, and Economy mail. In addition, information is available concerning unique mailing restrictions for other countries.

(c) *Track/confirm status:* The Delivery Confirmation™ or Signature Confirmation™ Service number allows access to information about the delivery status of any package shipped by Priority Mail®, first-class mail, or package services. Such delivery information as the date and time of delivery, attempts at delivery, and the name of the person who received the package can be obtained.

(d) *Address information:* Other services include address standardization, ZIP Code lookup, and city/state lookup. These services are available through the U.S. Postal Service Internet Customer Care Center. Once the user's registration is confirmed, the Address Informational User's Guide can be downloaded to provide the needed documentation.

In addition to these tools, express mail and global express mail shipping labels are available as well as customs forms.

2. ***Private Messenger or Delivery Services:*** Many organizations use a private messenger, delivery, or courier service when a guaranteed delivery time is required. Services available and fees charged by different services vary. The administrative professional should investigate these services to identify the messenger, delivery, or courier service that best meets the needs of the organization.

EXAMPLES:

Federal Express Corporation (FedEx) is a family of companies offering ground, freight, and overseas shipping services within an international network of over 210 countries that includes the Asia Pacific region, Canada, Europe, the Middle East, Africa, and Latin America and Caribbean region. Complete details of services offered can be found at the FedEx Web site www.fedex.com.

United Parcel Service (UPS) offers guaranteed delivery service of parcels to over 200 countries worldwide. A number of domestic and international service options are available to users. For example, UPS Next Day Air® guarantees overnight delivery by 10:30 A.M., noon, or end of day the next business day, depending on the destination to every address in all 50 states and Puerto Rico. Other service options can be found at the UPS Web site, www.ups.com.

3. ***Telecommunication Systems:*** Information distribution services available through telecommunication systems are popular alternatives to postal or delivery services, depending on the type of information to be distributed and the form in which it is required. Telecommunication systems have expanded from telegrams and mailgrams to the new frontier—the Internet.

    a. *Western Union services:* Money transfer and message services are available through Western Union. Consumers are able to quickly transfer money and send messages to more than 150,000 WU locations worldwide.

        (1) *Telegrams:* A **telegram** is a message delivered to the receiver through Western Union. Telegrams are used for any type of written communication—a message of congratulations, a memento of a special occasion, or business information. Messages received prior to 6 P.M. Eastern time (Monday through Thursday) will be delivered the next day to any point in the continental United States. Messages received on Friday before 6 P.M. Eastern time will be delivered the following Monday. In 2003 the basic fee to send a telegram message was $14.99.

        (2) *Mailgrams:* A mailgram is a message transmitted by Western Union to the post office that serves the ZIP Code of the addressee. At the post office, the mailgram is printed, inserted into an envelope, and included with the next regularly scheduled mail delivery. A mailgram is less expensive than a telegram.

        (3) *Money transfers:* Western Union provides a secure money-transfer service for consumers and businesses to transfer amounts of money to 150,000 locations around the world.

        (4) *Bill payments and money orders:* With Western Union's bill payment service, money orders and other electronic systems may be used to send bill payments.

        (5) *International messages:* The WU worldwide network enables international messages to be delivered to 150,000 agents around the world.

b. *Telephone technology:* Standardizing procedures for using telephone technology between and among organizations is very important to administrative professionals.

(1) *Telephone communication:* Using telephone communication effectively at the workstation is an extremely important aspect of business life. Personal traits such as politeness, courtesy, and tact are vital in placing calls and responding to telephone communication.

(2) *Procedures for telephone usage:* Here are some of the specific procedures the office professional needs to keep in mind:

(a) Answer the telephone promptly when it rings, preferably after the first or second ring.

(b) If you are going to be away from your desk for an extended period of time, forward your calls to another person or have your calls covered by a voice-mail network that will save messages.

(c) Take accurate messages so that correct information will be transmitted to other people in the organization. When people leave messages, they expect the information to be correctly transmitted.

EXAMPLE:

A telephone message with numbers transposed or an area code missing is of no value. The call cannot easily be returned. Names of callers should be verified for correct spelling as well.

(d) Place telephone calls with a specific purpose in mind. Know the name of the person you are calling and be ready to give message information if that person is not available to take the call.

(e) Read or listen to telephone messages as soon after arrival at the office as possible. Doing so helps you prioritize the return of telephone calls along with other informational tasks.

(3) *Voice mail:* A telephone system is greatly enhanced through the addition of a voice-mail network as a means of recording telephone messages received at a particular workstation. Most voice-mail networks are set up so that if the telephone is not answered by the third or fourth ring, the caller will automatically hear a prompt from the person being called requesting that a message be recorded. This type of system enables each person to receive messages directly instead of receiving these messages through an intermediary who may or may not record an accurate message. Here are some procedures that will be helpful in managing voice mail.

(a) Establish a daily schedule for responding to voice-mail messages. Accessing messages in the early morning, mid-day, and later in the afternoon will permit you to stay in touch with people who need information from you.

(b) Upon arrival at the office, check to see if voice-mail messages need to be accessed and responded to immediately.

(c) As you listen to messages, make notes of the calls received and the responses required. Even if you have to search for information, at least respond to each call and indicate when you hope to have the information to share.

c. *Facsimile (fax) transmission:* The way that information is distributed or communicated to or through the office sometimes necessitates quick responses in the form of documents or copies of documents.

   (1) Inquiries may require the immediate transmittal of copies of written documents with signatures. Fax machines can transmit copies of documents over telephone lines from one fax machine to another in a matter of minutes. Only a few seconds are usually required to transmit one page.

   (2) Separate telephone numbers may be assigned to fax machines so that once the connection is made to the other machine, the transmission should take only a few minutes and typically no more than a minute per page. The cost of fax transmission has been reduced greatly within the past few years.

   Domestic as well as international transmission is available, with the cost similar to that of a telephone call.

d. *Internet:* The Internet is the largest implementation of internetworking, linking millions of individual networks around the world. Web sites and external electronic communication are the most prevalent uses of the Internet.

   (1) *Electronic mail:* Most administrative professionals and busy executives find themselves part of the global network, the Internet, as well as their internal local area network (LAN), providing electronic mail capability for both external and internal communications. The primary reasons for electronic communication are speed in transmitting information, time savings, and reduction in the amount of paper involved in communications. Management of electronic information is very important.

      (a) *e-Mail technology:* The use of e-mail technology has expanded greatly in the past few years. e-Mail networks have enabled administrative professionals to more quickly and easily process and transmit information. e-Mail has become the primary method of sharing information throughout business organizations.

      (b) *e-Mail procedures:* Most electronic messages are stored on the individual's electronic mailbox. The administrative professional can assist the busy executive in accessing e-mail communications and sorting those that require immediate attention from others that can be delayed. Here are some of the decisions that need to be made about each message:

         • Is the message merely an item of information?

           Electronic file folders can be created and entitled *Reading Material* or *For Your Information*. All correspondence received can be moved from the electronic mailbox to the "read" folder. As the executive reviews this correspondence, he or she can decide whether it should be deleted or moved to an appropriate electronic folder for future reference.

         • If the item requires a response, who needs to respond to it?

           Depending on the nature of the inquiry, the "right" person should respond to the message as quickly as possible. Sometimes the message will need to be forwarded to another department or division for a response. The administrative professional can be especially helpful in letting the original sender know who will be responding to the message.

- Can an immediate response be sent?

  Sending an immediate response will enable you to handle the item only once. By clicking on "Reply to Sender," you can initiate a rapid response to the message. Be sure you have the appropriate e-mail address for the individual to whom you are sending the response. Word your response simply and concisely. The system will send the message on command. Your response is stored in "Sent Messages" in case you have to refer to it again.

- Do you need additional information before responding?

  If additional information is needed from the documents or files, the response may be delayed for a short while. Notify the original sender of the message if there will be a delay in locating the information. Once the information has been obtained, respond to the original message as quickly as possible.

- Should you check to see that the response was received?

  Make sure that the response was received. Most e-mail networks identify the date and time when a communication was sent as well as a return receipt showing the date and time that communication was received and read. When documents are attached to messages, be sure to have the receiver acknowledge that the complete document was received. However, remember to use the "return receipt requested" option sparingly.

- When should the message be deleted from the e-mail listing?

  Once the message has been read and the information is no longer needed, delete the item from the e-mail listing. Keep the e-mail network "clean" from a cluttered and sometimes outdated collection of information items.

(c) *Netiquette practices:* As more and more office communication is internally and externally distributed, etiquette guidelines should be followed. Etiquette practices for the electronic environment are often referred to as **netiquette.** The following are some of the basic practices that administrative professionals should follow in politely, courteously, and thoughtfully handling communication.

- Use a subject line so the recipient knows the topic of the e-mail before opening the message. Because of recent problems with viruses, many receivers choose not to open any messages that arrive from unknown senders with nondescript subject lines.

  EXAMPLE:

  IAAP INTERNATIONAL CONVENTION is a more descriptive subject line than just the word CONVENTION.

- Remember to follow the guidelines for well-written electronic mail messages (see Chapter 8).

- Avoid all caps when keying e-mail communications. A message or a portion of a message in all caps gives the impression that you are shouting. Use other means of emphasis such as boldface, underlining, or bulleted lists. Many e-mail systems today also have the option for different-colored fonts. If the e-mail system does not include boldface or underlining features, use the following substitutes:

Underlining: Key in an underscore (_) at the beginning and ending of words needing to be underlined.

Bolding: Key in an asterisk (*) at the beginning and ending of the words to be in bold.

Note: If the underscore and bold alternatives are used, include a note in the e-mail so the recipient understands the notation you used.

EXAMPLE:

Note at end of e-mail message:

*Words that are underlined: _words_*

*Words that are in bold: *words**

When an e-mail message is sent using a different e-mail program than the receiver uses, the receiver needs to be able to access the desired type fonts that produce underlining, boldface, or other features as needed.

- Abbreviations and emotion icons (emoticons) are for very informal communication. Even though e-mail is an informal communication, abbreviations and emotion icons should be avoided or used at a minimum in business e-mail.

- Never send **spam** (unsolicited e-mail); this is considered an Internet *faux pas.*

- Honor someone's private communication with you. Never send e-mail messages that contain personal information about others without obtaining their permission first.

- When using the reply option and the original message is being returned, your response should be at the beginning of the e-mail message, not at the end of the original message. Sometimes responses are interleaved within the original message. When this option is used, color code your response or use the bold or underscore to highlight your response. At the beginning, clarify to the receiver that your responses are interleaved in *bold* (note your response method).

EXAMPLE:

The following e-mail response is interleaved in bold.

Looking forward to your arrival on Monday. Hoping to have time to meet before the Executive Session at 6 P.M. When do you arrive? **Monday 10 A.M. Limo to Hotel Harrington by approximately noon.** *Can we meet before the meeting?* **Let's have lunch at the Harrington at 12:30 P.M.**

- Use antivirus software to maintain a virus-free environment. If you receive a virus warning, confirm it with reliable sources before acting upon it. Many virus warnings are hoaxes.

- At the end of an e-mail message, include a signature file with your name, title, company name, e-mail address, and telephone number. Many systems provide a signature option. Once your signature is saved in the system, you can easily affix your signature file to the end of every e-mail message you send.

- Do not clog the Internet by forwarding chain letters and other non-business material from the office. Uncontrolled use of the Internet is like sending and receiving "junk" mail through the U.S. Postal Service.

(d) *Employers' right to monitor e-mail:* Employers have become much more aware of the ways in which e-mail is used within the office—for personal as well as business purposes. An increasing number of organizations is monitoring employee use of e-mail for a variety of reasons. These include the possibility of sending proprietary information about products and services to other organizations without authorization, concern for employee productivity, and employer legal liability for specific types of information transmitted. Employers are also establishing new policies and procedures for e-mail usage within the firm. Administrative professionals need to be knowledgeable about such policies that are in effect and how e-mail usage is viewed within the organization.

Electronic mail can be extremely helpful, especially in terms of speed in communication and ease in getting a quick reply (see Chapter 8 for a review of composing e-mail messages).

(2) *Web site:* Many organizations provide information about their firms through Web sites. This new way of communication combines text, hypermedia, graphics, and sound to disseminate product, service, and other company information on the Web.

- The person in charge of an organization's Web site needs to be skilled in communication, artistic design, and technology as well as Web site management strategies. The person responsible for these activities is called a **Webmaster.**
- A **Web site** collectively consists of all the pages included for the company.
- The **home page** is the first page for the Web site and is registered on the World Wide Web (WWW) through a Web address—a uniform resource locator (URL).

See Chapter 4 in *Office Systems and Technology* for more information on Web technology.

The distribution of information, both internally and externally, depends on the nature of the information being communicated as well as the means that are available for such communication. Administrative professionals must take responsibility for making numerous important decisions about the communication and distribution of information within the organization as well as with external organizations.

Check Point—Section C

Directions: For each question, circle the correct answer.

C–1. A newspaper that is mailed once a month to a list of subscribers would be classified as

A) first-class mail
B) parcel post
C) standard mail
D) periodicals

C–2. One of the primary reasons for applying electronic communication to both external and internal business communication is to

A) transmit information as quickly as possible

B) increase the quantity of hard-copy documentation created

C) set priorities for information distribution

D) concentrate on domestic services available for the transmission of information

C–3. Which one of the following business practices illustrates the application of netiquette?

A) The most important points in an e-mail message should be keyed in all caps

B) Emotion icons should be used only in informal communication

C) A response to an original message should be keyed after the original message

D) Chain letters may be forwarded as long as they do not interfere with business communication

For Your Review

Directions: For each question, circle the correct answer.

1. Information that is not in usable format is of value only if
   A) the information is needed immediately
   B) available as hard copy
   C) transmitted electronically
   D) converted to the format required

2. The transmission of information must take place quickly enough for the information to be
   A) transmitted electronically
   B) current enough to meet the needs of the receiver
   C) distributed internally and externally
   D) available as hard or soft copy

3. In addition to transmitting information as needed, it is important that the information be
   A) accurate in expressing facts, data, and opinions
   B) distributed internally
   C) critiqued by an administrator
   D) distributed externally

4. Information that includes statistical data may be distributed best in a/an
   A) telephone message
   B) e-mail message
   C) written memorandum or letter
   D) face-to-face conversation

5. Which one of the following means would be appropriate for transmitting informal information that is needed within a few minutes?
   A) A letter sent by express mail
   B) An appointment for a face-to-face discussion
   C) A short report to be faxed the next morning
   D) An e-mail message

6. An organization may need to do which one of the following to handle information processing during a peak season?
   A) Inform clients of a slowdown in response time
   B) Increase working hours for staff
   C) Purchase a new computer system to speed up the process
   D) Streamline procedures to handle the extra work load

7. The intranet is an organization's
   A) external electronic network permitting employees access to Internet capabilities
   B) telephone communication system equipped with voice-mail messaging
   C) internal electronic network for communicating information to employees
   D) system for handling interoffice correspondence

8. Reducing the number of hard copies needed in the office is the main purpose of a/an
   A) telephone communication system
   B) Internet Web server
   C) mail distribution system
   D) electronic mail system

9. Which one of the following is a major difficulty in relying on telephone communication?

   A) Reaching the desired receiver with the information needed
   B) Leaving a telephone message with call-back information
   C) Practicing appropriate telephone etiquette
   D) Leaving a good impression with the receiver

10. When leaving an appropriate telephone message, the caller needs to

    A) provide a detailed message with all the information needed
    B) reference a previous call or message left
    C) plan the message in advance in case the receiver is not available
    D) access any pertinent information that needs to be shared

11. Transmitting information face to face is best when

    A) the receiver will be receptive to the information
    B) the information is critical to a particular business function or operation
    C) a quick "yes" or "no" response is needed
    D) only one specific topic needs to be discussed

12. The ZIP + 4 Code consists of

    A) classifications of domestic mail within the United States
    B) five digits representing global areas plus four digits for local delivery routes
    C) bar codes imprinted on envelopes
    D) five digits representing areas of the United States plus four digits for local delivery routes

13. Which one of the following statements represents an appropriate procedure for handling incoming mail?

    A) A paper trail must be created for mail that contains payments in the form of checks or cash
    B) Payments received need to be credited immediately by the administrative professional who sorts the mail
    C) Incoming mail is forwarded to a manager or executive for opening, dating, and time stamping
    D) The date the mail is received is considered less important than the date of the correspondence

14. The domestic mail delivery service that guarantees next-day and second-day delivery for items weighing up to 70 pounds is

    A) priority mail
    B) express mail
    C) first-class mail
    D) standard mail

15. A statement of account mailed to a domestic client would be considered

    A) priority mail
    B) standard mail
    C) first-class mail
    D) express mail

16. The R-D Furniture Outlet sends four-page flyers to a mailing list of local area customers once a month. These flyers, weighing approximately 4 ounces each, would be classified as

    A) standard mail—A
    B) periodicals
    C) package services
    D) standard mail—B

17. An R–D Furniture Outlet catalog is prepared once a year for distribution to customers. If these catalogs are mailed out, they will be classified as

    A) standard mail—A
    B) periodicals
    C) standard mail—B
    D) package services

18. The Illinois Division of the International Association of Administrative Professionals mails a membership directory to every Illinois chapter once a year. Which one of the following statements is true about this type of mailing?

    A) The ID president can enclose a short personal message

B) The directory can consist of un-bound pages

C) A letter on ID letterhead cannot be included with the mailing

D) A printed form for updating addresses can be enclosed with the directory

19. Ramirez needs to send stock certificates for 100 shares of stock to her sister. Which one of the following postal services would be best for sending the certificates?

A) Special delivery
B) Registered mail
C) Certified mail
D) Insured mail

20. The delivery status of any package shipped by Priority Mail™ through the U.S. Postal Service can be determined by

A) contacting the local U.S. Post Office
B) checking the postal receipt for the mailing
C) calculating the shipping cost for the package
D) accessing the delivery confirmation Web tool at the U.S. Postal Service Web site

21. Skolowski needs to transfer $2,000 to her cousin Warzawski in Prague, Poland. Which one of the following methods would provide the fastest service?

A) Global Priority Mail™
B) Global Express Mail™
C) Western Union's money-transfer service
D) Registered mail

22. What does a person generally expect will happen when leaving a telephone message?

A) The information will be transmitted correctly to the called person
B) The called person will promptly return the call

C) The message will be forwarded to someone else for response
D) A voice-mail network will be less effective in delivering the message

23. A major advantage in receiving messages through a voice-mail network is that

A) copies of documents can quickly be sent
B) the receiver does not have to record the message or make notes
C) the written message is transmitted promptly from an intermediary
D) the called person receives and hears the message exactly as recorded

24. If an e-mail message requires a response from someone else, the administrative professional should

A) forward the message to the person who should respond to it
B) place a copy of the message in an electronic file folder marked "For Your Information"
C) reply to the e-mail by letting the original sender know who will be writing the response
D) seek additional information before responding

25. A number of employers are beginning to monitor employees' e-mail usage during company time because they are concerned about the

A) number of employees who are using e-mail for company business
B) information contained in e-mail messages that are being transmitted on company time
C) deletion of e-mail messages from intranets
D) increased productivity of employees when using e-mail systems

Solutions

Solutions to Check Point—Section A

Answer	Refer to:
A–1. (C)	[Overview, A]
A–2. (B)	[A-1-a]
A–3. (D)	[A-2-e]

Solutions to Check Point—Section B

Answer	Refer to:
B–1. (A)	[B-1-a]
B–2. (C)	[B-2-a]
B–3. (D)	[B-3-b]

Solutions to Check Point—Section C

Answer	Refer to:
C–1. (D)	[C-1-c (1) (d)]
C–2. (A)	[C-3-d (1)]
C–3. (B)	[C-3-d (1) (c)]

Solutions to For Your Review

	Answer	Refer to:
1.	(D)	[A-1-a]
2.	(B)	[A-1-c]
3.	(A)	[A-1-d]
4.	(C)	[A-2-a]
5.	(D)	[A-2-b]
6.	(B)	[A-2-d]
7.	(C)	[B-1]
8.	(D)	[B-1-a]
9.	(A)	[B-2]
10.	(C)	[B-2-b]
11.	(B)	[B-3-b]
12.	(D)	[C-1-a]
13.	(A)	[C-1-b (3) (a)]
14.	(B)	[C-1-c (1) (a)]
15.	(C)	[C-1-c (1) (c)]
16.	(A)	[C-1-c (1) (e)]
17.	(D)	[C-1-c (1) (f)]
18.	(C)	[C-1-c (1) (f)]
19.	(B)	[C-1-c (2) (c)]
20.	(D)	[C-1-c (3) (c)]
21.	(C)	[C-3-a (3)]
22.	(A)	[C-3-b (2) (c)]
23.	(D)	[C-3-b (3)]
24.	(C)	[C-3-d (1) (b)]
25.	(B)	[C-3-d (1) (d)]

Chapter 11
Rules of Grammar

OVERVIEW

In many parts of the world, the English language is becoming the universal language of business, and some already view it that way. What this means is that the majority of business transactions are accomplished with English as the primary language, although there may still be times when knowledge of another language such as Spanish, German, or Chinese would be helpful in negotiations. Having the help of a translator may be a necessity in order to make sure that clear and meaningful communication takes place.

Conducting or assisting with business transactions requires administrative professionals to have an excellent command of formal language—from grammar to punctuation to other mechanics of writing and speaking. Impressions we create—both favorable and unfavorable—stem from the facility with which language is used in communicating with others. People from other countries have often been subjected to the fundamentals of different languages early in their education and are able to recognize the strength with which language is put into practice.

This chapter highlights basic rules of English grammar, word usage, punctuation, capitalization, number usage, and word division. These rules will help administrative professionals achieve consistency, accuracy, and proficiency in the way the English language is put to use in developing all types of business writing.

KEY TERMS

Apostrophe, 359
Colon, 360
Comma, 361
Complement, 356
Consecutive adjectives, 364
Coordinate adjectives, 363

Dash, 364
Direct object, 355
Ellipsis, 364
Exclamation point, 364
Gerund phrase, 358
Hyphen, 365

Indirect object, 355
Infinitive phrase, 358
Modifiers, 356
Parentheses, 366
Parenthetical expression, 362
Participle phrase, 358

A. Grammar and Word Usage

In business writing, many of the documents are expected to have a "conversational" tone and yet be formal. Formal English is characterized by adherence to language rules and specialized vocabulary. The purpose of the language guide that follows is to review the structure of English language, the rules that govern the language, and the language style that results in a well-written business document.

1. ***Primary Elements of a Sentence:*** A complete sentence must contain a subject and a verb (predicate). Most sentences also contain an object or a complement. The four components of a sentence are subject, verb, object, and complement.

   Secondary sentence elements encompass the use of modifiers, phrases, and clauses.

   a. *Subject:* Each sentence requires at least one *subject*. The subject of a sentence is a noun or noun equivalent that serves as the topic of the sentence. A simple subject consists of a single word, such as *manager*. A complete subject consists of the simple subject as well as any other words that modify that subject, such as *knowledgeable manager*.

   EXAMPLES:

   > *A knowledgeable <u>manager</u> coordinates the work of the entire office staff.* (noun used as subject)
   >
   > *<u>She</u> aspires to become a CPS.* (noun equivalent—pronoun used as subject)
   >
   > *<u>What you study</u> is important to pass the CPS examination.* (noun equivalent—noun clause used as subject)
   >
   > *<u>Studying</u> is important to pass the CPS examination.* (noun equivalent—gerund used as subject)
   >
   > *<u>To study</u> requires self-discipline.* (noun equivalent—infinitive used as subject)

   b. *Verb:* The *verb* of a sentence tells what the subject has done, is doing, or will be doing, or the verb can express a condition about the subject. When the verb expresses a condition, it is a *linking verb;* otherwise, it is an *action verb*.

   The verb must agree with the subject in number. If the subject is singular, the verb must be singular. If the subject is plural, the verb must be plural. Agreement between subject and verb is important. This is where writers sometimes have problems. Questions about agreement usually arise when verbs have plural compound subjects or when the subject is separated from the verb by other words. Typically, the verb follows the subject.

   EXAMPLES

   > *I always <u>ask</u> questions to ensure complete understanding.*
   > (present tense, singular, action)
   >
   > *He always <u>asks</u> questions to ensure complete understanding.*
   > (present tense, singular, action)

We <u>ask</u> questions of each other while studying.
They <u>ask</u> questions of each other while studying.
(present tense, plural, action)

I <u>asked</u> for a raise.
She <u>asked</u> for a raise.
(past tense, singular, action)

We <u>asked</u> for a new copier.
(past tense, plural, action)

I <u>will ask</u> for a new computer for the office.
I <u>am going to ask</u> for a new computer.
(future tense, singular, action)

We <u>will ask</u> for help during the tax season.
We <u>are going to ask</u> for help during the tax season.
(future tense, plural, action)

I <u>am</u> happy with the computer class you offer.
(present tense, singular, linking verb)

I <u>was</u> happy when the computer arrived.
(past tense, singular, linking verb)

We <u>were</u> happy when the computer arrived.
(past tense, plural, linking verb)

We <u>will be</u> happy when the computers arrive.
(future tense, plural, linking verb)

c. *Object:* Action verbs are usually followed by a **direct object.** The direct object of the verb completes the sentence by answering the question "what" or "whom" after the verb. The direct object is either a noun or a noun equivalent.

Verbs such as *buying, giving, asking,* and *telling* are followed by an **indirect object.** The indirect object names the receiver of the direct object, precedes the direct object, and answers the questions "to whom," "to what," "for whom," or "for what."

EXAMPLES—Direct Object:

Office professionals who are rushed usually make <u>mistakes</u>.
Make "what"? mistakes (noun)

Morrison likes <u>him</u> for a manager.
Likes "whom"? him (noun equivalent—pronoun)

Clare knows <u>what skills are required</u>.
Knows "what"? what skills are required (noun equivalent—noun clause)

Radkowski enjoys <u>hunting</u> every fall.
Enjoys "what"? hunting (noun equivalent—gerund)

The committee voted <u>to adjourn</u>.
Voted "what"? to adjourn (noun equivalent—infinitive)

EXAMPLES—Indirect Object:

Many employees gave <u>United Way</u> a fair-share contribution.
Gave "what"? contribution (direct object)
    "to whom"? United Way (indirect object)

Dr. Jones should give the <u>tree</u> a pruning.
Should give "what"? pruning (direct object)
"to what"? tree (indirect object)

Douglas bought <u>Mother</u> 50 stock certificates yesterday.
Bought "what"? certificates (direct object)
"for whom"? Mother (indirect object)

d. *Complement:* When the verb is a linking verb that expresses a condition about the subject, it usually is followed by a complement. A noun in the predicate that refers to the subject or is an adjective that describes the subject is known as a **complement.** A complement is related to the subject because of the linking verb.

A noun or noun equivalent is called a **predicate noun;** an adjective is called a **predicate adjective.**

The most common linking verbs are the various forms of the verb *to be*: *is, am, are, was, were, has been, might be.*

EXAMPLES:

Johanson is a dynamic <u>speaker</u>.
Is "what"? speaker (predicate noun)

My manager might be <u>unhappy</u> with the committee's decision.
Might be "what"? unhappy (predicate adjective)

2. *Secondary Elements of a Sentence:* Most sentences have modifiers, clauses, or phrases. These are considered secondary elements of a sentence.

a. *Modifiers:* Single words may describe or modify other words in the sentence. These **modifiers** usually add descriptive details or specific definition to key words and assist the writer in being more specific.

The most common modifiers are adjectives and adverbs. An *adjective* describes nouns or pronouns, whereas an *adverb* describes a verb, an adjective, or another adverb. The adjective or adverb is usually near the word it modifies. Many adverbs are formed by adding *ly* to an adjective.

EXAMPLES:

Our home office is located in Memphis.

Subject:	office
Adjective:	home (describes which office)

Jennings speaks quite clearly over the telephone.

Verb:	speaks
Adverb:	clearly (describes how Jennings speaks)
Adverb:	quite (describes how clearly)

Mack's extremely small frame makes it difficult to find a comfortable work area.

Noun:	frame
Adjective:	small (describes frame)
Adverb:	extremely (describes small)

b. *Clauses:* Clauses can be either independent or dependent. An *independent clause* contains a subject and verb (predicate) and can stand by itself as a sentence. A group of words that is not an independent clause is called a *sentence fragment.*

   (1) *Independent clauses:* When two independent clauses are connected with a conjunction (*and, but, or*) and no commas are used within either clause, a comma is placed before the conjunction.

   EXAMPLE:

   The new computer arrived this morning, and Micro-Systems will be out to-morrow to review the operations.
   (two independent clauses connected by the conjunction *and*)

   When two independent clauses that are related in meaning are not joined by a conjunction, a semicolon should be used to separate the clauses.

   Note: If a comma is inserted rather than a semicolon, a *comma-splice* error has occurred.

   EXAMPLE:

   Muhler is at the board meeting; she should be back at 4 P.M.
   (two independent clauses, no conjunction)

   Muhler is at the board meeting, she should be back at 4 P.M.
   (a comma-splice error; the comma must be replaced with a semicolon)

   When a comma is already in use within one of the independent clauses and a conjunction separates the two clauses, a semicolon needs to be placed before the conjunction.

   EXAMPLE:

   The new computer system includes typical hardware (a central processor, a monitor, a keyboard, and a mouse; but training will focus mostly on the application software.
   (two independent clauses—one using commas in a series—joined by the conjunction *but*)

   When the second independent clause is introduced with a conjunctive adverb like *however, therefore,* or *consequently,* a semicolon must separate the independent clauses and a comma is placed after the conjunctive adverb.

   EXAMPLE:

   The new computer system includes the typical hardware components; therefore, the training will include an orientation to the features of the system.
   (two independent clauses with no conjunction—joined by a semicolon—conjunctive adverb introducing second clause followed by comma)

   (2) *Dependent clauses:* A dependent clause also contains a subject and a verb (predicate); however, the clause is part of the sentence and cannot stand by itself as a complete sentence. A dependent clause is introduced by a conjunction (*since, when, because, if, after*) or a relative pronoun (*who, which, that*).

When a dependent clause begins a sentence, a comma always follows.

EXAMPLE:

If you are serious about taking the CAP® exam, you should register for the review course that begins next month.
(dependent clause beginning the sentence, followed by a comma)

A dependent clause included within a sentence is considered a sentence interrupter and may be surrounded by commas if it is deemed nonessential to the meaning of the sentence.

EXAMPLE:

Maria Johnson, who is our new director, will meet with the board of directors tomorrow.
(dependent clause within the sentence)

When a dependent clause appears at the end of a sentence, it may be introduced with such words as *if, as,* or *when.* No comma is needed between the independent clause and the dependent clause.

EXAMPLE:

Maria Johnson will meet with the board of directors when the results of her feasibility study is complete.
(independent clause followed by dependent clause)

Note: A dependent clause by itself, without the aid of an independent clause, is considered a sentence fragment.

c. *Phrases:* A phrase is a group of related words connected to a sentence by a preposition or a verb. Such a phrase cannot stand by itself because it has no subject or verb (predicate). Such phrases are modifiers and may or may not require punctuation marks.

(1) *Prepositional phrases:* Depending on what it modifies, a prepositional phrase functions like an adjective or adverb. The phrase begins with a preposition (*from, at, by, of*) and is followed by a noun or noun equivalent (the object of the preposition).

EXAMPLES:

The cabinet *by his desk* contains our procedures manual.
(prepositional phrase used as an adjective)

Mr. Klein spoke in a loud voice.
(prepositional phrase used as an adverb)

(2) *Verbal phrases:* A verbal phrase does not function as a verb. A **participle phrase** functions as an adjective, a **gerund phrase** functions as a noun, and an **infinitive phrase** functions as a noun, an adjective, or an adverb. The phrase consists of the verbal element plus the object or complement and modifiers of the phrase.

EXAMPLES:

Ashford, having passed the CPS® exam on the first try, feels very good about herself.
(verbal phrase—participle phrase modifying the noun *Ashley*)

Passing the CAP® exam opened new directions for Mason.
(verbal phrase—gerund phrase as the subject)

Davidson gave me plenty of work <u>to do</u> before she left.
(verbal phrase—infinitive phrase as an adjective modifying the noun *work*)

The students in the CPS® review course want <u>to review</u> grammar and punctuation rules.
(verbal phrase—infinitive phrase as an adverb modifying the verb *want*)

Check Point—Section A

Directions: For each question, circle the correct answer.

A–1. Administrative professionals who are rushed <u>make mistakes.</u> The underlined words are the sentence's

    A) action verb (make) and direct object (mistakes)

    B) indirect object of <u>who are rushed.</u>

    C) modifiers of <u>who are rushed</u>

    D) verb

A–2. *Maxwell is in executive session; she should be available at 4 P.M.* This sentence consists of

    A) one dependent clause and one independent clause

    B) two dependent clauses, no conjunction

    C) two independent clauses, no conjunction

    D) two independent clauses, connected with a conjunction.

A–3. *Rodriguez plans to attend the international convention in August.* This sentence contains

    A) a compound subject

    B) an infinitive phrase

    C) one dependent clause

    D) a gerund phrase

B. Punctuation

The use of correct punctuation is extremely important for the administrative professional. What is said or written can easily be changed by the misuse of a punctuation mark. This section includes a quick summary of the ways in which major forms of punctuation are used correctly in business writing.

  1. *Apostrophe:* The **apostrophe** is used to show possession and to form plurals. Its use in contractions and as a mark of punctuation or symbol is very important in business writing.

    a. *To show possession:* The apostrophe may be used to show ownership or possession.

        (1) *Singular nouns:* Add the apostrophe and an *s* to all singular nouns (unless the singular noun ends in *s*). For singular nouns that end in *s*, only the apostrophe is necessary. However, it is also correct to add an apostrophe and an *s*, particularly if the extra syllable is pronounced.

        EXAMPLES:

            author's manuscript
            (singular noun)

            boss' standards*
            (singular noun ending in <u>s</u>)
            (*boss's* is also correct)

James' invention*
(one-syllable proper name ending in <u>s</u>)
(*James's* is also correct)

*Once you decide how you prefer to show possession, be consistent throughout the document.

(2) *Plural nouns:* Add the apostrophe and an *s* to plural nouns that do not end in an *s*. For plural nouns that end in an *s*, add only the apostrophe.

EXAMPLES:

women's organization
(plural noun not ending in <u>s</u>)

accountants' pins
(plural noun ending in <u>s</u>)

b. *For plurals:* For the sake of clarity with small letters, the plural is formed by adding 's. An apostrophe is generally used to form the plurals of capital letters and numbers; however, just the capital letter and an *s* is sufficient. The only capital letters which should always have an apostrophe before the *s* are A, I, and U, primarily for clarity. Again, once you choose a style, be consistent throughout the document.

EXAMPLES:

a's	*A's*	*Bs or B's*	*1s or 1's*
b's	*I's*	*Cs or C's*	*2s or 2's*
c's	*U's*	*Ds or D's*	*3s or 3's*

c. *With symbols:* The apostrophe is used as the symbol for *feet* on business forms and in tables. As part of a sentence within a paragraph of a letter or a report, the word *feet* is spelled out in full.

EXAMPLE:

2' x 4' (meaning 2 feet by 4 feet)

A sentence within a letter would read: The board must be 2 feet by 4 feet.

d. *Contractions:* The apostrophe is used to indicate the omission of one or more letters.

EXAMPLES:

it's	*(it is)*
wouldn't	*(would not)*
can't	*(cannot)*

2. **Colon:** When the **colon** is keyed in text, it is followed by two spaces. The only exception is when the colon is used in indicating time (e.g., 4:30 P.M.).

a. *After an introduction:* A colon is used after a statement that introduces a long direct quotation, enumerated items, or a series introduced with the expressions *these*, *as follows*, or *the following*.

EXAMPLES:

Weinberg made the following motion: "I move that the bylaws of our organization be revised to waive local dues for emeritus members."

My presentation is divided into these three areas:

1. *Applying for the CPS® Examination*
2. *Reviewing for the Examination*
3. *Taking the Examination*

The 10 o'clock workshop sessions are as follows: information processing, communication, or integrated office systems.

b. *Time:* The colon is used to separate the hours from the minutes when time is expressed in figures, with no space after the colon. The time is always followed by a correct form of A.M. or P.M. When the time is an even hour, only the hour is used.

Variations for A.M. and P.M. are *a.m.*, *A.M.*, *am*, and *AM*; *p.m.*, *P.M.*, *pm*, and *PM*. For clarity, the more frequent use is with periods. Otherwise, *am* and *AM* could be mistaken for the word *am*. Be consistent with format, and type A.M. and P.M. notations in the same way.

EXAMPLES:

> *The staff meeting will begin at 2 p.m.*
>
> *We will meet Stevens at the office at 10:30 A.M.*

When the sentence has time both as an even hour and also as hours and minutes, write the even hour as only the hour (3 P.M.) and an hour with minutes as 3:15 P.M.

EXAMPLE:

> *The first film is scheduled for 3 P.M.; the second showing begins at 5:15 P.M.*

3. ***Comma:*** A **comma** is perhaps the most commonly used mark of punctuation in sentences. Proper use of commas improves the readability of sentences. Here is a summary of the ways in which the comma should be used.

a. *After an introductory group of words:* An introduction can be a word (*However, Therefore*), a phrase (*By hurrying, In case you did not know*), or a dependent clause (*As soon as the package arrives, When this meeting is called to order*). A comma is used to separate this introduction from the main clause.

EXAMPLES:

> *Finally, the meeting began at 3 P.M.*
> (introductory word)
>
> *Because of the weather, the company picnic will have to be postponed.*
> (introductory phrase)
>
> *As soon as the package arrives, deliver it to the accounting department.*
> (introductory dependent clause—adverbial clause)

b. *Series:* When three or more items are included in a series of words or phrases, a comma is used to separate the items. If a conjunction (*and, or, nor*) precedes the last word in a series, a comma is not necessary before the conjunction. However, the comma is often used before the conjunction for clarity. The basic decision is to follow the same rule throughout your writing; always insert the comma before the conjunction in a series, or always leave the comma out.

EXAMPLE:

> *Matthews ordered the paper, folders and gummed labels.*

or

Matthews ordered the paper, folders, and gummed labels.

Sometimes the items within the series contain conjunctions. Again, for clarity, a comma should precede the conjunction before the last item in the series.

EXAMPLE: *The shipment contained letter- and legal-size paper, pencils and pens, and rulers.*

If *et cetera* (*etc.*) is part of the series, use a comma before *et cetera* and after if *et cetera* or *etc.* is not at the end of the statement.

EXAMPLE: *The order for spring slacks, skirts, blouses, etc., from the Marks Department Store was shipped yesterday.*

If the series contains a series, semicolons are used to separate the main series while commas are used for the inner series.

EXAMPLES:

The Harris shipment on Friday included two blue, green, and gold chairs; one green sofa; and one glass sofa table.

The participants came from as far away as Juneau, Alaska; Bangor, Maine; and Honolulu, Hawaii, to attend the convention.

c. *Compound sentences:* When two complete sentences are connected with a conjunction (*and, but, or, nor*), a comma precedes the conjunction. Sometimes the conjunction is used because of a compound verb. In that case, the comma is not used because you do not want to separate the compound verb.

EXAMPLES:

Our administrative professional was out sick for one week, but we obtained an excellent replacement from Temporaries, Inc.

You should reconsider your decision to cancel the order and instruct us to reinstate it.
(subject: You; compound verb: should reconsider and instruct)

d. *Direct quotations:* A comma is used to set off a direct quotation (the exact words of a speaker), and quotation marks (" ") are placed around the exact words. Periods and commas are placed inside the quotation marks.

EXAMPLES:

Jackson said, "Pay the bill immediately."

"Pay the bill immediately," were Jackson's exact words.

Jackson said, "Pay the bill immediately," in a very emphatic tone.

e. *Parenthetical expressions:* A word, phrase, or clause that is not necessary to the grammatical completeness and meaning of the sentence is considered a **parenthetical expression.** This expression within the sentence is set off by commas, but only one comma is needed if the expression comes at the end of the sentence.

EXAMPLES:

Klein, however, is not applying for the position.
(parenthetical word)

Joan Smith, <u>I am sure</u>, will be able to handle the matter for you.
(parenthetical phrase)

I have prepared a cover letter, <u>a copy of which should be inserted in each booklet</u>.
(parenthetical clause)

f. *Apposition:* An *appositive* is a word, phrase, or clause that identifies or explains a noun, pronoun, or other term. An appositive is set off by commas unless it is at the end of the sentence; then, only one comma is necessary.

EXAMPLES:

The meeting will be on Wednesday, April 15, in Conference Room B. (<u>April 15</u> explains which Wednesday is meant and is the appositive.)

Sally Francis, our IAAP president, will attend the International Association of Administrative Professionals convention. (<u>our IAAP president</u> is the appositive; you can identify the appositive by asking, "Which Sally Francis?")

g. *Nonrestrictive clauses:* A nonrestrictive clause typically begins with *which*, *who*, or *whose*. The word *which* refers to a thing or place; the words *who* or *whose* refer to people. These clauses may be omitted without changing the meaning of the sentence. Nonrestrictive clauses are set off with commas.

EXAMPLES:

> *The formula, <u>which was tested at the Med-Lab Institute</u>, has really been an advancement for the medical profession.*
>
> *Emerson, <u>who can type 98 words per minute with 97 percent accuracy</u>, is being considered for the new position.*

A clause beginning with *that* usually is a restrictive clause, that is, essential to the meaning of the sentence. Therefore, no commas are placed around the restrictive clause. The word *that* is a demonstrative pronoun referring to a "thing" previously identified.

EXAMPLE: *The office design <u>that is the most conducive to effective communication</u> will be our first choice.*
(*that* refers to *design*)

h. *And omitted:* When two adjectives modify the same noun and the *and* is missing, a comma is used to replace the missing *and*. These two adjectives must be equal in rank; that is, they can be changed around and the meaning will not be distorted. We call these adjectives **coordinate adjectives.**

EXAMPLES:

> *Please order a <u>bronze, fluorescent</u> lamp for the office.*
>
> *Please order a <u>fluorescent, bronze</u> lamp for the office.*
>
> *The train is a quiet, smooth way to travel.*
> (The words *quiet* and *smooth* modify *way*.)
>
> *This is just a short, friendly reminder that your payment is now due.*
> (The words *short* and *friendly* modify *reminder*.)

However, if the first adjective modifies the combination of the second adjective plus the noun, the comma is not used. The adjectives are not equal in rank and must appear in this order or the sentence will not make sense. These adjectives are called **consecutive adjectives.**

EXAMPLES:

I need to hire a <u>dependable</u> <u>administrative</u> *assistant to help on this project.*
(The words *dependable* and *administrative* are both adjectives; *administrative* modifies *assistant,* and *dependable* modifies *administrative assistant.*)

The beautiful spring bouquet added a nice touch to the head banquet table.
(The word *beautiful* modifies the combination *spring bouquet.*)

4. *Dash:* Typically, a **dash** is used to emphasize one or more parenthetical words. For the dash to have any impact, however, you must be selective in substituting the dash for other punctuation marks. The forcefulness of the dash is greatly diminished if overused.

EXAMPLES:

O'Miria—an excellent physician—has been honored by her colleagues.
(The dash is used here instead of parentheses or commas to <u>emphasize</u> the words *an excellent physician.* With word processing software, the dash is typed with two hyphens and no spaces [the preferred style]. Once you have keyed in the next few characters or word followed by a space, the two hyphens automatically change to one long line [a dash] instead of two hyphens.)

Our favorite place to vacation—Alaska!
(The dash is used here instead of a colon. Another way to key in a dash is to type two hyphens with a space before and after.)

I like the new computer - the new ergonomic keyboard makes keying in text so much easier.
(The dash may be typed as a hyphen with one space before and after and is used here instead of a semicolon.)

Note: Once a style for typing a dash is selected, use the same format throughout a document; consistency is very important. Never type a dash as only one hyphen with no space before and after the hyphen. A single hyphen with no spaces is used within a compound word or in word division.

5. *Ellipsis:* Ellipsis marks are used to show the omission of words within a sentence. An **ellipsis** is typed with three periods, with a space before and after each period. If the ellipsis comes at the end of the sentence, the end-of-sentence punctuation is typed as normal (next to the word); then leave a space before typing the ellipsis. If the end-of-sentence punctuation is never typed, only the ellipsis is used.

EXAMPLE:

The president said, "With rising energy costs . . . we will keep thermostats at 72 degrees year round. . . ." She was very emphatic with this statement.

The president said, "With rising energy costs . . . we will keep thermostats at 72 degrees . . ."

6. *Exclamation point:* After a word, phrase, or sentence, an **exclamation point** is used for emphasis. The exclamation point used as end-of-sentence punctuation is typically followed by two spaces.

EXAMPLES:

The exam is in only two days!

Yes! I am impressed with that community project.

7. **Hyphen:** The **hyphen** is typically used for word division or in a compound word.

   a. *Compound adjective:* If two adjectives (descriptive words) precede a noun and together modify that noun, a hyphen is used to combine these adjectives into a compound word.

   Note: Do not confuse this rule with the *and*-omitted rule.

   EXAMPLE:

   The first-class mail is delivered to all departments by 10 A.M.
   (Together, *first* and *class* form a single adjective modifying *mail*.)

   b. *Replace "to" or "through":* In statistical writing, tables, or charts, the hyphen can be used to replace the words *to* or *through*.

   EXAMPLE:

   The report covers Tables 19-35.

   c. *Prefixes:* When a prefix is added to a word, the word may be written as a single word or as a hyphenated word. Preferred usage calls for words with prefixes to be spelled as single words without hyphens whenever possible. Typically, if a prefix is a word (e.g., *self*), a word with that prefix will be hyphenated.

   EXAMPLES:

   preemployment   nondiscriminatory
   (The prefixes pre and non are not words; therefore, preemployment and nondiscriminatory are not hyphenated.)

   self-imposed   self-addressed
   (The prefix self is a word by itself; therefore, anytime self is used as a prefix, it must be hyphenated.)

   d. *Word division:* The hyphen is used to indicate the division of a word at the end of a typed or printed line. Correct hyphenation rules must be followed in dividing words (see Section F in this chapter).

   EXAMPLE:

   When you are keying in a rather lengthy manu-script, rules for hyphenation must be followed.

   e. *Suspended hyphen:* In a series of hyphenated words having the same ending, the hyphen is retained with all the hyphenated words. One space follows each suspended hyphen.

   EXAMPLE:

   Either the blue- or green-colored chairs will match the décor of the new office.

   Note: A hyphen is typed with no spaces before or after it except if used as a dash or suspended hyphen or in word division.

8. *Parentheses:* **Parentheses** ( ) are used to enclose words or phrases that are needed for clarification but need to be deemphasized.

   a. *Enumerated items:* Enclose the number or letter in parentheses when the enumerations are continued in the same paragraph.

   EXAMPLE:

   The CPS® Examination will have three parts: (1) Management and Accounting, (2) Office Systems and Technology, and (3) Office Administration.

   b. *Instead of comma or dash:* If you wish to deemphasize an expression that is not necessary to the meaning or completeness of a sentence, you may use parentheses instead of a comma or dash to set it off from the rest of the sentence. The use of parentheses "quiets" the words included within the parentheses.

   EXAMPLE:

   The company picnic (scheduled for August 15) will be held at Tinley Park.

   c. *References:* When references to tables, pages, diagrams, or other similar materials are made for further clarification, these references are placed in parentheses.

   EXAMPLE:

   The section on buying stocks (pages 35–42) is very helpful.

   d. *Around a complete sentence:* If a complete sentence is placed in parentheses, the sentence begins with the left parenthesis and a capital letter and the ending punctuation mark would fall inside the right parenthesis.

   EXAMPLE:

   Dr. Carmichael's presentation on electronic records systems lasted over an hour. (However, the time was well spent!) After the presentation, time was allotted for a short question-and-answer session (requested by the audience).

   Note: Punctuation following a parenthesis within a sentence goes outside the parenthesis, and the first word within the parentheses is not capitalized.

9. *Period:* A **period** is a very commonly used mark of punctuation. Here is a review of the major ways in which the period is used in writing.

   a. *Ends of sentences:* A period marks the end of a complete declarative sentence. The period is typically followed by one or two spaces in business writing.

   EXAMPLE:

   I plan to attend the IAAP seminar on the office of the future. Reservations must be made by October 15.

   b. *Polite request:* Use a period to mark the end of a question that is a polite or courteous request. This type of question implies that the reader will be able to fulfill the request by performing some specific action.

   EXAMPLES:

   Will you please attend the meeting for me next week.

   Will you review the enclosed material and let me know your reaction by next Wednesday.

c. *Abbreviations:* Periods are to be used with personal and professional abbreviations, academic abbreviations, and seniority abbreviations. The ending period is followed by one space unless it ends a sentence; then there are two spaces. No space appears after a period within an abbreviation.

EXAMPLES:

Ms. Lee   Dr. Ross   Mr. Austen

Ph.D.   B.A.   D.D.S.

Frank Johnson, Jr. was present for the meeting.

d. *Numbers:* Use a period to denote the decimal point when designating amounts of money or fractions. Omit the decimal and two ciphers after even-money amounts. In a decimal fraction, the figures are considered as one number. Therefore, no space follows the period.

EXAMPLES:

We still owe a balance of $1,537.75 for our personal computer, which amounts to 48.5 percent of the total bill.

You gave a $50 donation this year, but you gave $80.50 last year.

e. *Enumeration:* A period follows each number or letter of an enumeration that is listed. The periods are to be aligned, and two spaces follow the period.

EXAMPLE: *Please include the following administrators on the invitation list:*

1. Mr. George White, Board of Directors
2. Ms. Martha Phiffel, Second Vice President
3. Ms. Kathy McDoughel, Director of Human Resources

The numbering feature in word processing may be activated to create a list of items or names. Once the numbering sequence has been selected, the numbers will increment to the next one each time Enter is depressed. An item that carries to the second line will be aligned under the first word in the first line. The space between the number and the first word depends on the tab set by the user. A ½-inch tab would leave three to four spaces between the number and the first word in the item.

f. *Outline:* A period may follow each letter or number used to introduce each item in an outline, depending on the style format chosen. The periods are to be aligned, and two spaces follow the period.

EXAMPLE:

I. Business Letters
   A. Styles
      1. Block Style
      2. Modified Block Style
      3. Simplified Style
   B. Format
      1. Margins
      2. Spacing
II. Memoranda

The automatic outlining format can be activated with tabs every ½ inch. In this example, an Enter after the first line would bring up II. A tab would change II to A, and the word *Styles* can be inserted. Another Enter and a tab would move the cursor to 1 on the next line for fill in, and so on.

g. *Paragraph headings:* When you use a paragraph heading, it is followed by a period and a dash or two spaces. The heading is always underlined. However, the heading should not be in italics.

EXAMPLE:

February usage. *The executive dining room was scheduled eight times during February for luncheon meetings.*

February usage.—*The executive dining room was scheduled eight times during February for luncheon meetings.*

10. *Question Mark:* A **question mark** is used at the end of a sentence that asks a direct question. The question mark is followed by two spaces.

EXAMPLE:

Will Julie Bennington be sitting for the CAP® Exam in May or November? If so, which testing site does she prefer?

11. *Quotation Mark:* **Quotation marks** ("") are used with direct quotations, titles, and single letters.

a. *Direct quotations:* Quotation marks are placed around the exact words that were spoken or written.

EXAMPLES:

Carlson said, "Since I did not get the promotion, I am going to resign."

Your advertisement must include the following: "Warning! Use of this product may be hazardous to your health."

b. *Titles:* Quotation marks are used to enclose chapters of books and titles of articles, lectures, or reports.

EXAMPLE:

My lecture, "Today's Electronic Office," is going to be published in OfficePro *as "The Electronic Office of the Future Is Here Today."*

c. *Single letters:* When reference is made to a single alphabetic letter, that letter may be placed in quotation marks for ease of reading.

EXAMPLE:

You only need to add an "s" to form the plural of all numbers.

Note: Periods and commas are the only punctuation marks that always go inside the closing quotation mark. The question mark, exclamation point, and closing parenthesis go inside the closing quotation mark only when they are part of the quotation. Semicolons and colons always go outside the closing quotation mark. If quoted material comes at the end of a sentence, the punctuation mark that ends the quotation is also used to end the sentence. This is true even when the punctuation mark for the end-of-quotation sentence and the end of the sentence are not the same.

EXAMPLE: *Did Carlson really say, "Since I did not get the promotion, I am going to resign"?*

12. *Semicolon:* The **semicolon** is used to separate compound sentences or a series within a series.

   a. *Compound sentences:* When a sentence consists of two complete sentences with no conjunction between the sentences, a semicolon is used to separate the sentences. (See Section B-3-c for use of a comma with a conjunction.)

   EXAMPLE:

   Our administrative professional attended a business writing seminar last month; however, she was away for only two days.

   Note: When punctuation is required within either of the sentences, follow correct punctuation rules. The conjunctive adverb *however* is an introductory word in the second sentence; therefore, it is followed by a comma.

   b. *Series:* When a series contains a series, semicolons are used to separate the main series and commas are used for the inner series.

   EXAMPLE:

   The fall order includes women's slacks, skirts, blouses, and sweaters; men's slacks, shirts, and sweaters; and children's pants, T-shirts, and sweaters.

13. *Underscore:* The **underscore** is used for underlining titles, specific words, paragraph headings, or single letters. An alternate method is to use italics in place of the underscore.

   a. *Titles:* In the body of text, titles of publications such as books, periodicals, magazines, newspapers, and movies are underscored or italicized, but not both.

   EXAMPLE:

   The president is an avid reader of the <u>Wall Street Journal</u>, <u>Money</u>, and the <u>Chicago Tribune</u>.

   The president is an avid reader of the *Wall Street Journal, Money,* and the *Chicago Tribune.*

   b. *Specific words:* An underscore may be used to emphasize a word, phrase, clause, or sentence. However, for the underscore to have any effect, be selective with its use.

   EXAMPLE:

   The <u>main</u> reason for wanting an upgrade on the word processing software in our office is because we exchange many of our documents with consultants who are using a more current version.

   c. *Paragraph headings:* All paragraph headings are to be underscored so they stand out from the balance of the material in the paragraph. Other headings (centered and side headings) may or may not be underscored.

   Note: The alternative use of italics is not used for paragraph headings.

   d. *Single letters:* When reference is made to a single letter within the alphabet, that letter may be underscored for ease in reading.

   EXAMPLE:

   You only need to add an <u>s</u> to form the plural of all numbers.

Check Point—Section B

Directions: For each question, choose the correct answer.

B–1. Which sentence is written and punctuated correctly?

A) Harris' order only included hanging folders, bond paper, and mailing labels.

B) Since the meeting begins at two, meet me at 1:30 pm to review the agenda.

C) The desk should be at least 2½' by 5'.

D) This local womens' organization meets the first Thursday evening of every month at 7:30 pm.

B–2. Which one of the following sentences is punctuated correctly?

A) Dr. Jones is pleased with the conference. (She called from Boston.)

B) Mr. Paris article *Management for the 21ˢᵗ Century* covers the importance of the administrative professional.

C) We need to finish these projects today; minutes of yesterdays board meeting, monthly stock report, the presentation for Mark's retirement dinner, and the Jagger Yancy report.

D) The next conference is in California. I need plane reservations because its a fast convenient way for me to travel.

B–3. Which one of the following correctly illustrates a paragraph heading?

A) Multiple selection criteria—Logical operators know that different criteria are used in making software decisions.

B) <u>Multiple selection criteria</u>—Logical operators know that different criteria are used in making software decisions.

C) Multiple selection criteria. Logical operators know that different criteria are used in making software decisions.

D) <u>Multiple selection criteria.</u>—Logical operators know that different criteria are used in making software decisions.

C. Capitalization

Proper capitalization is like having good manners. Improper capitalization makes a written document appear sloppy and difficult to read.

Note: An explanation of all capitalization possibilities is impossible in a review manual such as this. Therefore, only the most frequent use of capital letters will be covered in this section.

1. ***Beginning a Sentence:*** Capitalize the beginning of every sentence or expression that ends with a punctuation mark (period, question mark, or exclamation point).

EXAMPLE:

When is the meeting? Originally, it was scheduled for 9 A.M. tomorrow.

2. ***A Sentence Within Parentheses:*** When a complete sentence within parentheses stands by itself, the first word is capitalized. If, however, a sentence within parentheses is part of another sentence, it usually does not begin with a capital letter.

EXAMPLES:

A good synonym and antonym reference book is important to writers. (A popular reference book is <u>Roget's International Thesaurus</u>.*)*

The teacher requires several reference books (we need them for the next session).

3. ***Beginning a Quotation:*** The first word of a complete sentence from a direct quotation is to be capitalized.

    EXAMPLE:

    In the letter, Johanson wrote, "The stock will double within the year."

4. ***Pronoun I:*** The pronoun *I* is always capitalized to distinguish it as a word (a first-person pronoun) by itself.

    EXAMPLE:

    Judge Rand and I will take care of the banquet arrangements.

5. ***Titles of People:*** When a title is used as part of a person's name, it should be capitalized. This is also true for names of family relationships unless preceded by a possessive or used as a common noun. When any title is a descriptive word, it is not capitalized.

    EXAMPLES:

Part of the Name	Descriptive Word
Judge Matthews	*She is the new judge.*
Dr. Andrews	*Your doctor called.*
The President vetoed the bill. (U.S. president)	*The president resigned.* (a company president)
I called Mother.	*She is a grandmother.*

6. ***Books and Articles:*** The first word, nouns, pronouns, verbs, adjectives, adverbs, and prepositions of more than five letters are capitalized in titles of books, magazines, or newspaper articles.

    EXAMPLES:

    Title of Book: <u>Molloy's Live for Success</u>
    (for = preposition = not capitalized)

    Title of Book: <u>The World Is Made of Glass</u>
    (of = preposition = not capitalized)
    (Is = verb = capitalized)

    Title of Newspaper Article: "Communication—An Important Link Between Administrative Professionals and Executives"
    (An = article = first word of phrase capitalized)
    (and = conjunction = not capitalized)

7. ***Academic Courses:*** Specific high school or college course titles are capitalized; general subjects are not capitalized unless they are languages.

EXAMPLES:

Business Letter Writing	*communication*
Administrative Systems	*management*
Human Relations 101	*psychology*
Conversational Spanish	*language*
English	*literature*

8. ***Geographic Locations:*** Specific geographic locations and directions used to identify geographic areas are capitalized. When used to indicate direction, the word is not capitalized.

EXAMPLES:

Minnesota	*the Midwest*	*west of the Mississippi*
Savannah	*a Southerner*	*a southern custom*
Indonesia	*the Far East*	*in east China*

9. ***Organizations:*** Names (and abbreviations) of social organizations, business organizations, and clubs are capitalized. When the words *senior, junior, sophomore,* and *freshman* refer to organized groups or functions, they are capitalized. Articles *(a, an, the)* or prepositions *(of, for)* within the name are not capitalized.

EXAMPLES:

International Association of Administrative Professionals™ (IAAP)

League of Women Voters

American Management Association (AMA)

Junior Prom

Sophomore Bleacher Bums

10. ***Institutions:*** Specific names of public and private institutions are capitalized. When general reference is made to a whole class of institutions, the name is not capitalized.

EXAMPLES:

Gifford High School	*our high school*
Green Public Library	*the public library*
Daily Medical Clinic	*the medical clinic*

11. ***Groups:*** Names of national, political, religious, or ethnic groups are capitalized. Names of social and economic groups are not capitalized.

EXAMPLES:

English	*Finnish*	*Russian*
Democrat	*Republican*	*Independent*
Lutheran	*Jewish*	*Catholic*
Caucasian	*Asian*	*Native American*
upper class	*teenagers*	*senior citizens*

12. ***Departments in Organizations:*** Names of specific departments within your own organization are capitalized. Departments within other organizations are not capitalized unless the specific name of the department is being used.

EXAMPLES:

> *The interviews are being conducted in our Human Resource Department.*
>
> *Motorola's personnel department will be conducting all of the interviews on site.*

13. ***Objects:*** Names of specific objects (brand names, structures, documents, trade names, artifacts) are capitalized. Words that relate to general categories of objects are not capitalized.

EXAMPLES:

> *Kodak film* (only the brand name is capitalized)
>
> *Jefferson Memorial* (specific name of structure is capitalized)
>
> *Declaration of Independence* (specific name of document is capitalized, except for preposition *of*)
>
> *Halley's comet* (only the specific name of the comet is capitalized)

14. ***Elements of Time:*** Capitalize words designating specific months, days, holidays, events, and historic periods. Names of seasons are not capitalized.

EXAMPLES:

June	*Monday*	*December*	*fall semester*
Memorial Day	*Veterans Day*	*World War II*	*winter storm*
Halloween	*the Renaissance*	*the Stone Age*	*spring flowers*

Check Point—Section C

Directions: For each question, circle the correct answer.

C–1. Which one of the following sentences shows correct capitalization of words?

A) Carlotta is taking a course in management information systems from a University in West Texas.

B) The League of Women Voters is holding an open forum at the Newburg Public Library to discuss the state mandates with Senator Lewis.

C) The Mayor has an editorial about last week's article, "City services will be cut."

D) One hundred fifty Senior Citizens attended the first meeting on Wednesday, the 6th of June.

C–2. Which one of the following sentences applies correct capitalization rules?

A) Ramirez teaches an undergraduate Human Resources class this semester in the College of Business.

B) The President of the local chapter, Denise McDonald, will attend the international convention as a Delegate next August.

C) We need some samples of Kleenex tissue, Avery labels, and Pentel mechanical pencils as favors for the seminar next Monday.

D) The committee is submitting a formal Proposal to the International Board of Directors for the 200X international convention.

C–3. Which one of the following sentences correctly applies capitalization rules?

A) Our office will be closed on the following days to commemorate past events: the 4th of July, Columbus day, veterans day, Thanksgiving, and Christmas.

B) Our marketing director will be traveling to the Far East next month to promote the development of our latest product.

C) The U. S. Golf Association is promoting the inclusion of native Americans, african Americans, and Japanese-Americans in the major tournaments each year.

D) The book I enjoyed reading this Summer was <u>East Of Eden</u> by John Steinbeck.

D. Spelling

Executives expect administrative professionals to have good basic spelling skills to complement their facility with the English language.

Spelling words in the English language would be easier if a single letter or a combination of letters represented each sound. An administrative professional with good spelling skills is more efficient. Absolute correctness in spelling is not easy to achieve. However, most errors can be avoided if time and effort are spent:

- Memorizing the spelling of difficult words
- Using the software spell check tool, a standard dictionary, a specialty dictionary, or a word book when in doubt
- Proofreading carefully what has been written and keyed
- Reviewing spelling rules like those that follow

1. **Vowel Combinations ie and ei:** The grammar school rhyme is most helpful with this rule: "*i* before *e* except after *c*, or when sounded like *a*, as in *neighbor* and *weigh*."

EXAMPLES:

> *freight   receive   achieve   lien*

Exceptions to be memorized:

> *counterfeit   either   foreign   leisure   neither   weird*

2. **Ending ie:** When a word ends in *ie*, it is changed to *y* before the suffix *ing*.

EXAMPLES:

> *die   dying   lie   lying*

3. **Silent e Ending:** When a word ends in a silent *e,* drop the *e* before a suffix beginning with a vowel. The *e* is retained before a suffix beginning with a consonant except when the *e* is immediately preceded by another vowel other than an *e*.

EXAMPLES:

> *conceive   conceivable   achieve   achievement*
> *true   truly   imagine   imaginary*
> *definite   definitely   nine   ninth*

Exceptions: (retention of *e* before a vowel because of pronunciation)

> *changeable   noticeable   outrageous   vengeance*

4. **Silent e with Compounds:** Silent *e* is retained with compounds whether or not the second word begins with a vowel or a consonant.

EXAMPLES:

> *hereafter   household   heretofore*

5. **Word Ending ee:** When a word ends in *ee*, both *e*'s are retained when adding a suffix except when the suffix begins with an *e*. To form the plural of the word, add only an *s*.

EXAMPLES:

> *agree   agreeable   free   freed*
> *lessee   lessees   employee   employees*

6. **Word Endings cle and cal:** Words ending in *cle* are nouns; words ending in *cal* are adjectives derived from other words ending in *ic*.

EXAMPLES:

> *article   icicle   logical   comical*

Exceptions: (words that are both nouns and adjectives)

> *chemical   periodical   radical*

7. **Sounds ph, gh, ch, and i:** In many words, the *gh* and *ph* sound like *f*; the *ch* sounds like *k*; the *i* sounds like *y*.

EXAMPLES:

> *enough   physician   architect   companion*
> *laugh   multigraph   scheme   familiar*

8. **Endings cede, ceed, and sede:** There is no rule for verbs with any of these endings; the words just need to be memorized.

EXAMPLES:

> *accede   precede   exceed   supersede*
> *concede   recede   proceed   secede*
> *receded   intercede   succeed   superseded*

9. **y Ending Preceded by a Vowel:** When a word ends in *y* and is preceded by a vowel, the *y* is generally retained when adding a suffix. To form the plural of the word, add only an *s*.

EXAMPLES:

> *convey   conveyance   conveys*
> *display   displayed   displays*

turkey   turkeys
pulley   pulleys

10. **y *Ending Preceded by a Consonant:*** When a word ends in *y* and is preceded by a consonant, the *y* is generally changed to *i* when adding a suffix except when the suffix begins with *i*. To form the plural of the word, change the *y* to *i* and add *es*.

EXAMPLES:

rely	*relied*	*relying*	*relies*
liquefy	*liquefied*	*liquefying*	*liquefies*
remedy	*remedied*	*remedies*	
dictionary	*dictionaries*		

11. ***The Suffix* ful:** The suffix *ful* is spelled with only one *l*. The *l* does not double when adding another suffix except for the suffix *ly*. To form the plural of the word, add only an *s*.

EXAMPLES:

powerful	*helpful*	*cheerful*	*handful*
powerfully	*helpfully*	*cheerfully*	*handfuls*

12. ***Doubling the Ending Consonant:*** The ending consonant is doubled before adding a suffix in the following situations:

- The suffix begins with a vowel.
- The final consonant is preceded by a single vowel.
- The word is accented on the last syllable.

EXAMPLES:

gripping   pinned   controllable   occurrence

13. ***Compound Words:*** A compound word consists of two or more words that are written as one word, written as separate words, or hyphenated. There is no rule for the use of the hyphen; the decision is based on common usage. However, phrases used as adjectives are typically hyphenated before a noun.

EXAMPLES:

Closed (one word): *toastmaster   workbench*
Open (separate words): *attorney general*
Hyphenated: *public-spirited   one-half   hard-hat*

Check Point—Section D

Directions: For each question, circle the correct answer.

D–1.   From the following statements, select the one that includes correct spelling:

A)   The reciever of the communication is the individual who must decode the message that is sent.

B) When the bank teller examined the bill, she noticed an unusual mark that could make it counterfiet.

C) American companies are beginning to value the involvement of foriegn organizations in the marketing process.

D) Once the down payment has been processed and the papers signed, a lien will be placed upon the vehicle.

D–2. Select the statement that applies correct spelling techniques:

A) Immediately proceeding the seminar, Johansen will pass out the lesson booklet to members of the audience.

B) Preceding through the set of procedures in the manual, Johansen noticed space for an illustration on page 56.

C) The set of procedures handed out at the meeting this morning will supercede the ones that were already in the manual.

D) A good manager will try to intercede whenever a conflict needs to be resolved quickly.

D–3. In which one of the following statements are compound words correctly written?

A) One of the benefits of belonging to our group is the opportunity to meet well-known celebrities.

B) The toast master for the evening will be Joseph William Bryant, a recent graduate of the Longfellow Institute.

C) The cry from public spirited Americans has been the need for more attention to "the Basics."

D) Over all, the organization wide changes we are trying to implement will probably require a minimum of six months.

E. Number Usage

Numbers appearing within documents require you to follow rules of consistency throughout the document. The following guidelines should be helpful in deciding exactly how numbers should be written in business documents.

1. ***Numbers One Through Ten:*** The numbers from one through ten are usually spelled out; numbers above ten should be in figures.

EXAMPLES:

We ordered ten cases of yarn; however, only four were shipped.

Please send us 35 copies of your latest bulletin on health care.

2. ***Specific Numbers Ten and Under:*** Even though the number is ten or under, the following specific types of numbers should be written in figures: measurements, temperature readings, dimensions, election returns, market quotations, chemical terms, scores, and percentages.

EXAMPLES:

The temperature today is only 5 degrees.

The Rebels won the soccer game with a score of 5 to 2.

The room was 8 feet by 12 feet.

3. ***Sets of Numbers in a Sentence:*** Be consistent when several sets of numbers are included within the same sentence. Use figures for all numbers.

EXAMPLE:

In our firm there are 9 exempt employees and 28 nonexempt employees.

4. ***Money:*** Sums of money are expressed as figures.

EXAMPLES:

Correct	***Incorrect***
$5.41	*$5.41¢*
92 cents	*92¢ (unless used in material that contains many price quotations)*
	$0.92 (unless in a table with other dollars-and-cents figures)
$25	*25$*
	25 dollars
	$25.00

5. ***Percentages:*** Express percentages in figures followed by the word *percent*. Once you choose a spelling, be consistent throughout the document. If the percentage is used in technical material, the percent symbol (%) can be used.

EXAMPLE:

This group of merchandise will have a 35 percent markup.

EXAMPLE — Technical Material:

The federal government requires that this food product contain 95% natural ingredients; our product is 96.3% natural.

6. ***Mixed Numbers:*** Express mixed numbers (whole numbers and fractions) in figures with a space between the whole number and the fraction. Key in the fraction with a number, a slash, and another number (no spaces). If the only fractions within the document are symbols included in the word processing software you are using, these fractions may be used. In other words, be consistent with the format.

EXAMPLES:

The board should be 28¼ inches by 3⅜ inches by 1½ inches.
(All of these fractions are software generated: ¼ and ½ automatically appear when the characters are keyed in; ⅜ is a special symbol that must be inserted.)

The frame measures 5⅝ by 3¼ inches.
(The fraction ⅝ is not software generated; therefore, the same style must be used for both fractions even though ¼ can be software generated.)

Note: Creating fractions with word processing software programs may require you to override an automatic feature that automatically changes a fraction keyed in as 51/4 to 5¼. If all the fractions you are using are available in the software-generated symbols included in the software, you will not need to override the feature. Be consistent with the style you are using for all fractions.

7. ***Beginning Sentence with Number:*** When a sentence begins with a number, write the number as a word(s) or rearrange the sentence.

EXAMPLES:

> *Seventy of the administrative professionals belonging to the local chapter are going to the convention.*
>
> *The convention will be attended by 70 administrative professionals belonging to the local chapter.*

8. ***Hyphens in Numbers:*** Use hyphens in numbers between 21 and 99 when the numbers are written in words.

EXAMPLES:

> *twenty-one*
>
> *three hundred seventy-eight*

9. ***Two Numbers for One Item:*** If two numbers describe one item, express the smaller number as a word. Where this is impractical, separate the two numbers with a comma.

EXAMPLES:

> *We just purchased 30 twenty-cent stamps.*
>
> *In 2003, 5,654,098 packages were delivered by our company.*

10. ***Dates:*** The day and year in a date are expressed as figures unless used in rigidly formal writing such as an invitation or announcement. The day is written without a suffix such as *st, nd,* or *th* unless the day is written before the month (the 12th of July).

EXAMPLES:

> *The open house is Wednesday, June 19.*
>
> *The 19th of June would be a good date for the open house.*

11. ***Time:*** Time is written in figures unless used with the word *o'clock*. Variations for keying A.M. and P.M. are a.m., A.M., am, and AM; p.m., P.M., pm, and PM. For clarity, the more frequent use is with periods. Otherwise, am and AM could be mistaken for the word *am*. Be consistent with your format, and key A.M. and P.M. the same way. Do not use the two ciphers with the even hour.

EXAMPLES:

> *The meeting will begin at ten o'clock in the morning.*
>
> *The meeting will begin at 10 A.M.*
>
> *The time set aside for the meeting is 2 to 3:30 P.M.*

12. ***Grouping of Numbers:*** No commas should be used in large serial numbers, policy numbers, page numbers, or telephone numbers. It is permissible, and often desirable for clear reading, to insert spaces within large serial numbers or policy numbers. The number is usually clustered in groups of three or four digits. However, when copying a number, key in the number exactly as the originator keyed it. Area codes for telephone numbers are placed within parentheses, and the phone number is entered with a hyphen.

EXAMPLES:

Our insurance policy is No. 378 9605 789.

The telephone of the branch office is (815) 399-5678.

Assign the new job number 38976.

13. ***Expressing Large Numbers:*** A number in the millions or billions is typed as a combination of the figure and word. If a number in the thousands must be written out, write it in hundreds (a shorter form) rather than thousands.

EXAMPLES:

Our goal is 10 million orders for this fiscal year.

Sixteen hundred orders have already been placed.

14. ***Spelling Out Other Forms of Numbers:*** Spell out numbers when they appear as *first, second, third,* and so on.

EXAMPLES:

This is our third notice. Please call if there is a problem.

The best week for our vacation is the second week of August.

15. ***Numbers in Legal Documents:*** In legal documents, money is expressed in both words and figures.

EXAMPLES:

The defendant agrees to pay the sum of four hundred fifty dollars ($450) for services rendered.

16. ***Descriptive Numbers:*** Express numbers that follow such words as *chapter, volume, no., page, floor,* or *apartment* in figures. The word *number* is not used.

EXAMPLES:

Chapter 2 begins on page 56.

I moved to apartment 8 at the beginning of September.

17. ***Age:*** Age is expressed as a word unless days and months are given.

EXAMPLES:

Thomas is two years old.

Thomas is 2 years, 3 months, and 15 days old.

Aunt Mathilda will be eighty-five on her next birthday.

18. ***Street Names:*** A street name should appear the same as the way the city identifies the address or as it appears on the company letterhead.

EXAMPLES:

Harrison Interiors in Rockford, Illinois, is located on Sixth Street.

Ada International is located on 5th Avenue in Des Moines, Iowa.

19. ***Plurals of Numbers:*** Express the plural of figures by adding an apostrophe and an *s*, or just adding an *s* is sufficient. Generally, the apostrophe is used. Once you choose a style, be consistent throughout the document.

EXAMPLES:

7's or 7s   35's or 35s

Check Point—Section E

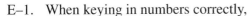

Directions: For each question, circle the correct answer.

E–1. When keying in numbers correctly,
   A) always use the fraction symbol when available; key in other fractions by using the slash
   B) use figures for all numbers when several sets of numbers are within the same sentence
   C) express a percentage as: 23%
   D) use figures for numbers under 10

E–2. Proofread the following sentences for correct number usage. Which one is correct?
   A) Twenty-five members attended the 4th of July picnic.
   B) We were surprised when the part cost only 75¢.
   C) When Grandpa was 69, he started writing chapter one of his memoirs.
   D) 1,500 patients received the vaccination today!

E–3. Proofread the following sentences for correct number usage. Which one is correct?
   A) The meeting is scheduled for June 5th at 2:00 P.M.
   B) The 1st letter referred to policy number 378,469,201.
   C) Their new address is Suite 3, 465 East Sixth Avenue, Eau Claire, WI 54701-1732.
   D) There should be 30 5-pound boxes of candy.

F. Word Division and Hyphenation

In word processing, the use of word wrap often negates the need for hyphenating words at the right margin. In some cases, words that extend beyond the right margin may be divided in order for the right margin to be somewhat even. The most desirable point for dividing a word is sometimes a matter of opinion. Basing word division on principles of pronunciation and spelling saves much time and effort.

You can develop a "feeling" for correct syllabication through careful observation and study of word pronunciation and spelling as well as through reference to a word book or dictionary. The following general suggestions were developed from word processing and business protocol.

1. ***Hyphenation with Word Processing Software:*** The purpose of hyphenation is to divide a word that is too long to fit within the right margin of the text. Ideally, a hyphenated word would keep the ragged right margin fairly even. Word processing software allows an entire word to wrap (or automatically be moved) to the next line whenever that word extends beyond the right margin or the word to be automatically hyphenated. If the hyphenation feature in the word processing software is activated, a long word can be divided between two lines. The hyphenation feature is programmed for automatic or manual functioning.

   a. *Automatic hyphenation feature:* When activated, the automatic hyphenation feature divides and hyphenates a long word according to the rules established within the word processing software program. The word processing hyphenations may or may not be consistent with the rules for word division as accepted by many business professionals. Therefore, it may be necessary to sometimes override the automatic hyphenation decision.

   b. *Manual hyphenation feature:* Manual hyphenation permits the administrative professional or user to decide where a hyphen should be inserted in a word. The manual function provides the user with the flexibility to follow accepted rules for word division. However, this process can take more of the user's time, particularly with lengthy documents.

c. *No hyphenation:* Word wrap is the word processing term used to indicate that a word that is too long to appear before the right margin will be moved to the beginning of the next line. A ragged right margin is preferred for business writing so the spacing between words remains uniform and consistent.

2. ***General Suggestions for Word Division:*** The following suggestions provide helpful cues in making word-division decisions.

a. Divide a word only when it is absolutely necessary.

b. When a word must be divided, it is best to have enough of the word on the first line to be able to conceptualize the entire word and to carry enough of the word to the next line to balance the division somewhat equally on both lines.

c. Avoid dividing a word at the end of the first line of a paragraph. The last word in the paragraph should *never* be divided.

d. The last word on a page should never be divided. Key in the complete word on the page where you achieve the best balance between the two lines of print.

e. Avoid dividing words at the end of more than two consecutive lines.

f. If you can possibly avoid it, do not divide a proper name. The pronunciation of a proper name is not always revealed by the spelling; there may be some doubt as to the correct syllabic division.

3. ***Word Division Rules:*** Specific rules for word division are helpful in making appropriate decisions in hyphenating words and checking the accuracy of automatic hyphenation. In the following examples, the period (.) identifies syllables where it is not advisable to divide a word, and the hyphen (-) identifies syllables where it is acceptable to have a word division.

a. Only divide words between syllables. Therefore, one-syllable words cannot be divided.

EXAMPLES:

One-syllable Words:

    cream   sound   king   milk

Correct Word Division:

    for-ward   mo.ti-va.tion   care-ful.ly

b. Words of four or five letters should never be divided, and the division of six-letter words should be avoided. A divided syllable should have three or more characters in the division.

EXAMPLES:

    a.lone   a.part-ment   co.her-ence
    vouch.er   caf.e-te.ri.a

c. Hyphenated words are to be divided only at the hyphen.

EXAMPLES:

self-ad.dressed   self-en.closed

d. Compound words should be divided between the elements of the compound.

EXAMPLES:

busi.ness-peo.ple   grand-fa.ther

e. The addition of the past tense to a word does not necessarily add an extra syllable.

EXAMPLES:

guessed   missed   laughed

f. When a word containing three or more syllables is to be divided next to a one-letter syllable, the division should come after the one-letter syllable.

EXAMPLES:

crit.i-cism   sep.a-rate   af.fil.i-ate

g. When there is a double consonant within a word, the word may be divided between the consonants. The pronunciation of the word will help you determine whether it is proper to divide the word at this point; that is, you could divide a word with a double consonant sound (see also Examples under *h* and *i*).

EXAMPLES:

bel.lig-er-ent   strug-gling   vac-ci-nate

h. When a final consonant is doubled before a suffix, the additional consonant goes with the suffix (see also Examples *g* and *i*).

EXAMPLES:

be.gin-ning   de.fer-ring

i. When the double consonant is the ending of a root word, separate the suffix from the root word (see also Examples *g* and *h*).

EXAMPLES:

ad.dress-ing   a.gree-ing

j. Words ending in *able*, *ible*, *ical*, *cian*, *cion*, *sion*, *gion*, and *tion* should be divided between the stem of the word and the terminating syllables.

EXAMPLES:

a.gree-able	*con-ta-gion*	*sus-pi-cion*
cler-i.cal	*mu.si-cian*	*am.bi-tion*
de.duct-i.ble	*ap.pre-hen-sion*	

k. Some word endings are *ble* and *cal* instead of *able*, *ible*, or *ical*. In these cases, the *a* or *i* is considered part of the preceding syllable.

EXAMPLES:

cha.ri-ta-ble   au.di-ble   fan-tas-ti-cal

l. When a word is to be divided at a point where two one-letter syllables (vowels) occur together, the division should be made between the vowels.

EXAMPLES:

e.vac.u-a.tion   grad.u-a.tion

m. A syllable that does not contain a vowel must not be separated from the remainder of the word.

EXAMPLES:

did.n't   would.n't

n. A date can be divided only between the day and the year, not between the month and the day. In this case, no hyphen is needed; the date (year) is just continued on the next line.

EXAMPLES:

September 18,   NOT: September
200X   18, 200X

o. Do not divide a proper name if you can possibly avoid it. If, however, a complete name cannot be keyed on one line, separation of the parts of the name must be made at a logical reading point. A title should not be by itself on a line. A middle name should be included with the first name. When a name is separated between two lines, no hyphen is used.

EXAMPLES:

Ms. Carla M.
Johnson

NOT:

Ms.   or   Ms. Carla
Carla M. Johnson   M. Johnson

p. If it is not possible to include a street address on one line, the address should be separated at a logical reading point. There are many variations of a logical reading point; you must use your best judgment. The city, state abbreviation, and ZIP Code can be separated between the city and the state but not between the state and the ZIP Code. No hyphen is needed for this type of separation.

EXAMPLE:

Harrisonburg,   or   Harrisonburg,
Virginia   VA 22801

q. Do not divide figures, amounts of money, figures from an identifying term, or abbreviations. Avoid dividing Web addresses.

EXAMPLES:

Correct	*Incorrect*	
34576539	*3457-*	
	6539	
$50,000	*$50,-*	*$*
	000	*50,000*

page 45	page 45
11 inches	11 inches
AT&T	AT-&T
www.amazon.com	www.amazon.-com

If you need to divide a long Web address, enter a space at the end of a segment so that the reader will not sense that a space would be inserted.

EXAMPLE:

| www.amazon.com | www.amazon.∧ com | ∧ = space |

Familiarity with the basic rules for word division and the automatic hyphenation feature within word processing programs will guide the user to hyphenate words correctly when word division is necessary.

Check Point—Section F

Directions: For each question, circle the correct answer.

F–1. Which statement is correct with regard to hyphenation with word processing?

A) The automatic hyphenation feature prompts the user to determine whether the word should be hyphenated

B) The automatic hyphenation feature hyphenates the word according to hyphenation rules established within the word processing software

C) The manual hyphenation feature provides the least amount of flexibility in following hyphenation rules as accepted by most businesses

D) The word processing feature relieves the office professional from having to know business word division rules

F–2. When dividing a word,

A) it is best to have enough of the word on the first line to be able to conceptualize the entire word

B) make sure the pronunciation of a proper name is followed

C) the last word on a page should contain most of the letters so the word is easily conceptualized without having to turn the page

D) the last word on a page can be divided

F–3. Which word or phrase is divided correctly?

A) Mr. John R. David
B) page 105
C) should- n't
D) $132, 050

For Your Review

Directions: For each question, circle the correct response.

1. *The administrative professional has the responsibility of coordinating various office tasks.* The subject of this sentence is
   A) responsibility
   B) administrative
   C) coordinating
   D) professional

2. *To examine an inactive file requires Rogers to fill out a request form.* The subject of this sentence is
   A) Rogers
   B) To examine
   C) file
   D) form

3. Agreement in number between subject and verb means that the
   A) subject can be singular
   B) verb can be plural
   C) subject and verb must both be singular or both be plural
   D) subject can be plural and verb singular

4. The direct object of the verb completes the sentence by answering the question
   A) what
   B) to whom
   C) for whom
   D) where

5. Which one of the following sentences includes a predicate noun?
   A) As a result of the class action suit, Bryant is determined to appeal to a higher court.
   B) Rowan appears unhappy with the jury's verdict, too.
   C) Michaelson is a powerful advocate for the business entrepreneur.
   D) Conrad will probably be appointed to the position of chief executive officer when Williams retires.

6. In an independent clause, an adjective modifies
   A) a verb
   B) a noun or pronoun
   C) an adverb
   D) another adjective

7. *The purpose of well-written business writing is to express ideas clearly and concisely.* Identify the adverbs in this sentence.
   A) business, clearly, concisely
   B) writing, clearly
   C) well-written, clearly, concisely
   D) well, clearly, concisely

8. *You should be a few minutes early to work each day if you want time to greet co-workers.* In this sentence, the independent clause is
   A) if you want time
   B) if you want time to greet co-workers
   C) early to work each day
   D) you should be a few minutes early to work each day

9. *When McCue entered the office suite on Monday morning* is an example of a/an
   A) dependent clause
   B) prepositional phrase
   C) introductory phrase
   D) independent clause

10. Which one of the following phrases shows correct use of the apostrophe to show possession?
    A) a womens' organization
    B) Dr. Maxwells' diagnosis
    C) the administrative professionals' responsibilities
    D) a writers' block

11. Which one of the following shows time correctly written?
    A) three-fifteen P.M.
    B) 4:22 P.M.
    C) 5:27
    D) 35 minutes after 4 P.M.

12. Three items are included in a series within a sentence. A comma is
    A) required before the conjunction
    B) not the correct punctuation to use
    C) considered nonessential in this sentence
    D) optional before the conjunction

13. Which one of the following statements illustrates a compound sentence correctly punctuated?
    A) Madison was on time for the Monday staff meeting, she was a few minutes late for her afternoon appointment.
    B) Madison was on time for the Monday staff meeting, but was a few minutes late for her afternoon appointment.
    C) Madison was on time for the Monday staff meeting, but she was a few minutes late for her afternoon appointment.
    D) Madison was on time for the Monday staff meeting but she was a few minutes late for her afternoon appointment.

14. *The new administrator, Jayne O'Rourke, will report for her first day on December 10.* The words *Jayne O'Rourke* are called a/an
    A) appositive
    B) nonrestrictive clause
    C) parenthetic expression
    D) coordinate adjective

15. Which one of the following statements includes a nonrestrictive clause correctly punctuated?
    A) The communication approach, that makes the most positive impression, is the direct approach.
    B) The communication approach that makes the most positive impression is the direct approach.
    C) The communication approach, which is used the most often in persuasive letters, is the indirect approach.
    D) The person, who communicates the most positive impression, writes the most concise message.

16. A dash is used to separate groups of words and to
    A) show the omission of one or more words in a sentence
    B) punctuate the end of a sentence
    C) deemphasize the words enclosed
    D) emphasize one or more words

17. *A well-written business letter should create a positive impression when the receiver reads the message.* The words *well-written* are hyphenated because they
    A) are always hyphenated
    B) represent a word that is missing
    C) modify a noun as a compound adjective
    D) appear before an adjective

18. *in the far east, universities generally include english as an important part of the business administration curriculum.* Which words in this sentence should be capitalized?
    A) far, east, english

B) in, far, east, english
C) english, business, administration
D) east, english, business, administration

19. Which words in the following statement need to be capitalized: *items on the office supply list include kodak film, xerox paper, bic pens, and memorex compact discs.*

A) items, kodak, xerox, bic, memorex
B) kodak, film, xerox, paper, bic, pencils, memorex
C) items, film, paper, pens, compact, discs
D) kodak, xerox, bic, memorex

20. Which one of the following sentences has all words spelled correctly?

A) The artical will appear in the next addition of the *OfficePro* periodicle.
B) The conveyence of the real estate will depend on the remedys provided by law.
C) A courteous, helpfull customer service representative is one of an organization's greatest assets.
D) The receiver of a business message needs to at least acknowledge the message within a brief time.

21. Which one of the following sentences is written with all words spelled correctly?

A) Construction workers must be sure to wear hard-hat headgear for protection as they work.
B) The final occurence of the solar eclipse will take place next Thursday.
C) Jameson relyed on Garcia to revise the final draft of the report.
D) In the golf tournament, Bixby conseded the match to Murphy after she hit a ball into the water hazard.

22. *On the 31st day of March, 200X, interest of six percent earned on the investment of five thousand dollars was recorded as twenty-five dollars.* The numbers in this sentence should be written as

A) March 31, 200X; $5,000; $25.00
B) March 31, 200X; 6 percent; $5,000
C) March 31, 200X; 6 percent; $25
D) March 31, 200X; 6 percent; $5,000; $25

23. Which one of the following sentences containing numbers is written correctly?

A) For the mailing, Ripley purchased one hundred fifty 37-cent stamps.
B) Seventy-five administrative professionals attended the CPS seminar.
C) July 17th will be an excellent day for the company picnic.
D) The meeting of the ad hoc committee is scheduled for today from 3:00 to 4:15 P.M.

24. The term *word wrap* in word processing means that a word too long for the right margin will be

A) hyphenated according to the word processing program
B) kept on the first line
C) moved automatically to the next line
D) kept on the first line if it is a proper name

25. A Web address contained in a paragraph

A) cannot be divided anywhere
B) needs to remain on the first line
C) can be divided but is best moved to the second line
D) can be divided by entering a space at the end of a segment within the address

Solutions

Solutions to Check Point—Section A

Answer	Refer to:
A–1. A	[A-1-b and A-1-c]
A–2. C	[A-2-b (1)]
A–3. B	[A-2-c (2)]

Solutions to Check Point—Section B

Answer	Refer to:
B–1. A	[B-1-a (1), B-3-b and B-9]
B–2. A	[B-8-d, B-9-a and B-9-c]
B–3. D	[B-9-g and B-13-c]

Solutions to Check Point—Section C

Answer	Refer to:
C–1. B	[C-1, C-5, C-9 and C-10]
C–2. C	[C-1, C-13 and C-14]
C–3. B	[C-1 and C-8]

Solutions to Check Point—Section D

Answer	Refer to:
D–1. D	[D-1]
D–2. D	[D-8]
D–3. A	[D-13]

Solutions to Check Point—Section E

Answer	Refer to:
E–1. B	[E-3]
E–2. A	[E-7 and E-10]
E–3. C	[E-18]

Solutions to Check Point—Section F

Answer	Refer to:
F–1. B	[F-1-a]
F–2. A	[F-2-b]
F–3. A	[F-3-o]

Solutions to For Your Review

Answer	Refer to:
1. (D)	[A-1-a]
2. (B)	[A-1-a]
3. (C)	[A-1-b]
4. (A)	[A-1-c]
5. (C)	[A-1-d]
6. (B)	[A-2-a]

7.   (D)   [A-2-a]

8.   (D)   [A-2-b (1)]

9.   (A)   [A-2-b (2)]

10. (C)   [B-1-a (2)]

11. (B)   [B-2-b]

12. (D)   [B-3-b]

13. (C)   [B-3-c]

14. (A)   [B-3-f]

15. (B)   [B-3-g]

16. (D)   [B-4]

17. (C)   [B-7-a]

18. (B)   [C-1, C-7 and C-8]

19. (A)   [C-1 and C-13]

20. (D)   [D-1]

21. (A)   [D-13]

22. (D)   [E-4, E-5 and E-10]

23. (B)   [E-7]

24. (C)   [F-1-c]

25. (D)   [F-3-q]

Chapter 12
Business Etiquette

OVERVIEW

Today's workplace environment demands that office professionals be more aware of appropriate business etiquette to apply in specific types of situations. Such business and social events as the civil rights movement, the entry of women and minorities into the workplace, the globalization of the economy, and the passage of legislation like the Americans with Disabilities Act have greatly affected individual and organizational behaviors. Mastering business etiquette has become imperative.

The new reality is that every act that occurs in business has become more visible and telling. With downsizing and rightsizing initiatives that have taken place in many organizations, fewer layers of management have resulted in shorter lines of communication between top management (the decision makers) and employees at lower levels. With smaller support staffs, administrative professionals have to find new ways to outclass the competition.

Business etiquette has military origins, based on hierarchy and power. **Social etiquette** is rooted in chivalry—the concept that females must be protected. Men and women must now be treated as peers in the workplace. People of different ethnicities and backgrounds must be awarded opportunities to succeed in business. Business professionals with disabilities must be treated with the same respect accorded any other professional. The new Golden Rule is "treat others as you would like to be treated."

Being courteous and polite, and showing respect for others, results in positive first impressions and many times to long-lasting relationships. Experts say that most business professionals decide within the first four minutes they spend with someone whether or not to establish an ongoing relationship. Because we transmit and receive messages on both subliminal and conscious levels, body language and behaviors play a critical role in determining how others respond to us. We need to use business etiquette to advantage in all business relationships.

KEY TERMS

Business etiquette, 393
Developmental disability,
  411
Disability etiquette, 409

Disabled, 411
Gratuity, 405
Guest, 398
Host, 398

Networking, 396
Power meals, 404
Social etiquette, 393
Tab, 405

A. Conducting Business

Success in conducting business depends on a number of factors. Being professional is defined by the way one dresses as well as by the rapport that develops among superiors and co-workers.

1. ***Business Attire:*** The way you dress for business affects the impression you will make with business associates. Attire is classified as either business dress or casual dress. What does your company allow? Is there a dress-down policy—perhaps for a certain day of the week or time of year, such as Fridays during the summer months? Here are some suggestions for business attire that will assist in creating a more professional atmosphere.

   a. *Personal appearance:* Be concerned about maintaining a neat, clean, and professional appearance. Clothes that are wrinkled or unkempt may communicate carelessness about the work situation or the requirements of the job.

   b. *Conservative business attire:* Some organizations have conservative dress codes with men wearing suits and ties and women wearing suits and dresses. Uncertainty about a business situation may lead the administrative professional to be more conservative in dress and practice impeccable grooming. Overuse of cosmetics including strong colognes and perfumes is considered unprofessional.

   c. *Casual business attire:* A recent joint study by Levi Strauss & Co. and the Society for Human Resource Management indicates that 90 percent of office workers enjoy the opportunity to wear casual business attire for work. The word *casual* does not mean the way people dress on Saturdays. Men might wear a polo-style shirt with a sweater and khaki pants. For women, a turtleneck shirt with navy or khaki slacks would be appropriate. Sloppy, unclean, or suggestive clothes are off limits. Jeans or sneakers may not be appropriate.

   d. *Use of jewelry:* Tattoos on the body or piercings on the face or ears may interfere with your physical appearance when on the job. During the normal business day, covering tattoos and removing some earrings may help an employee be more professional in appearance. Wearing quality but conservative jewelry will meet with approval. Large rings worn on the right hand may interfere with a firm handshake when greeting people.

2. ***Introductions and Greetings:*** Business professionals need to know how to properly make introductions. Greeting business co-workers as well as visitors is extremely important and helps them "feel at home" in your organization. Nametags, worn on the right shoulder, make introductions easier.

   a. *Making introductions:* Few people know how to properly introduce others. When introducing yourself to someone, stand up, smile, walk toward the person, and extend your right hand for a handshake. A man does not have to wait for a woman to extend her hand first.

(1) *Introducing higher-ranking individuals:* A person of lesser importance, in terms of rank within the organization, is introduced to a higher-ranking individual. This applies whether the person of lesser importance is male or female.

(2) *Using courtesy titles and personal names:* The person to whom the introduction is made is mentioned first; the name of the person being introduced is mentioned last. When meeting a business associate for the first time, use a title and the last name until you are told to do otherwise. Using only first names may reflect a business style that is too casual.

EXAMPLE:

"Ms. Heath (with greater authority), I would like you to meet Mr. Kaszmer (with lesser authority)."

Note: When you are not sure if a woman is married, use the title "Ms." (pronounced "Miz"). If a woman does not want to be called by this title, she should tell you the courtesy title she prefers.

A client or visitor is more important than anyone in your organization and should be treated as a person of greater authority.

Using courtesy titles such as Dr., Ms., and Mr. with full names in making introductions enhances credibility and professional identity. After an introduction, respond with a greeting, such as:

"I'm happy to meet you, Ms. Heath," or
"I am so pleased to meet you, Mr. Kaszmer."

Sometimes you will only be given the individual's first name or a nickname. In this case, you simply use the first name or nickname. Depending on the situation, the use of nicknames is often encouraged.

(3) *Pronouncing difficult names:* If you are introduced to someone with a name that is unfamiliar to you and difficult to pronounce, ask politely how to correctly pronounce his or her name. "Jr." after a man's name indicates that he has the same name as his father. The Roman numeral III or IV after a man's name signifies that he is the third or fourth generation to have the same name as his predecessors. These titles are usually included in introductions.

EXAMPLES:

Martin Luther King, Jr.
Davis Love III

b. *Greetings:* An introduction is usually accompanied with a handshake. The accepted physical greeting is a firm but not overpowering handshake. In business, it does not matter whether a man or a woman offers to shake hands first. Usually, a handshake takes no longer than about three seconds. Nametags can be very helpful in addressing people you meet. When you shake hands, your eye follows the line of your arm to the other person's right side—where the nametag should be. Read the name as you shake hands.

3. ***Business Language:*** In many countries including the United States, business is generally conducted in the English language. Many Americans speak and write only English. Therefore, they may not be sensitive to the difficulties of bilingual individuals who try to use English for business purposes. Sometimes people speak too fast or loudly, which does not help other business associates to understand better.

American business language is also very idiomatic. International visitors may not easily understand sports terms such as *touch base, ballpark figures, team players,* and *game plan.* If language becomes a barrier for any of the participants, ask for a clearer explanation of the information being presented. Sometimes a translator needs to be available if participants have difficulty with English interpretation and meanings.

4. ***Business Networking:*** Business gatherings offer excellent opportunities to meet and talk with businesspeople with whom you have common interests. To give you the best opportunity for networking, prepare beforehand by learning more about the information that will be discussed as well as the individuals who will be at the meeting.

   Networking requires you to circulate among the participants, introduce yourself with a one-line description of your business, and learn something about each person you meet. A few minutes spent with each one provides the opportunity to become acquainted and perhaps exchange business cards. Information gathered by listening during networking functions may be invaluable in forming longer-lasting relationships.

5. ***Business Cards:*** As an important part of networking and communications within the corporate setting, business cards provide contact information about you—your name, title, company or organization, telephone and fax numbers, and e-mail address. A business card can be used as an attachment to a report or other document or enclosed with a gift sent to a business associate.

   a. *Presenting business cards to associates:* When you present your business card to a business associate, you are using the card to introduce yourself. The best time to personally deliver the card is at the end of a conversation. Present the card with the print side up so the other person can read it, and say something that connects the card with your specialization or work assignment. Here are a few suggestions for presenting a business card in a courteous, tactful manner.

      • Wait to present a business card to a senior executive until you are asked.

      • Do not give your business card to everyone if you are with a large group of people. Present your card only to people you want to contact later.

      • Carry a few business cards with you to social and business functions. If you are asked for one but do not have a card, apologize and write out the information on a piece of paper.

      • Business cards should not be passed during a meal function. If you are asked for one, you may pass one to the individual as discreetly as possible.

   Your business card will not be refused. The recipient may place it in a wallet or a pocket for convenience. In the United States, this is not meant to be a sign of disrespect, as it might be in some other cultures.

   b. *Receiving business cards from others:* Often an associate will present you with a business card in return. When you receive a business card, hold it in front of you for a moment, look at it, and then look at the face of the person who presents you the card. Later, you want to associate the name on the card with the face of the person you met.

   Typically, business cards are exchanged only if both you and the person you met want to be able to make contact later.

Check Point—Section A

Directions: For each question, circle the correct answer.

A–1. Which one of the following descriptions would be classified as business casual dress for a woman in an administrative position?

   A) A navy-blue suit with skirt and fashionable jewelry
   B) Dress shoes that are the same color as the suit and are polished to a gleaming shine
   C) Pressed slacks with a matching blouse and sweater
   D) Clean blue jeans with an attractive sweatshirt

A–2. Which one of the following greetings would be the most appropriate if you were introducing Dr. Ellen Johanson, a client, to Maria Delgado, an administrative professional in the office?

   A) "Ms. Delgado, I would like you to meet Dr. Ellen Johanson, the president of J-H Associates."
   B) "Ellen, I would like you to meet Maria, my administrative assistant."
   C) "Maria, I would like you to meet Ellen Johanson from J-H Associates."
   D) "Dr. Johanson, I would like you to meet Maria Delgado, my administrative assistant."

A–3. Business networking during a business conference or meeting provides an opportunity to

   A) learn something about each person you meet
   B) announce a major award that you have just won
   C) collect as many business cards as you can from the people in attendance
   D) act as a host for the event

B. Workplace Etiquette

The office environment (or climate) reflects the attitudes and feelings of the people who are employed there. You want to make the office environment a more pleasant place in which to work. Disrespectful, abrasive, and discourteous treatment of office professionals is passed along from the top. A recent study showed that 40 percent of new management hires fail in their first jobs because of their inability to build good relationships with peers and subordinates. Here are some pointers that enable administrative professionals to help create an office climate more conducive to teamwork and mutual respect.

1. *Greetings to Co-workers:* When you arrive at the office, smile and greet co-workers in passing. Come in a few minutes early so that you have time to talk and visit with people before the workday begins. Whether you are the president of an organization or an inventory clerk, you need to show respect and courtesy to everyone regardless of position. It is considered rude not to greet people when you enter the office—yours or someone else's. Using courtesy titles like Mr. or Ms. or first names depends on a company's culture. Using words like "Babe" or "Dear" in the office is unacceptable verbal behavior.

2. *Sharing Recognition:* When you have worked with others on collaborative or team projects, be ready to share recognition for the work accomplished. Never take credit yourself for something the team achieved—praise that you give for the work of others will be rewarding to you, too.

3. **Respecting Personal Space:** The work area assigned to an individual, whether it is a private office or a cubicle, is that person's private space during the workday. When you visit someone at his or her work area, you are the **guest**. When others visit you, you are the **host**.

    a. *As a guest:* When you visit someone at his or her work area, you need to respect that person's privacy. The following tips will help make a good impression.

- When entering the work area, never put your briefcase, documents, or handbag on someone else's desk; this demonstrates that you may be trying to take over that person's space.
- Make an appointment so that the host will reserve the time to meet with you. Stay within the time frame. If more time is needed, schedule another appointment.
- Be punctual in keeping your appointment. "Surprise" visits are not appropriate for conducting business.
- Do not make yourself more comfortable than the host.

    b. *As a host:* When another person visits you at your work area, your initial task is to greet the visitor and make him or her feel welcome and comfortable. Here are some tips to help you be an effective host.

- When the visitor arrives, meet the visitor yourself, shake hands, and escort him or her to your office.
- If you are busy when the visitor arrives, have a co-worker or an administrative assistant escort the guest to your office.
- When the visitor enters the office area, stand up and come around the desk to shake hands.
- Indicate where you would prefer the visitor to sit during the meeting.
- Lead the discussion during the visit.
- Bring the meeting to a close, and summarize what was covered and the action to be taken.
- Escort the visitor out of the office or to the elevator; for security reasons, never leave a visitor to find his or her own way.

    c. *As a co-worker:* Respect toward a co-worker can easily be shown through use of words like *please* and *thank you.* As you work closely with your co-workers and observe them working on various assignments, you can show courtesy and understanding by heeding some of the following tips:

- If a colleague is hard at work on an assignment, try not to break that person's concentration.
- Do not enter the closed office of a co-worker or superior. Your business may not be important enough to interrupt the other person.
- When you are conversing with a co-worker, use your body language to indicate to that person that it is time to return to work.
- If your work space is in a cubicle area, make it as personalized and neat as possible. Arrange pictures of family and pets, plants, and other personal decorations neatly; however, use some restraint.
- Enter another person's cubicle area or private office only after receiving permission.

- Even though you may hear others talking nearby, respect their privacy; do not interrupt or involve yourself in their discussion.

- In a modular office area, do not shout over the walls or call across the office.

- Avoid discussing such sensitive issues as religion, politics, health, dieting, or personal problems in the office.

4. ***Communication Etiquette:*** In business today, the majority of a worker's time is spent communicating—verbally and in writing. This section looks at the different ways in which administrative professionals communicate in business and appropriate etiquette that needs to be displayed in these types of situations.

a. *Telephone etiquette:* The telephone is used many times during the workday. Courtesy shown while answering the telephone or making telephone calls will be reflected in the impressions received by the person on the other end of the line.

- Identify yourself and your department or organization when answering a call. "Good afternoon, Marketing Division, Glenda Hilgenberg speaking."

- Rather than asking "Who's calling?" you should probably ask "May I tell Ms. Grant who is calling?"

- If you need to screen calls for another office professional, indicate that the person being called is not available at the moment and then ask for the caller's name and message. If it is a call that needs to be taken care of immediately, you can usually say something like "Oh, one moment please, here she comes now!"

- Use voice mail to screen callers, too, especially if you do not want to be interrupted. You can easily return calls that need responses as soon as you become available.

- When making a phone call, announce yourself at the beginning of your call: "Hello, this is Robert Watson from Triple-E Corporation. May I please speak to Christine Choi?"

- Use a speakerphone only when you need to continue the conversation while doing something directly related to that call or need to involve one or more people in your office. Always ask permission before you initiate use of the speakerphone. Use of a headset eliminates the possibility of eavesdroppers and still affords the use of your hands at a computer keyboard or to work with document pages that pertain to the telephone conversation.

- Return all telephone calls personally, or have someone else in your office return the call. Do so even if you are just acknowledging that you received the call but are not yet ready to respond with information.

- Enable a caller to easily leave a voice-mail message. Give the caller a few options such as leaving a message or calling another extension or the operator. Too many options or being placed on hold for long periods of time are usually annoying to the caller.

- When you are the caller, leave a voice-mail message that is brief, to the point, and complete so that the person called will find it easy to respond.

Telephone calls interrupt our workday. Know why you are calling before you place the call; quickly get to the point of your discussion. Wasting someone's time, especially on the telephone, is rude.

b. *Electronic communications:* Some forms of electronic communications can cause annoying or inconvenient circumstances when trying to communicate with others.

There is a need for more effective use of cellular phones, e-mail, fax, and other forms of electronic communications.

(1) *Cellular phone etiquette:* With more than 120 million cell phone users in the United States alone, etiquette practices for answering and making calls are needed. Many times a cell phone is considered a convenience, especially when you are running late for an appointment. At other times, a cell phone is a necessity—particularly for immediate contact with a business associate. However, a cell phone should not be viewed as a status symbol or a companion for loneliness. The following ideas stress the need for some control in the use of cell phones for business communication.

- When riding on public transportation, avoid loud, animated, or extended conversations. Keep the voice low and at a conversational level.
- To avoid disturbing others, the ringer should be set as low as possible or to vibrate instead of ring.
- Cell phone conversations are out of place at social events like concerts, plays, movies, or lectures or in public places like restaurants, theaters, medical offices, and emergency rooms.
- Cell phones should never be used or allowed to interrupt a business meeting.
- Never have any emotional cell phone conversations in public.
- People you are with should take priority over your responding to a cell phone call. A caller can leave a message that you can return later when it is more convenient for you to speak.
- Tell the person you are calling that you are using a cell phone so he or she can anticipate distractions. If the connection fails, the person will know to wait for a call-back.
- Do not use cell phones when they impede your ability to drive or walk. A "walk-around" or "hands-free" kit should be purchased if you need free hands while you talk.

EXAMPLES:

In 2002 about 41 state governments in the United States were considering proposals to restrict or ban the use of cell phones while driving. A number of states have already enacted legislation that makes talking on a cell phone while driving illegal.

The New York City Council has passed a law against using cell phones during live performances and in museums. Violators may have to pay a $50 fine.

- Maintain at least a 10-foot zone from anyone while talking on a cell phone.
- Never "multi-task" by making calls while shopping, waiting in line, or conducting personal business.
- Demand "quiet zones" and "phone-free areas" at work and in public areas.

(2) *e-Mail etiquette:* International Data Corp. (IDC) recently projected the number of e-mail boxes around the world will grow from 505 million in 2001 to 36 billion in 2005. Since more workers will gain e-mail access over the next few years, e-mail etiquette will become even more important. The same

boundaries should be used for e-mail as those that are used when meeting with a person face to face.

- Avoid jokes and emoticons (those little "smilie" faces). They may be considered unprofessional and are most likely to be misinterpreted. Use emoticons sparingly—at the ends of statements to refer back to a previous statement.

EXAMPLES:

> :-) *a smiley face*
>
> ;-) *wink; slight sarcasm*
>
> 8-) *eye glasses*
>
> :-e *disappointment*

- Do not send a message in all caps, which is viewed as SHOUTING.
- Every e-mail message should begin with a courteous, polite greeting, which lets the receiver know he or she is the right person to receive this message.

EXAMPLES:

> *Dear Joe:*　　　*Dear Dr. Brumley:*
>
> *Hi, Susan!*　　　*Greetings, Roman!*

- Do not send abusive, harassing, or threatening messages.
- When you are upset or angry about a business matter, review the message you plan to send after you have had time to calm down and think about the situation.
- Use e-mail in a professional manner. Remember to control forwarding of messages. Sometimes you will need to ask the sender's permission to forward the message to another person.
- Remember that all laws governing forms of written communication including copyright, defamation, and discrimination also apply to e-mail.
- Do not use excessive and unnecessary punctuation. One exclamation point at the end of the sentence, rather than three or four, should be sufficient.
- Abbreviations used in an e-mail message should be those that are already common ones to use in English, such as FYI (for your information) or BTW (by the way).

EXAMPLE:

An abbreviation like TNSTAAFL may do nothing but confuse the reader. This abbreviation stands for "There's no such thing as a free lunch."

- Include a signature file at the end of the e-mail message that includes name, address, telephone and fax numbers, and e-mail address. By doing so, there will be little misunderstanding as to the originator of the message. Just using e-mail addresses can often be confusing.
- Maintain "threads" of communication (links) with others so that you can reply more easily and quickly to e-mails you receive.
- Quoted material within an e-mail message should be indicated with this symbol at the beginning of each line <.

EXAMPLE:

<and do you agree with the proposal to
<investigate the legal services that
<are available?

Yes. Please complete the request for a confidential report.

(3) *Fax etiquette:* When you send a fax, always include a cover sheet stating the total number of pages, the date, to whom the fax is being sent, from whom the fax is sent, and your telephone and fax numbers in case there are problems with the transmission.

(4) *Correspondence:* Most business professionals work diligently at polishing their written communication skills. Here are some tips for using appropriate etiquette in developing written correspondence.

- Write thank-you notes by hand. You can never send too many of them. This gesture will be remembered.

- A short, sincere style for writing congratulatory and thank-you messages will be most effective. A brief message will convey sincere thoughts to the recipient.

  EXAMPLE:

  A technique often used by business professionals in congratulating someone on a publication or a program presentation is to write a short congratulatory message right on the article or program and hand or mail it to the person.

- Polish your business letter-writing skills. Administrative professionals are expected to use correct grammar, punctuation, spelling, and other writing mechanics.

- Do not waste a person's time with a long letter. Brief messages and concise letters will receive more prompt attention than long, wordy ones.

- Do not say "thank you" in your message unless the receiver has actually done something worthy of thanks. Such trite comments as "thank you for taking the time out of your busy day" or "thank you for reading this letter" are inappropriate. Show appreciation for the reader's consideration of the contents of your message, but saying "thanks" would be for doing nothing.

- Be direct in choosing words, and use as few words as possible. As you proofread your message, see if you can eliminate unnecessary words.

  Do not say:

  "If you have any questions, do not hesitate to call me, and I will be happy to answer them."

  Instead, say:

  "Please call if you have any questions or need additional information."

- If you address someone in the salutation with just the first name (Dear Joseph), you need to sign the letter with your first name, or you are talking down to the receiver. Your full name appears on the signature line, anyway.

c. *Business meetings:* All business meetings require careful preparation, respect for all participants who will be present, and a basic knowledge of meeting etiquette. Meetings are another opportunity for participants to make positive impressions by what they say, what they don't say, and nonverbal cues they display. Some suggestions for applying appropriate meeting etiquette include the following:

- Do your homework before a meeting so you will be prepared for the presentation, discussion, and dissemination of information.

- Being on time or a few minutes early shows respect for the others attending the meeting. This extra time gives you an opportunity to introduce yourself to the participants at the meeting and a chance to gather the materials to be discussed.

- If the presiding officer (or chair) starts meetings on time or as soon as a quorum is present, participants will be more apt to be punctual, too.

- If you are not sure where to sit, ask the person in charge of the meeting where you should sit. Shake hands with your associates, and introduce yourself to people you do not know.

- During the meeting, be attentive and listen carefully. Do not dominate a discussion; give others an opportunity to speak, too.

- Maintain good posture, and stay alert. Body language communicates your interest in the people who are attending the meeting and the topics being discussed.

- Dress professionally for the meeting. Be sure your shoes are polished. Keep suit jackets and ties on during the meeting.

- Accept no telephone calls during the meeting. A telephone call should not take precedence over your talking with the person who is facing you.

- Turn off cell phones and pagers during the meeting. If you are on call or expect an urgent call, switch your phone or beeper to vibrate mode (instead of ringing mode) before the meeting begins. To minimize any disruption, sit near the door if you may have to leave the room. Let the meeting chair know ahead of time that you may be called out.

- Only one person should speak at a time during the meeting. In a formal meeting, an authority like *Robert's Rules of Order* is often used as the guide to parliamentary procedure, which allows each person to speak during the meeting, even if the person has a minority viewpoint.

- At the end of the meeting, shake hands with your associates. If you are the chair of the meeting, be sure to thank participants for coming. Remind them of the next meeting, if one is scheduled.

Workplace etiquette needs to be practiced throughout the entire workday. When it is your turn to provide the office treats, be a contributor. A small gift to a person who helps you with a special project is an excellent gesture. If you need to make personal appointments (doctor, dentist, hair) for the beginning or end of the day, find out how you should handle the work time you missed by working late or through a lunch hour. Through all of this, most importantly, remember to respect those around you and try to keep the office environment a pleasant one in which to work.

Check Point—Section B

Directions: For each question, circle the correct answer.

B–1. Which one of the following statements illustrates an acceptable way to greet a co-worker when you enter the office?

A) "Good morning, John! Don't you think it's time to start work?"

B) "Good morning, Dear! What's on the agenda for today?"

C) "Hello, Joanna! Let me see a picture of your new baby before we start working."

D) "Joseph, let's get started on that Rothman report right away."

B–2. When you are a guest in someone else's office, you should

A) put your briefcase on the desk or work table prior to sitting down

B) make an appointment so the host will reserve some meeting time for you

C) stop in the office at least ten minutes before you would like to meet to see if the host is in

D) make yourself just as comfortable as the host is

B–3. When using a cell phone to call a business associate, appropriate etiquette would be shown by

A) excusing yourself from talking with a business associate to make the call

B) calling from an evening performance by the Stage Coach Players since you were unable to contact this person during the day

C) making the call after work as you are walking down the street toward the parking garage

D) keeping your conversation short and your voice conversational and low as you are taking the commuter train home

C. Business Dining and Entertaining Etiquette

Many business meetings involve continued discussions during or after a meal function. The meeting's purpose and time frame will help to dictate what meal would be appropriate. Some organizations see these meal functions as **power meals**. One problem business people frequently encounter is how to handle the tab gracefully and tactfully.

1. *Meal Functions:* Business etiquette as well as social etiquette is required when meal functions with clients or other business associates are scheduled. The purpose of the meal function needs to be clear to all who are participating.

   a. *Breakfast:* Starting the day with a breakfast meeting is an ideal way to handle an urgent business matter, to review an upcoming event, or to meet with someone who prefers meeting early in the morning. You need a good reason for someone to meet with you as early as 7 A.M. Such power breakfasts are usually 45 minutes to 1 hour.

   b. *Luncheon:* Lasting for up to two hours, luncheons are ideal for entertaining clients or establishing business contacts. Lunch is usually a lighter meal, perhaps served with wine or beer. Some companies may have strict policies against consumption of alcoholic beverages on company time. A good idea is to follow the host's lead and, if still unsure, ordering soft drinks may be the best choice. Immediately after the appetizer is served, business discussions can begin, according to the meeting agenda.

Work can continue directly after lunch, either at that location or moved to the office after a short break. Lunch is a common male-female business dining situation.

c. *Afternoon tea:* A relatively new "power" meal is afternoon tea. This is an excellent time to become better acquainted with someone with whom you wish to establish a business relationship. Afternoon tea is a healthy alternative to meeting for cocktails. Business matters can be discussed outside the office without breaking up the middle of the day.

d. *Business dinner:* Dinners are often used to further develop and solidify an existing business relationship or as a special treat for out-of-town business clients. Dinner should never be the first meal with a client unless that person is from out of town or has specifically requested a dinner meeting. With the client's knowledge, the dinner should be planned ahead of time for about two hours between 5:30 and 8 P.M. so that a large amount of the client's personal time is not monopolized with evening meetings. Typically, the dinner should be the main meal of the day. If business is to be discussed at dinner, discussions should begin before a second drink is served.

e. *Business brunch:* In the United States, little business is conducted on Sundays. However, some business meetings might be held over brunch on Saturday or Sunday, especially if foreign visitors are here for only a short stay. In such a case, a business brunch might be the most appropriate function to organize.

2. ***Paying the Bill:*** Whoever benefits from the business association pays the bill (the **tab**), regardless of gender. If you invite a client, you need to pay. If a client invites you, you still should pay. The person who extends the invitation may pay if there is no clear beneficiary. Here are some ways of tactfully handling the check so that paying the tab does not become an issue.

a. *Arranging payment:* Arranging payment ahead of time with the restaurant manager is a tactful way of being sure that the check will not be brought to the table at the end of the meal. After the meal is over, you can discreetly pay the bill.

b. *Extending an invitation:* A woman who is hosting a male client should put the burden of payment onto her company to avoid raising the social issue of "the man always pays."

When you extend the invitation, say: "I'd like you to be my company's guest at dinner." In this way, the guest knows immediately that your company will pay.

c. *Receiving an invitation:* A client may extend an invitation for you to come to a private club. In this case, you should not even try to pick up the check because the club probably only accepts payment from the member. Instead, reciprocate with an invitation at a later date or ask the client the amount of your share of the bill; then, if appropriate, you can pay the client that portion.

3. ***Tipping Practices:*** A **gratuity** (or tip) should be merited. Typically, people who are service providers, such as wait staff in restaurants or taxi drivers, depend on tips to augment their salaries. Good service should be generously rewarded. However, when service personnel are rude or inattentive to customers or clients, the amount of the gratuity should be reduced. Perhaps no tip at all should be left. You may even want to discuss the situation with the manager. Here are some tipping practices that are commonly found in business today.

a. *Acceptable gratuities:* The accepted percentage for a gratuity for good service in U.S. business is 15 percent.

EXAMPLES:

> *Bellperson or porter: $1 per bag; $2 if something special is brought to the room*
> *Doorman: $1 or $2 for hailing a taxi*
> *Concierge: $5 per day for special services*
> *Parking valet: $2 for bringing the car around*
> *Taxi or limousine drivers: 15 percent*
> *Housekeeping/maid service: $2 or $3 per night; pay directly to person*
> *Wait staff, room service, and bartenders: 15 to 20 percent*
> *Catering service for home entertaining: 20 percent*
> *Strolling musicians who play specific requests: $1 per request*

b. *Added service charge:* Many U.S. restaurants and caterers add a service charge or gratuity of about 15 to 17 percent to the bill when a minimum number of six or eight are being served. When this gratuity is automatically added, you know that the wait staff and hosts will be sharing it. An additional gratuity is not required.

4. ***Dining Etiquette:*** When invited for a meal, arriving promptly is expected. When a cocktail hour is held before the meal, arriving a few minutes late is permissible. You need not call ahead, even if you are 30 minutes late; however, you do need to arrive on time for the dinner.

a. *Place settings:* In a typical place setting, the fork is placed to the left of the dinner plate, and the knife and spoon are placed to the right of the plate. If you have more than one fork or spoon, use the outside fork or spoon first. The bread plate goes on the left. Glasses as well as cups and saucers are placed to the right.

b. *Eating the meal:* When sitting at a banquet table, you may begin eating when two people to your left and two people to your right are served. Reach only for items placed in front of you on the table. Other items may require someone to pass them to you. Pass items to the right; offer items to the left.

When eating, the fork is held in the right hand and is used for eating. The knife is used to cut or spread something. When using the knife, the fork is shifted to the left hand. The continental style of dining (the knife and fork are never switched and the tines of the fork are held downward) is acceptable, too. Some foods may be picked up and eaten with the fingers such as:

Corn on the cob	Spareribs
Clams	Lobsters
Small sandwiches	Crisp bacon
Bread and rolls	Chicken wings
Canapés	Shoestring potatoes
Olives	Small French fries
Cherries	Some fruits

Large sandwiches should be cut before eating. The best rule to follow in eating with your fingers is the example shown by your hosts.

Check Point—Section C

Directions: For each question, circle the correct answer.

C–1. If Sveigny, an attorney, invites Rogers, a client, to lunch to discuss an important business matter, the person who should pay the tab is

A) Sveigny
B) Rogers
C) Sveigny and Rogers should each pay half
D) Rogers' company

C–2. Which one of the following statements would be appropriate for a businesswoman to use when she wants to invite a male client to dinner?

A) "I would like you to be my guest at dinner tonight."
B) "I would like you to be my company's guest at dinner tonight."
C) "Please join me for dinner tonight at the Emerald Club."
D) "Let's have dinner together tonight."

C–3. When a minimum number (six to eight persons) meet for a business dinner, many U.S. restaurants and caterers

A) issue individual checks to enable guests to pay for their own dinners
B) suggest a gratuity of 10 percent for the wait staff
C) prefer that the guests do not add a gratuity to the total bill
D) add a service charge or gratuity to the total bill

D. Giving and Receiving Gifts

The giving and receiving of gifts is a very important consideration in doing business with other domestic and international organizations. In some societies, giving gifts is viewed as a necessary business practice. In others, however, giving gifts is considered in a similar vein as bribing business associates. People who represent political organizations or who are elected to office may not be allowed to accept gifts.

1. *Giving Gifts:* Presenting a gift is seen as a thoughtful gesture but usually is not required. Once a business deal has been closed, business gifts are sometimes presented. In these types of situations, gifts are usually unwrapped immediately and shown to those who are present.

   a. *Types of appropriate gifts:* Sometimes the best gifts come from your own organization or country. Holiday seasons are often seen as appropriate times to give or exchange gifts, but they do vary from country to country. Presenting a gift, however, should be treated specially and not necessarily be expected. Here are some situations in which gift giving is appropriate.

      (1) Business gifts may be presented after a transaction has taken place. Oftentimes, these are gifts that depict the organization or result from the business deal.

      (2) Holiday gifts that you may exchange with your business associates may be useful items for the office or gift certificates. Remember that *holiday* does not mean just Christmas! Before giving a gift of liquor or wine, you need to find out if such a gift is appropriate.

(3) When you visit a business associate's home, flowers, a potted plant, or a bottle of wine are always appreciated. Flowers could even be sent in advance, but be careful about the types and colors of flowers given.

EXAMPLE: *The color yellow depicts death in some countries.*

(4) Another popular gift is lunch or dinner out. Tickets to a concert or theatrical performance or a gift certificate from a local retailer are other popular choices.

b. *Types of inappropriate gifts:* Careful thought should be given to the selection of gifts for business associates and their families. Giving an inappropriate gift can affect the impression the host develops of you and your organization. Here are some ideas usually considered inappropriate.

(1) What gifts to purchase for children should depend on the values held by the parents. You may not know whether or not the parents would approve of certain types of gifts or toys such as a holster and gun set or a video game.

(2) Cologne, perfume, lingerie, or other articles of clothing are inappropriate gifts because they are seen as too personal.

2. ***Receiving Gifts:*** Gifts that you receive need to be acknowledged with a thank-you note. A business associate who sends you a card in the mail, along with a gift certificate from a local bookstore, will not know for sure that you received the gift unless you acknowledge it.

Check Point—Section D

Directions: For each question, circle the correct answer.

D–1. An American business representative needs to be cautious in giving a gift to a business associate in another company because a gift

A) may be viewed as a bribe
B) may not be viewed as a personal gift
C) is usually presented before the business transaction takes place
D) is required in most business dealings

D–2. Which one of the following gifts would be appropriate to give a business associate after a business transaction has taken place?

A) Replica of a toy gun and holster for the business associate's child
B) Cotton-blend sweater that is imported

C) New perfume mist just being marketed
D) Letter opener with the company logo on the handle

D–3. Which one of the following is an appropriate acknowledgement for a gift certificate from a local bookstore that you received from a business associate?

A) Accepting the gift card and using it to buy a bestseller
B) Writing a thank-you note to the business associate within a day or two
C) Telephoning the business associate and leaving a message that you appreciated receiving the gift card
D) Writing yourself a reminder to send a thank-you note next week

E. Disability Etiquette

Disabled people are now the largest and most diverse minority in our society. The passage of the Americans with Disabilities Act required employers to make appropriate accommodations for disabled personnel. Thus, seeing the disabled function effectively in the workplace has become much more commonplace. Knowledge of **disability etiquette** is essential for administrative professionals to capitalize on the skills and competencies possessed by the disabled that support work assignments to be accomplished.

1. *Practical Tips for Working with Disabled:* Persons with disabilities deserve the same respect extended to anyone else. Behaving naturally should enable people to feel more comfortable in work situations involving the disabled. The application of common sense and courtesy as shown in the following suggestions helps keep difficult situations from recurring.

   - If you offer assistance, wait until the disabled person accepts the offer before doing anything. The disabled person will inform you of the type of assistance needed.
   - Speak directly to the disabled person, not to a third person.
   - Always offer to shake hands with the disabled person.
   - Identify yourself and others to a visually impaired person. Be sure to let him or her know when you are leaving the room.
   - Treat adults as adults.
   - Don't shout. Disabled persons have very sharp senses to compensate for those that are impaired.
   - Don't move, lean on, or touch a wheelchair without asking permission of the person occupying the chair.
   - Don't touch or distract a working guide dog.
   - Listen carefully to a person with a speech impediment. Be patient, and give the person a chance to finish comments before trying to respond.
   - Speak as you would normally. Using phrases such as "running around" to someone in a wheelchair or "see you later" to someone who is visually impaired will usually not offend the disabled person.

2. *Etiquette for the Disabled:* Disabilities range from being unable to walk and use motor functions to being able to use the senses (sight, hearing, speaking, and thinking). Applying a few helpful suggestions will assist administrative professionals in creating a workplace climate that is conducive to accommodating individual differences in work situations.

   a. *Wheelchair etiquette:* The wheelchair is considered an extension of the person who uses it. These tips also may apply to people who use crutches, canes, or walkers.

      - Keep your hands off the disabled person's wheelchair.
      - Respect the disabled person's personal space.
      - When conversing for any length of time with someone in a wheelchair, seat yourself so you can talk with the person eye to eye.
      - Do not move crutches, walkers, or wheelchairs out of reach of the person who uses them. If you do move them, place them within sight to avoid any panic.

- Offer to help first before acting. Push a wheelchair only after asking the disabled person if you may do so.
- If you are planning a social function, find out whether the location has access for wheelchairs. Considerations include steep inclines, obstacles, and time to reach the location.

b. *Visual impairment etiquette:* Visual impairment ranges from partial sight to complete blindness. Here are a few guidelines that will help you communicate better with a visually impaired person.

- Do not pet, distract, or interfere with guide dogs without explicit permission from the owner.
- Allow guide dogs to accompany their owners at all times into all stores and buildings.
- Leave items exactly as you found them in an environment (office, home) familiar to a blind person.
- Offer assistance if you think it might be helpful. Sometimes a person who is blind prefers to go along unaided. At other times, the person may need help crossing a busy street or moving down a crowded hallway.
- If the person wants your help, offer your elbow. You will be walking a step ahead, and your body movements will indicate any change in direction, stopping, or starting.
- Hesitate, but do not stop before stepping up or down. You might want to say, "Step up" or "Step down."
- Be aware of half-opened doors that can be a hazard to a blind person.
- Give directions using the blind person as the reference point. If you are helping the person cross a street, indicate the name of the street and left or right directions, like this:

  > "You are on the corner of Second Street and Lincoln Highway, facing Lincoln Highway. You will need to cross it, turn to your right and cross Second Street, then proceed west one block to First Street."

- When helping the person into a car or taxi, place his or her hand on the inside door handle, letting the person get into the vehicle alone.
- When accompanying a blind person, do your best to describe the area, especially the terrain and any spatial relationships.

c. *Hearing loss etiquette:* Hearing loss is not such a severe disability as blindness but has become extremely common. Here are some tips that may be helpful in working with people who are experiencing some hearing loss.

- Before you begin to speak, notice if the person has a hearing aid in one or both ears. Try to speak in a normal tone, without shouting, so you can tell how much the person can hear.
- Be sure you have the person's attention. Wave your hand, tap the person's shoulder, or use some other signal in a gentle manner.
- If the person depends on lip reading to understand what is said, face the person to whom you are speaking and make sure that he or she can see your lips clearly.
- Repeat yourself if necessary, write down the message, or get someone to sign for you.

- Keep your hands away from your face, and don't eat or chew while you are speaking.

- Reduce background noises by turning off the television or radio or closing a door.

- Bend down to get a little closer to the ear of the listener, but don't speak directly into the ear. Don't touch the listener nor shout your message.

- In a group setting with others laughing at a joke or story the hearing-impaired person did not understand, take time to explain the story or tell him or her that you will explain it later. You don't want the hearing-impaired person to think that others are laughing at him or her.

d. *Developmental disability etiquette:* In the workplace, the person who is challenged with a **developmental disability** may need your patience and understanding in adapting to the work environment. The key is to treat people with these types of disabilities as normally as possible. The same standards need to be set for them as for other employees. Here are a few other guidelines that should be helpful.

- Touching often signals approval of whatever behavior is being demonstrated. Be careful about touching the person.

- Ensure that the messages you are sending with body language and tone of voice are nonthreatening. Be firm, but pleasant. Speak with a smile on your face and in your voice.

- Use positive language to get your point across. Instead of saying, "You made a mistake," try saying "How about doing it this way?"

- If the person does not seem to understand your message, repeat the information in simpler words and be patient.

Remember that disabled persons are often as anxious to put you at ease as you are to put them at ease. Avoid using terms such as *victim*, *crippled*, *invalid*, and *handicapped*. The correct word to use is **disabled**.

Check Point—Section E

Directions: For each question, circle the correct answer.

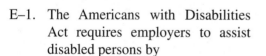 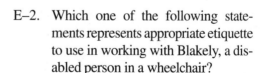

E–1. The Americans with Disabilities Act requires employers to assist disabled persons by

A) making reasonable accommodations for the disabled person to be employed in business

B) creating a section of the office for the disabled person to work

C) providing disabled persons with skills to qualify for positions in business

D) requiring employers to meet a specific quota when hiring disabled persons

E–2. Which one of the following statements represents appropriate etiquette to use in working with Blakely, a disabled person in a wheelchair?

A) Assume that Blakely will need your help moving down the hall to her office

B) When you see Blakely coming down the hall, walk over and push the wheelchair for her

C) Ask Blakely first if she would like some assistance going down the hall

D) Stop the wheelchair physically, and ask her if she needs help

E–3. Stevens has a visual impairment that requires her to have Rex, a guide dog. You see Stevens standing between the front door of the building and the first-floor elevator. Which one of the following strategies would be appropriate for you to use?

A) Stop to say hello, and reach down to pet Rex

B) Offer your elbow, and indicate that you will help her get to her destination

C) Offer assistance by saying something like "Hello, Stevens! I'm Jonathan Wakely in the Marketing Department. Can I be of some help to you?"

D) Tell Stevens that Rex cannot come into the building

F. International Etiquette

If you are traveling on business to a foreign destination or welcome visitors from other countries, it is a good idea to learn as much as you can about their cultures and make appropriate allowances in your plans for meetings and social events during the visit.

1. ***Eliminating Stereotypes:*** Sometimes you need to forget about what you think you already know about people from a particular culture. Stereotypes are generalizations you make about others, often based on bad experiences you have had, that may or may not be true. Here are some common generalizations that you need to eliminate from your thinking:

   - The siesta is a part of all Latin cultures.
   - Visitors from abroad are eager to eat in American restaurants that serve their favorite foods.
   - Signs, gestures, and loud English will bridge language gaps.
   - People from Asian cultures are remote and inscrutable whereas Germans are cold and extremely efficient.
   - Oriental people are basically shy.

   With appropriate research, administrative professionals will find that all of these generalizations are untrue. In Italy, Spain, and some Latin cultures, for example, the siesta is an important part of the day, with businesses closing for two or three hours during the heat of the day. Those same businesses, however, stay open into the evening hours to accommodate customers. Use of signs and gestures that are acceptable in one country may be obscene in another culture.

2. ***Greeting Business Associates:*** Meeting business associates from other countries requires you to be familiar with public behaviors like handshaking, bowing, and making eye contact.

   - In America, kissing as part of the greeting is considered unacceptable. Handshaking is the general type of greeting that takes place in France; however, kissing on both cheeks (across genders) is expected by colleagues in the workplace.
   - Germans do not expect to be greeted by strangers in the office environment. Hugging and kissing on both cheeks is only expected among good friends or family members.
   - In Japan, a bow called an "ojigi" (oh-jee-ghee) is a way of greeting someone, saying "thanks" or "I'm sorry," or asking for a favor.
   - Swedish people like to maintain eye contact as much as possible and lower the tone of their voices.

3. ***Building Relationships First:*** In most countries, other than the United States and Germanic countries, it is important to build relationships before conducting business. This is especially true in high-context cultures like China, Japan, and Greece. Time is required to build these kinds of relationships. Sometimes Americans appear to be willing at the beginning of a negotiation to be competitive and take risks but do not always live up to the implied promise of an ongoing friendship or, at least, a business or personal relationship.

   Some business people from other cultures view Americans as persistent, abrupt, and impatient in getting things done. Another complaint others have is that Americans want to put people from other cultures on a first-name basis as quickly as possible.

4. ***Language:*** Jokes may not be interpreted by people in other countries the way you intended. Use of jargon often leads to misunderstanding the intended meaning of the message that is being conveyed. Nonverbal cues, like the gestures described here, may be misinterpreted as well.

   - *Using the crooked index finger to beckon someone:* In some cultures, someone is beckoned with the arm extended and the fingers making an inward sweeping motion.
   - *The "thumbs-up" sign:* In Brazil, this gesture is acceptable to show that things are going well. This sign means "OK" in France.
   - *Clapping hands or snapping fingers:* Sometimes this gesture is used to summon wait staff to the table. However, visitors need to refrain from doing so. In France, snapping fingers is considered a vulgar gesture. Chinese people do not like to use their hands while speaking.
   - *The V for victory sign:* This gesture is considered an insult in England if the palm is turned inward.
   - *Showing the soles of shoes:* This gesture is considered an insult in many Asian countries and in parts of the Middle East.
   - *Arms folded over the chest:* In some cultures, this gesture shows rudeness in communicating.
   - *The OK sign:* In Brazil, the OK sign (forming a circle with first finger and thumb) is considered a vulgar gesture. The same sign means "zero" or "useless" in France.
   - *The "arms akimbo" position:* In Singapore, standing tall with hands on hips is perceived as an angry or aggressive posture.

5. ***Attention to Time:*** Time takes on new meanings in different cultures. In some cultures, attention to time is very important. Americans tend to believe that people should be on time for appointments and meetings. A meeting will start on time whether all of the attendees are present or not. When visiting a foreign business, be prompt in keeping appointments. You may find that your foreign counterpart is not on time; be patient and wait. Pay close attention to time, but be understanding when your foreign business associates have a different view toward time.

6. ***Personal Space:*** Asians stand farther away during conversation, preferring a larger personal space. Many people of Mediterranean descent, as well as Latinos, prefer to stand so close that Americans may take a step back. People of Asian cultures do not like to be touched.

EXAMPLES:

Putting your arm about the shoulders of a Japanese person would not be appreciated.

Slapping a Korean on the back during a conversation and saying, "Good job," would be very disconcerting to that person.

An Asian shopkeeper might put change on the counter rather than in your hand.

Touch, such as touching a shoulder or patting an arm, is part of French business etiquette.

A Chinese person, especially one who is older, dislikes being touched by another person.

7. ***Working Schedules:*** In the United States, the work day is typically 8:30 or 9 A.M. to 5 P.M., Monday through Friday. Retail establishments are open on Saturdays, Sundays, and some holidays. Although businesses in many countries function on a similar time schedule, some of the variations include a break in the middle of the day to accommodate a longer lunch or a siesta. Work begins again in mid-afternoon but extends into the evening hours. Break times will vary, too, depending on the nature of the business and the work schedule.

8. ***Holidays:*** Of course, the celebration of holidays will change from country to country. Research on a particular country will yield a list of holidays that are celebrated in that country. People in European countries, for example, go on "holiday" for at least one month during the summer. Many businesses close during this period of time to allow all employees to go on vacation, which is certainly a resource-saving measure. Business travel to a foreign country should be scheduled so that disruptions caused by holidays will not be experienced.

9. ***Food Customs:*** The main meal in America comes at the end of the work day, whereas in many foreign countries the main meal is served at noon. Therefore, sometimes a longer break in the work day comes in the early afternoon. The evening meal in America is served around 7 P.M. In Spain, for example, supper begins about 10 P.M. and ends the day. The English have tea at 4 P.M. in the afternoon, and high tea is served later in the evening as a substitute for supper.

    a. *Differences in foods:* Not only is there a difference in the types of meals that are served, but there are differences in the foods as well. Here are some examples of American foods that foreign business associates might find distasteful.

    EXAMPLES:

Marshmallows	*Corn on the cob*
Pumpkin pie	*Pecan pie*
Sweet potatoes	*Grits*
Hot dogs	*Crawfish*

    Some foods thought to be of foreign origin have really developed in the United States and have become Americanized. Pizza is believed to have originated as an American menu item rather than an Italian one. Chop suey is a dish that Chinese think is American and Americans think is Chinese. Fortune cookies are known to be an American invention as well. Here are some examples of foreign delicacies that Americans may or may not enjoy.

    EXAMPLES:

Japan	horse meat
England	kidney pie
Mexico	toasted grasshoppers
Middle East	sheep's eyes

b. *Rules of etiquette:* Here are some general rules of etiquette to follow when confronted with unfamiliar food in a foreign land:

- If you don't recognize the food, don't ask—taste it. If you are asked for your opinion, say something positive like "It is very flavorful."

- Politely refuse if you know what it is but don't want to try it. You might say something like "I know this is a delicacy, but I have tried it before and I would prefer to eat the . . . ."

- If a refusal to eat the food would offend your host or others, cut it up into small pieces and move it around on your dish so that it appears you are eating it.

In European countries, the main entrée is served at the beginning of the meal. A formal Chinese banquet consists of many more courses than Americans would expect. Many of the Chinese delicacies are served later in the meal, so eating sparingly during the first few courses is a necessity in order to enjoy the later courses.

In Japan, soy sauce should not be added to the rice and no sugar or cream should be added to Japanese tea. No tipping is required in restaurants in Japan.

c. *Religious beliefs:* Religious orientations will dictate the types of food that are acceptable in particular cultures. Muslims do not drink alcohol or eat the flesh of any animal that scavenges (pigs, goats, lobsters). Therefore, respect the food and beverage choices of business associates who are following their religious convictions.

General questions about international etiquette, and particularly about specific countries, may be answered by performing an Internet search under key words like "international etiquette," "business etiquette," or the name of the country. The consulates for foreign countries also have Web sites with helpful information about the country. The following Web sites may also offer information about specific countries and cultural customs for the business traveler:

www.executiveplanet.com
www.geocities.com
www.odci.gov/cia//
www.webofculture.com

Check Point—Section F

Directions: For each question, circle the correct answer.

F–1. A business traveler may form a stereotype about people from a different culture such as which one of the following?

  A) A visitor from abroad prefers to eat only foods native to his or her own country

  B) People from Asian cultures are distant and shy in their dealings with others

  C) The siesta is a part of all cultures

  D) People from Germanic cultures are warm and friendly

F–2. The saying, "Rome wasn't built in a day," would describe the attitude and orientation of which one of the following business associates?

A) George, an English business manager, who wants to enter into a contract with your company for automobile parts

B) Gustav, a construction engineer from Germany, who wants to get the bid on your company's new headquarters

C) Kim, a Chinese businessperson, who wants to purchase computer components from your company

D) Henri, a French architect, who is considering your company as a potential supplier

F–3. Which one of the following gestures reflects etiquette that should be practiced in an international setting?

A) Asking for a 1 P.M. appointment in Mexico City, even though you know the business is closed from noon to 2 P.M.

B) Being on time for a 10:30 A.M. appointment in Athens, Greece, even though you know you will have to wait at least a half-hour for your counterpart to show up

C) Standing close to your Asian counterpart during a business conversation

D) Being a half-hour late for an appointment in Paris, France, because you know that your French counterpart will be late

For Your Review

Directions: For each question, circle the correct answer.

1. Findings from a joint study by Levi Strauss & Co. and the Society for Human Resource Management indicate that most office workers enjoy
   A) conservative business attire to adhere to the dress code
   B) casual attire such as jeans and sweatshirts to work
   C) wearing casual business attire for work
   D) overusing cosmetics when preparing for work

2. Which one of the following practices will complement personal appearance in a business setting?
   A) Wearing small rings on the right hand
   B) Selected body tattoos or piercings
   C) Casual attire for the office
   D) Use of a strong perfume

3. When you are introducing yourself to a business associate, you should
   A) wait for the other person to extend his or her hand first
   B) wear a nametag on the right shoulder
   C) stand up, smile, and greet the person
   D) stand up, approach the person, and extend the right hand for a handshake

4. Which one of the following examples shows the correct way to introduce Mr. Schmidt, a business associate with greater authority, to Ms. Tolski, an associate with lesser authority?

   A) "Ms. Tolski, I would like you to meet Mr. Schmidt."
   B) "Mr. Schmidt, I would like you to meet Ms. Tolski."
   C) "Ruth-Ellen, I'd like you to meet Jason."
   D) "Let me introduce you to each other."

5. When a woman does not want the title *Ms.* to be used with her name,
   A) she should be called by her first name
   B) the title *Mrs.* should be used as the preferred title
   C) she should indicate the title she prefers to use
   D) she should just use her surname

6. The accepted physical greeting when business associates are introduced is
   A) pronouncing the person's name as best you can
   B) reading the associate's name as shown on the nametag
   C) shaking hands firmly with only male business associates
   D) shaking hands firmly with a man or a woman

7. Your purpose in presenting a business card to a business associate is to
   A) introduce yourself and your specialization
   B) request help in developing a business relationship
   C) distribute cards to as many people as possible
   D) disseminate information about your organization

8. What should you do when a business associate presents you with a business card?

A) Tell the person you will read the card later

B) Look at the card and then at the face of the person who handed it to you

C) Tuck the card into your pocket

D) Refuse the card if you prefer not to do business at this time

9. A recent study showed that a large percentage of people newly hired as managers fail in their first jobs because of an inability to

A) perform specific work tasks involving the computer

B) recognize the contributions of others to task performance

C) collaborate with others on specific assignments

D) develop positive relationships with co-workers

10. To help develop a pleasant office environment, respect and courtesy need to be shown to

A) collaborators on team projects

B) primarily subordinates

C) everyone at all levels within the organization

D) top executives in the organization

11. Which one of the following shows a guest's respect for privacy when entering someone else's office?

A) Making an appointment so a given amount of time is reserved for the meeting

B) Arriving for the meeting only a few minutes late

C) Putting a briefcase and/or documents on the host's desk

D) Staying beyond the appointment if more time is needed

12. To be an effective host when someone else visits your office, you should

A) let the guest choose a comfortable place to sit

B) allow the guest to find his or her way to your office

C) lead the discussion during the visit

D) end the meeting the moment the appointment time is over

13. If you are screening calls for another office professional, indicate that the person being called

A) can also be reached on the voice-mail network

B) is not available but would appreciate a message

C) is not available at the moment

D) is working on a project and cannot be disturbed at this time

14. Mason is discussing an important business transaction with Gomez, a client, when Mason's cell phone rings. What should Mason do?

A) Say, "Excuse me a moment," and answer the phone call

B) Answer the phone, and then tell Gomez how important it was to answer this call

C) Ask someone else in the office to answer the cell phone call for you

D) Let the cell phone system record a message so you can continue talking with Gomez

15. An abbreviation included in an e-mail message needs to be

A) quoted within the message

B) commonly accepted for ease of interpretation

C) explained within the message

D) omitted from the e-mail message

16. Messages that will receive prompt attention tend to be those that are

A) long and wordy

B) at least three paragraphs in length

C) self-explanatory in presenting details

D) brief and concise

17. If the presiding officer starts a business meeting on time, participants will tend to

A) be on time for the meeting

B) call in when they cannot attend

C) be more attentive during the meeting

D) accept the use of *Robert's Rules of Order* during the meeting

18. A breakfast meeting is an excellent way to
A) entertain an important client
B) become better acquainted with a prospective client
C) handle an urgent business matter
D) solidify an existing business relationship

19. The bill for a business dinner hosted at a nearby restaurant should be paid by
A) the client, whether male or female
B) whoever benefits from the business association
C) the person who extended the invitation to dinner
D) the project manager for the performance of a contract

20. Gifts that you receive need to be
A) reciprocated with a gift of equal value
B) returned so no one will suspect bribery will influence your business judgment
C) acknowledged with a thank-you note
D) preferably liquor or wine

21. If you offer assistance to a disabled person,
A) begin to help the person as soon as possible
B) assume that the disabled person will accept the offer
C) tell the disabled person what assistance you will give
D) wait until that person accepts the offer before doing anything

22. When accompanying a visually impaired person, describe the surrounding area so that the person is aware of
A) any spatial or distance relationships
B) directions from your point of view
C) other people who might be able to assist the person
D) any changes you have made in the physical placement of furniture

23. Taking time is considered important in building associations when doing business in
A) Germany
B) the United States
C) Japan
D) Canada

24. The use of a nonverbal cue such as the "OK" sign
A) is generally understood around the globe
B) may be misinterpreted by a business associate from another country
C) takes on the same meaning in different cultures
D) is considered an insult in most international settings

25. Which one of the following is an example of cultural preference for personal space?
A) Food delicacies differ worldwide
B) The main meal of the day in many countries is the noon meal
C) The work schedule in the United States is generally 8:30 or 9 A.M. until 5 or 5:30 P.M.
D) People of Asian cultures do not like to be touched

Solutions

Solutions to Check Point—Section A

Answer	Refer to:
A–1. (C)	[A-1-c]
A–2. (D)	[A-2-a (1) and A-2-a (2)]
A–3. (A)	[A-4]

Solutions to Check Point—Section B

Answer	Refer to:
B–1. (C)	[B-1]
B–2. (B)	[B-3-a]
B–3. (D)	[B-4-b (1)]

Solutions to Check Point—Section C

Answer	Refer to:
C–1. (A)	[C-2]
C–2. (B)	[C-2-b]
C–3. (D)	[C-3-b]

Solutions to Check Point—Section D

Answer	Refer to:
D–1. (A)	[D and D-1]
D–2. (D)	[D-1-a (1)]
D–3. (B)	[D-2]

Solutions to Check Point—Section E

Answer	Refer to:
E–1. (A)	[E]
E–2. (C)	[E-1 and E-2-a]
E–3. (C)	[E-2-b]

Solutions to Check Point—Section F

Answer	Refer to:
F–1. (B)	[F-1]
F–2. (C)	[F-3]
F–3. (B)	[F-5]

Solutions to For Your Review

Answer	Refer to:
1. (C)	[A-1-c]
2. (A)	[A-1-d]
3. (D)	[A-2-a]
4. (B)	[A-2-a (1) and A-2-(2)]
5. (C)	[A-2-a (2)]

6.	(D)	[A-2-b]
7.	(A)	[A-5-a]
8.	(B)	[A-5-b]
9.	(D)	[B]
10.	(C)	[B-1]
11.	(A)	[B-3-a]
12.	(C)	[B-3-b]
13.	(B)	[B-4-a]
14.	(D)	[B-4-b (1)]
15.	(B)	[B-4-b (2)]
16.	(D)	[B-4-b (4)]
17.	(A)	[B-4-c]
18.	(C)	[C-1-a]
19.	(B)	[C-2]
20.	(C)	[D-2]
21.	(D)	[E-1]
22.	(A)	[E-2-b]
23.	(C)	[F-3]
24.	(B)	[F-4]
25.	(D)	[F-6]

Practice Exam

Directions: For each question, circle the correct answer.

1. Creating a new record involves
   A) redesigning an existing record
   B) establishing the value of the record
   C) justifying the need for the new record
   D) retaining the record for a specified period of time

2. Which one of the following would be considered a conventional format for a record?
   A) Microform
   B) e-Mail message
   C) Compact disc
   D) Magnetic disk

3. Electronic mail has become an appropriate means of transmitting business information
   A) internally within the organization as well as externally to another organization
   B) internally within the organization
   C) externally to other organizations
   D) from superiors within the organization to employees at all levels

4. The most cost-effective storage equipment when comparing cost per filing inch is
   A) a programmable high-density storage system
   B) vertical file cabinets
   C) microform storage equipment
   D) high-density open-faced shelving

5. Which one of the following would be considered a problem with an existing records system?
   A) Tracing the use of specific records throughout the organization
   B) Lack of a tracking system for documents that have been removed from the files
   C) A relatively small number of records to be maintained
   D) The number of records personnel needed to maintain the organization's records

6. A basic principle in developing a computer database is that
   A) only data items on a specific topic will be included in the database
   B) data fields will be duplicated in additional sets of files
   C) a subscription fee will be required for regular access to the database
   D) once a data item is correctly entered, it will be ready for user access

7. When a document is borrowed from the files, a record needs to be kept showing the
   A) name of the person who issued the document
   B) name of someone who is requesting the document
   C) date on which the document was borrowed
   D) tracking of the document

8. The confidential nature of an organization's business and the need to be careful with client information could best be reviewed for new employees in a/an
   A) article in the monthly newsletter distributed to all employees

B) news release to the local newspaper

C) presentation by the organization's chief administrator at the next staff meeting

D) orientation training program for new hires

9. One of the primary reasons for maintaining a business archive is to

A) permit public and private users to have access to the records

B) restrict researchers' efforts to use the records and documents that are stored in the archive

C) store historical records and documents in a no-access environment

D) permit only company personnel to have access to the documents stored in the archive

10. Procedures embedded in software programs that restrict individual access to records are known as

A) passwords

B) physical security measures

C) logical security measures

D) user identification procedures

11. One rule of caution you should follow in using a personal password is to

A) record the password in an easy-to-access location

B) change your password often

C) inform a close co-worker of your password

D) assign a string of characters as a user identification code

12. A security feature that would deter someone from altering an original document is

A) a unique watermark appearing within the security paper used for the document

B) a magnetic strip on the original document

C) encryption of the original message on the document

D) the word VOID appearing on the area where someone might try to alter the document

13. When quantities of a business form need to be readily available to more than one department or division within the firm, the forms are referred to as

A) copyrighted forms

B) nonstock forms

C) stock forms

D) reproduction forms

14. When quantities of a copyrighted business form need to be produced,

A) permission must be sought from the copyright holder to produce copies of the form

B) a quantity of the form may be produced without the permission of the copyright holder

C) the form needs to be produced in multiples of 1,000

D) the form needs to be considered a stock form

15. The in-house design of business forms, brochures, and other professional pamphlets is possible with the help of software programs for

A) database management

B) communication

C) desktop publishing

D) networking

16. The first filing unit in a personal name is the

A) first name or initial

B) surname

C) middle name or initial

D) title

17. When a personal name is hyphenated such as Mary-Ellen Harrison or Joanne Hilton-Carter,

A) the two words are considered two indexing units

B) only the first word is considered an indexing unit

C) the hyphen is a part of the preceding filing unit

D) the two words are considered one indexing unit

18. Index each of the following names. Then, decide which one should be filed <u>last</u>.
    A) Prime Minister, Commonwealth of Great Britain
    B) State of Georgia Motor Vehicle and Transportation Dept.
    C) Grayslake (Illinois) City Clerk's Office
    D) Green Bay Packers

19. The Library of Congress system catalogs books with one or two alphabetic letters and a series of numbers for subcategories. This code is a/an
    A) alphanumeric code
    B) straight numeric code
    C) duplex numeric code
    D) decimal numeric code

20. In subject filing, a piece of correspondence is analyzed first to determine the
    A) correspondent's name under which the correspondence should be filed
    B) main topic covered in the correspondence
    C) account number referred to in the correspondence
    D) date on which the piece of correspondence was prepared

21. Decisions made in handling inconsistencies in filing systems should be
    A) discussed and presented at office staff meetings
    B) basic in developing electronic filing systems
    C) cross-referenced within the files
    D) documented in the organization's filing policies and procedures

22. The listener's ability to understand the message is affected most by
    A) nonverbal messages sent by the listener to the speaker
    B) the speaker's ability to clearly enunciate words

C) the attention being paid to the speaker
D) the development of the message to be sent

23. The words or symbols selected to convey the message can be
    A) verbal—spoken words
    B) nonverbal—gestures, facial expressions
    C) a combination of verbal-nonverbal communication
    D) encoded in more than one way

24. The biggest challenge in taking a telephone message for a co-worker is to
    A) write down an accurate and complete message
    B) remember to ask the caller if he or she would like to leave a message
    C) find out the best time for a return call
    D) reassure the caller that you will deliver the message

25. Stevenson uses a cell phone on a daily basis to keep in touch with clients. When Stevenson walks into a meeting, she should remember to
    A) be discreet in answering a cell phone call after the meeting starts
    B) answer promptly to avoid disturbing others at the meeting
    C) use a hands-free telephone kit to receive calls
    D) switch the cell phone to silent mode during the meeting

26. The goal of constructive criticism is to
    A) compliment a person on a "job well done"
    B) defend the need for self-improvement within the organization
    C) critique and evaluate job performance and report back to the individual
    D) balance ideas for performance improvement between positive remarks about the person's contributions

27. Whenever a co-worker or a manager criticizes you, you need to
    A) defend your position with a comment about your hard work
    B) accept the criticism graciously and put it in a positive context
    C) voice your own opinion of your work ethic
    D) complain to a higher administrator in the office

28. Once the listener has gained a basic understanding of the information being presented, evaluating the logic and validity of that information leads the listener to
    A) content listening
    B) empathic listening
    C) critical listening
    D) perceptive listening

29. Research studies show that the average person remembers what percentage of what is heard during the listening process?
    A) 10 percent
    B) 25 percent
    C) 50 percent
    D) 75 percent

30. Which one of the following statements expresses nonverbal communication over which you would have control?
    A) Making character judgments of others based on the clothes being worn
    B) Determining the social status of someone in another culture based on clothing being worn by that person
    C) Being insensitive to personal space preferred by others
    D) Considering importance of time in another culture

31. A formal meeting set up so that business executives from different geographic regions can meet through telephone communications is called a
    A) teleconference
    B) video conference

C) computer conference
D) data conference

32. The primary objective of a data conference is to permit participants to
    A) use computer terminals to transmit information to other group members
    B) view one another on closed-circuit television
    C) speak with others directly from their offices
    D) have simultaneous access to a document for review and editing

33. The parliamentarian's responsibility is to ensure that the meeting is conducted so that
    A) all items of business are thoroughly discussed
    B) a specific time frame is planned for the meeting
    C) the basic principles of parliamentary procedures are followed
    D) motions may be made by any person attending the meeting

34. The required number of voting members who must be present to transact business at a business meeting is called the
    A) minutes
    B) quorum
    C) agenda
    D) majority

35. The minutes of a meeting need to be distributed to the members before the next meeting to give members the opportunity to
    A) approve the contents of the minutes
    B) help write the minutes
    C) compare them with the agenda for the next meeting
    D) review the minutes for accuracy

36. Gutierrez has served as a member of the House of Representatives from her district for 15 years. She has announced her retirement as of July 1. The state legislature is planning a special recognition of her many years of service.

Which one of the following would be a formal way of recognizing her service?

A) Petition from the citizens in her district

B) Formal announcement of her retirement mailed to the newspapers in her district

C) Resolution to be presented at the next session of the legislature

D) Letter sent to her by the Speaker of the House

37. Collins, a senior-level executive, has just been invited to give the keynote address at next year's Women in Management conference and has asked you to assist in the preparation of the speech. Which one of the following should be determined first as you prepare to help Collins prepare her presentation?

A) Possible topic(s) to be covered in the presentation

B) Number of people attending the conference

C) A topical outline of the presentation

D) Honorarium to be paid for the presentation

38. When a research report is presented to a group of professionals, an appropriate presentation technique is to present

A) the highlights of the research with electronic slides

B) an abstract of the research

C) an exact copy of the presentation in the form of a handout distributed at the beginning of the session

D) a question-and-answer session for the participants to become involved in the discussion

39. Nonverbal behavior observed when communicating with someone from another culture indicates

A) clear understanding of the verbal message being conveyed

B) the way space is perceived by that person

C) physical gestures that are universally understood in different cultures

D) the nonjudgmental nature of a response

40. A secondary source of information when researching a specific topic would be

A) an article in yesterday's issue of *The New York Times*

B) a questionnaire you plan to use to survey 150 administrative professionals in your geographic area

C) an interview schedule you have established for interviewing ten administrative professionals

D) your observation of the procedures used to perform a specific task in your business

41. The library classification system in which a book is assigned an alphanumeric code based on 21 major areas of knowledge is the

A) Dewey Decimal system

B) interlibrary consortium

C) Library of Congress system

D) vertical file service

42. You are designing a research study in which you plan to survey 300 women who are corporate executives. Which one of the following information sources will provide you with the names and addresses for women executives selected?

A) Web site for the International Association of Administrative Professionals

B) *Standard and Poor's Register of Directors and Executives*

C) Web site for Resourcelinks Business Directory

D) Barron's

43. The information in a Web site reference needs to be evaluated in terms of the

A) number of pages or paragraphs of material included at the Web site

B) subjectivity of the information presented

C)   technical language used throughout the material

D)   specific audience to which the
Web site is aimed

44. Which one of the following statements
is written in passive voice?

A)   In the last weekend of October,
clocks need to be turned back one
hour.

B)   In the last weekend of October,
you need to remember to turn back
your clocks one hour.

C)   The last weekend of October is
when time changes back one hour.

D)   Daylight savings time means that
you must turn clocks back one hour
in the fall.

45. Which one of the following sentences
uses words correctly?

A)   When the explosion occurred, the
sound affects were heard for miles.

B)   Any change in our flight schedule
will effect our arrival time in Los
Angeles.

C)   The change in flight schedules
affected the arrival time in Los
Angeles.

D)   The affect of the explosion was
felt throughout the neighborhood.

46. A comma-splice sentence consists of
two independent clauses

A)   with no punctuation between the
clauses

B)   joined by a comma

C)   joined by a conjunction

D)   joined by a conjunctive adverb

47. In writing a business message, supporting details are presented to act as a
buffer when which one of the following
approaches is applied to the writing?

A)   Deductive approach

B)   Direct approach

C)   Inductive approach

D)   Outlined paragraph composition

48. Spell check software programs enable
the user to

A)   check grammar at the same time
words are being keyed in

B)   highlight a word with strikethrough

C)   revise word usage in the document
text simultaneously as the spell
check is running

D)   add new words to the electronic
dictionary as the spell-check is
running

49. The receiver of a negative letter is expected to be

A)   unreceptive to the message

B)   neutral to the outcome of the
message

C)   receptive to the message even
though it presents a "no" response

D)   accepting of the message being
conveyed

50. The variable information in a repetitive
letter is

A)   wording that stays the same on
each letter produced

B)   the context of the message itself

C)   the body paragraphs of the message

D)   any text that must be inserted on
each letter to complete the message

51. A business report that primarily includes text material in word form is referred to as a/an

A)   statistical report

B)   narrative report

C)   technical report

D)   analytical report

52. The process of researching a trend involves examining

A)   the pros and cons of a specific issue or topic

B)   several alternatives to solving a
problem

C)   chronological events taking place
over a period of time

D)   logical style used in preparing a
report

53. Tompkins plans to investigate how desktop publishing software is being used to
create communication pieces throughout
the company. She is developing a questionnaire that includes questions for sur-

veying employees at all organizational levels. Tompkins is conducting

A) secondary research
B) preliminary research
C) experimental research
D) primary research

54. The international standard format for the date line is shown in which of the following date lines?

A) 10/14/200X
B) 14 October, 200X
C) October 14, 200X
D) 14 October 200X

55. Which one of the following is the correct placement of the attention line in a business letter?

A) The R-and-T Corporation
   Attention Ms. Arlene Gustafson
   1254 South Park Drive, Suite 4B
   Madison, WI 53715-1374
B) Attention Ms. Arlene Gustafson
   The R-and-T Corporation
   1254 South Park Drive, Suite 4B
   Madison, WI 53715-1374
C) The R-and-T Corporation
   1254 South Park Drive, Suite 4B
   Madison, WI 53715-1374
   Attention Ms. Arlene Gustafson
D) The R-and-T Corporation
   1254 South Park Drive, Suite 4B
   Attention Ms. Arlene Gustafson
   Madison, WI 53715-1374

56. Which one of the following complimentary closings would be considered the most formal?

A) Yours truly
B) Truly yours
C) Cordially yours
D) Sincerely

57. A copy of a business letter is being sent to one or more persons, and the recipient of the letter needs to be informed. Which one of the following is added to the letter to show this?

A) Blind copy notation
B) Copy notation

C) Attention line
D) Enclosure notation

58. A short report that is developed as internal communication may be formatted as a/an

A) business letter
B) manuscript
C) electronic mail message
D) memorandum

59. Once incoming mail is received within departments, an administrative professional has the responsibility to

A) credit accounts for payments received
B) sort the mail by classification
C) sort the mail by priority
D) handle domestic mail first

60. Phillips needs to send a 3.5-pound parcel to Wilkinson in Frankfurt, Germany. The information is needed for a meeting in ten days. Which one of the following mail classifications would be the most economical to use?

A) First-class mail
B) Global Priority Mail
C) Global Express Mail
D) Parcel post

61. Hodgkins plans to mail Meyers copies of documents for a real estate transaction. He wants to receive proof of delivery (a return receipt). Which one of the following postal services would be most appropriate?

A) Certified mail
B) Registered mail
C) Insured mail
D) COD mail

62. United Parcel Service is a private delivery company that offers a variety of services such as Next Day Air®, which offers guaranteed overnight delivery service to

A) over 200 countries worldwide
B) any address in all 50 states and Puerto Rico

C)   a selected number of foreign sites

D)   any address in the contiguous 48 states

63. A telephone message with a telephone number but a missing area code

A)   becomes a high-priority item

B)   needs to be checked in terms of the name of the caller

C)   is of little value to the receiver of the message

D)   can be responded to easily if the caller's name is known

64. The indirect object of a sentence identifies

A)   when an action is taking place

B)   the receiver of the action taking place

C)   what action is happening

D)   where an action is taking place

65. *The open work area features modular units that can be rearranged.* Identify the adjectives in this sentence.

A)   features, modular, rearranged

B)   open, modular, rearranged

C)   work, features, modular

D)   open, work, modular

66. Which one of the following statements illustrates a comma-splice error?

A)   A personal digital assistant helps with keeping a record of your appointments. It also records messages, a to-do list, and a monthly calendar.

B)   A personal digital assistant helps with keeping a record of your appointments; it also records messages, a to-do list, and a monthly calendar.

C)   A personal digital assistant helps with keeping a record of your appointments it also records messages, a to-do list, and a monthly calendar.

D)   A personal digital assistant helps with keeping a record of your appointments, it also records messages, a to-do list, and a monthly calendar.

67. *The file folders by the lateral file need to be sorted and arranged alphabetically.* The phrase *by the lateral file* is a/an

A)   infinitive phrase

B)   gerund phrase

C)   prepositional phrase

D)   participle phrase

68. When you create a list of people who will be attending a meeting, which one of the following word processing features will be helpful in developing this list?

A)   Outlining

B)   Numbering

C)   Paragraphing

D)   Hyphenation

69. Which one of the following statements correctly uses capitalization?

A)   Sarah Edmonds is the new judge for our district.

B)   The new Judge, Sarah Edmonds, will take Office officially on January 15.

C)   The DeKalb County district court will begin its next session in january.

D)   The Judge identified for the next appointment is Sarah Edmonds.

70. Which one of the following statements correctly applies spelling rules?

A)   The published artical will be placed in the files for later referance.

B)   The executives definitly want to include a session on business etiquete in the convention program.

C)   The conveyance of the warranty deed will take place at the closing, which will be scheduled for the end of the month.

D)   The human resources manager relyed on the advise of the interviewer when deciding on the candidate's application.

71. Which one of the following sentences correctly applies the number rules?

A)   Our new vinyl siding will protect your home against extremely hot temperature as high as 110 or as low as $-24°$.

B) The contract calls for the sum of $50,000.00 to be paid for services rendered by March 15th of next year.

C) The diversity in our information technology workforce is shown by these figures: 9 Asians, 15 African-Americans, 12 Caucasians, and 3 Native Americans.

D) 158 members of the American Business Management Association attended the annual conference; in addition, 8 people were identified as special guests.

72. A word may be divided (hyphenated) at the right margin when

A) at least one letter of the word will remain at the right margin

B) at least one syllable of the word will remain at the right margin

C) it is the last word of a paragraph

D) the word extends beyond the right margin

73. Which one of the following persons should be treated as a person of greater authority?

A) The manager of the department initiating the meeting

B) A top-level executive within the organization

C) A client of the organization

D) An administrative professional assisting the person in charge of a business meeting

74. Networking with business associates is more effective when you

A) learn something about each person you meet

B) exchange business cards as quickly as possible

C) use idioms when speaking about business information

D) use only the English language in communication

75. Respect toward co-workers can be shown by

A) being sympathetic to a colleague who is hard at work on a project

B) calling across a modular office area to get a co-worker's attention

C) discussing such issues as religion or personal health in the privacy of your office

D) not involving yourself in a conversation colleagues are having nearby

Solutions to Practice Exam

Note: The reference includes the chapter number first, followed by the appropriate outline section in the chapter.

Answer	Refer to:	Answer	Refer to:
1. (C)	[1-A-2-a (3)]	22. (B)	[4-A-3-a (2) (b)]
2. (B)	[1-B-1-a]	23. (C)	[4-A-3-b (1)]
3. (A)	[1-B-1-a (2)]	24. (A)	[4-B-1-c]
4. (D)	[1-C-1-d (5)]	25. (D)	[4-B-3-d]
5. (B)	[1-D-1-a]	26. (D)	[4-C-2-a]
6. (D)	[1-E-1-a]	27. (B)	[4-C-2-b (1)]
7. (C)	[2-A-5]	28. (C)	[4-D-1-b (2)]
8. (D)	[2-B-2-b]	29. (C)	[4-D-2-c]
9. (A)	[2-C-2]	30. (A)	[4-E-1-e (1)]
10. (C)	[2-D]	31. (A)	[5-B-1-b (3) (a)]
11. (B)	[2-D-1-a]	32. (D)	[5-B-1-b (3) (d)]
12. (A)	[2-D-4-a]	33. (C)	[5-B-3-b]
13. (C)	[2-E-3-a (1)]	34. (B)	[5-B-3-b (2) (b)]
14. (A)	[2-E-3-d (2) (b)]	35. (D)	[5-B-4-c]
15. (C)	[2-E-4-e]	36. (C)	[5-B-5-a]
16. (B)	[3-A-2]	37. (A)	[5-C-1]
17. (D)	[3-A-2-c]	38. (C)	[5-C-2-b]
18. (D)	[3-A-3, 3-A-8, 3-A-9]	39. (B)	[5-D-2-a]
19. (A)	[3-C-2]	40. (A)	[6-A-5]
20. (B)	[3-D-1]	41. (C)	[6-B-1-a (2)]
21. (D)	[3-E-1]	42. (B)	[6-C-4-c]

Answer	*Refer to:*	*Answer*	*Refer to:*
43. (D)	[6-D-3]	60. (B)	[10-C-1-c (1) (b)]
44. (A)	[7-A-5-b]	61. (A)	[10-C-1-c (2) (f)]
45. (C)	[7-A-7-h]	62. (B)	[10-C-2]
46. (B)	[7-B-1-a (3)]	63. (C)	[10-C-3-b (2) (c)]
47. (C)	[7-B-2-a (2)]	64. (B)	[11-A-1-c]
48. (D)	[7-C-5-a (2)]	65. (D)	[11-A-2-a]
49. (A)	[8-A-3]	66. (D)	[11-A-2-b (1)]
50. (D)	[8-A-6-b]	67. (C)	[11-A-2-c (1)]
51. (B)	[8-D-1-a]	68. (B)	[11-B-9-e]
52. (C)	[8-D-2]	69. (A)	[11-C-1, 11-C-5]
53. (D)	[8-D-2-b (2)]	70. (C)	[11-D-9]
54. (D)	[9-A-1-a]	71. (C)	[11-E-3]
55. (A)	[9-A-1-c]	72. (D)	[11-F, 11-F-1]
56. (C)	[9-A-1-g]	73. (C)	[12-A-2-a (2)]
57. (B)	[9-A-1-k]	74. (A)	[12-A-4]
58. (D)	[9-E]	75. (D)	[12-B-3-c]
59. (C)	[10-C-1-b (2)]		

Glossary

Abstract Concise summary of all key points in an article or reference that can be prepared in outline or paragraph format. (9)[1]

Abstract language Quality of language where meanings can be interpreted differently by different people, even in the same type of situation. (7)

Accession record Official log listing the names to which numbers have already been assigned. (3)

Accession register List of records in an archive that controls access to documents and retrieval of documents from the archive. (2)

Acronym Word formed with the initials of words in a set phrase or name. (7)

Active records Those records that are accessed and utilized in the current administration of business functions. (1)

Ad hoc committee Group of people assigned on a temporary basis to investigate a particular event or problem that has occurred within the organization. (5)

Agenda List of items of business to be presented and/or discussed during a formal meeting. (5)

Airmail service Postal service offered for international mail. (10)

Almanac Book or publication, usually published on an annual basis, that includes factual information about international and national events of the year; also called a *fact book*. (6)

Alphabetic filing system Classification system based on the 26 letters of the alphabet as the primary divisions. (3)

Alphanumeric code Combination of alphabetic characters and numbers used in a filing code. (3)

Analytical report Written document that presents basic information and facts as well as an analysis and interpretation of primary data obtained through formal research. (8)

Apostrophe Mark of punctuation (') used to show possession, form plurals, and make contractions. (11)

Appendix Supplementary research material (sample questionnaire, sample letters written to respondents, and detailed data analysis) not included in the body of the report. (8)

Archive Collection of documents of historical or administrative value to an organization. (6)

Area codes Numeric codes that represent geographic zones for telephone networks across the United States. (3)

Attachments Copies of documents affixed electronically to an electronic mail message and sent to the receiver of the message. (9)

Attention line In a business letter addressed to a company or organization, the line beginning with the word *attention* followed by the name of a specific individual who should receive the letter; attention line is placed a double-space below the inside address or as the second line in the inside address. (9)

Audio conference Formal meeting set up so that several business executives from different geographic locations can "meet" through telephone communications; another term for teleconferencing. (5)

Authenticity Proof that the document is the work of the stated author or source. (2)

Bar codes Envelope imprints that contain ZIP Code information to enable mail to be processed more quickly. (10)

Bibliography Alphabetical list of all information sources used for a report, including sources for citations included in the report; list of all references consulted by the author that contributed to the content of the report. (8) (9)

Biometric identification system Authentication technique that matches unique physical characteristics of a person against a database. (2)

Blind copy notation Notation placed on copies of a business letter a double-space below the last notation at the left margin, but not on the original copy, when a copy of the letter is sent to another person and the recipient of the letter need not be aware of this. (9)

Block codes Groups (blocks) of numbers that are reserved for records that have a common feature or characteristic. (3)

---

[1] The number in parentheses after each entry indicates the chapter location in the text.

Block letter style   Format used when all lines of a business letter begin at the left margin, even the date line, the complimentary closing, and the signature line. (9)

Body   Detailed information included in the paragraphs of a business letter. (9)

Body language   Most prominent element in nonverbal communication that refers to posture, facial expressions, eye contact, gestures, and physical movements; the study of nonverbal body motions and communication is known as *kinesics*. (4)

Bound printed matter   Subclass of package services that includes advertising, promotional material, directories, or editorial material securely bound with permanent fastenings. (10)

Buffer   Beginning paragraph in a negative letter that sets the stage for the information that follows. (8)

Business archive   Facility that houses records being retained for research or historical value. (2)

Business etiquette   Acceptable behaviors applied in specific types of business situations when conducting business, carrying out workplace assignments, dining with and entertaining business associates, giving and receiving gifts, and working with disabled people. (12)

Calling card call   Long-distance telephone call that allows the caller to charge the service to a specific account number. (4)

Certificate of mailing   Proof of mailing that can be purchased for a mailed item. (10)

Certified mail   Proof of mailing and delivery that may be purchased for a first-class item with no dollar value of its own. (10)

Channel   Connecting device between the speaker (sender) and the listeners (receivers) through which the message is sent. (4)

Charge-out (tracking) system   Procedures to be followed when any records need to be borrowed from hard-copy files. (2)

Chronological style   Preparation of a written document according to the sequence in which events occurred. (8)

Chronological system   Filing system that utilizes calendar dates as the significant divisions of the system. (3)

Coding   Making notations on a record to indicate exactly how the record will be stored (names, numbers, or character strings). (2) Procedure used in research to assign a number to each response classification. (8)

Collaboration   Members of a team working together to accomplish a specific goal or task. (7)

Collect call   Operator-assisted telephone call that will be paid by the person or company receiving the call. (4)

Collect-on-delivery (COD) mail   Sending an item so that the buyer must pay the postage, COD fee, and price of the item shipped in cash or personal check upon receipt. (10)

Colon   Mark of punctuation (:) used after an introduction or in separating hours from minutes in time. (11)

Color coding   Identifying alphabetic letters, numbers, or topics with specific colors to aid in filing and locating specific records and files. (2)

Comma   Mark of punctuation (,) used to separate parts of sentences, such as after an introductory group of words, in a series, in compound sentences, in direct quotations, and in parenthetical expressions. (11)

Committee   Group of people who are meeting to accomplish a specific task. (5)

Complement   Additional words in a sentence that serve as modifiers and help complete the meaning of the sentence; noun in the predicate that refers to the subject or an adjective that describes the subject. (7) (11)

Complex sentence   Statement that includes one independent clause and one or more dependent clauses. (7)

Complimentary closing   Formal or informal expression, such as *Sincerely* or *Cordially yours*, included a double-space after the last paragraph of a business letter. (9)

Compound-complex sentence   Statement consisting of two or more independent clauses and one or more dependent clauses. (7)

Compound sentence   Two independent clauses joined by a comma and a conjunction or a semicolon. (7)

Computer conference   Formal meeting set up so participants can use computer terminals to transmit information to other members of the group for either simultaneous or delayed response. (5)

Conciseness   Writing in a brief but comprehensive manner, using as few words as possible to express the information presented. (7)

Concrete language   Use of words or terms that are precise in meaning. (7)

Conference   Formal meeting of a group of people with a common purpose. (5)

Conference call   Telephone call among three or more people in different locations arranged through a firm providing conference call services. (4)

Conferencing   Use of telephone and computer systems to create networks necessary in order to meet with others without having to leave the office. (5)

Confidentiality   Maintenance of information contained in business records so that it is used only for intended purposes. (2)

Consecutive adjectives   Modifiers that are not equal in rank and must appear in a specific order or the sentence will not make sense. (11)

Constant information Printed or electronically imaged data on a business form; information that remains the same on each document. (1) (2)

Content listening Process of gaining an understanding of the information being presented. (4)

Convenience motions Motions that affect the comfort of the members of the group that is meeting. (5)

Convention Type of conference that is typically sponsored by a professional association. (5)

Coordinate adjectives Modifiers that are equal in rank; that is, they can be changed around and the meaning will not be distorted. (11)

Copy notation Notation that appears a double-space after the enclosure notation at the left margin when a copy of a business letter is sent to one or more persons. (9)

Copyediting Revision of a draft or a document for consistency, conciseness, and grammatical accuracy. (7)

Credit card call Long-distance telephone call that allows the caller to charge the service to a specific account number. (4)

Critical listening Evaluating the information being presented in terms of logic, validity, and implications for individual performance. (4)

Criticism Evaluative message that communicates positive and/or negative reactions to a specific act or performance. (4)

Cross-reference Card, sheet, or folder used whenever a record could be filed in more than one place in the files to indicate the location of the original document or complete file. (2)

Cuts Number of tabs (projections) extending across a set of folders: single-cut (one tab), third-cut (three tabs), and fifth-cut (five tabs). (1)

Dash Mark of punctuation (—) used to emphasize one or more parenthetical words. (11)

Data collection Accumulation of data or facts from primary and secondary sources to analyze a research problem thoroughly and evaluate possible solutions to the problem. (8)

Data conference Formal meeting using computers arranged so that two or more participants simultaneously have access to a document for review and editing. (5)

Data integrity Maintenance of accurate information or data within the system. (1)

Decimal-numeric system Filing system that expands a simple numeric arrangement in which the major divisions of a subject (topic) are subdivided and assigned a number, followed by a decimal point and one or more digits for further subdivisions. (3)

Decoding Process by which the listener (receiver) interprets the meaning(s) of the message. (4)

Decryption Process of decoding data that has been encrypted into a secret format. (2)

Deductive approach Writing a business letter so that the main idea is presented first, followed by facts and details and a positive, forward-looking closing statement; also referred to as a *direct approach*. (7) (8)

Descriptors Key words that are precise or imprecise in the way they describe other words. (7)

Developmental disability Mental impairment that may result in limited capacity to function in a workplace environment or in society. (12)

Dewey Decimal classification system Most widely known decimal-numeric filing classification system primarily used for cataloging library books into ten general categories. (3) (6)

Dictionary Reference book that provides the correct spelling, meaning, usage, and syllabication of all words recognized in a specific language. (6)

Digital signature Proof in the form of identity information, document fingerprints, and date/time information that a document has never been altered since it was signed. (2)

Direct access Procedures that permit a person to go directly to the storage system (file cabinet or computer storage) and locate a file. (2)

Direct approach Writing a business letter by presenting the main idea first, followed by facts and details and a positive, forward-looking closing statement; also referred to as the *deductive approach*. (8)

Direct-distance dialing Placing a long-distance call to another telephone number without the intervention of an operator. (4)

Direct object Noun or noun equivalent following an action verb that completes the sentence by answering the question "what" or "whom" after the verb. (11)

Direct personal channels Face-to-face conversations, telephone calls, meetings, and conferences best used when personal contact is necessary for sharing information. (4)

Direct quotation In a business document, citing a passage verbatim (word for word) from an information source. (9)

Directories Listings of companies, associations, organizations, individuals, or products arranged alphabetically, geographically, or by subject. (6)

Disability etiquette Acceptable behaviors to apply in specific types of situations involving disabled persons, such as wheelchair etiquette, visual impairment etiquette, hearing loss etiquette, and developmental disability etiquette. (12)

Disabled Modifier used when referring to an individual who is physically, visually, or developmentally impaired or who has severe hearing loss. (12)

Diversity Characteristic of members of a workforce that consists of people with different personal characteristics, physical abilities, and employment opportunities. (5)

Document camera   Smart podium equipment that projects hard copy or transparencies as visuals on a projection screen in front of the room. (5)

Documentation   Process of giving appropriate credit to information sources within the text (footnotes, endnotes, or in-text citations) and in bibliographic form at the end of the report. (9)

Double-strikethrough   Word processing software feature used to highlight words that have been deleted from the text by drawing a double-line through each letter or word that is being highlighted for change. (7)

Duplex numeric system   Filing system in which file numbers may have two or more sets of code numbers separated by a dash, comma, period, or space. (3)

Electronic blackboard   Device used with teleconferences to transmit visuals to other locations that consists of a pressure-sensitive blackboard, microphone, and speaker at one location and a television monitor, microphone, and speaker at additional locations as well. (5)

Ellipsis   Punctuation that shows the omission of words within a sentence—three periods with a space before and after each period (. . .). (11)

Empathic listening   Understanding the speaker's emotions and feelings about the topic of the presentation. (4)

Empathy   Ability to understand the feelings or emotions of another person. (7)

Emphasis   Greater importance attached to a particular fact or idea. (7)

Enclosure notation   If material is enclosed with a business letter, the word *enclosure* or *attachment* (abbreviated or keyed in full) appears a double-space after the reference initials at the left margin. (9)

Encoding   Process of assigning and organizing symbols such as words or gestures to formulate the message to be sent. (4)

Encryption   Translation of data into a secret code that is unintelligible without a deciphering device. (2)

Encyclopedias   Set of one or more general reference books that provide detailed information on a wide variety of topics arranged in alphabetical order. (6)

Endnotes   Reference citations that are indicated in the text with superscripts but appear on a separate page at the "end" of the report. (9)

Environment   Context in which communication encounters take place. (4)

Etiquette references   Publications that feature conventional requirements of social behavior and conduct as established for specific occasions. (6)

Exclamation point   Mark of punctuation (!) used for emphasis after a word, phrase, or sentence. (11)

Express mail   Fastest mail delivery service for any item weighing up to 70 pounds, which guarantees next-day delivery and second-day delivery. (10)

External report   Written document that will be disseminated outside the organization; sometimes referred to as a *radial report*. (8)

Fact book   Book or publication, usually published on an annual basis, that includes factual information about international and national events of the year; also known as an *almanac*. (6)

Feedback   Receiver's response to a message that helps the sender determine whether the message sent was truly received and understood. (4)

Fiche   A sheet of film containing miniature images arranged in rows and columns on a card. (1)

Files integrity   Characteristic of records and files that remain factual, accurate, and truthful. (2)

Filing segment   One or more filing units (the total name, a number, or a subject) used for filing purposes. (3)

Filing standard   Procedure to follow in establishing consistent filing rules and developing the documentation needed to support the rules applied within a given organization. (3)

Filing unit   A number, a letter, a word, or any combination of those that form a character string used for filing. (3)

Findings   Results of a research study that are summarized immediately following the presentation of the data as a capstone to the data analysis section of the report. (8)

First-class mail   Class of mail that includes personal and business correspondence, handwritten and printed messages, bills, statements of account, post cards, printed forms filled out in writing, and business reply mail not requiring the highest priority and weighing no more than 13 ounces. (10)

Footnotes   Reference citations that are indicated in the text with superscripts and are included at the "foot" (bottom) of the page where the reference is made. (9)

Formal meeting   Meeting planned and scheduled in advance so that participants know ahead of time the agenda items to be presented and discussed. (5)

Fragment   Incomplete sentence that is missing a subject or a verb (predicate). (7)

Geographic filing system   Classification system in which records are arranged alphabetically according to geographic locations. (3)

Gerund phrase   Verbal phrase that functions as a noun. (11)

Glass ceiling   Invisible barrier to advancement to higher-level corporate positions, usually experienced by women and members of minority groups. (5)

Glossary Alphabetical list of terms defined for the reader. (8)

Goodwill Positive, clear, and courteous communication climate that develops when people work together within the organization or with others outside the organization; favorable attitude and feeling exhibited toward an individual and/or his or her organization. (7) (8)

GPO Access U.S. Government Web site that provides the official, published electronic version of public information available daily to the general public. (6)

Gratuity Tip that is paid to service providers to augment their salaries. (12)

Guest Person who visits another business associate at his or her work area. (12)

Guide words Arrangement of the words DATE, TO, FROM, and SUBJECT keyed in at the beginning of a memorandum. (9)

Guides Inserts for file drawers that indicate file sections and serve as dividers for groups of records. (1)

Hanging indent Type of indentation in which the first line of each entry is flush left and the second and succeeding lines are indented at least one-half inch (one standard tab). (9)

Header Descriptive phrase that automatically appears within the top margin on each page of a report. (9)

Home page First page for a Web site that is registered on the World Wide Web through a Web address—a uniform resource locator (URL). (10)

Horizontal report Communication at the same administrative level that may be distributed from department to department or division to division within the organization. (8)

Host Person who receives business visitors in his or her own work area or office. (12)

Hyphen Mark of punctuation (-) used for word division or in a compound word. (11)

Impersonal channels Written memoranda, notices on bulletin boards, and electronic mail messages used to communicate a small amount of information about a single topic that needs to be transmitted quickly in a simple, straightforward manner. (4)

Important records Documents that contribute to the continued smooth operation of an organization and can be replaced or duplicated if lost or destroyed in a disaster but with a considerable expenditure of time and money. (1)

Inactive records Those records no longer referred to on a regular basis but still of limited importance. (1)

Incidental motions Motions arising from pending questions that must be decided before the question to which the incidental motion pertains is decided. (5)

Index Publication that contains a list of particular topics or subjects that have appeared in newspapers, periodicals, or other sources with specific references to the source. (6) Alphabetical list of names and subjects appearing at the end of a reference that contains page numbers where the names or subjects appear within the publication. (8)

Index record Card that contains reference information indicating where the original file or document in a numeric or alphanumeric classification system is located. (1)

Indexing Deciding what names, numbers, or character strings need to be used in filing a record. (2)

Indirect access Procedures that require a person to consult a relative index to locate the name, subject, or number under which a file is stored. (2)

Indirect approach Writing a business letter that conveys a negative response or some other form of bad news so that the details are presented first as a buffer, followed by the decision and a forward-looking closing statement; also referred to as an *inductive approach*. (7) (8)

Indirect object Noun or pronoun following a verb that names the receiver of the direct object, precedes the direct object, and answers the questions "to whom," "to what," "for whom," or "for what." (11)

Individual folder File folder that includes all correspondence for one correspondent, subject, or account. (1)

Inductive approach Writing a business letter that conveys a negative response or some other form of bad news so that the details are presented first as a buffer, followed by the decision and a forward-looking closing statement; also referred to as an *indirect approach*. (7) (8)

Infinitive phrase Verbal phrase that functions as a noun, an adjective, or an adverb. (11)

Informal meeting Discussion by a small number of people (two to five) about a particular business issue or concern. (5)

Information banks Collections of information specific to a particular profession or field, usually available through computer networks by subscription. (6)

Informational report Written document in which facts are presented in an organized, structured manner. (8)

Inside address Name of the person to whom a business letter will be sent, along with the person's complete address. (9)

Inspecting Examining a record to ensure that it has been released for filing by an appropriate authority within the firm. (2)

Insured mail   Additional postal protection up to $500 against loss or damage for express, first-class, priority, and standard mail as well as package services. (10)

Intelligent retrieval   Efficient searching of document content through the use of an index of words (descriptors) contained in the document. (1)

Intended meaning   Sender's interpretation of the information conveyed in a message, which may or may not be the same as the receiver's interpretation. (4)

Interactive channels   Face-to-face conversations, telephone calls, and meetings that allow for questions and concerns to be immediately addressed and information readily exchanged. (4)

International mail   Postal service, such as Global Express Guaranteed and Global Express, available for mail being sent to foreign countries. (10)

Interview guide   Document that contains an interview plan and the questions that need to be asked during the interview. (6)

Intranet   Organization's internal network for electronically communicating company policies, procedures, news items, and data/information available to employees. (10)

Itinerary   Travel plan that specifies all details concerning a business trip. (9)

Jargon   Technical language pertinent to a specific profession or group. (5) (7)

Library of Congress classification system   Alphanumeric filing classification system developed in the early 1900s used for cataloging library books according to 21 major areas of knowledge that includes one or two alphabetic letters and a series of numbers that designate subdivisions within categories. (3) (6)

Library consortiums   Networks of public and university libraries that link the online services of the libraries. (6)

Library mail   Subclass of package services that permits qualifying institutions (libraries, universities, zoos, research institutions) to mail educational and research material. (10)

Listening   Mental process that involves sensing, seeing, and interpreting what is being communicated. (4)

Listening process   Set of related physical and mental activities usually considered in sequence that involves different types of listening. (4)

Logical security   Procedures embedded in software programs to restrict individual access to records. (2)

Logical style   Preparation of a written document according to patterns of reasoning. (8)

Mailgram   Electronic message forwarded from Western Union to the post office that serves the ZIP Code of the address for next-day delivery to any address in the United States. (10)

Main document   Contents of a form letter prepared for the mail-merge function. (8)

Main motion   An item of business presented to a group in the form of a motion that has the lowest precedence in rank among all types of motions. (5)

Media mail   Subclass of package services that includes books of at least eight pages, film, printed music, printed test materials, sound recordings, play scripts, printed educational charts, medical information, and computer-readable media. (10)

Microform   Any record that contains reduced images on film. (1)

Microprinting   Words in an area of a document that appear to the reader as a solid line and can only be read under magnification. (2)

Middle-digit system   Numeric filing system typically used for numbers with six digits or fewer in which the middle digits are the primary indexing unit. (3)

Minutes   Official report of a meeting that summarizes the business that has been transacted, reports that have been presented and discussed, and any other significant events occurring during the meeting. (5) (9)

Miscellaneous folder   File folder at the end of a file group that houses the group of records that have not yet been assigned individual file folders. (1)

Mixed punctuation   Basic punctuation style in which a colon is inserted after the salutation and a comma follows the complimentary closing. (9)

Mnemonic code   Numeric code assigned to an item that takes on additional meaning about the item. (3)

Modified block letter style   Format used for business letters where the date line is centered or may end at the right margin, the complimentary closing and signature line begin at the center point of the line of writing, paragraphs may be blocked or indented, and all other parts of the letter begin at the left margin. (9)

Modifiers   Words that describe other words in the sentence, adding descriptive details or specific definition to those words. (11)

Narrative reports   Written documents that primarily include text material (words). (8)

Netiquette   Etiquette practices for the electronic environment. (10)

Networking   Circulating among the participants at a business gathering to become acquainted, make introductions, and learn more about each person contacted. (12)

News release   Announcement about a business event that is written in the direct approach. (9)

Noise External, internal, or semantic distractions that can occur at virtually any time or point in the communication process. (4)

Nonessential records Documents that are not necessary for the restoration of the business and have no predictable value. (1)

Nonrecords Documents prepared for the organization's convenience or temporary use but that normally are not saved and are disposed of after use. (1)

Nonrestrictive clause Clause beginning with the relative pronoun *which* that does not add meaning to the sentence, may be considered parenthetical, and is set off by commas. (7)

Nontechnical reports Written documents that refrain from using technical language to convey information to people who do not have backgrounds in a given subject area. (8)

Nonverbal communication Aspect of the information exchange that is beyond words—body language, paralanguage, space and distance, touch, and apparel. (4)

Numeric filing system Indirect-access system that consists of various combinations of numeric codes assigned to names of individuals, organizations, or subjects. (3)

Official Airline Guides (OAGs) Travel and transportation guides available through subscription for all domestic and international airline flights. (6)

Open punctuation Basic punctuation style in which no punctuation is keyed in after the salutation or the complimentary closing. (9)

Optical character recognition (OCR) Process whereby a document is scanned and the data converted to digital form for processing by the computer. (1)

Oral communication Exchange of information between speakers (senders) and listeners (receivers) in which those roles are shared. (4)

Out folder Folder inserted into a file when someone charges out an entire file folder of documents. (1)

Outline Key words from a document that are coded in descending order using Roman numerals, letters of the alphabet, and numbers at different levels. (9)

Package services Class of mail intended for catalogs, merchandise, and other printed material that can be sent as parcel post, bound printed matter, media mail, or library mail. (10)

Paralanguage Communication effect of speed, intensity, volume, accent, and even silence on spoken words in the message. (4)

Paraphrasing Rewriting the original author's words or ideas while maintaining the author's intended meaning. (9)

Parcel post Subclass of package services that includes merchandise, books, circulars, catalogs, and other printed matter with a maximum weight of 70 pounds. (10)

Parentheses Marks of punctuation ( ) used to enclose words or phrases that are needed for clarification but need to be deemphasized. (11)

Parenthetical expression Word, phrase, or clause that is not necessary to the grammatical completeness and meaning of the sentence and is set off by commas. (11)

Parliamentary procedures Application of a set of rules and principles for conducting formal meetings efficiently and orderly; appropriate conduct of business meetings as specified in specific references. (5) (6)

Participle phrase Verbal phrase that functions as an adjective. (11)

Passwords Assignment of user IDs (string of characters) to gain access to records. (2)

Perceived meaning Receiver's interpretation of the information conveyed in a message, which may or may not be the same as the sender intended. (4)

Period Mark of punctuation (.) that is commonly used after declarative sentences, polite requests, abbreviations, and numbers in enumerations, among other uses. (11)

Periodic transfer The physical movement of records from active storage to semiactive or inactive storage as of a specific date each year. (1)

Periodicals Class of mail that includes publications such as newspapers, magazines, and other periodical publications whose primary purpose is transmitting information to a subscription list. (10)

Perpetual transfer The physical movement of records from active storage to semiactive or inactive storage at any time an event has been completed or a case closed. (1)

Person-to-person call Operator-assisted telephone call from one person to another person that is charged to the caller only if the person being called is able to answer the call. (4)

Personal interview Technique used to obtain responses to open-ended questions from a population or sample of individuals. (8)

Petition Formal statement signed by those who are eligible to sign such a petition asking for a specific action to be taken. (5)

Physical security Procedures that restrict access to records through the use of hardware, facilities, or electronic storage. (2)

Plagiarism Use of information or ideas from secondary sources by writers who intentionally refrain from including documentation giving the original author appropriate credit. (9)

Posted record   Card record used to record or post information that updates, changes, deletes, or adds data to the record. (1)

Power meals   Planned meal functions (breakfast, luncheon, afternoon tea, dinner, brunch) that involve business discussions during or after the meal. (12)

Praise   Communication that acknowledges the effective work of others. (4)

Précis   Concise summary of all key points in an article or reference, typically prepared only in a paragraph format. (9)

Predicate adjective   Modifier that follows a linking verb in the predicate and describes the subject of the sentence. (11)

Predicate noun   Noun or noun equivalent that follows a linking verb in the predicate and refers to the subject of the sentence. (11)

Primary research   Gathering original information to use as current data in a report. (8)

Primary sources   Research studies such as surveys, interviews, and experiments that yield actual data that can be analyzed. (6)

Primary value   The appraisal assigned to records that are active in nature and needed for current operations. (1)

Priority mail   First-class mail that weighs up to a maximum of 70 pounds and has a maximum size of no more than 108 inches in length and distance around the thickest part combined and is deliverable within two to three days. (10)

Private key   Code known only to the recipient of a message that is used to decode (decrypt) the message. (2)

Privileged motions   Motions that take precedence over all other motions, such as a motion to take a recess or a motion to adjourn. (5)

Progress report   Written document that outlines steps already completed in a project and others that still need to be completed. (8)

Proposal   Plan that includes information such as *what* the new development is, *why* it is important to the continued efficient operation of the business, *how* it will be used, and *how much* implementation will cost. (8)

Proxemics   Way people structure their space or territory. (4)

Psychological style   Preparation of a written document according to the receiver's needs. (8)

Public key   Code available to everyone that is used as the basis for encrypting a message. (2)

Public library   Collections of books and other informational publications housed in a local library and available to everyone who resides in a particular community or geographic area. (6)

Purging   Process of automatically deleting the contents of an electronically stored record. (1)

Question mark   Mark of punctuation (?) used at the end of a sentence that asks a direct question. (11)

Quorum   Required number of voting members who must be present to transact business. (5)

Quotation marks   Marks of punctuation (" ") that are used with direct quotations, titles, and single letters. (11)

Records   Official documents of the company or organization valuable enough to be retained and stored in a format for future use and distribution. (1)

Records center   Depository for an organization's vital, inactive, and/or active records. (2)

Reference citations   Notations within the text to give appropriate credit to the originator of specific information that is quoted or paraphrased from secondary information sources. (9)

Reference initials   Administrative professional's initials alone or the writer's initials followed by the initials of the administrative professional who prepared the business letter keyed in at the left margin a double-space below the signature line on the letter. (9)

References   Alphabetical list of all information sources that were directly cited within the body of the report; also referred to as *works cited*. (8)

Registered mail   Additional postal protection available for valuable items, money, checks, jewelry, bonds, stock certificates, and important papers sent by first-class mail. (10)

Relative index   Card containing reference information for files using a numeric or alphanumeric classification system; a backup for numeric and alphanumeric systems that consists of cards filed alphabetically, providing a complete list of names or subjects already included in the filing system; individual cards or computer listing of all names in alphabetic order to which numbers have been assigned. (1) (2) (3)

Resolution   Formal expression of an entire group's appreciation, congratulations, or sympathy directed toward a particular individual or group. (5)

Restrictive clause   Clause beginning with *who*, *which*, or *that* necessary for the completeness of the sentence and that does not require a comma before and after the clause. (7)

Salutation   Greeting to the receiver of a business letter, such as *Ladies and Gentlemen, Dear Sir* or *Madam*, and *Dear Sales Manager.* (9)

Scheduled reports   Written documents issued at regular, stated intervals—weekly, monthly, or quarterly. (8)

Secondary research   Investigation to gather information that others have written and prepared as the basis for primary research. (8)

Secondary sources   Published and unpublished documents written by others who have studied the research topic. (6)

Secondary value   The appraisal assigned to records that may have historical or archival importance and are held in semiactive or inactive storage. (1)

Semantics   Meanings assigned to the words used when communicating with others. (4)

Semicolon   Mark of punctuation (;) that is used to separate compound sentences or a series within a series. (11)

Sequential files   Straight numeric filing system in which files are arranged in consecutive order, from the lowest number to the highest number; also known as *serial files*. (3)

Serial files   Straight numeric filing system in which files are arranged in consecutive order, from the lowest number to the highest number; also known as *sequential files*. (3)

Shading   Technique for highlighting words or sections that have been added to a document. (7)

Signature file   Sender's information inserted at the end of an electronic mail message that includes the sender's name, title, company name, e-mail address, telephone number, and fax number. (9)

Simplified letter style   Format that is similar to the block letter style with all lines beginning at the left margin, but the salutation and complimentary closing are omitted and a subject line is included before the body paragraphs. (9)

Slang   Expressions that are idiomatic (peculiar to a particular language) that cannot be translated literally into another language. (7)

Social etiquette   Acceptable behaviors exhibited in specific types of personal situations, such as courtesy, politeness, and respect for other individuals. (12)

Soundex code   Alphanumeric code that includes an alphabetic letter (the first letter of the name being coded) and three numbers representing the consonant sounds in the name. (3)

Spam   Unsolicited electronic mail messages that are sent through the Internet. (10)

Speaker   Source of a message known as the sender. (4)

Special delivery   Payment of regular postage plus an extra fee that assures immediate delivery within prescribed hours and distances. (10)

Special handling   Postal service available for unusual mail and packages sent by first-class mail, priority mail, and package services that require preferential handling and will be delivered with regularly scheduled mail deliveries. (10)

Special reports   Written documents prepared on demand that concern unusual or nonroutine requests for information. (8)

Standard mail   Class of mail that includes printed matter, flyers, circulars, advertising, newsletters, bulletins, catalogs, and small parcels not required to be sent by first-class mail or periodicals; two subclasses of standard mail exist—A for mail of less than 16 ounces and B for mail of more than 1 pound. (10)

Standing committee   Group of people appointed for a definite term and assigned specific objectives to accomplish within that period of time. (5)

Station-to-station call   Telephone call placed from one telephone number to another telephone number. (4)

Statistical reports   Written documents that include primarily numerical data. (8)

Strikethrough   Word processing software feature that highlights words that have been deleted from the text by drawing a line through each letter or word that should be changed. (7)

Subject filing system   Classification system in which records are arranged in alphabetical order according to topics or categories. (3)

Subject line   Descriptive phrase that tells what the letter, memorandum, or electronic mail message is about. (9)

Subsidiary motion   Motion that assists, modifies, or disposes of the main motion and that must be acted on before the group returns to the main motion. (5)

Tab   Projection on a file folder or guide for placement of a label with a typed caption. (1) Bill for a meal function normally paid by whoever benefits from the business association. (12)

Technical reports   Written documents designed for conveying information to professionals within the field who will understand the specialized vocabulary and terminology included in the documents. (8)

Teleconference   Formal meeting set up so that several business executives from different geographic locations can "meet" through telephone communications. (5)

Telegram   Message delivered to the receiver through Western Union. (10)

Telephone tag   Situation that occurs when two people keep trying to reach each other by telephone without success. (4)

Terminal-digit system   Numeric filing system in which the primary indexing units are the last digits (terminal digits) in the number. (3)

Thesaurus   Lexicon (dictionary) of similar words or information that focuses on synonyms and antonyms; reference that is helpful in determining other words that have the same meaning as the one being conveyed in the message. (6) (7)

Tone   Manner in which a certain attitude is expressed. (7)

Track changes   Word processing software feature that permits editing functions (delete, insert, or move text) and creation of comments that show the writer exactly what editing changes are being recommended. (7)

Transparency   Acetate sheet containing an image burned or drawn on it that can be projected on a screen or wall. (5)

Underscore   Mark of punctuation (_) used for underlining titles, specific words, paragraph headings, or single letters. (11)

Unity   Coherent flow of ideas existing throughout a document—within sentences, within paragraphs, and between paragraphs. (7)

Useful records   Documents used in the operation of the organization that can be easily replaced. (1)

Variable information   Data to be filled in and inserted on a business form; information that is inserted on a document and changes each time the form is filled in. (1) (2)

Vertical report   Written document prepared for someone at a higher level within the organizational structure of the company or for someone at a lower level. (8)

Videoconference   Formal meeting set up for a scheduled date and time in which participants are able to communicate with each other by viewing and listening to one another on closed-circuit television. (5)

Vital records   Documents that are essential for the effective, continuous operation of the firm and are irreplaceable. (1)

Voice-mail system   Telephone message system that permits callers to record messages digitally according to prerecorded instructions. (4)

Web site   All the Web pages, collectively, for a specific company or organization. (10)

Webmaster   Person in charge of an organization's Web site who needs to be skilled in communication, artistic design, technology, and Web site management strategies. (10)

White Pages   Alphabetic listing of all telephone numbers assigned within a given city or area. (4)

Widow/orphan line   One line of a paragraph by itself on the top or bottom of a page of a document. (9)

Word book   Alphabetical list of the most frequently used words that indicates the spelling, syllabication, and recommended hyphenation. (6)

Works cited   Alphabetical list of all information sources that are directly cited within a document; also referred to as *references*. (8)

Writing style manuals   References that provide assistance in preparing formal reports requiring documentation (footnotes, endnotes, or in-text citations and bibliographies). (6)

Yellow Pages   Classified section of the telephone directory that uses a subject index of products and services as the basis for presenting information about provider organizations. (4)

ZIP + 4 Codes   Zone Improvement Program Codes that are used by the U.S. Postal Service to expedite mail deliveries throughout the United States. (3) (10)

Index